THE PHYSICAL GEOGRAPHY OF LANDSCAPE

Roy Collard

Director of Studies, Oundle School

Unwin Hyman

To Jane

Published by
UNWIN HYMAN LIMITED
15–17 Broadwick Street
London W1V 1FP

Reprinted 1989
© Roy Collard 1988

British Library Cataloguing in Publication Data

Collard, Roy
  The physical geography of landscape.
  1. Landforms. Formation
  I. Title
  551.4

ISBN 0–7135–2734–X

Designed by Geoff Wadsley.
Cover picture of the Ogwen Valley, Snowdonia
  from Bruce Coleman Ltd.
Typeset by August Filmsetting, Haydock, St Helens
Printed in Great Britain by Butler & Tanner Ltd.,
  Frome, Somerset

Bibliography: Lists of useful books, including all those
titles referred to in the text, are included at the end of
each chapter. The lists are divided into two; the first
section contains books of general relevance to the subject while the second section in each case contains
books of a more advanced nature.

    Some words and phrases in the text have been set in
bold type. These key terms have been identified for the
purposes of aiding understanding and for ease of revision. Many of them have been defined in the Glossary
on page 282.

Contents

Preface

If, in writing this book, I have produced nothing more than an aid to passing examinations then I have failed. My hope is that I might engender, in some readers at least, a curiosity about landscape that will go well beyond the demands of an examination syllabus and extend into a much longer-term interest. An understanding of landscape involves study not just of geography, but also of ecology, industrial archaeology, agriculture, geology, anthropology and economic and social history; but further than that, an appreciation of landscape demands study of the literature and art which a landscape has inspired.

As a physical geography text, I hope this book is of value both to those whose base is in the sciences and to those who prefer to deal with words rather than formulae and statistics. Unlike some other textbooks, this one is not based upon a systems framework, but rather uses systems theory when and where it is most appropriate. Throughout the text I have tried to stress the vital role of man as a geomorphological agent and the impact of landscape-forming processes on human activities. With this end in mind, I have included an entire chapter on human impact.

In producing the book I am indebted to Sue Richards and James Crookes, who have made many helpful suggestions in reading the text, and also to those people who have, over the years, developed my curiosity about the subject. Not least amongst them are Tom Palmer, who taught me A-level, Rex Walford, who taught me to enthuse about my subject, and Tony Land who taught me to understand it. Most of all I am utterly indebted to Jane, Samuel and Hannah who suffered many lonely holidays on the North York Moors whilst I was locked away in my study, writing.

RAC
Oundle, September 1988

Fig 1.1 Natural events and human disasters. Florence, 1966, Colombia, 1985, and San Salvador 1986.

Earthquake toll still rising in devastated city

By Mark Fazlollah in San Salvador

THE CITY of San Salvador began burying its earth-quake dead yesterday. The International Red Cross reckoned the toll so far at 350, with 5,800 more ...f thousands homeless.

...rmed at ceme-
...ose who had been
...d the bodies of
...ut most of the
... victims still
... in the concrete
...nd twisted steel
...he downtown area
...Salvador capital.
...amilies were vainly
...the city's morgues
...e bodies were buried
...ed.
...people already knew
...t. Roberto Uria Ramos

THOUSANDS FLEEING VALLEYS NEAR VOLCANO IN COLOMBIA; MORE ERUPTIONS REPORTED

RESCUE WORK LAGS

500 May Be Trapped Alive in a Buried Town — 19,000 Homeless

By JOSEPH B. TREASTER
Special to The New York Times

BOGOTA, Colombia, Nov. 16 — Thousands of people, fearing another volcanic eruption, today fled several owns in the area where an avalanche f mud earlier this week buried an en-e town.

FLORENCE CUT OFF BY FLOODS

◆

Emergency plans to move art treasures

21 DEAD: 50,000 MEN ON RESCUE WORK

JOHN WALLIS
Daily Telegraph Staff Correspondent
ROME, Friday.

THOUSANDS of people were homeless tonight and at least 21 are known to have died in the storms and floods which have caused chaos in Italy from the Alps to Sicily.

1

Introduction: Aspects of Landscape

Extreme Natural Events

In case any reader is unsure about the need for a greater knowledge or understanding of the changes that occur in the physical landscape, the disasters headlined in Fig 1.1 should remove any doubts. Most of us, though, will never experience a natural disaster of the type mentioned here; mercifully they are very rare in Britain and only increase significantly in numbers as one moves into the tropics or towards the margins of the tectonic plates (see Chapter 2). Nevertheless we can probably all recall experience of equivalent events of a much lower magnitude, be it the overtopping of its banks by a local stream, the collapse of a nearby railway embankment, a momentary shake of the earth's crust or a particularly angry sea. Each of these occurrences may represent an extreme natural event for the particular locality, and a little reflection on one's experiences should lead to an appreciation that such events usually have a greater impact on the landscape than years of gradual wearing away by everyday processes. It is hardly surprising, therefore, that considerable effort and resources have been directed towards research into **extreme natural events**. However, as we shall see in later chapters, man is not especially adept at either predicting or preventing them. Nature retains the ability to catch us unawares.

In focusing on extreme natural events though, we should not avert our attention more than temporarily from the everyday processes that operate in the landscape for they, too, effect change. It is these processes which may help return a landform to its former, or a new, equilibrium after a disaster has occurred. It is these processes which wear down the uplands, transport the debris to the rivers and empty it into the sea. It is these processes which we can actually observe and measure. They carry out the spade work, the natural disasters take the glory.

Change

The Cycle of Erosion

Geomorphology is the name given to the study of the shape or form of the earth's landscape. Throughout the discipline's existence its practitioners have always needed to address themselves to the knotty problem of how change occurs within the landscape. This is not just a debate about whether isolated events of great magnitude effect more short-term change than the continuous everyday processes. It is also a debate about long-term change as students attempt to clarify the ultimate outcome of current denudation.

The ideas of the American geomorphologist, W M Davis, dominated this debate in the first 50 years of this century. He envisaged a **cycle of erosion** in which landscape was gradually worn down to a featureless plain which he termed a **peneplain**. Uplift of land from the sea initiated the cycle and could initiate a second cycle once the first was complete. Such cycles would take millions of years to accomplish and would proceed through a series of stages of youth, maturity and old age, each of which Davis and his followers recognised in different landscapes of today (see Fig 1.2).

Such rigidity in our interpretation of landscape has been abandoned in the latter half of this century, not least because the observation and measurement of the processes that sculpt the surface indicate that many of Davis' suppositions were incorrect. For example, Davis made the assumption that the velocity of a stream is dependent only on its gradient. Study of Chapter 6 will indicate that modern research suggests otherwise. Similarly, the assumption that drainage density is simply a function of time has been challenged; in fact, it reflects a whole range of different variables. The supposition that all slopes decline over time has also been questioned. Many have been shown to retreat in parallel and some isolated cases even reveal localised steepening.

Change over Different Time Scales

Despite recent opinion, our understanding of the long-term development of the landscape has gained much from Davis' pioneering work and it should not be underestimated. Few could deny, for instance, that differences in relief are gradually being reduced by the processes of erosion and weathering. However, rather than seeing a landscape as having reached a particular stage in the inevitable decline towards senility, we tend

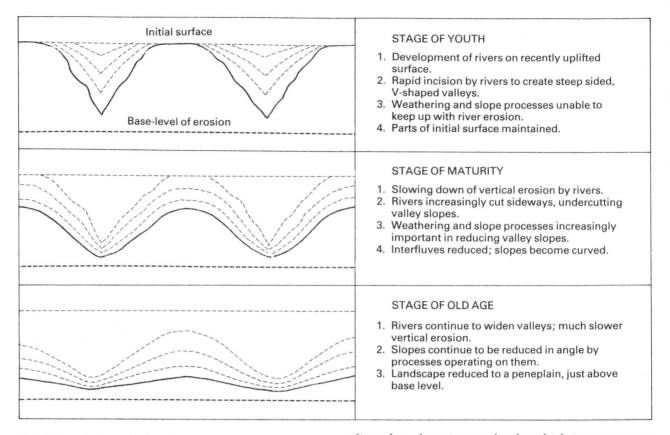

Initial surface Base-level of erosion	**STAGE OF YOUTH** 1. Development of rivers on recently uplifted surface. 2. Rapid incision by rivers to create steep sided, V-shaped valleys. 3. Weathering and slope processes unable to keep up with river erosion. 4. Parts of initial surface maintained.
	STAGE OF MATURITY 1. Slowing down of vertical erosion by rivers. 2. Rivers increasingly cut sideways, undercutting valley slopes. 3. Weathering and slope processes increasingly important in reducing valley slopes. 4. Interfluves reduced; slopes become curved.
	STAGE OF OLD AGE 1. Rivers continue to widen valleys; much slower vertical erosion. 2. Slopes continue to be reduced in angle by processes operating on them. 3. Landscape reduced to a peneplain, just above base level.

Fig 1.2 Stages in the cycle of erosion.

to see the landscape as a combination of landforms, produced by processes working at different rates and at different periods of time.

Thus we see the major relief features, the uplands and the lowlands, as almost timeless observers of human history, being created and destroyed by both tectonic events and surface processes operating over millions or tens of millions of years. It is this scale which gives us the upland surfaces which have been uplifted from seas of earlier geological eras, the strata which have been folded into the escarpments and hills of south east England, the intrusions which have emerged as the moorlands of Dartmoor or Rannoch, and the faults which delineate the Central Lowlands of Scotland.

Superimposed upon these, we can observe relict landforms of considerable age carved by processes no longer operating. In Britain, the obvious example would be the landforms moulded by the glacial, fluvio-glacial and periglacial processes of the Pleistocene Ice Age, and within this group we must not exclude the imprint on the landscape of the higher sea levels of warmer interglacial periods (see Chapter 7). We must look not only to the U-shaped troughs, corries and meltwater channels (see Chapters 8 and 9), but also to the raised shorelines and beaches as evidence of this time scale.

At the next scale we can observe the processes that have operated since the ice retreated 10 000 years ago. Rivers have cut down into Ice Age deposits, and have

adjusted to changing sea levels, which in some cases has meant rejuvenation (see Chapter 6). Present-day shorelines have been created as the new sea level has eroded cliffs and deposited beaches (see Chapter 7). Vegetation patterns have changed as a reflection of an improving climate, and in turn have generated soil development and thus have exerted some control over the stability of slopes (see Chapter 3).

Finally, we have the study of the processes of today, some of which are merely continuations of those that have evolved over thousands or millions of years. In looking at landforms it is the detail that we see change rather than their actual form. Thus we observe river banks collapsing, meanders migrating, slope debris sliding, coastal sediment drifting, beach profiles waxing and waning with the seasons. We also see, more than ever before, human actions interfering with natural processes, so much so that some commentators are concerned about man's increasing efficacy as a sculptor of landscape.

Perhaps the easiest way of understanding landscape change, then, is to see it operating on each of these scales, as shown in Fig 1.3. We may be inclined to overestimate the processes which we see operating in our lifetime but we would be unwise to look only at this time scale, for change on all four of the scales identified in Fig. 1.3 continues to occur. The Mexican earthquake of 1985 should, perhaps, be seen as evidence of change across the longest time scale.

It is difficult to identify current change in the British landscape on the next time scale, for climatic records are too scanty and opinion too divided to know

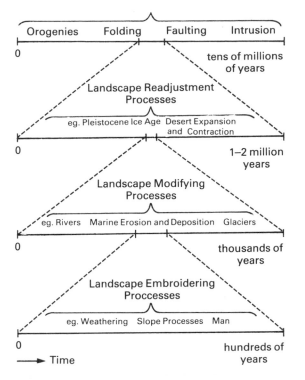

Fig 1.3 Different scales of operation of the processes in a landscape.

whether we are currently declining into an Ice Age or undergoing a long-term warming of our atmosphere. Perhaps we should regard the gradual adjustment of the steepness of ice-riven slopes in the glaciated uplands of northern Britain as evidence at this scale, as processes slowly seek to eradicate the imprint of ice as they have the evidence of Ice Ages of former geological periods such as the Ordovician.

Isostatic readjustment of the land, as it rises as a consequence of its release from the Pleistocene ice sheets, is an example of the third time scale. Evidence suggests that the Grampian Mountains, for instance, are rising by four millimetres a year as a result of this. The continuing adjustment of rivers to post-glacial sea levels is also a process operating on this time scale.

Current Change in the Landscape

Several questions still remain, however. Davis' theory answered some of these; we must also attempt to provide solutions. How drastic is the change that is currently occurring? Is landscape in a constant state of change? Is all change gradual or does it proceed by fits and starts?

How drastic is change?

The significance of present processes really depends on which global environment you happen to inhabit. At plate tectonic margins events of importance on macro time scales occur today with surprising frequency. Even a scanty knowledge of recent Icelandic history will exemplify this – the island of Surtsey emerging from the ocean in 1963, the devastating eruption of Heimeay occurring in 1973 and the constant burbles and emissions of Krafla happening throughout the 1970s. Inhabitants of certain coastlines and river valleys may similarly feel that their environment is still a very volatile one. The frequency of floods on rivers such as the Ganges and the Yangtse, and even the Yorkshire Ouse, certainly suggests a dynamic landscape, as does the speed of cliff erosion at Barton-on-sea and Holderness in Britain. Landscapes in which recent man-induced changes have occurred may be equally fickle. For the majority of the British population, though, the physical environment which they inhabit appears virtually changeless, with the attrition and abrasion of today's weathering and erosion processes inducing only a handful of noticeable alterations during a lifetime.

Concepts of equilibrium

A part of this apparent changelessness undoubtedly reflects the fact that many landscapes have reached an **equilibrium** with the tectonic, climatic or human forces that created them. For example, a particular slope process may have been engendered by certain climatic conditions which produce a debris slope whose angle of repose is maintained by a soil and vegetation combination in harmony with the climate, and so long as this angle and protection are maintained the slope is unlikely to change its form. Only a major intervention by man, a tectonic event or a distinct change in climate is likely to disturb the equilibrium.

However, one may well question why so much continental denudation appears to be occurring when one observes the millions of cubic metres of sediment that are discharged into the oceans each day. Surely some of this denuded sediment must be derived from such apparently stable slopes as the one mentioned here. The answer is that it probably is, for soil creep may well be occurring, especially on slopes of five degrees or more.

The point is that the permanence of the equilibrium really depends on which time scale we use to view the landscape. Observed over a short time scale, say a week or a day, no change may be visible; equilibrium could therefore be said to be **static**. Viewed across a longer period of time, say a hundred or even a thousand years, the slope may be seen to be in equilibrium with the climate, but even so it undergoes various alterations in profile due to the slope processes operating. If we view each change as a minor fluctuation from the basic form to which the slope tends to return after any disturbance, we can still regard the slope as being in equilibrium, a condition usually referred to as **steady state equilibrium** (see Fig 1.4).

If looked at over an even longer time scale, say a million years, the slope may still be in equilibrium even though its form is actually changing. This changing or **dynamic equilibrium** means that an overall balance

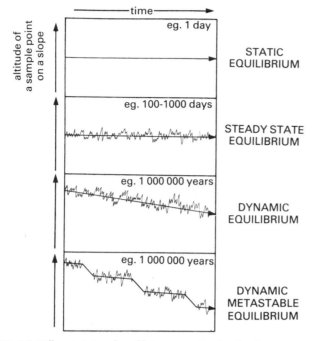

Fig 1.4 Different states of equilibrium operating in a landscape.

still exists between process, form and climate, but as they operate the processes are slowly altering the slope profile. A major change brought about by tectonic uplift or a change in climate could, of course, completely upset the equilibrium at this time scale. However, as Fig 1.4 suggests, a new stage of equilibrium could in time be achieved, the culmination of a series of events, in which **dynamic metastable equilibrium** could be said to be operating.

This understanding of different types of equilibrium helps us to put into perspective the changes caused by extreme natural events. Depending on their magnitude and their outcome they may be responsible for an oscillation from average form at any one of the time scales. Obviously, very large events may be seen as one in 100 000 or one in 1 000 000 year events, in which case the equilibrium they are disrupting needs to be seen as a dynamic one. On the other hand they may be no more than one in 100 or one in 500 year events, causing relatively temporary disturbance to the steady state.

Thresholds of Change

At whatever time scale we are investigating a landscape our understanding may benefit from the study of natural **thresholds**. In the long term a landform may pass from one dynamic equilibrium to a very different one when a natural threshold is passed. For instance, two adjacent river systems may exist for tens of thousands of years, each in its own state of dynamic equilibrium, until headward erosion by a spring in one basin causes sufficient undermining of the narrowing watershed for a threshold to be passed. Suddenly, one river system finds some of its headwaters diverted into the adjacent basin – river capture has occurred. Eons of

erosion have built up to one sudden change demanding a new state of equilibrium to be reached in which each river system is adjusted to the new energy conditions. Thresholds are perceptible at much shorter time scales, too. Take, for example, a meandering river which suddenly breaks through to create an oxbow lake, the rock fall which suddenly transforms a coastal arch into a stack, or the overland flow which becomes sufficiently fierce for gullying to begin. In each case a threshold has been passed, the equilibrium has been shattered. Whether the disturbance of the equilibrium is temporary or permanent will depend on local circumstances and the scale at which the event is observed. For man, the understanding of thresholds, and when and why they occur, is vital. If man is disturbing the normal operation of a natural process it could prove very useful if he knew whether he was accelerating a process towards a major threshold.

Landscape Systems

What is a System?

So complex are the interactions and interrelationships between the various parts of the landscape that over the past two decades or so geomorphologists have often resorted to **systems theory**, which was first developed in the biological sciences to aid their understanding.

A system is simply a series of materials, components or variables linked together by flows or processes. Thus if the human body is a system, it could be said to consist of materials such as skin, hair and flesh, of components such as brain, heart and liver, of variables such as intelligence, height and strength linked by flows of such fluids as blood and lymph and processes such as digestion, the transmission of nerve impulses and respiration. Or, if applied to a drainage basin, a system could consist of materials such as rock, soil and water, of components such as river channel, hillslope and vegetation, of variables such as size, shape and elevation, linked by flows of sediment and water and processes such as mass movement, channel transport and throughflow.

The model can be applied at any scale – thus the universe, the earth and atmosphere, the tropical rain forest zone, a glaciated upland landscape, a drainage basin, a beach or even a back garden are all appropriate systems. The ideal scale and unit by which to classify landscape is the drainage basin, but we can sub-divide this into a series of sub-systems such as individual slopes, the river channel and the flood plain (see Fig 1.5).

Sources of Energy

In order to function, systems require energy. The human body derives this from its consumption of food and drink, the river basin from its intake of solar energy (see Fig 1.6). Most natural systems also benefit from the force of gravity which allows, for example, the

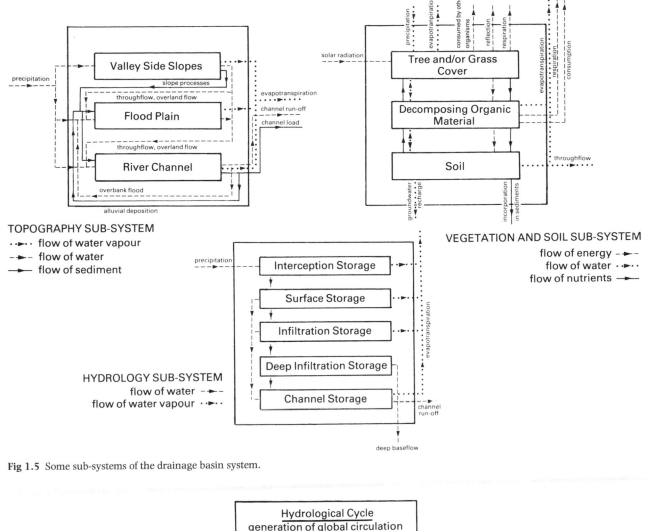

Fig 1.5 Some sub-systems of the drainage basin system.

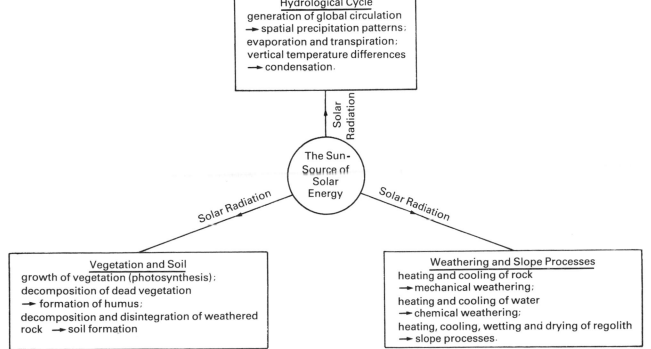

Fig 1.6 The dependence of a natural system (the drainage basin) on solar energy.

potential energy afforded by a certain elevation to be converted into the kinetic energy of motion. This, then, is a source of energy from within a system. A similar internal energy source within the earth-atmosphere system is the spin of the earth which causes air and water to move across the surface.

Systems are often classified into three types – those that are **closed to energy and matter**, an almost impossible case to exemplify naturally except perhaps the universe, those that are **open to energy** but not to matter, for example the earth-atmosphere, ignoring the odd meteorite and space shuttle, and, the most frequently occurring in nature, those **open to energy and matter**. Thus, in a drainage basin, inputs of solar energy and precipitation, which may contain both solids and solutes within it, occur as do outputs of evapotranspiration, river discharge, sediment, organic debris, radiation and deep outflow.

Black Box, White Box and Grey Box Systems

A further classification of systems refers to the way in which we perceive them. A **black box system**, as Fig 1.7 shows, is one in which we take a simple view, identifying inputs and outputs from a box into which we cannot see. Thus we do not observe the processes and flows which transform each input into an output. Such a box may be imposed upon us because we have insufficient knowledge or because we choose to view a system in this way as its simplicity is appropriate to our purpose of study.

At the other extreme, a **white box system** has transparent sides and we can view every detailed reaction and transformation that is occurring. An intricate knowledge permits this, but it may need a computer to envisage it, for the human brain has considerable limitations, as does a page of this book, in attempting mentally or visually to represent the drainage basin.

Between black and white there is a wide range of **grey boxes**, of course, for the depth of our knowledge and the need for different levels of complexity vary greatly. One hopes that the increase in understanding

of the landscape that has occurred over the last few decades means that we all have the opportunity of looking at it through the sides of a less and less darkened box.

Feedback within Systems

Within a system two processes may operate, at any scale, which greatly elucidate our study of the natural environment, namely **negative** and **positive feedback**. If negative feedback is able to operate in a system or in any of its sub-systems, it can be said to be self-regulating. In other words, if any change is introduced, for example in the amount of sediment or run-off discharged into a river channel, the system is capable of absorbing the change and returning it to its former equilibrium with minimal disturbance. However, if positive feedback is operating, a change that occurs may be too great for the system to regulate, a threshold may be passed and sufficient alterations may be engendered for an entirely new equilibrium to be reached, effectively altering the previous system. Extreme natural events, climatic change or human interventions are often inputs of such significance that the natural system cannot cope with them and positive feedback loops are set in operation. Many examples of both types of feedback are given in later chapters (see Chapters 3 and 12 for instance).

Types of System

To enable us to understand further the workings of the most sophisticated systems, Chorley and Kennedy have identified three major types appropriate to landscape study. **Morphological systems** are the simplest, in which the component materials of a system are identified as well as the structural links existing between them. Their aim is to show the layout of a system. Applied to a drainage basin, we may thus see either of the systems in Fig 1.8 as a morphological one.

Cascading systems proceed to a further stage of explanation by indicating how energy and matter flow or cascade through the system, eventually transforming input into output. The hydrological cycle or the solar energy cycle are obvious examples. Both are valuable to the geographer in demonstrating how chain reactions can reverberate through a natural system.

Process-response systems fuse the essential elements of the two preceding ones by demonstrating how the energy or material, as it flows through the system, affects the various components. Without doubt this is the most valuable to the geomorphologist for it explains clearly how the components of the system respond to change and, even more important, how intricately interrelated they all are (see Fig. 1.9).

It is not the intention of this book to look at the landscape only in terms of a series of systems and subsystems as some books do. Systems are used as one of several approaches to study, and their use is emphasised in those contexts where it is most illuminating and most relevant.

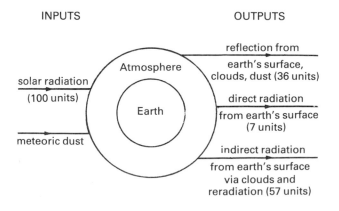

INPUTS   OUTPUTS

reflection from earth's surface, clouds, dust (36 units)

Atmosphere

solar radiation (100 units)

Earth

direct radiation from earth's surface (7 units)

meteoric dust

indirect radiation

from earth's surface via clouds and reradiation (57 units)

Fig 1.7 The earth atmosphere as a black box system.

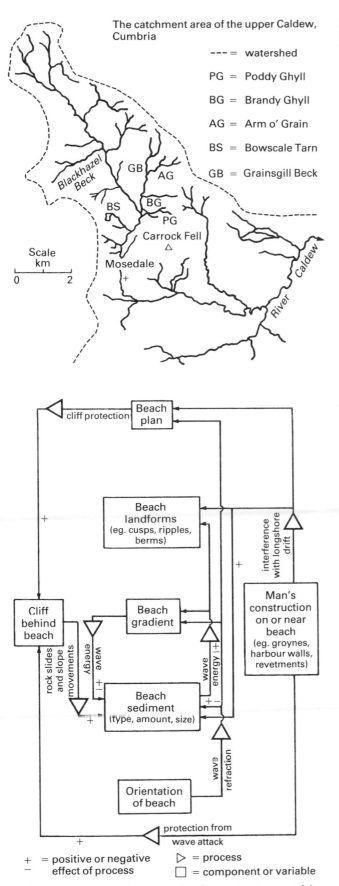

The catchment area of the upper Caldew, Cumbria

--- = watershed

PG = Poddy Ghyll

BG = Brandy Ghyll

AG = Arm o' Grain

BS = Bowscale Tarn

GB = Grainsgill Beck

Scale
km
0   2

Fig 1.9 A process response system: a beach – its components and the interaction of its processes.

+ = positive or negative
−   effect of process

▷ = process

☐ = component or variable

Fig 1.8 The drainage basin as a morphological system.
(a) (*left*) The series of channels that composes a drainage network.
(b) (*below*) The components of a drainage basin and their linkages.

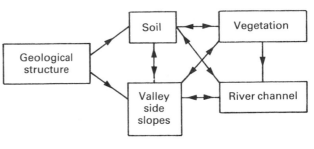

Scale

Considerable space has already been given in this chapter to the topic of time scales and their relevance to our study. As a framework to help us it is useful to refer to the **geological time scale**, reproduced in Fig 1.10. This divides the last 590 million years into three great eras, the Palaeozoic, the Mesozoic and the Cenozoic, each of which is subdivided into periods whose length varies considerably.

We are currently experiencing the Quaternary period. It is thought that the earth is at least 4500 million years old, which may cause one to wonder why geological time details only the last 500 million. The answer is simply that most of the present surface of the earth is formed of rocks no older than this and few present features pre-date the Cambrian period. There are, of course, exceptions even in the British landscape, such as the Charnwood Forest of Leicestershire, the Long Mynd of Shropshire and parts of the Lleyn Peninsula and Anglesey, but as one can see from the rocks and events listed in Fig 1.10, much of Britain is much more recent in origin. It should not be inferred from this, though, that one needs only to look at the surface strata to explain the form of the landscape.

An appreciation of spatial scale is also vital to an understanding of landscape and the processes that form it. Wherever possible in the text, dimensions and sizes have been given and it will aid understanding if these features can be envisaged, perhaps in comparison to more familiar dimensions such as the five or six metres of a Rolls Royce car, the 100-metre running track or the 600 kilometres between London and Edinburgh. It is essential that we always consider the spatial impact of a particular process; localised events, for instance, need not have local outcomes. A river flood originating with snowmelt in an upland area may have repercussions many kilometres away, an earthquake may set in motion tsunamis that traverse the Pacific, and the erosion of a cliff may encourage sedimentation elsewhere on the coast. Events are linked across space. There are no closed systems within the landscape.

Fig 1.10 The geological time scale.

Time	Era		Period	British Examples	Orogeny or mountain building
0.01	CENOZOIC	Quarternary	Holocene	Alluvium, Peat	
2			Pleistocene	Glacial deposits	
5.1		Tertiary	Pliocene	Crag	
24.6			Miocene	not present in Britain	Alpine folding
38			Oligocene	Sedimentaries of Hampshire and Isle of Wight	
65			Eocene	London Clay	
144	MESOZOIC		Cretaceous	Chalk Upper and Lower Greensand Gault and Wealden beds, i.e. many of the Sedimentaries of South and East England	
213			Jurassic	Upper Jurassic – oolitic limestone of Cotswolds and Northamptonshire Lower Jurassic – Lias – shales and limestone from Dorset to North Yorkshire	
248			Triassic	sedimentaries of North West Midlands and Cheshire eg. Keuper Marls and Bunter Sandstones	
286	PALAEOZOIC		Permian	Magnesian Limestone New Red Sandstone	Hercynian Orogeny (eg. parts of Cornwall, S. Ireland)
360			Carboniferous	Coal Limestone of Pennines, Mendips, the Peak District, parts of North Wales Millstone Grit of Pennines	
408			Devonian	Mostly sandstones, but also limestones and shales. Mostly in Devon eg. Old Red Sandstone	Caledonian Orogeny (Scotland, Scandinavia)
438			Silurian	Shales, slates, sandstones and limestones eg. Welsh and Scottish borders (Wenlock limestone)	
505			Ordovician	Shales, gritstones, sandstones and some limestones eg. in Lake District (Skiddaw slates) Also volcanic rocks eg. Borrowdale volcanics	
590			Cambrian	Very hard sandstones, slates, gritstones, eg. in North Wales (Llanberis slates), Shropshire, North West Scotland	

millions of years B P (before present)

Measurement and Observation

It is sometimes said of W M Davis and other early geomorphologists that too much of their work was **deductive**, in other words explanation was based on theoretical evidence. Ideas were developed that were well balanced and logically argued but that were based on virtually no collection of data from the field. Modern geomorphologists have more than made up for this deficit of data by devising brilliant methods of measuring almost every landscape form and process. Their reasoning is **inductive**, theories are developed which are based on solid fact. They work from the particular to the general rather than vice versa.

Fieldwork for the Amateur

This, of course, means that every student of physical geography is expected to participate in the collection of data through fieldwork to gain a full understanding of the operation of landscape processes. Every assignment in the field must be logically structured, though, if it is to be worthwhile. It is no good just going out and measuring anything that moves.

Aims must be clarified before the project is designed, preferably with the establishment of a hypothesis that can be tested and then accepted or rejected. Methods of measurement can then be chosen, which will raise the vital questions of how best to take a valid sample of readings from the field.

Sampling

The design of a sample needs to take account of variation over both time and space. Beach movements, river flows and slope processes, for instance, all vary markedly from year to year, season to season, day to day and even hour to hour. A sufficiently broad time span must be chosen, therefore, to prevent the readings being unrepresentative. This may provide problems for the amateur who has limited time at his or her disposal and who is rarely able to take a continuous log of readings, but adequate compromises can be devised. For example, in a basin hydrological study all the readings can be collected during and after one storm in order to gain a basic understanding of the character of the basin. Measurements of beach or slope profile could be taken at regular intervals during three separate weeks at three different times of the year to provide a useful comparison.

In this last case one is combining two of the three usual methods of sampling, namely systematic and stratified. The sample is **systematic** because it occurs at regular intervals and **stratified** because it divides the year into periods and samples each one. These techniques can also be applied spatially. A river, for example, could be divided into upper, middle and lower course, or into segments of different orders (see Chapter 5), to provide a stratified sample. Systematic sampling along the river channel or across the valley could then be carried out, depending on the aim of the operation.

Random sampling is used less widely in physical than in human geography. Its value may be in sampling stones on a river bed or in taking sediment samples from a deposit. Quadrat analysis is often helpful, in which a square metal frame, usually with sides of 0.5 metre, is randomly thrown on to the study surface, the co-ordinates of the point from which it is thrown having first been selected by the use of random number tables. Samples can then be collected from within the quadrat.

Methods, Results and Conclusions

In each chapter of this book, methods of field measurement are described, most of which can be carried out by sixth-formers. In some cases, if resources are not available, makeshift equipment may need to be devised. Students will often be capable of designing much more practical techniques of measurement than those suggested here. There is nothing sacred about a method just because it is used by a professional.

Numerous methods of analysis are available to clarify the trends apparent in the body of collected data. Statistical techniques such as correlation and the chi-squared test may be appropriate, but simpler techniques are often more effective, such as the calculation of the mean, median or mode used in conjunction with a measure of the range of the data, such as the standard deviation or inter-quartile range. Graphical and cartographic techniques are equally valuable. A geographer has so many techniques available that he or she must not fail to take advantage of their variety. For more detail, the reader should refer to one of the texts on techniques mentioned in the books listed at the end of each chapter.

A critical, but often underemphasised, stage in any field project is the drawing of conclusions. This does not just involve the acceptance or rejection of the

Fig 1.11 The procedure of carrying out a fieldwork project.

AIM:	To investigate the pattern of shingle and sediment on a beach
NULL HYPOTHESIS:	There is no variation in the size of shingle and sediment across the beach
ALTERNATIVE HYPOTHESIS:	The size of shingle and sediment varies across the beach
METHOD:	Map beach Lay out transects across beach Collect samples of beach material Measure axes of stones in sample, sieve finer material
RESULTS:	Graph results; map if necessary Analysis, with appropriate statistical method
CONCLUSION:	Interpret results Accept or reject null hypothesis Consider appropriateness of methods and accuracy of results

Photo 1.1 Langdale Pikes, as depicted by a camera in 1988.

Photo 1.2 The same view as 1.1, as painted by A. Heaton Cooper (1863–1929).

hypotheses but should also include consideration of wider issues such as an evaluation of the methods of data collection. Were they sufficiently refined to measure the object of study? Were they employed at the correct time? Was the sample size appropriate? Were the methods sufficiently objective or were the results prone to vary according to who operated them?

Methods of analysis should be similarly evaluated. The implications of the project should also be discussed in the conclusion. What further questions does the result of this project raise? How could the project be followed up? What are the wider implications of the result, for example for management of a natural process or hazard? The student is likely to benefit far more fully from a project in which the range of conclusions is broad and far-reaching than one which simply demonstrates a text-book principle in the field and proceeds to no further observations.

The Importance of Observation

It is all very well to discuss field techniques, some of which are quite sophisticated, but comprehension of landscape processes is best achieved through careful observation and thought. We all come into contact with situations from which we can learn. Taking time to observe the effects that a bridge is having on the flow of a river, noting how roadside embankments move and change over time, recording where and how water is flowing during a heavy storm or even how the stone of a building has been etched and weathered will pay great dividends. A solid foundation to one's understanding of how landscape processes operate will then allow far more meaningful field projects to be devised, and far more useful conclusions to be drawn from them.

The Relevance of Landscape Study

Understanding the physical landscape is just one aspect of a study which embraces almost every subject in the school curriculum. To comprehend the landscape fully, one also needs to be a student of ecology, of economics, of history, of agriculture and industry and, indeed, of art and literature, for an aesthetic appreciation of the landscape will go as far in reaching an understanding of man's response to the landscape as will the study of any other aspect. The view in Photo 1.1 will be seen to have quite different challenges depending on who is looking at it. The physical geographer may seek an explanation of the landforms in the photograph, the ecologist may see it as a series of different habitats, the land economist in terms of its possible yields, the farmer as a source of income, the historian may require explanation of the field patterns and the style of building, the student of literature as an inspiration for Wordsworth, Coleridge or Southey, and the artist may view it in his own individual way as the painting reveals (Photo 1.2).

The variety of interests which each of these views represents shows how vital it is that landscape study is taken seriously. It is as much a source of recreation and inspiration as it is a source of livelihood and sustenance. The conflicts which rage around British landscapes today, between farming and conservation, tourism and forestry, quarrying and water supply, the Ministry of Defence and the inhabitants of an area, can best be resolved if our knowledge is maximised. As much as anything, that knowledge must include an understanding of the physical processes of landscape and the effect of human activites upon them.

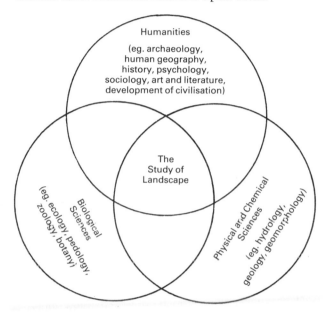

Fig 1.12 Landscape study: the interaction of many disciplines.

Further Reading

Process and Landform, A Clowes and P Comfort (Oliver and Boyd, 1982).

An Introduction to Environmental Systems, G Dury (Heinemann, 1981).

Dynamic Earth Series, *Geographical Magazine* (November 1983 – February 1985).

Systematic Physical Geography, M D Newson and J D Hanwell (Macmillan, 1982)

Techniques in Physical Geography, M D Newson and J D Hanwell (Macmillan, 1973).

Techniques and Fieldwork in Geography, B J Lenon and P G Cleves (Unwin Hyman, 1986).

The Study of Landforms, R J Small (Cambridge, 1978).

Natural Disasters, A Wijkman and L Timberlake (Earthscan, 1984).

Disasters, J Whittow (Penguin, 1980).

Guide to the Lakes, W Wordsworth (1810).

Other References

Physical Geography: A Systems Approach, R J Chorley and B A Kennedy (Prentice Hall, 1971).

The Geographical Cycle, W M Davis, *Geographical Journal* 14, 481–504 (1899).

2

Earth Structure and Landscape

The Structure of the Earth

Shape and Size

Proponents of the flat earth theory have been dealt two major blows in the history of their existence, the first with Columbus' circumnavigation of the globe and the second, and more earth shattering, with satellite photography. How many people in the developed world have not seen the glorious blue and white spectacle of the photographed globe? The earth is spherical. Strictly speaking it is not a perfect orb, for the polar diameter is 0.33 per cent less than the equatorial diameter, but if the scale is reduced, irregularities such as this and the 20 kilometre difference between Mt Everest and the deep Mariana Trench of the Pacific Ocean disappear. The perfect smooth sphere of a classroom globe is totally accurate at its scale. The circumference, of approximately 40 000 kilometres is, in more comprehensible terms, about eight times the distance between London and New York.

The Earth's Interior

Many children may have been excited by the prospect of a journey to the centre of the earth, stimulated by the Jules Verne novel or film which describe such an under-

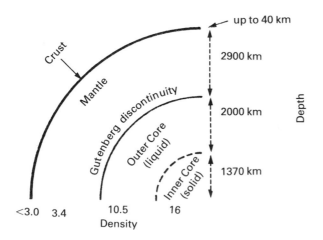

<**Fig 2.1** The structure of the earth.

taking. But such fantasy is likely to remain fictitious, for, as yet, man has drilled no further than 800 metres below the ocean bed, the equivalent in an orange of not even reaching the pith beneath the peel, and the economic viability of delving any deeper is likely to be in doubt for a long time into the future.

Our knowledge of the interior of our planet has to rely on more subtle forms of investigation, most particularly on the study of the path of earthquake waves as they pass through the earth's interior, or on evidence from volcanic eruptions of subterranean materials. The simple model of the earth's interior, shown in Fig 2.1, is the result of such research, with the earth consisting of a series of concentric shells of molten and solid rock. As geomorphologists we are most concerned with the outer layer, the **crust**, as it is changes in the surface of the crust that form our landscape, but we must not ignore the processes and form of the **mantle** and **core** for they may also determine what happens on the surface.

The crust is a thin layer, its depth usually less than one per cent of the earth's radius or between 40 and 50 kilometres, although this varies considerably around the globe. The two layers of crust, **continental** and **oceanic**, differ considerably from each other. The former is thicker, usually 35–40 kilometres, although under high mountain ranges it may be nearly twice that, but it produces only fragments of a shell for it occurs only where there are large land masses or continental shelves or beneath certain shallow seas. The oceanic crust is more complete, forming 60–70 per cent of a shell, but is rarely thicker than six kilometres. It is much more recent in origin than its partner and is made of denser material, primarily basaltic lava, which in turn provides a further contrast to the continental crust, in which granitic rocks are dominant. (Fig. 2.2.)

From his study of earthquake waves a Yugoslavian scientist determined a break point between the crust and the mantle to which his name has been given, the **Mohorovicic Discontinuity**. More useful a line, however, is the one between **lithosphere** and **asthenosphere** which separates the crust and rigid uppermost parts of the upper mantle from a zone of weaker, more plastic rocks at a depth of about 100 kilometres. The asthenosphere extends down to approximately 240 kilo-

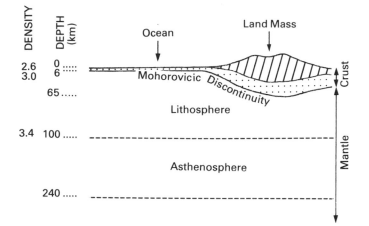

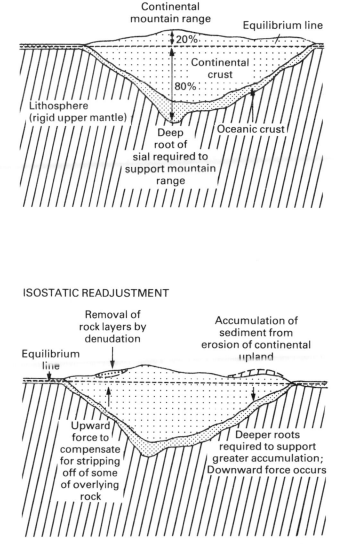

metres beneath the surface and its pliable nature aids our understanding of how vast plates of lithosphere are able to move.

Fig 2.2 The structure of the outer layers of the earth.

The Theory of Isostasy

Although the upper parts of the mantle are rigid, they can deform slowly and this property allows us to use a simple analogy of less dense islands of continental crust 'floating' on the denser mantle beneath (see Fig 2.3). Any floating object needs to displace some of the material that supports it and thus, where continental crust is thick, it is necessary for the 'island' to have deep roots of crust extending down into the mantle. The crust is thus in equilibrium, for the displacement needs to balance the 'floating' continent. This concept has been known since 1889 as **isostasy**. From this principle it follows that if some of the crust is removed, for example by surface erosion, the crust should rise to achieve a new balance above and beneath the equilibrium line, and if additional crust accumulates, for example due to the deposition of sediment, the crust should sink (see Fig. 2.3). Such a theory may at first sight seem of peripheral or even negligible interest to the geomorphologist, but the importance of isostatic equilibrium and adjustment will be seen in later chapters on glaciation and sea level changes.

Plate Tectonics

The Theory

A theory which proposes that America is gradually drifting away from Europe is an immense stimulation to anyone's imagination, and wild visions immediately occur of a widening Atlantic and of the USA one day colliding with the USSR as the Pacific Ocean closes in. But, of course, one's imagination has little respect for facts, for any drift that is taking place is occurring so slowly that even in a century the displacement may be only a metre or two; significant change will take millions of years. Theories which suggest that continents alter their locations over time were not taken seriously until an Austrian meteorologist, Alfred Wegener, published a book on **continental drift** in 1915, and even

Fig 2.3 Simplified diagrams to demonstrate the principles of isostasy and isostatic readjustment.

then the majority of the world's geoscientists dismissed the idea as scornfully as Galileo's society dismissed ideas that the earth was round. Despite persistent attempts by the author and his followers to produce adequate evidence for the theory that an ancient continent of Pangaea had split into smaller continents over the past 200 million years, it did not gain wide respect until the 1960s. By then, sophisticated data collection techniques had been developed by British and American scientists, such as Blackett, which allowed more convincing evidence to be assembled. The basic ideas of Wegener's continental drift have now been absorbed into the widely accepted theory of **plate tectonics**, which suggests that it is not just the continents that are moving but large sections, or plates, of the oceanic crust as well. Seven enormous plates of lithosphere stretching down into the upper mantle have been identified with a further series of much smaller ones as shown in Fig 2.4. Even if we accept the existence of these plates, how should this prove that continents have actually changed their positions?

There are effectively two types of evidence which we can examine: first, that which supports Wegener's theory that the continents have actually drifted, and second, that which shows that it is the movement of the plates that has caused the drift.

The Evidence

For continental drift

The simplest piece of evidence is obtained by glancing at a map of the world. The great bulge of Africa seems to

fit so snugly into Central America, with Brazil safely tucked up into the Bight of Biafra and the Cape of Good Hope cradled in the cupped hand of Southern Argentina and Chile, that extra evidence would seem almost irrelevant. Thus one can gradually piece together the continents into a giant jigsaw which Wegener termed Pangaea, an ancient 'supercontinent' whose constituent pieces are seen in Fig 2.5. If one accepts that sea levels have constantly changed in the past, then the fact that an even closer fit can be seen at 200 metres, or even 2000 metres, below present-day sea level acts as further confirmation. But this is not proof, merely substance for the already converted, and dissenting scientists have astutely pointed out that the Iberian Peninsula prevents the neat fit of Europe into Africa unless some unknown mechanism, of which there is little obvious evidence, has moved Spain and Portugal anti-clockwise since the drifting of the Americas.

However, geological structure can provide us with further circumstantial evidence: for example, the form and pattern of the ancient fold mountains of north west Scotland, Norway, eastern Greenland, northern Newfoundland and the coast of New England are sufficiently similar to suggest that they were once a continuous mountain range, now isolated from each other by the splitting of the continents. This would also have allowed the downfaulted trenches of the Great Glen of Scotland and the Cabot Strait of Canada to have originated in a similar location, and certainly the similarity of their fault lines would not prevent this.

Then there is the evidence yielded by rocks. Unusual violet quartzites, Devonian in age, occur in both Brazil and South Africa at locations which the jigsaw would have once placed adjacent. Could the great thicknesses of similarly composed lava in the Drakensberg Plateau

Fig 2.4 The distribution of tectonic plates.

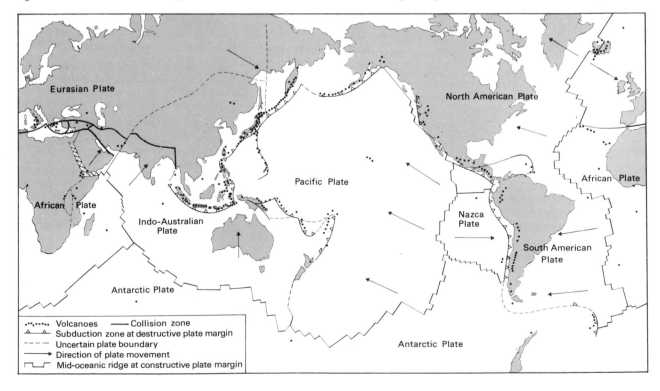

The single land mass of Pangaea, beginning to drift apart. The modern continents are shown in their probable position at the time.

Fig 2.5 Pangaea as it was 200 million years ago. (© B.G.S.)

in South Africa and those of south Brazil once have been joined? Is the occurrence of rare glossopteris leaf fossils in coal deposits in compatible locations in South America, South Africa, India and Australia just a coincidence? Can we dismiss the fact that island deposits in Yampi Sound, Australia bear a remarkable likeness to deposits at Singhbhum in India, two locations that would have been joined in Wegener's Pangaea?

The Ice Age of the late Carboniferous, some 290 million years ago, provides us with further useful, if scanty, evidence. It seems logical to assume that an ice cap extending northwards from the South Pole would reach approximately the same latitude on each continent, and yet analysis of deposits remaining from this glaciation are distributed in a far from logical latitudinal pattern, as Fig 2.6 shows. If, however, we assume that the continents were in their Pangaea locations at the time, the pattern of deposits seems to follow a much more rational distribution.

If the ability to measure ancient magnetic forces of the earth had been at Wegener's disposal in the early twentieth century, he might not have met such deaf ears, for it is the evidence of **paleomagnetism** that has persuaded many geoscientists of recent years that continental drift is feasible. Certain rocks, notably igneous and some sedimentary, retain a magnetisation which reflects the direction of the earth's magnetic pole at the time the rock formed. The magnetic north pole is currently positioned in north Canada, some distance from the rotational pole, but it is known to be mobile having frequently changed its position. We can locate the pole at various times in the past by the study of magnetisation within certain rocks of known age, and by measuring this paleomagnetism in rocks of many different ages we can show that the magnetic pole has

moved across the globe in what is known as a **polar wandering curve**. If we repeat this process for rocks through the ages on a different continent we should, if our method is correct, produce the same polar wandering curve. However, when the method is carried out in both Africa and South America two quite different, but approximately parallel, curves are produced, as Fig 2.7a shows. It is not until we fit our continental jigsaw together, as in Fig 2.7b, that we discover that the two curves coincide, and coincidence is essential unless we are to suggest that the earth has two magnetic south poles.

For plate tectonics

Do we now have sufficient evidence to support the conclusion that the continents have moved?

If we do, we still need to proceed further to silence Wegener's critics, for we need to provide evidence of the process by which the continents drift. This, in turn, means we must show how the plates on which the continents sit can move. The mechanism for plate movement occurs at certain of the plate margins where molten rock from the asthenosphere is forced upwards, perhaps by convection currents, and on reaching the sea bed solidifies and pushes apart the two plates that meet there. These junctions are termed **constructive margins** and occur in the form of **mid-oceanic ridges**, for example down the centre of the Atlantic and Indian

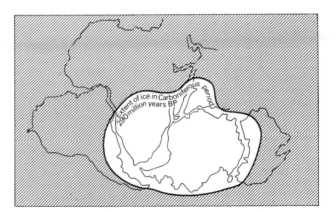

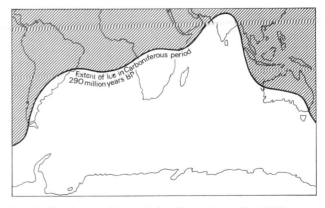

Fig 2.6 Distribution of ice in Carboniferous times. (© B.G.S.)
(a) The continents in their pangaea positions.
(b) The continents in their present positions.

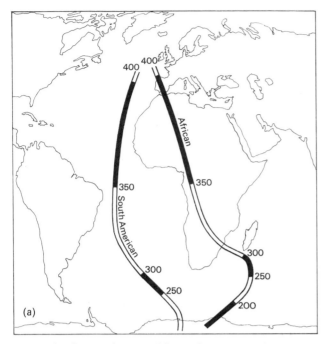

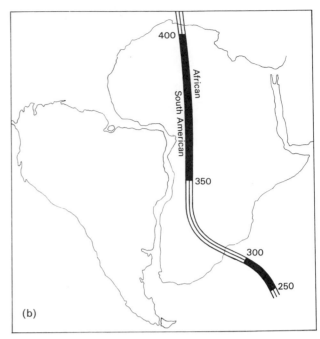

Fig 2.7 The changing location of the south magnetic pole.
(a) Africa and South America in their present positions.
(b) Africa and South America in their positions during an early geological period (250–400 million years BP).

Oceans. Proof that such ridges exist is easily obtained by submarine surveys, but proof that their emerging magma forces apart continents in a process of **ocean floor spreading** is more difficult to assemble. Much research has been carried out on the Atlantic. Iceland lies across the mid-Atlantic Ridge and is largely the product of countless eruptions along it. The symmetry in the ages of its ancient lavas around the currently active central depression suggests that it is being forced outwards. On a larger scale, paleomagnetic analysis of the ocean bed right across the Atlantic reveals that a

regular striped pattern of present and reversed polarity exists, as shown in Fig 2.8.

It has been proposed that as igneous rock emerges from the mid-oceanic ridge it takes on a magnetisation according to the current magnetic field of the earth. As this systematically reverses over time the ocean bed will consist of a series of alternating magnetic stripes, almost exactly symmetrical on each side of the ridge. At a similar scale, the oldest rock on each island in the Atlantic has been dated by Wilson and once again the data show that the age of rock increases with distance

Fig 2.8 Schematic diagram of the ocean bed to demonstrate the pattern of magnetization of the rocks. Note that the pattern of magnetic stripes does not coincide perfectly with the periods of normal and reversed polarity, but that there is a broad relationship.

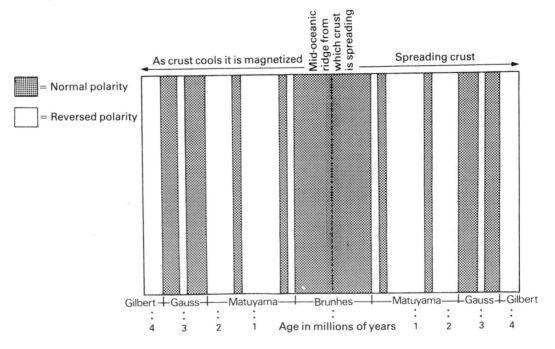

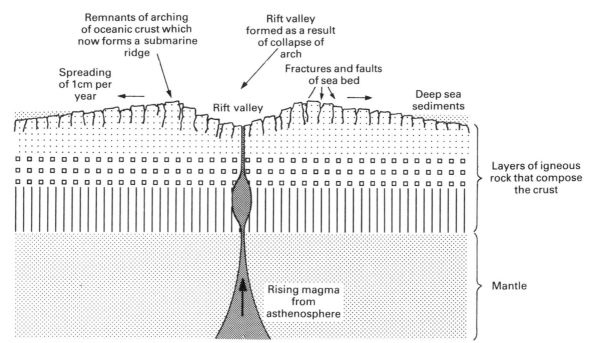

Fig 2.9 Cross-section of a mid-oceanic spreading ridge. (© B.G.S.)

on each side of the ridge, thus suggesting that ocean floor spreading has been a more or less continuous process.

So, there seems to be a considerable body of collected data to support not only Wegener's continental drift but also the theory that the continents move on giant lithosphere plates which are being forced apart at mid-oceanic ridges.

The Effects on Landscape

You might by now have questioned what all this has to do with physical geography, and in particular the geography of landscape. How can a process such as plate tectonics, to which scales of global proportions and millions of years are appropriate, be relevant to our concern with twentieth century landscape? Some eminent geomorphologists would say there is no relevance. Others, however, justify its study by showing its relevance to the underlying structure of many landscapes and, whilst it may not affect the detail or even the surface of some current landforms, in many cases it has produced the basic foundations.

Many of the features produced by the movements of tectonic plates are to be found on or near to their margins, and as far as man is concerned this may be of greater significance when the margin is on or near to land. Three types of margin are usually identified, the constructive, the destructive and the conservative.

Constructive margins

Constructive margins are almost always found beneath oceans and produce the mid-oceanic ridges referred to previously. As magma rises from the asthenosphere the crust above it arches up until eventually the centre of

the arch collapses into a **rift valley**. This is slowly widened through the centuries as the magma breaks through and solidifies on the sea bed. The ridge today will therefore appear as a broad rift valley with the remnants of the former arch reaching 2000–4000 metres above the sea bed on each side of the rift valley (Fig. 2.9). This vast submarine trench is rarely straight or continuous as the enormous compression and tension have produced cracks known as transform faults, sometimes 100 kilometres long, which cut perpendicularly across the valley, as Fig 2.10 shows.

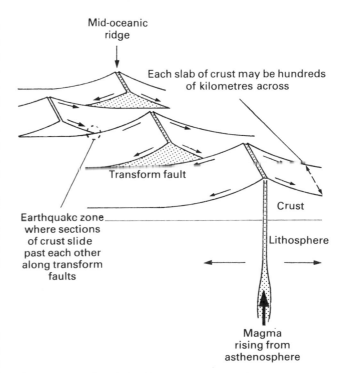

Fig 2.10 Transform faults along a mid-oceanic ridge.

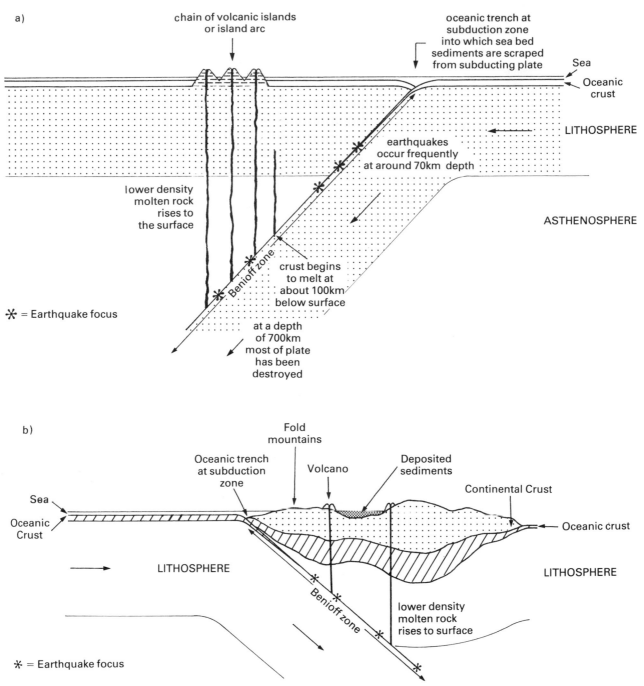

Fig 2.11 Destructive plate margin or subduction zone.
(a) Where oceanic plate meets oceanic plate.
(b) Where oceanic plate meets continental plate.

These submarine locations are so remote that direct influences on landscape are few, except where volcanic eruptions on and around the ridge have been of such magnitude that they produce volcanic islands emerging from the sea. The chain of islands in the mid-Atlantic, from Iceland south through Ascension Island to Tristan da Cunha, is a prominent example. There is little evidence that constructive margins exist within continents, although some geologists have suggested that the East African Rift Valley is an ancient margin, and others believe that the Red Sea and Gulf of Aden may be a developing margin that will eventually split Asia from Africa.

Destructive margins

Little has been said so far of the consequences on the earth of all this newly created crust which is developing at the constructive margins for, surely, if the shell of the globe is growing the earth must be expanding its circumference; unless, that is, there are other locations on earth where the crust is being destroyed. It is in support of this latter idea that **destructive margins** have been identified at various plate junctions where one plate can be seen to be sliding down beneath another, having been forced against it by the movement initiated at a constructive margin. This subterranean sliding is known as **subduction**, with the more mobile of the two plates sliding at an angle of approximately 45 degrees down into the mantle (see Fig. 2.11). It is easy to get the impression that this movement is as smooth as a conveyor belt, but a plate of lithosphere of perhaps 100 kilometres thickness does not behave like well-lubricated machinery. Its uneasy, lumbering path of collisions, compression and tension will produce a series of earthquakes not only at the junction of the plates where compression is high, but through much of the **Benioff Zone**, which is the name given to the belt of seismic activity on the descending slab of lithosphere. Below 700 kilometres earthquakes cease, for by this depth the lithosphere plate has been melted by the high temperatures of the mantle, and thus finally the crust has been destroyed.

A series of distinctive features occurs at destructive margins, their nature dependent on whether the margins are of two plates of oceanic crust, two of continental crust or one of each. Where two oceanic plates meet, the resultant features may rarely be seen but are nevertheless dramatic. **Oceanic trenches** such as the 10 kilometre deep Tonga Trench of the Pacific may stretch for many hundreds of kilometres along the sea bed at the point of contact of the two plates. Chains of volcanic islands, known as **island arcs**, are often found close to such margins, located above the non-subducting plate. They result from the upwelling of magma from the melted subducting plate which forces its way through cracks in the crust to erupt into andesite volcanoes, which in the most extreme cases penetrate above the ocean to produce island chains such as Indonesia or the Kuril Islands, north of Japan. To explain why the melted magma wells up rather than being absorbed into the mantle we must remember that the material of the crust is less dense than that of the mantle and, on melting, it will ascend.

Where oceanic crust meets a plate of continental crust, for example where the Pacific plate collides with the South American, the results are even more dramatic. As the oceanic plate subducts beneath the continental, a 4500 kilometre long trench has formed from Panama to Tierra del Fuego. Significantly, the great thicknesses of sediment on the American plate have, in the last 200 million years or more, been squeezed and contorted into the **fold mountains** of the Andes, due to the continued compression and collision. In the same way that subducted crust rose to form island arcs, so here it wells up to produce the volcanoes of the Andes range such as Cotopaxi in Ecuador and Nevado del Ruis in Colombia which erupted spectacularly in 1985 (Fig 2.11b).

The consequences of the collision of continental plate with continental plate are not difficult to deduce given the above knowledge, but the complexity of the processes that occur must not be underestimated for

they are still only partially understood. In simple terms, colliding continents, such as Eurasia with Africa and India, are likely to produce immense uplift and, most likely, highly contorted fold mountains such as the Alps and Himalayas. It is not within the scope of this book to delve any further into the operating mechanisms, and students should refer to the bibliography for easily accessible sources that do.

Conservative margins

Some geoscientists identify a third form of margin, the **conservative**, best illustrated by the junction between the North American and Pacific plates, as in Fig 2.12. At such margins crust is neither being created nor destroyed, hence the term conservative. Effects may nevertheless be dramatic. The world famous San Andreas Fault lies along such a junction, and movement along it has already destroyed San Francisco once, in 1906, and may do so again as the Pacific plate continues to slide alongside its North American neighbour.

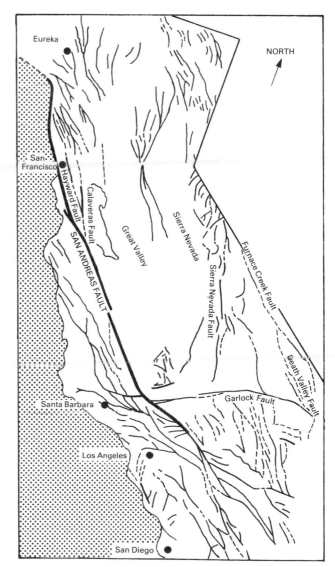

Fig 2.12(a) California showing major fault lines.

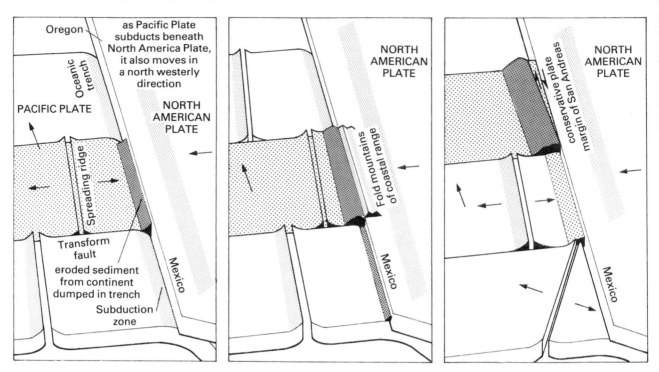

Fig 2.12(b) Diagrammatic map of plate margin to explain origin of San Andreas Fault.

The Effects on the British Isles

Plate tectonics theory, then, has provided us with an explanation of many features of the world landscape, most significantly fold mountains, volcanoes and volcanic islands. It is clear from Fig 2.4 that the vast majority of the world's active earthquakes and volcanoes lie along the margins of the plates. A British geomorphologist, however, may well ask if this has any relevance to our islands.

As far as today's movements are concerned, Britain is remote from active zones and more or less free from earthquakes and volcanoes as a result. It is for this reason that nuclear waste has been sent to Britain for disposal and storage from nations in more volatile, plate margin locations, such as Japan.

Although man's understanding of plate tectonics is still in its infancy, the processes themselves have been occurring continuously, perhaps since the formation of the earth 4500 million years ago. Thus, Britain's landscape is able to bear witness to both destructive and constructive phases in the history of the earth's crust, and examples of many of the plate margin features described above can be found in the British Isles. The present constructive phase which has created the Atlantic Ocean may well have been preceded by a phase of subduction and the closing in of an ocean which itself had been created by an even earlier period of plate movement. Much of this, of course, must be conjecture, but geologists believe, for example, that the Caledonian Mountains of Scotland were created in a previous period of subduction, that Scotland was once part of what is now the Americas and became attached to

Britain in a plate collision some 500 million years ago, and that the Snowdon and Scafell ranges may once have been island arcs in a former ocean. It is not just the movement of European and American plates that has affected Britain, for the plate collision which created the Alps caused so much disturbance that waves within the crust spread right across Europe up-folding the chalk and other sediments of south east England into undulating downland.

The seas around us also bear witness to plate movement. Rift valleys formed in a similar way and at a similar time to the mid-Atlantic Ridge, but on a smaller scale, produce deep trenches in the North Sea, down the west coast of Ireland and Scotland and north into the Norwegian Sea. Indentations in the coastline such as the Solway Firth, Cardigan Bay and the Bristol Channel may also owe their existence to the creation of rift valleys and their subsequent drowning.

Conclusion

Throughout this discussion it may have been implied that the theory of plate tectonics now has universal support. Although a substantial majority of geoscientists support it, there is some dissent. Some have questioned the measurements of paleomagnetism, indicating their wide degrees of error and challenging the validity of drawing such positive conclusions from readings in ancient rocks which are never more than faint. If we cannot trust these readings then vital evidence for the theory vanishes. More recently, some geoscientists have looked to other even more revolutionary theories which we must be careful not to treat in the same way as the early critics received Wegener. One of these is the expanding earth thesis, which, whilst supporting the idea of continental drift away from an ancient Pangaea, suggests that the creation of new crust is in fact causing the earth to expand in size. The strongest point in favour of this is that if one tries to reconstruct Pangaea from a jigsaw of today's continents, it is much more neatly achieved if the pieces are placed on a globe some 20 per cent smaller than today's.

Earthquakes

Introduction

The Times, 19th April 1906: SEVERE EARTHQUAKE AT SAN FRANCISCO

A few minutes of disturbance, caused by one of those mysterious commotions in the earth whose operation we can only dimly fathom, have sufficed to change the glorious possibilities of San Francisco's future. What we call the solid earth is in fact a shivering jelly, perpetually vibrating to shocks great and small. In its interior forces are at work of which we know but little.

The Times, 24th November 1980: BIG DEATH TOLL FEARED AS EARTHQUAKE ROCKS ITALY

The Trieste Observatory reported that it had registered two shocks, one with an intensity of 6.5 on the Richter Scale and one of 4.9 degrees... the earthquake's epicentre was located in Eboli, a small poverty-stricken town near the spectacular bay of Salerno.

The two short extracts above, from the same newspaper but 74 years apart, demonstrate not only how much the experts' understanding of earthquakes has deepened during this century, but also how much greater is the public's knowledge of earthquakes, for the front page of *The Times* in 1980 is able to use terms like '**Richter Scale**' and '**epicentre**' without further explanation. This pursuit of explanation has been stimulated by a demand to lessen the immense impact on man that earthquakes can have, an impact that can be just as great now as it was in 1906 when the despatch to *The Times* shown in Fig 2.13 was written.

The Mechanics of Earthquakes

Earthquakes occur when the normal movements and minor adjustments of the crust are concentrated into a single shock, or a series of sudden large shocks in a short period of time. This means that rather than the crust absorbing the tension or compression that is brought about by movements of the tectonic plates, a rupturing takes place and the rock slides along new cracks or along pre-existing fault lines. This movement generates **seismic** energy which travels from the focus of the earthquake through the earth in three different types of wave, the **P** or **primary wave**, the **S** or **secondary wave** and the surface waves, of which there are two types, the **Love** and the **Rayleigh**.

The contrast between the P and S waves is clearly seen in Fig 2.14. Underground waves travel much faster than surface waves, and the deeper into the mantle they penetrate the faster they can travel. The core has an important effect on their movement. It does not

Yesterday morning shortly after 5 o'clock the city of San Francisco was visited by an earthquake of the most violent kind, followed three hours later by a second shock which completed the ruin wrought by the first. A large part of the city seems to have been completely wrecked, the damage being greatest in the business quarter. Unknown numbers of people were crushed under the falling buildings, while the more fortunate rushed panic-stricken into the streets in their night attire. Then, as nearly always happens in such cases, the horror of the situation was immensely aggravated by fires breaking out at many points among the debris of the ruined buildings. The earthquake broke the water-mains, thus rendering the firemen almost powerless to cope with the flames, while the gas-mains, also destroyed by the shock, contributed powerfully to the conflagration. A fresh easterly wind was blowing, as if to destroy what small chance remained of saving the rest of the town. Dynamite was freely used in the attempt to check the spread of the flames by blowing up houses, but the fire seems to have overleaped every gap, and so far as can be judged at present there is nothing to prevent the destruction of the whole of San Francisco, one of the finest, largest, and busiest cities in the United States, covering an area of some 30,000 acres and with a population of over 350,000 souls.

Fig 2.13 Extract from *The Times*, Thursday 19th April 1906.

allow the penetration of S waves, probably because of its liquid nature, and refracts and slows down the P waves which are normally the fastest moving type.

The movement and tracking of these waves has been enormously important not only in helping us to trace the focus of an earthquake, but also in adding to our knowledge of the internal composition of the earth (see Fig. 2.16).

To pinpoint the **focus** of an earthquake or the more useful epicentre, which is the point on the earth's surface immediately above the focus, readings are required from three separate wave recording instruments, or **seismographs**, positioned at different stations on the globe. From each of these locations circles can be drawn, the radius being the calculated distance of the focus from the seismograph. The three circles meet at the origin of the earthquake, as Fig 2.15 shows. For the outside world the news received by the seismograph may be the first of the earthquake, for, as in the case of a 'quake in remote Irian Jaya in 1976, it may take at least two weeks for word of mouth to penetrate from the disaster.

The Location of Earthquakes

Earthquakes are most common along the margins of tectonic plates where compression and tension in the crust are greatest, and most earthquakes of recent years, for example in Algeria, southern Italy, Iran, Mexico, El Salvador, Turkey, Yugoslavia and

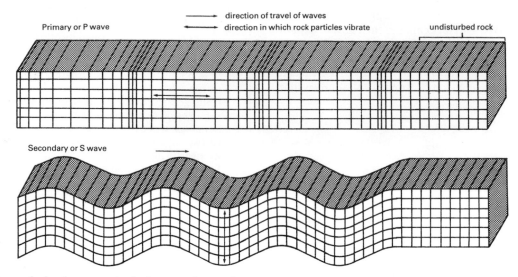

Fig 2.14 The methods of movement of primary and secondary waves. (© B.G.S.)

Nicaragua, can be located on Fig 2.4 in such places. However, there are plenty of exceptions, for some devastating earthquakes, such as that at Bucharest in 1977 and those in central China, occur inside plates, probably at ancient weaknesses in the crust, possibly along old fault lines or at former plate margins. Even Britain is not free from the earthquake hazard. As recently as 19th July 1984 a shock recording 5.5 on the Richter Scale, with its epicentre in North Wales, rattled teacups in the BBC canteen in London, and on Boxing Day, 1979 the Borders of Scotland and England were severely shaken. Even greater events have preceded these. In 1382 Canterbury Cathedral suffered considerable damage, and in 1580 Dover Cliffs and many Kent churches were diminished in size. The exact cause is not known, although certain ancient fault lines are thought still to be active, notably the Great Glen, the Neath Disturbance in South Wales and various submarine ones.

The Effects of Earthquakes

The effects of earthquakes on human activity are well documented and the misery that results is imprinted on most of our minds by television or newspaper photography. Their effect on landscape is less frequently recorded by the media. New fault lines may be opened, fault scarps created, old fault lines reactivated, and vertical or horizontal displacement may occur along them. In February 1931 an earthquake in Napier, New

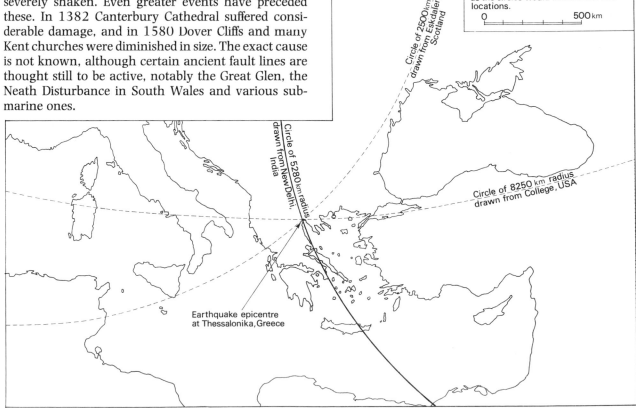

Fig 2.15 The epicentre of an earthquake plotted from three seismometers.

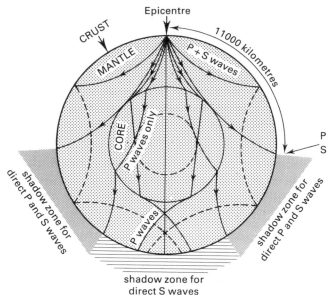

Epicentre

CRUST

MANTLE

11000 kilometres

P + S waves

CORE

P waves only

P waves

shadow zone for direct P and S waves

shadow zone for direct P and S waves

shadow zone for direct S waves

Fig 2.16 The paths of primary and secondary waves through the earth's interior.

——— P and S waves

– – – Indirect P and S waves

P waves take 14 minutes to reach here
S waves take 25 minutes to reach here

Zealand raised an area of the coast by two metres, sufficient to reclaim naturally a lagoon on which an airport now stands. Rocks may be changed in character, perhaps, by frictional heat altering their chemistry, or by stress and strain creating new lines of weakness within them. The indirect impact on landscape may be even more significant. The earthquake which accompanied the eruption of Mt St Helens in 1980 sent a glacier sliding down the mountain side which later contributed to the flooding of the Toutle River.

Similarly, avalanches, debris slides, mudflows and dam bursts can be triggered, all of which eventually bring about greater alteration to the landscape than the earthquake itself. The indirect consequences of submarine earthquakes are also profound, for the movement of the sea bed can generate waves, known as **tsunamis**, which, on reaching shallow water near land, can create massive walls of water whose erosive capabilities are immense. With the Pacific Ocean and its continental margins experiencing some 80 per cent of all the world's shallow earthquakes and nearly all its deep ones, it is not surprising that most Pacific islanders from Japan to New Zealand are well aware of the dangers of tsunamis.

Earthquake Monitoring

There is nothing more stimulating to research into earthquake prediction than a massive disaster, and at most recent events there have been nearly as many research scientists on the scene as relief workers. The most beneficial effect of the San Francisco disaster of 1906 was that it not only stimulated research into the measurement of seismic waves, but also eventually led Richter in 1935 to lay out his scale of earthquake magnitude. Because the energy release of earthquakes varies so much a logarithmic scale was used by Richter, the highest recording on which was in 1960 when 8.9 was registered in Chile. Extensive monitoring of all earth tremors now occurs throughout the world, and each tiny piece of information gleaned may help a little in the quest for accurate prediction. The location of

active zones is well known and the mathematical probability of movement along them within the next 100 years has often been calculated, but it is of little use to the inhabitants of an earthquake zone to know that movement will occur, say, one year in thirteen, for that year could be a long or a short time coming. Consequently, local monitoring in areas most susceptible to 'quakes takes place. This can help identify smaller foreshocks, notice the creation of new cracks or the upward expansion of rock surfaces, or even observe changes in animal behaviour. For over 20 years now a massive movement of the San Andreas fault in California has been predicted, a period of inactivity long enough to make inhabitants blasé about precautions and thus increase the potential effects.

The San Andreas Fault provides us with an interesting example of how man might attempt to modify the potential effects of an earthquake. A scheme has been proposed in which a series of holes would be drilled along the fault line, several kilometres deep at approximately half-kilometre intervals. Large quantities of liquid, conceivably sewage water, could then be pumped into the holes with the intention of increasing pressure so as to trigger off an earthquake or series of earthquakes of low magnitude. Thus, the tension could be released and hopefully major devastation could be avoided. Such attempts to trick nature need to be very carefully planned, for unpredicted consequences can often leave man with the losing hand.

Faulting and Landscape

Several times already in this chapter we have referred to faulting, and it is appropriate that we should now examine this process in more detail. A **fault** is a fracture of rock strata caused by compression or tension, which in turn are the result of crustal movement. The fracture will be accompanied by vertical or horizontal displacement of rock as it slides along a fault plane.

Effects of Faulting

By examining the effects of faulting on landscape we should be able to assess how important these movements are. The degree to which a fault shapes a landform will depend on a variety of the fault's characteristics. The size of the fault or fault zone is a predominant

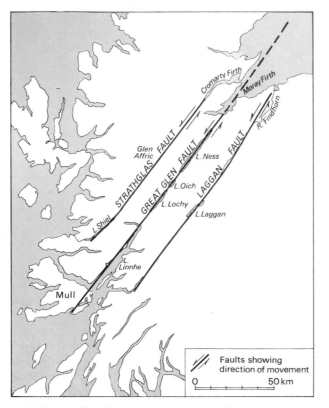

Fig 2.17 Great Glen, showing major fault lines. The major relief features of the region are dominated by the great wrench faults of Laggan, Strathglas and the Great Glen.

influence, and to clarify this point one needs only to contrast the insignificant impact of a hairline fracture of a few metres cutting across a rock surface with the influence that the Great Glen series of faults has had on northern Scotland. Not only have these Great Glen faults created a major NE–SW trending trench which virtually divides Scotland into two islands, but the high density of fault lines has also created a swathe of fractured rock, or **shatter belt**, so deep that glaciers have been able to carve the vast basin of Loch Ness, with its water capacity of nearly 7500 million m³. The loch stretches between virtually straight walls for an impressive 37 kilometres, continuing a line begun by the small basins of Loch Lochy, Loch Oich and Loch Linnhe to the south west (Fig 2.17).

Between these two extremes of scale are many faults of intermediate size, for example the one which forms the impressive western escarpment of Cross Fell in the Pennines. Here, the vertical displacement of a fault line has allowed the Vale of Eden to develop at the foot of Cross Fell which towers some 500 metres above it, and which itself is part of a massive **fault-tilted block** of rock which makes up the northern part of the Pennines.

Although the scale of the faulting is of great relevance, the actual type of fault that occurs is important. In Fig 2.18, not only are different types of vertical displacement illustrated, but also different types of horizontal movement. It is not difficult to imagine that in many cases both vertical and horizontal movement

may occur. It goes almost without saying that the shape of a landscape feature could be dictated by the type of fault.

A third relevant consideration in our analysis of faulting and landscape is the time when the faulting actually occurred. In some cases the effects may be fresh from a recent earthquake, such as the 1.5 metre high **fault scarp** that remains near Meckering, Australia from a 1968 earthquake. Other fault scarps, however, may have been obliterated and their influence reduced to irrelevance, or, as in the case of Giggleswick Scar in North Yorkshire, diminished in grandeur. This once mighty scarp, that may have reached up to 1000 metres, is now a lowly 90-metre **fault line scarp**, which is the term given to fault scarps that have moved from their original location.

Millennia of erosion and weathering may exploit weaker strata to such an extent that the original effect of the faulting can be reversed, as in Fig 2.19, to produce an **obsequent fault line scarp** such as the Mere Fault in the Vale of Wardour in Wiltshire. Some geomorphologists suggest that this process can continue even further to produce a **resequent fault line scarp** whose orientation reflects the original one.

Another facet of timing is whether the faulting occurred during an important plate-moving phase such as a major mountain-building period or **orogeny**. If so, the effects are likely to be profound. The two great

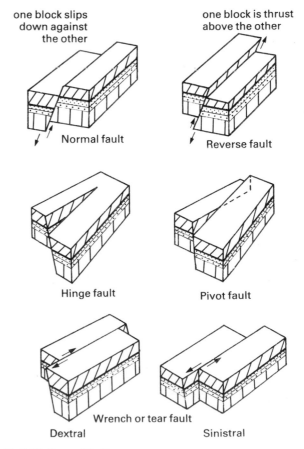

Fig 2.18 Types of fault.

events in the history of the **tear fault** of the Great Glen, its initiation and its later horizontal displacement of some 100 kilometres, both occurred in great orogenies, the first in the Caledonian, the second in the Hercynian. Movements are still occurring there, such as that around Inverness in 1769, but these have insignificant effects compared to those of the past for, as far as we can tell, Britain is not experiencing a major orogeny at present.

Fault lines rarely occur in isolation and, in any assessment of the impact of faulting on landscape, it is essential to consider the different patterns of association of fault lines with each other. We have aleady implied that a high density of faults, as in a shatter belt, is likely to have a more drastic effect than an isolated, individual fault. Another example of high density faulting is when faults occur in more or less parallel lines, causing **block faulting**, when sections of rock strata between them are uplifted or downthrown. As Fig 2.20 shows, three major features, **horsts**, **rift valleys** and **basin and range topography** may result.

Of these features there is probably most controversy over rift valleys. The theory that suggests they result from magma doming up the crust and causing related subsidence has been dealt with in connection with mid-oceanic ridges and may be relevant for some continental troughs such as the Rhine, but other more traditional theories rely on the processes of compression and tension in the crust. Thus, compression-theorists argue that blocks slide down fault planes caused by being squeezed from each side, whilst the tension-theorists hold that the valley is created as two great masses are pulled apart and blocks slide down into the trough left between them. Whatever the cause, the effects can be profound as the great rift valleys of the Rhine, Jordan and East Africa bear witness. Britain, too, has its rift valleys, in the Midland Valley of Scotland and the valley of the River Clwyd on the Welsh Borders, although neither is a spectacular example on a world scale. Hollywood cowboy films provide the easiest way of viewing basin and range topography, for it is best exemplified in the south west USA. Series of fault scarps separate basins from each other, and it does not take too much imagination to visualise, in Fig 2.20a, the lone cowboy drifting across the downfaulted basins of Nevada or Utah past cacti and sagebrush, quite unaware of the awaiting ambush in the range above the fault scarp. (See also Photo 2.1.)

Faulting alone, though, may leave little imprint on scenery, and we need to consider what other processes have been working to exploit the fault since its initiation and in what ways the fault has affected these processes. A glacier or a river, for instance, may have its path dictated by a fault that may otherwise have remained unnoticed. What better example of a fault-guided valley such as this could one have than Moffatdale, in Photo 2.2? Here, a glacier has used the weakness provided by fault-induced fracturing to erode a valley remarkable for both its depth, which plummets some 200 metres lower than tributary valleys which lacked the faulting advantage, and its straightness.

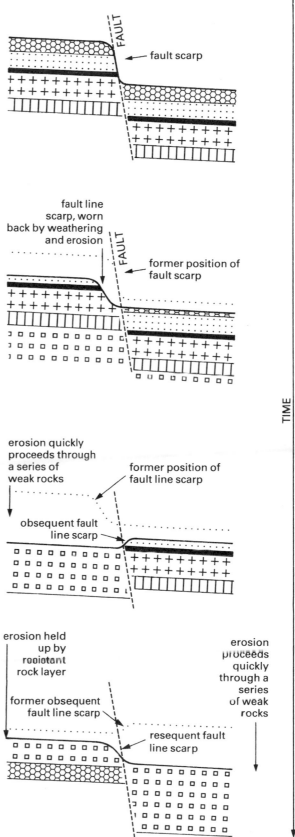

Fig 2.19 A possible evolution of a fault line scarp.

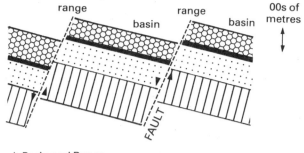

a) Basin and Range

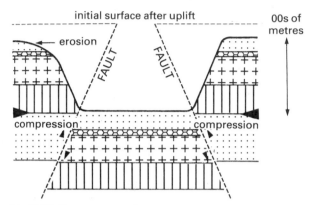

b) Rift Valley: compression

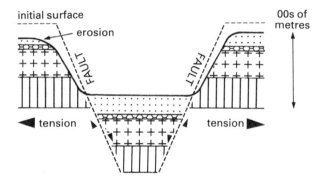

c) Rift Valley: tension

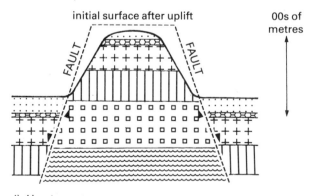

d) Horst

Fig 2.20 Possible outcomes of block faulting.
(a) Basin and range topography – in this case the blocks are tilted, producing asymmetrical basins.
(b) Rift valley – caused by compression of strata from each side.
(c) Rift valley – caused by tension in earth's crust.
(d) Horst – uplifted block, e.g. the Black Forest of southern Germany.

Fault-guided river valleys are more numerous than glacial examples, but rarely as spectacular, although the upper part of Cound Brook near Church Stretton in Shropshire makes a dramatic example.

Another process which exaggerates faults is coastal erosion, and on the southern coast of the Gower Peninsula it is possible to see many inlets, such as Mewslade Bay, that owe their existence to small fault lines running perpendicular to the coastline. Where fault lines run parallel to the coast they can produce strikingly straight boundaries to the land such as the 40 kilometre stretch between the Black Isle and Tarbat Ness at the north-east end of the Great Glen. Faulting can produce a seemingly unnatural straightness of line, so clearly demonstrated in the outline of Loch Ness. In addition, faulting has the ability to juxtapose rocks which appear as unlikely bedfellows and whose contrasts may result in sudden, sharp changes in an otherwise smooth landscape.

In our assessment, then, we have examined five characteristics of faulting which may determine its impact: the scale, the type, the time that it occurred, the pattern of faults and the processes which have exploited them. One is not always more important than another, for some or all of these characteristics working together or against each other are likely to determine the present impact.

Photo 2.1 Basin and range country, northern Nevada, USA. Notice the flat semi-arid plain of the basin and the sudden change of slope at the distant fault scarp.

Folding and Landscape

One has only to compress a large paperback book between one's hands to simulate the possible contortions that folding of rock strata can produce. **Folding**, like faulting, is another response to the constant movement and readjustment of tectonic plates, and its effects on landscape are similarly controlled by a series of conditioning factors.

First, it is essential that one establishes the importance of scale. Tectonic movements have created the

Photo 2.2 Moffatdale, Southern Scotland: this glaciated trough follows a fault line.

great fold mountain ranges, and are also responsible for inducing many of the less striking uplands whose more gentle uplifiting took place many hundreds of kilometres from plate margins. These smaller folds still play a prominent part in defining scenery, but then there are other folds that do not, for many a cliff or boulder has tiny folds locked into its strata and their presence offers little more than localised resistance.

There are many types of fold; the classification in Fig 2.21 represents a continuum from the simplest to the most complex rather than a set of clear-cut groups to which folds must adhere.

The major differences between the types, as the experiment with a book will show, reflect both the amount of pressure exerted from each side and the rigidity of the rock strata. The extreme case of **nappe structure** is best seen in the Alps where the collision of two great continents provided far too much pressure for any simple effects. It is hardly surprising that the shape of the fold will strongly influence the surface of the land, especially if the folds are large enough to produce mountains or hills. Of particular importance are likely to be the degree of symmetry and the steepness of the sides of the fold. The **scarp and vale topography**, so

Fig 2.21 Types of fold.

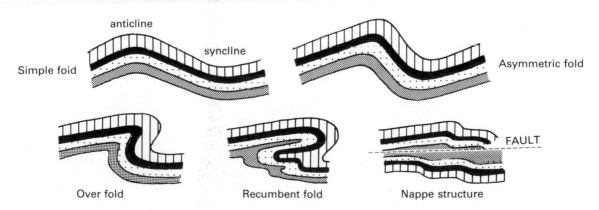

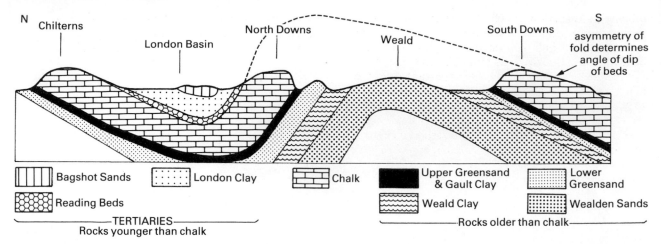

Fig 2.22 Cross-section through southern England to show asymmetrical folding of the chalk and associated sedimentary rocks.

typical of the chalk and related sedimentary rocks of south-east England, is very much a product of **asymmetrical folding**, for this produced the gentle angle of the beds that forms the **dip slope** of so many escarpments (see Fig. 2.22).

The most direct effect of folding is the production of a series of **anticlines** and **synclines**, or ridges and troughs, which, if preserved, are usually referred to as **normal** or the **Jura pattern of relief**. An example of this is to be found in the Gower Peninsula of south Wales, where a series of NW–SE trending anticlines forms ridges such as Cefn Bryn, and separate intervening river valleys that have exploited the synclines. Normal relief, however, does not always occur as frequently in a landscape as does **inverted relief**. Here, understanding is once again aided by simulation in the squeezing together of any solid block such as a piece of plywood between your hands. Although some uparching will occur, sooner or later the outer side of the block will start to crack as its particles are stretched apart. In the same way the underside, on the inner part of the fold, will experience a packing together of particles and, effectively, a strengthening. Transfer this principle to anticlines and synclines and you will appreciate that the crest of the anticline will be weakened by tension cracks and joints which are easily exploited by elements of weathering and erosion, whilst the strengthened syncline will be more easily able to resist mechanical forces. Add to this the likelihood of greater frost action at the greater altitude on the anticlinal ridge and you have an environment for virile denudation which in time can reduce the anticline to a lower relief than the resistant syncline (see Fig 2.23).

There are plenty of good examples of inverted relief in the sedimentary rocks of southern England. The Vale of Pewsey near Marlborough in Wiltshire, where rivers have found the anticlinal axis easier to follow than the syncline, is now some 200 metres deeper than the hills of the former syncline to the north. However, the above explanation does not cover all the methods by which the inversion of relief can come about. Suppose, for example, that beneath the uppermost rock layer there is a thick layer of unresistant rock. Passage to it for the denuding processes will be uninhibited once the tension cracks have appeared on the anticline, and the entire process of inversion will be accelerated. R.J. Small cites the example of the downs near Winchester where a weaker rock underground is leading to an

Fig 2.23 Evolution of inverted relief.

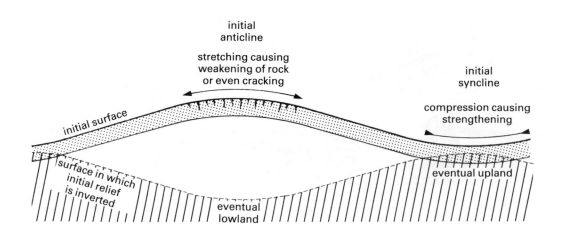

anticline's destruction. As Fig 2.24 shows, streams on the anticline's sides are cutting through the surface layers of Upper Chalk and once through this are able quickly to erode headwards and sideways, helped by slope collapse, thanks to the less resistant layers of Middle and Lower Chalk beneath. Once breached in this way the anticline will not be able to retain its upland status indefinitely. So, although the type of fold is important in controlling scenery, it is essential that one also considers the subsequent development of the fold after its creation.

Once again, then, we must be careful not to ignore the passing of time. It may be that the so-called young fold mountains of today, such as the Alps and the Himalayas, of only 30–40 million years, produce some of our loftiest peaks, but the ancient folds of the Scottish mountains and Appalachians, worn down by erosion of ten times this duration, may once have boasted equal, or even greater, grandeur.

In a final consideration of folding, one must place the process near the head of a list of major landscape influences, for a glance at any regional geology text will indicate that there are very few geological cross-sections that show no sign of folding. In the short history of the earth sciences much time has been given to attempts to unravel the contortions of folded strata, most notably the nappe structures of the Alps, and Fig 2.25 ably demonstrates that the influence of folding on landscape is rarely straightforward!

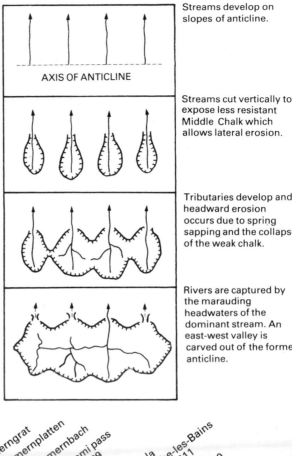

Fig 2.24 A possible sequence of events in anticline inversion.

Streams develop on slopes of anticline.

Streams cut vertically to expose less resistant Middle Chalk which allows lateral erosion.

Tributaries develop and headward erosion occurs due to spring sapping and the collapse of the weak chalk.

Rivers are captured by the marauding headwaters of the dominant stream. An east-west valley is carved out of the former anticline.

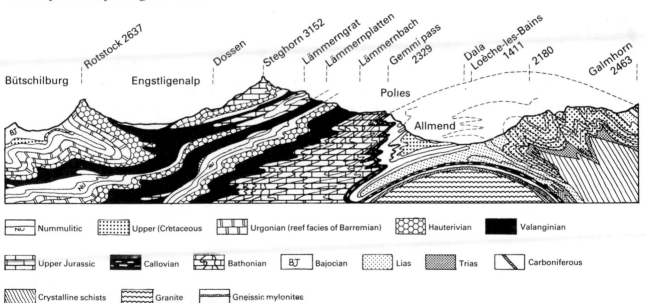

Fig 2.25 Cross-section of a series of nappe structures in the Swiss Alps.

Vulcanicity

Of the three great landscape building processes that are associated with the great orogenies and active regions of tectonic plates, probably the most spectacular in the public's mind is vulcanicity. Volcanoes such as the magnificent eruptions of Vesuvius, Krakatoa, Etna and Mt St Helens will immediately come to mind. As usual, however, the headline events are in danger of dimming into insignificance the many other processes that occur almost unnoticed, but whose outcome may be equally dramatic over the longer time scale. For the vulcanologist is interested in any movement of magma beneath, or above, the earth's surface, and in order not to allow film stars like Vesuvius to overawe us, we shall deal first with subterranean movements of magma, or **intrusive vulcanicity**, as it is most usually called.

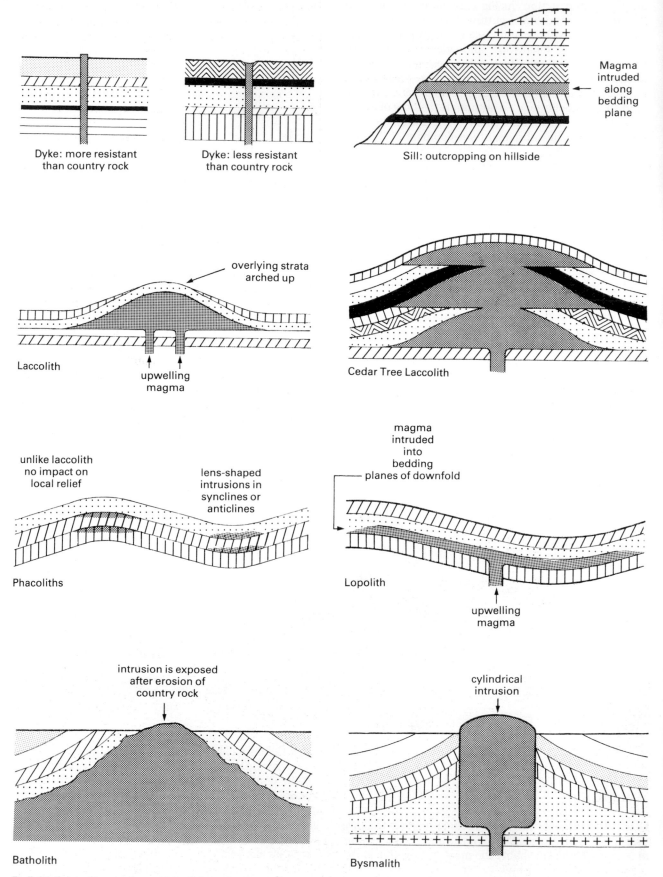

Dyke: more resistant
than country rock

Dyke: less resistant
than country rock

Sill: outcropping on hillside

Magma
intruded
along
bedding
plane

overlying strata
arched up

Laccolith

upwelling
magma

Cedar Tree Laccolith

unlike laccolith
no impact on
local relief

lens-shaped
intrusions in
synclines or
anticlines

Phacoliths

magma
intruded
into
bedding
planes of downfold

Lopolith

upwelling
magma

intrusion is exposed
after erosion of
country rock

Batholith

cylindrical
intrusion

Bysmalith

Fig 2.26 Types of igneous intrusion and their effects on relief.

Intrusive Vulcanicity

Here, more than anywhere else, a textbook's simple classification can do as much to impair field identification of geomorphological features as it can to help, for most of the easily viewed British examples are much more complex than any of the straightforward diagrams might suggest. However, we shall look first at a simple classification, and then see how the features actually manifest themselves and attempt to analyse their impact on landscape.

When molten igneous rock has forced its way through country rock it may solidify underground in a variety of shapes. A horizontal plane of magma making use of bedding planes in sedimentary rock will produce a **sill**, such as the dolerite Great Whin Sill in north-east England. On the other hand, a path that cuts vertically through rock strata, often via a pre-existing cleavage line or weakness, will lead to a **dyke** such as the Cleveland Dyke on the North York Moors. Other intrusive features have a much broader third dimension, however. Thus, **laccoliths**, such as those of the Eildon Hills in the Scottish Borders, are dome-like, as are the much larger scale **batholiths**. Other forms, **bysmaliths**, **phacoliths** and **lopoliths**, are included in Fig 2.26 for the sake of completeness rather than because they are widely distributed.

So much then, for the simple review of form. The

Photo 2.3   The Eildon Hills from Scott's View, Scottish Borders: the trachyte laccolith projects some 200 metres above the surrounding area.

impact on landscape is rarely as clear-cut. Scale, again, is an important consideration, for the most frequently occurring intrusions are the tiny dykes and sills which can be observed as crystalline veins on rock outcrops but whose influence is very localised. At the other end of the hierarchy are the massive features such as the giant granite batholith which underlies most of Britain's south-west peninsula, its exposure producing a profound effect on landscape from Dartmoor through the cliffs of Land's End to its emergence above the sea as the Scilly Isles. Between these two extremes intrusions may form a hill or may give rise to some local doming of the overlying strata or may merely form an irregularity on a hillside. The Cleveland Dyke, however, despite extending 40 kilometres across the North York Moors, has little impact on the scenery at all except for a series of scars where it has been quarried as roadstone by man. Intrusions of any size may, however, not be noticed by the casual observer at all for the features are, by definition, subterranean and a considerable amount of erosion may still need to occur in order to expose them.

The extent of an intrusion may partially depend on the fluidity of the magma, for if the silica content is high and the material acidic, flow from the point of origin will be restricted; on the other hand the basic tholeite of the Cleveland Dyke probably spread from a volcano in Mull several hundred kilometres away.

Consideration must also be given to the contrast in character between the rock of the intrusion and that of its surroundings. In the simple case, whether erosion

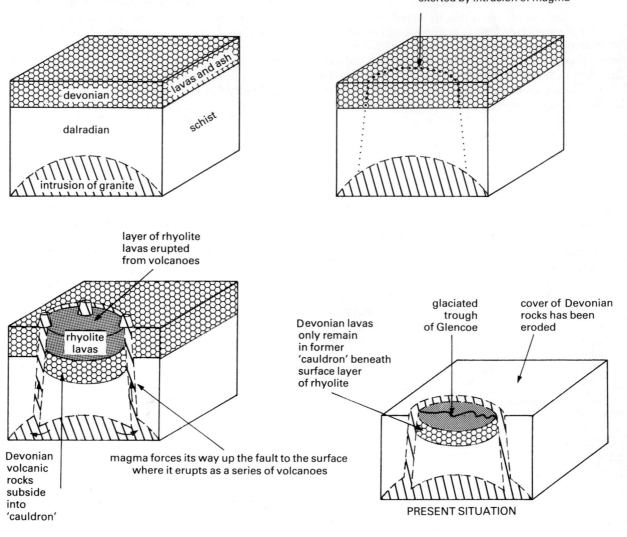

ring fault developing in
response to heat and pressure
exerted by intrusion of magma

lavas and ash

devonian

dalradian

schist

intrusion of granite

layer of rhyolite
lavas erupted
from volcanoes

rhyolite
lavas

Devonian
volcanic
rocks
subside
into
'cauldron'

magma forces its way up the fault to the surface
where it erupts as a series of volcanoes

Devonian lavas
only remain
in former
'cauldron' beneath
surface layer
of rhyolite

glaciated
trough
of Glencoe

cover of Devonian
rocks has been
eroded

PRESENT SITUATION

Fig 2.27 Stages in the development of the volcanic rocks of Glencoe.

transforms a dyke into a trough or leaves it as an out-standing ridge will depend on whether it can offer greater or lesser resistance than the country rock. Many a wave cut platform in the Isles of Arran and Skye demonstrates this principle. On a larger scale, the Eildon Hills, which provided Sir Walter Scott with what he considered so splendid a view, are able now to protrude above the Silurian rocks of Lauderdale only because the laccolith that forms them has proved more resistant than the rocks around it (Photo 2.3). It is not surprising that intrusions often prove more resistant, for not only are they often composed of strong materials such as granite, basalt and dolerite but heat, pressure and friction caused by their intrusion may have weakened the rocks into which they were injected. Thus cracks and joints may surround the intrusion, although it should be pointed out that in some cases melting and re-formation may actually strengthen the immediate surroundings.

Finally, for the sake of perspective, we should not shy away from the most complex effects of vulcanicity, and to face this challenge, let us consider what the impact on landscape has been in the Glencoe area. As Photo 2.4 shows, the mountains to the south of Glencoe produce an impressively rugged landscape and they owe their existence to a period of Devonian vulcanicity about 300 million years ago. Over 1000 metres of lava, **tephra** and ash were laid down from a series of volcanoes and covered an area much greater than the relatively small area of volcanic rocks to the south of Glencoe that remains today. As Fig 2.27 shows, the reason why the Glencoe lavas have been preserved is their subsidence into a vast **ring fault** of approximately 11 kilometres diameter.

This fault formed as a response to the pressure caused by the intrusion of a great mass of granite about the same time as the surface volcanoes were erupting. The rocks enclosed within the fault slid down into the unstable subterranean depths in a process known as **cauldron subsidence**. Molten rock was then able to rise to the surface through the ring fault to solidify into the ring dyke, a section of which forms the 800 metre high ridge of An t-Sròn. Lava from the volcanoes associated with the dyke infilled the cauldron from above, and as Fig 2.28 shows, most of the lava has been removed over the last 300 million years although it still remains in sufficient thickness to produce the three magnificent ridges of the Three Sisters. Virtually none of the Devonian volcanic rocks on the outside of the ring fault remains today. This example of the interaction of intrusive vulcanicity with extrusive leads us neatly into a consideration of **extrusive vulcanicity**.

Extrusive Vulcanicity

When bodies of molten rock erupt onto the earth's surface they usually do so with such devastation and spectacle that one is in danger of overestimating their relevance. **Magma**'s entry onto the surface, at which point we usually begin to call it **lava**, can be through any pre-existing crack such as a joint or fault, or, if the eruption has sufficient power, through a rupture or fissure of its own making. The most celebrated eruptions are, of course, those which create or occur from volcanoes and it is with this feature that we shall begin.

Volcanoes

Like so many other eruptions since, the magnificent performance that Mt Pelée in Martinique staged on 8th May 1902 was preceded by many rehearsals over the previous months. For instance, three days previously 'a stream of burning lava rushed down the side of the mountain from a height of 4400 feet (1340 m) following the dry bed of a torrent and reaching the sea, five miles from the mountain, in three minutes'. But this was thought by some to be a sideshow, for the volcano of Soufrière on neighbouring St Vincent was showing much more sign of preparation for a big eruption, with earth tremors producing detonations that ricocheted around the local islands, and vast columns of **scorial dust** and stones pouring from its crater. It was only the most cautious who fled from Martinique, and not

Photo 2.4 The Three Sisters, Glencoe: ancient lavas preserved by a remarkable interaction of extrusive and intrusive vulcanicity.

Fig 2.28 Cross-section of mountains on the surface of the 'cauldron' of Glencoe, to the south of the trough of Glencoe.

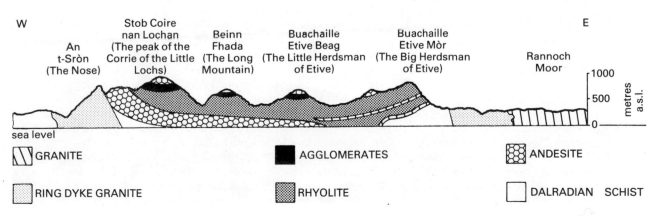

surprising, for since 1851 it had been thought that the volcano was extinct. Even trade continued as normal, with the British steamer, *Roddam*, anchoring off St Pierre, Martinique's capital, at 8 am on 8th May. 'The captain reported that he... was talking to the ship's agent.. in a boat alongside, when he saw a tremendous cloud of smoke glowing with live cinders rushing with tremendous rapidity over the town and port. The former, in an instant, was completely enveloped in a sheet of flame, which rained fire on board the steamer. The agent had just time to climb on board when his boat disappeared. Several men of the *Roddam's* crew were quickly scorched to death. By almost superhuman efforts the cable was slipped, and steam being still up, the vessel backed out from the shore. Ten of the *Roddam's* men were lying dead, having been burned out of all human semblance, among the black cinders which covered the deck to a depth of six inches. Two more died. The burning cinders continued to fall upon the ship for six miles after she was under way.' If this destruction befell a ship, imagine the plight of the 30 000 inhabitants of St Pierre at Mount Pelée's foot.

From this one example, much can be learnt of the character of volcanoes.

First, like so many extreme natural events, their eruptions are sudden and unpredictable and their largest displays are of the highest order of magnitude. Even all the sophisticated monitoring of volcanoes in

Photo 2.5 Mont Pelée, Martinique: the famous eruption of 1902, showing the vast glowing cloud of ash and tephra known as nuée ardente.

the 1980s could not cheat Mt St Helens out of claiming several lives in May 1980 (Photo 2.6), nor Soufrière out of being allowed the last laugh in 1979 when failing to erupt despite the evacuation of the island and the assembly of millions of dollars worth of seismic equipment there. Both St Helens and Pelée have shown us that a period of 50 or even 120 years is insufficient to describe a volcano as **extinct**; it is merely **dormant**, awaiting a period of activity. It is the ancient cores of volcanoes which litter northern Britain, such as Arthur's Seat near Edinburgh, that are truly extinct.

Second, Pelée shows us that the materials emitted during an eruption can show great diversity. The solidifying lava may produce the most permanent record, but an explosive mixture of a wide range of gases, such as hydrogen sulphide, chlorine and sulphur dioxide, may produce much of the immediate spectacle and destruction. As the solid cap of rock inside the crater is blown off by the eruption, blocks of shattered rock may shower the local environs, as, too, may globular lumps of burning lava that are flung out to land as **volcanic bombs**. These fragments, whether molten or solid, are known as **tephra** or **pyroclasts**, or if they are fine, as **lapilli**. Mt St Helens is estimated to have thrown dust 80 kilometres into the air, and many observers of Pelée report the announcement of the disaster by a hail of stones about the size of walnuts. An especially famous type of pyroclast, and a speciality of Vesuvius, is **pumice** which has a light, mousse-like nature which it owes to its origin as a bubbling scum on the surface of viscous lava. Even the term lava covers a wide variety of form,

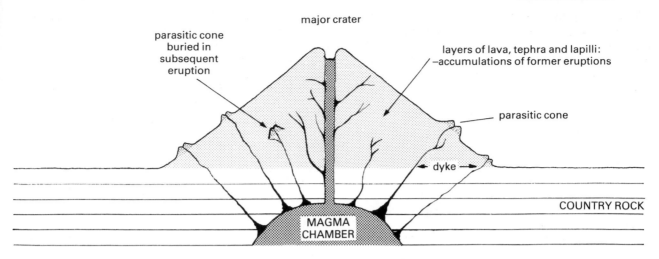

Fig 2.29 Cross-section of an idealised composite volcano.

for different amounts of each mineral give it different properties, the lower the amount of oxygen and silica the less viscous is the lava. The lava at Pelée was so viscous, so silica-rich or acidic, that during a later eruption of 1902 it cooled rapidly into a massive column of rock, towering for its short life 210 metres upwards. The fluidity of lava is also determined by its temperature, its gas content and the amount of solid fragments that it is transporting. These, in turn, will affect the colour, surface, texture and even resistance of the rock it produces. Notable examples of this are two contrasting types of basaltic lava, **aa** and **pahoehoe**, which, although similar in chemical structure, produce quite different effects. The former cools into an extremely irregular, clinker-like surface of sharp edges whilst the latter characteristically buckles up into a series of cord or rope-like pleats. Differences in the methods of flow, the speeds at which they solidify and the shape of the gas bubbles contained within appear to be responsible for these particular contrasts.

It is by no means true that every eruption will produce the full range of possibilities; indeed, the less well documented may be so slight that only clouds of steam or dust are emitted, but in the most celebrated eruptions the full variety may be demonstrated. The glowing cloud, or **nuée ardente**, of Mt Pelée showed how hot gas, burning cinders and ash could combine into a fearsome rush of air that obliterated all obstacles in its path, and it was this that the captain of the *Roddam* observed (Photo 2.5).

The form of the volcano itself will depend upon the constituents of previous eruptions, for the ash, cinders, pyroclasts and lava will compose the mountain's slopes. Many of Hawaii's volcanoes, such as Mauna Loa, have gently sloping sides, slightly convex in shape, built by less viscous basalt lava which emerges from a series of fissures on the volcanoes' sides as well as from the central vent. Few volcanic cones are as easily described as this, for their shape reflects a varied history of emissions, none of which may be similar in its products, some of which may add to the cone, perhaps altering

the angle of rest of its sides, whilst others may drastically alter the form by blasting away the side of the mountain, as happened at Mt St Helens in 1980. Thus, the term **composite volcano** is given to volcanoes like Vesuvius made up of mixed layers of tephra, lapilli and lava.

Fig 2.29 shows a cross-section of a model composite cone, but of course its symmetry, its **parasitic cones**, the angle of its sides and the thickness of its layers are generalisations that few real examples can repeat. Some cones may consist almost entirely of ash or **scoria**, as the cinder-like fragments are sometimes known. The 400 metre high scoria cone of Paricutin, which originated in a Mexican farmer's field in 1943 and within nine years had engulfed two villages, provides a dramatic example, but even this contains some solidified lava in its structure.

A third principle to be learnt from Mt Pelée is that it is not just the volcanic cone that is shaped by an eruption, but a much broader swathe of landscape that can be affected. Lava flows may spread many kilometres from their point of origin, and it was this that caused drastic measures to be taken in 1983 when explosives were used to divert the ravaging flow of Mt Etna. Ash and cinders can travel even further. They can transform rivers into mud flows or dam lakes, like the 60 metre high dam that blocked Spirit Lake after the St Helens eruption. Such inputs into the river system can have effects which reverberate hundreds of kilometres away in the form of flood discharges and high sediment loads. Avalanches, too, may be set in motion as glaciers or snowfields are melted and fractured; blasts of steam during an active period of Bandai, Japan in 1888 were sufficient to release avalanches that devastated 70 square kilometres of land.

A fourth point that emerges from a modern-day look at Pelée is that a volcano's form can change considerably even over a relatively short period of time, A **caldera**, for instance, is a volcanic cone which has undergone considerable modification. The evolution of Crater Lake, Oregon, in Fig 2.30, shows how the once 4000 metre high Mt Mazama suffered massive explosions 6500 years ago during which 40 cubic

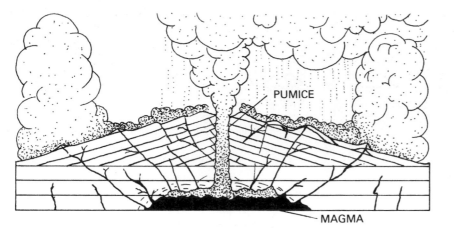

PUMICE

MAGMA

Following end of
magma eruptions, violent
emissions of pumice
occurred.

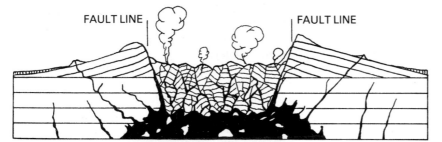

FAULT LINE   FAULT LINE

Crater collapsed
into vacated area
of magma chamber.

Crater of newly
formed caldera flooded.
Wizard Island formed
from rising magma.

Fig 2.30 The evolution of Crater Lake Oregon.

kilometres of pumice were violently disgorged, allowing the top of the cone to collapse into the vacated
chamber. Today's caldera has a crater over 9 kilometres across and some 1300 metres deep. Evolution of
form also produces strange, isolated stumps such as
Bass Rock in the Firth of Forth, which represents the
resistant plug of lava from around which the easily
erodible cone has long since been removed.

Other extrusive features

It would be misleading to give the impression that central vent volcanoes such as Pelée are the only routes for
emerging lava, for many outpourings occur from
fissures or cracks in areas where tension is stretching
the crust. It is usually basaltic lava that is emitted, and
in areas such as the Antrim Plateau of Northern Ireland or the Deccan Plateau of northern India, areas of
many hundreds of square kilometres have been blanketed by lava that may be up to 2000 metres thick.

One aspect of volcanoes that an eye-witness account
of Mt Pelée cannot tell us is why volcanic eruptions
occur where they do. As we have already seen in this
chapter, many volcanoes are associated with tectonic
plate margins, but careful study of Fig 2.4 will reveal

Photo 2.6 Mount St. Helens, Washington, USA. On May 18th
1980, the side of the mountain was blown out at the beginning of a
series of explosions which sent 16 cubic kilometres of rock and dust
up to 25 kilometres into space.

examples of active volcanoes in plate interiors some distance from their margins. It is probable that many of such volcanoes exist above **hot spots** in the mantle, which are narrow shafts of rising magma at centres of intense heat below the crust. As the plate moves across such a spot, magma may be able to break through the crust to produce a volcano, or series of volcanoes, such as the Hawaiian Islands. Other volcanoes, such as Mt Kenya and Mt Kilimanjaro, may also be located away from constructive or destructive margins, but are at points of intense tectonic activity, although, in the case of the East African Rift Valley, this may well be a former plate margin.

Rock Classification

Throughout this chapter reference has been made to three classes of rock, and before proceeding any further it will prove useful to examine these classes in greater detail.

Igneous Rock

Igneous rock is the original form from which all others derive, and it owes its origin to the various volcanic

upheavals described. If classification is essential to the advancement of any science, then geologists have been keen to advance theirs, for there are many possible ways of categorising igneous rock. The table in Fig 2.31 amalgamates and simplifies some of these and, although examples of each type are included, it is unlikely that many of these will be encountered as frequently as **granite**, **basalt** or **gabbro**. The two bases of the classification are the degree of acidity of the rock and the location of its cooling. As both of these characteristics are relevant to the rock's resistance and structure it seems appropriate that a geomorphologist should understand them.

Sedimentary Rock

Sedimentary rock is composed either of particles of other rocks derived by processes of denudation, or of organic material. Their agglomeration into a rock relies mostly on compression over a long period, but chemical activity is also important in holding them together.

The classification adopted in Fig 2.32 relies on mode of formation. Those that are **mechanically formed** are made up from rock fragments of various sizes that have

				>10% free quartz		quartz-free
				ferromagnesian minerals increase (e.g. olivine, pyroxene) →		
Rate of cooling	Location of cooling	Size of crystals		Acid (>66% silica)	Intermediate (52–66% silica)	Basic (45–52% silica)
slow	underground	large	Plutonic	**GRANITE**	Diorite	**GABBRO**
slow in centre	partially underground	medium	Hypabyssal	Micro-granite	Quartz-porphyry	**DOLERITE**
fast	surface	small	Volcanic	**RHYOLITE**	**ANDESITE**	**BASALT**
				viscous	runny	Viscosity when molten
				light	dark	Colour
				light	heavy	Density

Fig 2.31 Classification of igneous rocks.

	INCREASING SEDIMENT SIZE →				
MECHANICALLY FORMED or CLASTIC SEDIMENTS	ARGILLACEOUS <0.002 eg. clays 0.002–0.062mm eg. marl, shale		ARENACEOUS 0.062–2mm eg. sandstones, gritstones		RUDACEOUS >2mm eg. breccia, conglomerates
CHEMICALLY FORMED	CARBONATES eg. dolomite	CHLORIDES eg. rock salt	IRONSTONES eg. haematite	SILICATES eg. flint	SULPHATES eg. gypsum
ORGANICALLY FORMED	CALCAREOUS eg. most limestones	CARBONACEOUS eg. coal	FERRUGINOUS eg. ironstone	PHOSPHATIC eg. guano	SILICEOUS eg. diatomite

Fig 2.32 Classification of sedimentary rocks.

been eroded or weathered, such as sand, clay or gravel particles, before being reconstituted, perhaps with the aid of a natural cement which is chemically precipitated in the gaps between the particles. If a rock is **organically formed** it is the end product of the physical and chemical amalgamation of the remains of organisms such as microscopic sea creatures in the cases of **limestone**, **flint** and **chert**, ancient plants in the case of **coal** and **peat**, or minute water plants or diatoms in the case of **diatomaceous earth**. Evaporation and precipitation from solutions of salts produce most of the other, **chemically formed**, sedimentaries, one of the most familiar of which is **magnesian limestone** which is principally composed of the chemical compound magnesium carbonate.

Metamorphic Rock

Metamorphic means, literally, changed in shape or form, and a sedimentary or igneous rock whose chemical or physical structure is altered by heat or pressure becomes a metamorphic one. Such rocks are most common in zones of tectonic activity, where faulting, folding or vulcanicity produce the necessary force for the change and, thus, it is usual to find examples of them near to plate margins. They are less readily classified than other rocks, partly because the degree of metamorphism will vary and therefore one particular type of rock can lead to a wide variety of products, many of

which are so radically transformed that the original rock is barely discernible. The table in Fig 2.33 lists the most common examples and their origins.

Rock Character

Generalisations about the types of rock are not necessarily helpful and few will be made. It is useful to say that sedimentary rocks are usually laid down in distinct beds, and the **bedding planes** which separate them may be of relevance to their subsequent denudation. Igneous rocks may contain similar horizontal, parallel planes but these are not caused by bedding but by expansion of the rock when an overlying rock burden is removed by denudation. These potential lines of weakness are sometimes termed **pseudo-bedding planes** or **sheet joints**. Both sedimentary and igneous rocks may contain **joints**, which are fractures cutting through the rock strata at almost any angle. Their presence is vital to the later development of the rock outcrop, a fact which is well borne out by the influence of the hexagonal pattern of jointing in basalt and the regular joints in many limestones. Like cracks in cooling toffee, joints may be formed by a process of contraction, either as molten igneous rock cools or as a recently emerged sedimentary dries out. Joints of many different orientations can also be produced by tectonic movements, perhaps by tension during folding. Their relevance to the development of inverted relief has been outlined above. Joints may survive metamorphosis but very often the fresh melting and fracturing will destroy them. Nevertheless, metamorphic rocks contain their own lines of weakness for denudational processes to attack, notably the **cleavage lines** of slate.

The resistance, both physical and chemical, of a rock varies so widely within each category that generalisation is rarely fruitful. However, because of their origins, metamorphic rocks are usually very hard but this, of course, may give them only physical, and not necessarily chemical, strength. Igneous and metamorphic rocks are generally crystalline, whereas sedimentaries are more likely to be granular, and as will be seen in the next chapter, various properties of the crystal and grains may be relevant to a rock's breakdown.

There is an enormous range of ages amongst British rocks. Most of the sedimentaries that form the landscape of lowland Britain are relatively young, but the Carboniferous limestone and Old Red Sandstone of upland Britain provide a strong contrast. If one were to include the drift deposits of boulder clay and alluvium as sedimentary rocks in this category, many of the surface materials of eastern England would be extremely young in age. The igneous rocks are of a wide variety of ages, although even the most recent are at least 50 million years old, and include the gabbro of the Black Cuillins, the granite of Arran and the basalt of the lava plateau of Antrim. Similarly, with major tectonics being so distant in British geological history, the majority of metamorphics are extremely old, most tracing their origins back to the Caledonian and Hercynian orogenies.

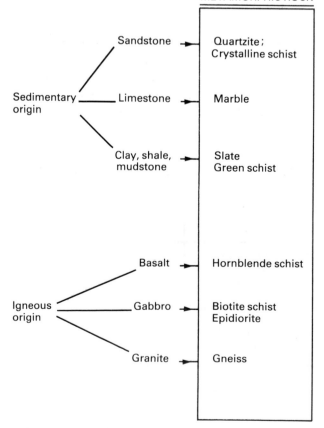

METAMORPHIC ROCK

Sandstone → Quartzite; Crystalline schist

Sedimentary origin — Limestone → Marble

Clay, shale, mudstone → Slate Green schist

Basalt → Hornblende schist

Igneous origin — Gabbro → Biotite schist Epidiorite

Granite → Gneiss

Fig 2.33 Classification of metamorphic rocks.

Questions

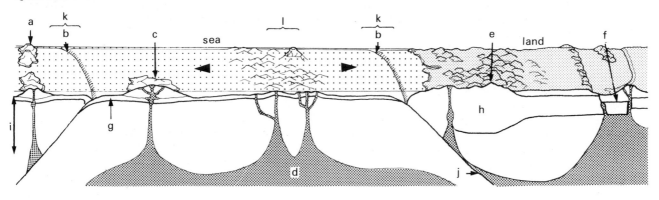

Fig 2.34 shows a theoretical cross-section of the lithosphere, with examples of many of the features mentioned in this chapter.

1 Try to identify each of the features labelled a–1.

2 For each of the types of volcano shown, explain a likely method of formation.

3 On a tracing of the earth's surface from the diagram, draw isolines which denote the areas most liable to earthquake damage.

4 Identify the areas which you would regard as most likely to be heavily populated. Is there any correspondence between these areas and those identified in 3?

Fig 2.34 Cross-section of earth's surface to show a series of tectonic features.

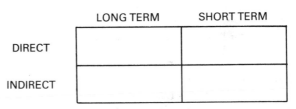

Fig 2.35 The impact of an earthquake or volcanic eruption.

5 Make an enlarged copy of Fig 2.35 and fill in details of the likely effects of *either* a volcanic eruption *or* of an earthquake on human activities; use the classification shown.

Further Reading

The Story of the Earth, F W Dunning et al. (HMSO, 1981).
Volcanoes, P Francis (Penguin, 1976).
Plate Tectonics, D C Heather (Arnold, 1979).
On the Rocks, R Muir Wood (BBC, 1978).
Glencoe, National Trust for Scotland (1979).
Fundamentals of Geomorphology, R J Rice (Longman, 1977).
The Study of Landforms, R J Small (Cambridge, 1978).
Rocks and Relief, B W Sparks (Longman, 1971).
Continental Drift, D H and M P Tarling (Penguin, 1971).

Earthquakes S van Rose (HMSO, 1983).
Volcanoes, S van Rose and I Mercer (HMSO, 1974).
Tectonic Processes, D Weyman (Unwin Hyman, 1981).
Geology and Scenery in Scotland, J B Whittow (Penguin, 1977).

Other References

The Origin of Continents and Oceans, A Wegener (Methuen, 1967).

3

Rocks and Landscape

Introduction

At first sight it may appear that rock type is the dominant influence on most landscapes. Elementary study of physical geography, with its emphasis on limestone and granite landforms, does little to alter this impression. As we shall see later in this chapter, in some cases rock type does exert considerable control, but for many landscapes rock type is just one of a myriad of factors that determine its shape. Indeed, in some deserts and glacial landscapes rock type is almost immaterial.

As geomorphologists, rather than **geologists** or **lithologists**, we are more concerned with the ways in which the characteristics of rocks respond to the processes of erosion and weathering than with the detailed study of rocks themselves. By examining the major method of rock breakdown, namely **weathering**, we should thus be able to derive a sufficient understanding of rock characteristics for our needs.

Weathering

The effect of weathering is easy to observe in whatever environment you live. The gradual mellowing of the sharp colours of brickbuilt housing estates, the constant appeals for money from the deans of our cathedrals to restore decayed tracery and gargoyles or the natural carvings of the Valley of the Rocks in north Devon (see Photo 3.1), the tors of Dartmoor or the limestone pavements of the Yorkshire Dales all serve as evidence of the potency of weathering.

Weathering is brought about by a rock's direct or indirect contact with elements of the weather, that is, precipitation, heat and cold. Weathering is always taken to mean the breakdown of a rock in the place where it is located, but not to involve the removal of the weathered material. **Erosion**, on the other hand, by the moving forces of ice, rivers and the sea involves wearing down and removal of the rock. It is important that the difference between the processes is clarified. **Denudation** is a useful term which is sometimes used to cover both processes and is particuarly applicable when both are acting together and the junction between them is blurred.

Photo 3.1 The Valley of the Rocks, Lynton, North Devon: grotesquely weathered outcrops of sandstone.

Types of Weathering

For the sake of convenience, processes of weathering are usually placed in three classes – **chemical, mechanical** and **biological**. Chemical weathering involves the chemical reaction of some or all of the constituents of a rock with air, water or an infiltrating solution. The result of the reaction may be simply a change of colour, a slight change in the rock's minerals or the complete chemical breakdown and rotting of the rock. Physical or mechanical weathering involves the disintegration into constituent parts rather than the decomposition of a rock and is most frequently associated with extremes of temperature. Biological weathering is carried out by organic elements and can lead either to mechanical or chemical breakdown. Undoubtedly there is great overlap between the classes; for example, it is not easy to decide conclusively whether salt weathering, which involves the chemical processes of evaporation and crystallisation followed by the exertion of pressure on a rock, is more chemical than mechanical. Similarly, is hydration, which involves the absorption of water by rock minerals and their subsequent expansion and exertion of pressure, predominantly mechanical or chemical? The confusion of this overlap is compounded by the fact that the processes rarely operate in isolation from each other and may well all occur together (see Fig 3.1).

Mechanical or physical weathering

Frost weathering: there are many forms of weathering associated with frost, several of which will be dealt with in Chapter 9. It will suffice here to mention the most common, **freeze-thaw** or **frost shattering**. This process will occur in a variety of locations, commonly in high latitudes but also in high altitudes regardless of latitude. It also occurs in temperate latitudes such as ours, chiefly in winter, and has been reported on rare occasions in deserts at night following massive outgoing radiation after intense daytime heating.

The process is a simple one, observed on roads and buildings in most British winters; it caused particular havoc to infrequently used country roads in the period of record low temperatures in December 1981. Water enters the rock through joints, faults, cleavage lines, cracks or pores and, on freezing, increases its volume by 9.05 per cent. This exerts immense pressure on the surrounding rock. Observations have suggested that the maximum effect is felt at $-22°C$ when the pressure can reach an incredible $2100\,kg/cm^2$, although of course most rocks will give way a long time before this is achieved. Granite has an absolute maximum tensile strength of $70\,kg/cm^2$. In fact, it is thought that, on average, frost action operates at a pressure of no more than $14\,kg/cm^2$.

Frost shattering can operate during a variety of time periods. An overnight frost may be sufficient but a **frost**

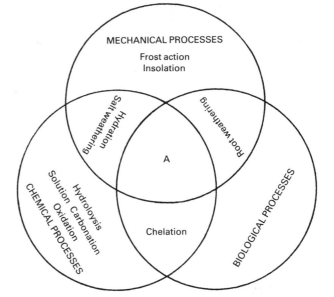

Fig 3.1 The problem of classifying methods of weathering.

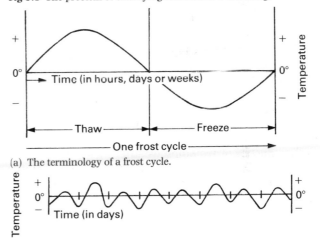

(a) The terminology of a frost cycle.

(b) A potent freeze-thaw environment.

Fig 3.2 Frost cycles.

cycle of several days of sub-zero temperatures may be just as effective, as may the onset of a cold season of constantly low temperatures in a high latitude climate. Perceptible damage really occurs only after the duration of a large number of cycles, and their frequency rather than their duration is probably of more importance to their potency (Fig 3.2).

The most common landscape feature associated with frost shattering is the **scree** which is so frequently found on the valley side slopes of the glaciated valleys of upland Britain, most notably the great screes of Langdale or the Great Stone Chute of the Black Cuillins of Skye. These screes are made up of angular fragments of rock, sometimes millions of cubic metres in total volume (Photo 3.2). Their sheer size plus the well established vegetation suggest that many of the British screes are not the result of present processes but probably formed in the tundra period which followed the last glaciation. Even so, in many British uplands frost action is sufficiently common either to add to the screes or at least to break down further the scree fragments.

Photo 3.2 Wastwater screes, Cumbria. These screes plunge beneath the surface of this 90 metre deep lake.

As well as screes, another feature of a frost-shattered landscape is the castellated appearance of mountain ridges and tops where frost has exaggerated the jointing pattern. In the Italian Dolomites such castellation of the magnesian limestone is reflected in the graphic names, Cinque Dita, the Five Finger Nails. Glacial arêtes are commonly sharpened and given jagged teeth by frost action, as anyone who has attempted to walk along Striding Edge can bear witness. Areas of large pieces of frost-shattered rock scattered across flatter upland areas of temperate regions or, more commonly, across landscapes of higher latitudes are, rather logically, termed **blockfields** or **felsenmeer** (Photo 3.3).

Insolation weathering: this form of mechanical weathering appears to be more effective in theory than in reality. The theory postulates that repeated heating and cooling of a rock leading to alternate expansion and contraction will exert such pressure that the rock will eventually weaken and possibly break down. Rock's poor performance as a heat conductor supports the theory, for this means that the heat of the day is concentrated in the outer zones of the rock and this is the region where night-time radiation most effectively reduces temperature. The process is thus most likely to occur on exposed surfaces of tropical latitudes, most specifically in deserts where daytime temperatures can reach 70°C. Presumably the same conditions could also occur in temperate conditions, although rock surfaces not covered by soil and vegetation are rarely found in the same location as high daytime temperatures in such regions.

The efficacy of **insolation weathering** was very much challenged in the inter-war years by the laboratory experiments of first Blackwelder, and later Griggs, who came to the conclusion that persistent heating and cooling of fragments of rock produces negligible weakening even over simulated long periods of time, and only becomes noticeable when it is combined with the action of water and thus chemical weathering. However, real world evidence for the process does exist, particularly in hot deserts where **exfoliation** and **granular disintegration** are thought to be its result. As the name suggests, exfoliation is the peeling off of leaf-like layers from a rock aided in particular by its poor

Photo 3.3 Blockfield or felsenmeer, Mont Blanc, France. The blockfield is an area of large boulders produced by frost shattering of the bedrock.

conduction of heat (see Fig 3.3). Granular disintegration is a more localised effect when certain grains, more prone to expand than others, exert pressure on those surrounding them and force them to break off.

Pressure release: as a method by which rocks are weakened, this process deserves mention here and yet it cannot be strictly regarded as weathering, as no element of weather is involved. It is much akin to the relief felt by a chair when your body is removed from it. That particular upward release is obviously infinitesimal, but imagine the same release felt by a rock stratum when an overburden of, say, a three kilometre thick layer of ice melts or a 100 metre thick overlying rock band is eroded. This **pressure release** or **dilatation**, a sort of 'breathing out', leads to the formation of joints in the rock which often reflect the former topography. The granite batholith of Dartmoor contains such horizontal joints, or **pseudo bedding planes**, formed after the removal of the country rock which once covered the massive underground dome. The presence of such sheet joints may well encourage the occurrence of exfoliation in tropical conditions.

Fig 3.3 The operation and effect of exfoliation.

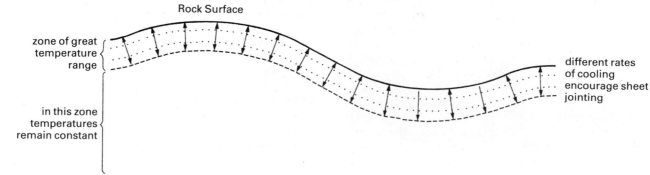

Rock Surface

zone of great temperature range

in this zone temperatures remain constant

different rates of cooling encourage sheet jointing

Salt weathering: it has already been mentioned that this process does not sit exclusively in the mechanical weathering class, but as it relies heavily on the exertion of pressure it seems appropriate to include it here. The process requires solutions of salt to evaporate and crystallise in a confined space so that the expanding crystal weakens the rock structure. Good conditions for this process to occur exist in coastal locations, where pores, cavities and joints in exposed cliffs trap sea spray, or in arid areas where solutions are drawn through rocks by capillary action to the surface. The most likely outcome is the gradual granular disintegration of the rock.

Chemical weathering

Carbonation and solution: many minerals are soluble under certain conditions, but very often they require preparation via the action of another process, such as oxidation, to enhance the effect of solution. One of the most potent combinations of process is that of **carbonation** and **solution**. Anyone foolish enough to have poured concentrated sulphuric acid onto a piece of Carboniferous limestone will have witnessed the power of the combined effects of these processes, although the devastating effect of this experiment would take natural forces many decades to equal.

The process is most easily studied in limestone landscapes where very weak acid solutions, provided initially by rainfall, carbonate the limestone minerals which become bicarbonates. Like all bicarbonates, they are soluble in water so the limestone is effectively dissolved. The two most commonly attacked minerals are calcite ($CaCO_3$) and dolomite ($CaMg(CO_3)_2$).

$$CaCO_3 + H_2CO_3 \longrightarrow Ca^{++} + 2HCO_3^-$$

calcite + carbonic acid $\longrightarrow$ calcium + calcium bicarbonate

$$CaMg(CO_3)_2 + 2H_2CO_3 \longrightarrow Ca^{++} + Mg^{++} + 4HCO_3^-$$

dolomite + carbonic acid $\longrightarrow$ calcium + magnesium + calcium bicarbonate

The weak acid solutions needed for the carbonation process have various origins, most common being the carbonic acid from the dissolving of carbon dioxide, from the atmosphere or the soil, in water. Other acids may also occur; for example, in highly polluted urban air weak nitric and sulphuric acids may be present. This probably explains why rates of limestone weathering in the Pennines have fallen since the late nineteenth century with the cleaning up of the air of the industrial towns of West Yorkshire and Lancashire. It is not only limestones that are affected by carbonation. Other minerals, notably certain feldspars, can be weakened by the same process.

Hydrolysis: for this important, and very common, method of weathering to occur no acids are required. Pure water is sufficient for a chemical reaction of rock minerals and water to occur. The hydrogen (H^+) or the hydroxyl (OH^+) ions of the water react with the mineral ions and both water and mineral decompose. A rock which is susceptible to the process is granite, which, like most igneous rocks, contains silicates, usually in the form of feldspars. These silicates undergo a complex series of changes in which they are converted to clay minerals (such as kaolin in the case of Dartmoor granite), silica and hydroxides. These hydroxides may then be subjected to carbonation and further breakdown. Silicates are the most common rock-forming minerals and their precise chemical structure will determine the nature of the resultant clay minerals. Illite and montmorillonite are two common examples, although most people are more familiar with kaolinite, not least because of its occurrence in the granite outcrops of Cornwall where it is extracted as china clay.

The effect of **hydrolysis** on a rock may vary. Changes of colour or slight weakening of the rock may be the only observable alterations, but in certain cases effects may be far more profound. The presence of orthoclase (potassium) feldspar in Dartmoor granite, for example, acts as the Achilles' heel. The weakening and removal of this mineral may reduce the rest of the rock to a litter of mica flakes and quartz crystals as the rock decays grain by grain.

Hydration: the process of **hydration** is usually less devastating than hydrolysis, and, rather than being a complex chemical reaction and breakdown, merely involves the absorption of water into the existing minerals. One of the most frequently quoted examples is the hydration of anhydrite to form gypsum. In some cases the effect of hydration may be no more than a change of colour, but very often it can cause expansion of a mineral as the water is absorbed; in this way the rock may be weakened, may show signs of cracking, and granular disintegration may occur. Hydration may also add to the potency of salt weathering as alternate wetting and drying of the salt crystal in a confined space may exaggerate the pressure that is created by initial crystallisation.

Oxidation: this process frequently accompanies one of the other processes of chemical weathering, hardly surprising as, like the others, it operates most effectively through the medium of water. The reaction of a mineral with atmospheric or soil oxygen dissolved in water to form oxides or hydroxides is the basis of the process, and the minerals most commonly affected are iron, manganese, sulphur and titanium. A common effect may be the 'rusting' of the elements of iron in a rock, as blue-grey becomes reddish-brown and ferrous compounds become ferric. As well as this superficial change, the chemical structure of the rock may have been so altered as to allow other processes to attack it more easily.

To have divided chemical weathering into individual processes is as misleading as it is helpful and it must not imply that each process occurs individually and is easily isolated. All of the processes described rely heavily on the presence of water in the rock and it is likely therefore that the processes will act together if water is

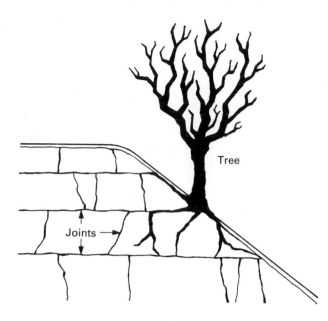

Fig 3.4 The effect of tree roots on joints.

present. This may happen simultaneously or, alternatively, the result of one process may allow others to follow it more easily. Thus it is likely that one process will reinforce another.

Biological weathering

Most methods of so-called biological weathering should, perhaps, truly be termed **bio-mechanical** or **bio-chemical**, but because they all rely on organisms for their existence they can usefully be grouped under one heading.

The detrimental effect that Virginia Creeper may have on the plaster or mortar of Cambridge colleges or large country houses is a simple form of biological weathering. A more virulent case of the same process is the growth of tree or plant roots into cracks or joints in rock strata; this puts such pressure on the strata that block disintegration may be facilitated, (see Fig 3.4).

The burrowing of animals, specifically rabbits, moles, badgers and foxes, is an indirect form of weathering as it allows an easy path for water to the rock beneath. A more disturbing, although still indirect case, is to be found in the game parks of southern Africa, notably the Luangwa National Park of Zambia in the 1970s and in the parks of Namibia and South Africa in the 1980s. Elephants, protected by law from the poacher's gun, have expanded in numbers so rapidly that their demands for food have outweighed the natural balance of the region. Trees are trampled, grass around water holes never allowed to regrow, and in the drought years of the early 1980s this led to soil erosion and eventually the exposure of the underlying rock which has then been left open to the ravages of tropical weathering.

Chelation is a complex biochemical process of rock breakdown in which chelating agents are released from the humus in the soil and carry out a change in the chemical structure of the rock. As well as dead organisms, live ones are also active, for example lichens are rich in chelating agents and this probably accounts for the increased rate of weathering of some lichen-covered rock outcrops.

Factors Affecting the Type and Rate of Weathering

As geomorphologists seeking to explain changes in the shape of the landscape we are really more interested in the effects of weathering than in the physical or chemical processes themselves. If we are to appraise the importance of weathering it is useful to consider what factors will determine whether a particular process will take place and, more important, the speed at which that breakdown will occur (see Fig 3.5).

Rock structure

A frequent misconception is that hard rocks like granite have a high resistance to weathering. Obviously this is a valid statement when concerned with mechanical

Photo 3.4 Elephant damage, Tsavo National Park, Kenya. The death of these trees will further reduce soil protection in this fragile landscape.

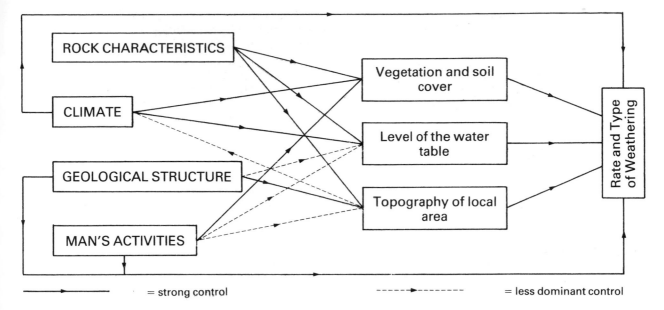

= strong control   = less dominant control

Fig 3.5 The dominant and intermediate factors controlling aspects of weathering.

Photo 3.5 Hexagonal jointing on the basalt coastal platform of Staffa near Fingal's Cave. The joints split the rock into blocks up to half-a-metre across.

processes, for the strength of a rock to resist pressure from ice, salt, or root growth is essential. However, many weathering processes are not going to respect a rock's strength if there is a path into the rock which can be exploited. The easiest route is provided by a physical weakness such as a joint, a shatter belt or cleavage line or by a weakness of chemical composition. A rock is only as strong as its weakest link.

Physical vulnerability is best exemplified by jointing. The regularity of Carboniferous limestone's vertical joints coupled with its horizontal bedding planes provide the necessary weakness to create **block disintegration** (see Fig 3.6). Similarly, the hexagonal joints of basalt dictate the form of the pillars of the Giants' Causeway or of Fingal's Cave (Photo 3.5). Linton's

theory of tor formation on Dartmoor relies heavily on variations in joint density, the rock being least resistant in those parts of the rock where the jointing pattern is most dense. Joints, of course, will facilitate all processes of weathering, and when they occur in a regular cuboidal pattern they may well give rise to spheroidal weathering.

Another physical weakness can be provided by the colour of the minerals that make up the rock. The darker the rock, for example basalt, the more insolation is absorbed and the greater the likely effect of heat expansion and contraction.

Chemical weakness may be the result of a variety of different causes. Limestones are vulnerable to carbonation because of the common constituent of calcite, while granites are affected by hydrolysis because of the presence of orthoclase feldspar. As silicates form over 90 per cent of all rock-forming minerals on the earth's surface, their ability to resist carbonation, solution, oxidation, hydration and hydrolysis is vital. The minerals in acid rocks are usually more stable against chemical attack than those in basic rocks, thus quartz is more

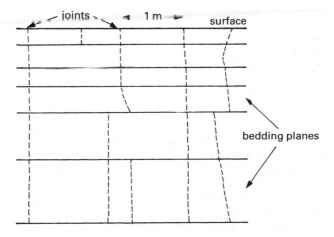

Fig 3.6 The massive structure of Carboniferous limestone.

stable than hornblende which in turn is more stable than the very soluble carbonates such as calcite. Grain size is another important aspect of composition but its effect is not always straightforward. It can be argued that large grains produce large void spaces between them and thus increase the possibility of the trapping of water for chemical or frost attack. Alternatively, it can be argued that the finer grains increase the surface area of the rock open to attack (see Fig 3.7).

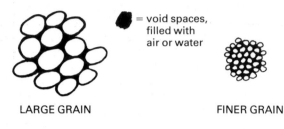

Fig 3.7 The effects of different grain size.

The water absorption capacity could thus be seen to be vital to a rock's resistance, a capacity which is determined by the degree of **primary permeability**, or **porosity**, and the degree of **secondary permeability**, that is the extent to which a rock can be permeated through joints and fissures.

Climate

Along with rock character, climate is undoubtedly one of the major controlling forces of the type and rate of weathering. It is hardly surprising that this is so, with almost every process requiring water, usually from rainfall, and/or a change in temperature, to operate. According to the chemist van't Hoff the speed of a chemical reaction increases two and a half times with each rise of temperature of 10°C, a principle which is most easily demonstrated by dissolving salt, sugar or instant coffee in water, and which helps to explain the increased potency of chemical weathering in tropical humid climates where not only temperatures of above 25°C are usually present but also vast supplies of fresh water. This potency can be clearly seen by studying Peltier's graphs of rainfall and temperature which indicate the strength of chemical breakdown in the wet and warm areas of the world and which, in turn, help to explain the very deep weathering down to 100 metres in parts of West Africa, (Fig 3.8).

Frost action's climatic requirements are rather different, the most important prerequisite being a temperature which fluctuates freely above and below 0°C. Thus, extreme cold, perhaps in the form of three months below − 5°C, is not necessarily as effective as a shorter winter period of more moderate temperatures. Similarly, a very cold climate may produce most of its precipitation in the form of snow, which is incapable of much frost action until it melts in spring, whereas a milder cold climate with a large proportion of rainfall may be more efficacious.

Insolation weathering needs large and violent fluctuations of temperature, for example, between day

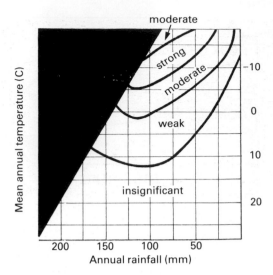

(a) Frost action.

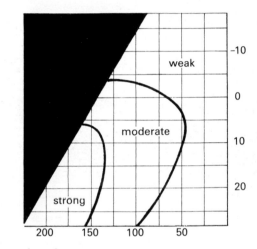

(b) Chemical weathering.

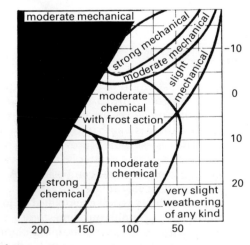

(c) Weathering regions.

Fig 3.8 The relationship between climate and weathering. (after Peltier)

the likelihood of carbonation at low temperatures.

Two other important elements of climate are rates of evaporation and wind strength and direction. The former is particularly influential in desert weathering, the latter will affect exposure and thus temperature.

Soils and vegetation cover

Soils are themselves a product of weathering and it may therefore seem contradictory to suggest soil as a control on the occurrence of weathering. However, the depth and type of soil cover are undoubtedly of direct relevance, although their effect can be one of either regulation or of activation. If frost shattering or insolation weathering on a rock eventually lead to the formation of a soil cover then that soil may effectively protect the rock from further breakdown, thus the operation of the process has regulated its further occurrence. Alternatively, chemical breakdown of a rock leading to a soil cover may intensify the operation of the process by allowing more plants to grow, thus producing more humus and in turn more soil acids which may encourage further chelation and carbonation; in this case positive feedback could be said to be occurring (see Fig 3.9). The presence of deep soils and regolith in tropical, humid areas may also add to the explanation of Peltier's classification, for they inhibit insolation weathering and promote chemical weathering in such climes.

Photo 3.6 Tombstone weathering in Northamptonshire. This early 19th Century headstone, made of local sandstone, shows many signs of weathering.

and night in hot deserts where a diurnal range of surface temperature of 30°C is not impossible.

The effect of climate on weathering is not as simple as it may first seem from Peltier's diagrams. It is not possible to divide the world into broad bands of temperature and rainfall and thus classify weathering patterns, for the macro scale pattern is disturbed by meso scale climatic variations, such as proximity to the sea, altitude and aspect, and by microclimatic influences.

These influences may be best demonstrated by the differential weathering noted on tombstones in a churchyard. Comparisons of degree of weathering can easily be made by looking at the freshness of inscriptions and state of the stone in different parts of the cemetery, for example in shade and sunlight, north facing and south-facing, and even at different heights from the ground on the tombstone itself.

Another reason why broad and simple classifications must be interpreted with caution is that certain chemical processes can operate very effectively in cold conditions. For example, hydration may be very active in periglacial conditions because of the presence of active supplies of fresh water; low temperatures do not inhibit its operation. Similarly, water at 0°C can hold twice as much carbon dioxide as it can at 30°C, which increases

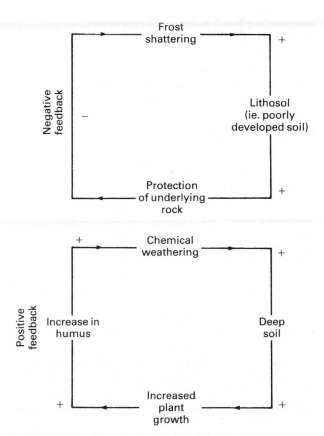

Fig 3.9 Positive and negative feedback: the relationship between soil and weathering.

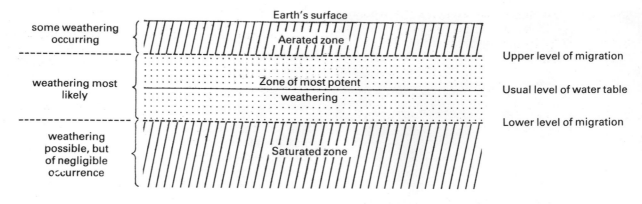

Fig 3.10 Weathering in relation to the migrating water table.

The influence of vegetation is inextricably bound with those of soil and climate. The degree of shade and protection in different seasons, the depth of roots and the acidity of the humus will all determine how effectively a process operates.

The level of the water table

Once again, there is no clear relationship between the factor and the process. Traditionally it has been considered that weathering occurs above the **water table** and thus that the latter's fluctuation and position are vital in determing the **basal weathering front**. The argument to support this, for chemical weathering at least, is that water below the water table would quickly become saturated with weathered solutes or sediment and so would not be able to accomplish any further decay. However, there is so much evidence of deep weathering in the humid tropics that some of this must be occurring below the water table, and certainly it has been proved that hydrolysis can occur there. Ollier comes to the conclusion that limestone solution caves can be formed, albeit very slowly, in the deep phreatic zone beneath the water table.

It thus seems reasonable to conclude that beneath the water table chemical weathering is reduced but certainly not eradicated.

As important an aspect of hydrology as the level of the water table is the presence of efficient drainage, for chemical weathering processes require a constant supply of fresh, oxygenated and unsaturated water.

Geological structure

The relevance of joints has already been examined, but other aspects of geological structure are also of importance. At the larger end of the scale the **angle of dip** and the breadth and variety of the rock strata are obviously important. The gentler the angle of dip, the greater the surface exposure of a particular bed to weathering. Thus, various patterns could occur (see Fig 3.11). In the extreme case of a nil angle of dip, that is, horizontal bedding, the sequence of beds is vital.

The grotesque etchings of the weathered gritstone outcrops of the Bridestones of the North Yorks Moors

Photo 3.7 The Bridestones, North Yorks Moors. The individual beds of gritstone have been picked out by differential weathering.

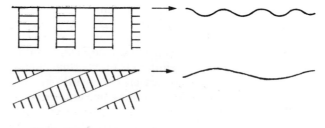

Shaded beds are less resistant, more easily weathered

Fig 3.11 The effect of bedding on weathering.

show just how vital is the sequence of beds, for the weakest ones have been picked out to produce deep indentations in the tor, as can be seen in Photo 3.7.

The resistance of the rock may also be affected by past folding and faulting. Intense, tight folds can harden the rock but at the same time tension cracks may appear which offer an entrance for water. Tiny fault lines may similarly encourage decay, and, on a larger scale, shatter belts provide ample weakness for weathering to attack.

Topography

The relief of the landscape is often a factor to be considered in an analysis of weathering. The relationship between slope angle, weathering and **mass wasting** will be dealt with more fully in Chapter 4, but a few points can be made here. For weathering of fresh rock to continue to its full potential, weathered material needs to be removed relatively soon after its development. If a slope is too shallow the processes of mass wasting will be too gentle for this to occur. On very steep slopes the removal may be almost immediate but, if the weathering process is at all strong, slope replacement is likely to occur as a scree develops to mask the rock face. Intermediate slope angles are thus likely to enhance weathering, not least because of the additional likelihood of their providing a more constant throughflow of water.

Other important elements of **topography** are the **aspect** of a slope and its altitude, both having indirect effects through their controls on climate. Whether a north-facing aspect increases or decreases frost shattering really depends on the average temperature of the location. If protection from the sun consistently keeps the temperature below 0°C day and night then frost shattering may be decreased, but if that protection causes it to fall below 0°C for only certain periods of time then frost shattering may well be increased. In deep glaciated valleys such as Great Langdale the north-facing slope may cast a permanent shadow across the south-facing side and thus extend the same effects, as shown in Fig 3.12.

Man's activities

By the extraction of resources man can easily disturb the natural rate of weathering. The most dramatic examples are caused by open-cast mining and quarrying in temperate countries where bare rock surfaces are exposed to the elements. A visit to a granite quarry such as Rubislaw in Aberdeen or Meldon on Dartmoor would confirm this. On a lesser scale, the continuous removal of peat for fuel on the island of Harris disturbs the natural system both by exposing bare rock and by disturbing the acid content of the soil.

The acidity of rain is increasing dramatically, and in parts of Canada and Sweden highly acid rain arriving

Photo 3.8 Cleopatra's Needle, Victoria Embankment, London. These ancient hieroglyphics are far less crisp now after a century or so in Central London than they were after 3000 years in the arid air of Egypt.

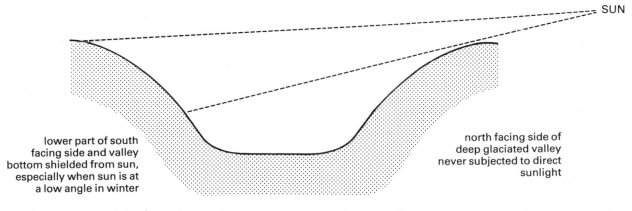

lower part of south facing side and valley bottom shielded from sun, especially when sun is at a low angle in winter

SUN

north facing side of deep glaciated valley never subjected to direct sunlight

Fig 3.12 Effect of aspect on weathering.

from industrial areas in countries to the south is increasing the rate of decay of old buildings. One has only to examine the pink granite of Cleopatra's Needle in London to see the damage caused to its ancient hieroglyphic engravings by a century or so of polluted air compared to three millenia of preservation in the purer air of Egypt that was its location until 1878 (Photo 3.8).

Thus, the rate and type of weathering can depend on a lot more than rock type, although undoubtedly this, along with climate, is usually the dominant control.

Rates of Weathering

The speed at which a rock weathers in its natural location is probably too hard to estimate as, relative to the lifespan of man, decay is extremely slow. However, various methods have been employed to overcome this difficulty, some relying on observations from the real world, others on the results of experiments.

The most accurate empirical data are derived from edifices of stone whose date of erection can be precisely determined. Thus, much evidence has been obtained by Barton from the pyramids and tombs of Egypt, and interesting comparisons can be made between the rates of decay in the semi-arid climate of the lower Nile valley with those of the more arid upper Nile. In Britain, evidence from medieval cathedrals and churches can also be used; with detailed chronicles of building alterations and additions available for most cathedrals, this can be a useful source. More commonly, gravestones are utilised, as precise dating is possible and the source is plentiful.

Experimental data are derived from the subjection of rock tablets to various laboratory tests, for example repeated freezing and thawing to simulate frost action, or immersion in weak acid solutions to simulate carbonation.

All the data on rates of weathering must be interpreted with caution, particularly those from laboratory experiments. Empirical data can also be misleading, for the length of period which is studied can seriously alter the results, as can the peculiar geomorphological history of the chosen sample. The selected data in Fig 3.13 give a guide to the rates of weathering for one example, Carboniferous limestone in the British Isles. There is a certain consistency of results, but we must be cautious, both because the results show mean rates in post-

glacial times and this may hide considerable fluctuation as the climate has ameliorated, and because other of Sweeting's measurements have shown considerable disagreement with those shown here. However, we may at least derive a general idea of the rate of weathering.

As a broader guide, Young suggests the contrasts between various climates shown in Fig 3.14. What they gain in simplicity they do, of course, lose in their accuracy.

Practical Exercises

Many of the techniques referred to in the previous section could be adapted for school use, perhaps for incorporation into a sixth form project.

A possible investigation might take one rock type, say Jurassic limestone, and attempt to discover its susceptibility to weathering. Your choice of rock type would obviously depend on the location of your home but a rock that is commonly used as a building stone is best chosen, thus chalk is a non-starter. The following steps might be taken:

1 Locate a churchyard where tombstones are of various ages but mostly of one rock type.
2 Set up the null hypothesis that there is no significant difference between the rate of weathering of north-facing tombstones with that of west-, south- or east-facing ones.
3 Select a sample of stones, say 50 north facing and 16 or 17 of each of the others. These should be chosen randomly and stones of all ages should be included.
4 A scale of the degree of weathering should then be devised, such as the following:
   Class 1 – No sign of rock weathering.
   Class 2 – Slight weathering; some letters showing wear.
   Class 3 – Moderate weathering; surface may be pitted, letters legible.
   Class 4 – Serious weathering; letters difficult to read.

Fig 3.14 Rates of weathering in different climates (after Young).

Climate	Years required for retreat of 1 metre
Humid Tropical	10^{2-3}
Humid Temperate or Subtropical	10^{3}
Semi-arid	10^{3-4}
Arid	10^{7}

Fig 3.13 Rates of weathering of Carboniferous limestone in the British Isles.

Researcher	Year	Nature of measurement	Rate	Rate per year
McKENNY HUGHES	1886	glacial erratics on pedestals	15–18 ins/10000 yrs	0.035–0.045 mm/yr
GOODCHILD	1890	tombstones	1 in/250–500 yrs	0.05–0.10 mm/yr
SWEETING	1964	$CaCO_3$ content in springs	—	0.04 mm/yr

Class 5 – Severe weathering; letters almost indistinguishable
Class 6 – Extreme weathering; no letters remaining, rock disintegration.

The stones should then be placed in these categories by filling in the table shown in Fig 3.15.

Fig 3.15

Class	North facing	East facing	South facing	West facing
1				
2				
3				
4				
5				
6				

5 The two distributions could then be plotted and compared as histograms, or the chi-squared test could be used to test the null hypothesis in 2. Many other spatial patterns of weathering could then be studied as suggested above.

6 The second part of one's investigation could attempt to conclude how rapid rock weathering has been. First, use the tombstones once again by using the inscribed date and freshness of the lettering to conclude the depth of weathering since the erection of the stone. One may be able to use a micrometer to assess this or a pair of calipers to assess the reduction in thickness of a block of stone.

7 Locate the quarry which provided most of the stone by referring to the Victoria County History. Visit the quarry, collect some samples and carry out some basic experiments such as simulating a frost cycle by the use of a household freezer. By using local climatic statistics from a Meteorological Office or RAF station the number of frost cycles per year could be calculated and, from this, decay over one year, five years or a decade could be simulated.

Weathering: in conclusion

What, then, are the effects and importance of weathering? Its place in landscape formation is often only superficial; compared with the effects of river and glacial erosion its importance may be only minimal. There are exceptions, of course, large-scale examples being ably provided by the **blockfields** of northern Canada and the **mushroom** and **pedestal rocks** of the Tibesti Plateau in the Sahara.

The many and obvious effects of weathering are not easy to summarise. Weathering may round off edges or create jagged ones (Fig 3.16), it may create rounded hollows on vertical or horizontal surfaces, it can flute, honeycomb, exploit or widen joints or it can reduce rock to a pile of rubble or sand grains; it can even dissolve altogether or transform the rock into clay minerals and eventually soil. The regolith of rock waste and soil which commonly carpets slopes in temperate regions is a consequence of the interaction of chemical, mechanical and biological weathering on the bare rock beneath. The products of weathering are thus very diverse: from the major landforms such as tors and screes to the clays and solutes that make up the load of a river.

Case Studies

In the second half of this chapter, three groups of rock will be examined and their effects on landscape studied. The three are chosen deliberately to present as wide a range of landscapes as possible and to demonstrate the diversity of relationships that can occur between rock type and relief.

Limestone

In the case of **limestone** the relationship is an especially interesting one, and is usually considered to be stronger than it is for most other rocks. Indeed, some authorities would go so far as to say that limestone controls relief, or in other words, rock type plays a far more important role than any of the other factors in determining the form of the landscape. The reason for the strength of this statement is that limestone produces a series of landforms that are not often found on other rocks, and most forms of limestone produce very distinctive landscapes which are easily distinguishable for their shape, their soils and their flora. This is far less true for other rocks.

With the exception of dolomitic or **magnesian limestone**, most British limestones are organically formed, the majority having been laid down in the sea. They may be formed of millions of fragments of shells and skeletons of small marine organisms, as in the case of chalk, or from ancient coral reefs. Another form of organic origin is the deposit laid down in springs and caves, of which **tufa** is a common example, and

Fig 3.16 Two possible effects of weathering.

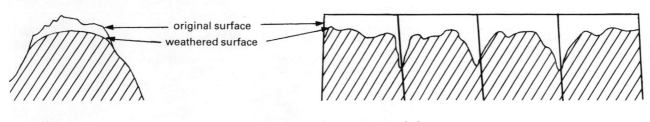

(a) Rounding off.   (b) Creating jagged edges.

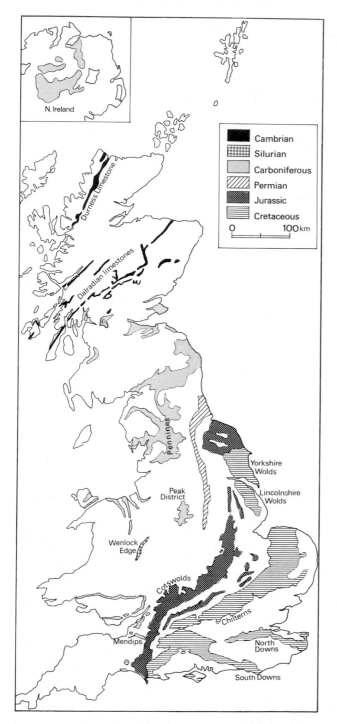

Fig 3.17 The major British limestones.

PERIOD OF FORMATION	AGE	EXAMPLE
CAMBRIAN	c. 500m	Durness area, NW Scotland
SILURIAN	c. 400m	Wenlock Edge, Shropshire and other parts of Welsh Borders
CARBONIFEROUS	c. 300m	Pennines, Peak District, Mendips, Gower Peninsula, parts of N Wales
PERMIAN	c. 250m	Magnesian limestone of Durham coast
JURASSIC	c. 175m	Cotswolds, Lincoln Edge, southern parts of N York Moors
CRETACEOUS	c. 100m	Chalk – N and S Downs, Chilterns, Salisbury Plain

stalactites and stalagmites a usual form. Magnesian limestone, or dolomite, is the only major limestone which is not predominantly calcium carbonate. Its chemical, rather than organic, origin means that its composition is mostly of the mineral dolomite, a double carbonate of calcium and magnesium.

Careful study of the table and map in Fig 3.17 will reveal the variety of limestones found in the British Isles, a variety which reflects not only a spectrum of appearance but also of rock character, particularly hardness, and of age. The three most commonly found in Britain are **Carboniferous limestone**, **chalk** and **Jurassic** (or **oolitic**) **limestone**.

Karst landscape

Outcropping extensively in the Pennines of North Yorkshire, the Peak District of Derbyshire, the Mendips of Somerset and the Gower Peninsula of South Wales, Carboniferous limestone produces what is usually termed **Karst scenery**. This provides support for those who consider that limestone controls landscape, for Karst is a region of western Yugoslavia which includes landforms similar to those of northern England, as indeed does the Grands Causses area of France, north Jamaica and the Guilin area of south-west China; these are all similar landscapes and yet totally contrasting environments. It must be mentioned, however, that many Karst landscapes are not on Carboniferous limestone, for example the Grands Causses area is Jurassic in age and most of the European examples are younger than ours. For the sake of convenience all Karst landscapes, regardless of age, will be dealt with here.

The British Carboniferous limestone is hard, usually grey in colour, and is divided by a regular system of

Photo 3.9 Cowside Gill, North Yorkshire. Notice the horizontal bedding of the Carboniferous limestone.

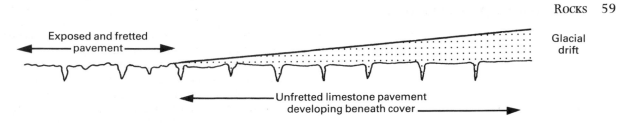

Exposed and fretted pavement

Glacial drift

Unfretted limestone pavement developing beneath cover

Fig 3.18 Limestone pavement, exposed and unexposed.

joints into **massive** blocks. It is the joints and their distinct control of landscape that are the most unifying characteristic of Karst scenery. The joints give the rock a permeability which prevents much surface drainage, although rivers can appear on the surface where upland peat bogs and deposits of glacial drift occur or where the water table is temporarily or permanently at the surface. This latter situation occurs in parts of the Burren of County Clare where permanent lakes such as the Ballyeighter Loughs exist in surface depressions. The rock's hardness and lack of surface downcutting mean that it often forms upstanding relief, which, in the cases of Ingleborough, Pen-y-Ghent and Whernside, reaches 900 metres. The scenery of this area of North Yorkshire is punctuated by bare outcrops, scree slopes, thin soils and the almost perfect horizontal bedding of the rock, as can be seen in Photo 3.9 of Cowside Gill.

Certain distinctive landforms are associated with Karst, one of the most striking being the **limestone pavement**. The natural paving stones, or **clints**, have in effect very irregular surfaces and are divided into roughly rectangular blocks by groove-like **grykes** which may be deceptively deep and which often provide unique habitats for rare orchids. In the case of the pavement above Malham Cove it is thought that formation occurred beneath a cover of glacial drift and soil. Joints were widened by the collaboration of carbonation and solution, the speed of the process increased by the extra supply of carbon dioxide and bacteria in the soil. This process probably began well before the last glaciation, the glacial advance being responsible for the stripping off of much of the soil and loose debris and its partial replacement by glacial till. Where the cover was not replaced, the exposed pavement has been subjected to much fretting, a process which probably accounts for the great surface irregularity (see Fig 3.18). Solution is slower on the exposed clints, but frost action and chelation encouraged by lichen growth will be much faster. As individual calcite crystals are etched out from the clints, small depressions may form which act as traps for rainwater which stagnates and, in turn,

Photo 3.10 Limestone pavement, Malham, North Yorkshire. The exposed pavement continues to weather. Notice the regularity of the jointing of the Carboniferous limestone.

speeds up the chemical breakdown – another example of a positive feedback mechanism. The etching and fretting of successive layers of limestone can be clearly seen in Photo 3.11 of the Aran Islands.

Persistent widening of one particular master joint, perhaps by a surface river as it sinks underground, may lead to the formation of **swallow holes** which are funnel-shaped features with deep shafts leading down from a surface depression. These shafts provide pot-holers with some of their most claustrophobic experiences, hanging upside down in a dark, wet, vertical tube with little room to move. Ingleborough has numerous examples of such pots, notably Gaping Ghyll but also the less famous Christmas, Bar and Disappointment Pots. The shafts, or **ponors**, commonly lead down to extensive **underground cave systems** such as the famous, commercialised examples at Castleton in Derbyshire and Cheddar in Somerset, or the much explored caves of Gaping Ghyll whose main chamber has dimensions similar to those of York Minster. The tunnels that lead to the caves often reflect the horizontal bedding planes of the limestone and the infiltrating water uses joints, or sometimes faults, to travel deeper into the rock. In this way the water produces a sequence of tunnels in a series of steps as in Fig 3.19.

In parts of the Burren in County Clare, however, the caves are consistently at one level, perhaps because a layer of impermeable chert blocks deeper penetration or because the water table retains a permanent level. The role of the water table in cave formation is much discussed, the usual view being that the solution is concentrated at the level which the water table usually attains, for here lateral flow is at its greatest. In fact, cave formation is not confined to this zone. It will also take place above it, when the water table migrates, and well below it, albeit at a very slow rate and under certain specific conditions. Thus, one may detect cave galleries at various levels within the limestone, reflecting former rainfall regimes. As water penetrates underground it becomes increasingly saturated with lime, and under certain conditions some of this may be redeposited. Dripping water from a cave's roof engenders **stalagmites** growing up towards the descending **stalactites** at a rate of about half a metre a century, or in the case of Ingleborough Cave at about ten centimetres a century. The redeposition of lime will also occur in some surface streams at waterfalls, where sheets of tufa extend beneath the blanket of water such as at Jannet's Foss near Malham.

Enclosed surface depressions, from the tiny hollows on clints to massive features whose diameter can be measured in hundreds of metres, are another Karstic landform. The majority have a scale somewhere between the two extremes and are known as **dolines** in Yugoslavia, **sotch** in France and **shake holes** in North Yorkshire. Solution at the surface is an important process in their formation, but the large ones are too enormous to be explained by present rates of decay alone. One explanation, shown in Fig 3.20, is that the hollows have developed beneath a cover of glacial drift or soil, and evidence from Malham shows that where

Photo 3.11 Limestone pavement, Aran Islands, Ireland. This close-up reveals the peeling off in layers of the Carboniferous limestone.

Photo 3.12 Hunt Pot, Pen-y-Ghent, North Yorkshire: a swallow hole in summer, the stream virtually dry.

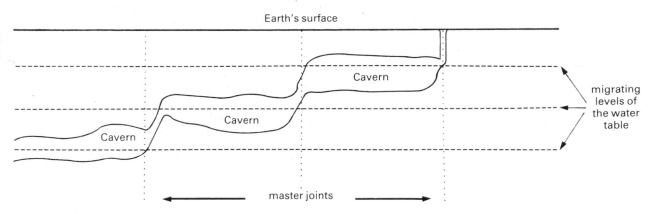

Earth's surface

Cavern

Cavern

Cavern

migrating
levels of
the water
table

master joints

Fig 3.19 The relationship of underground caves and the water table.

cover is absent so are the hollows, and where drift is two or three metres deep the hollows are best developed. The same intensification of chemical weathering occurs here as it does in the development of a submerged limestone pavement, and once the hollow is deep enough and the sides sufficiently steep, slope mass wasting will occur to deepen the hollow until an equilibrium slope angle is reached. If the hollow becomes a focus for surface run-off, further deepening may occur as debris is removed and solution is revitalised. The doline then becomes similar in form to a swallow hole.

An alternative hypothesis to this is often put for-ward, particularly for similar features in the Burren and the Grands Causses. This suggests that underground caverns collapse through continued solution weathering of the roof. This eventually leaves a depression on the surface. In extreme cases the hollows are so large, for example Parsons Pulpit and Douky Bottom in the Malham area, that weathering under former climates has to be resorted to for explanation. This might include the tropical rainy conditions of the late Tertiary or the periglacial conditions that followed the last ice age. In other cases, such as the vast **poljes** of Yugoslavia, the features owe their size as much to the

Photo 3.13   The Drunken Forest, Mulu National Park, Sarawak: well-developed stalagmites and stalactites in a tropical Carboniferous limestone cave.

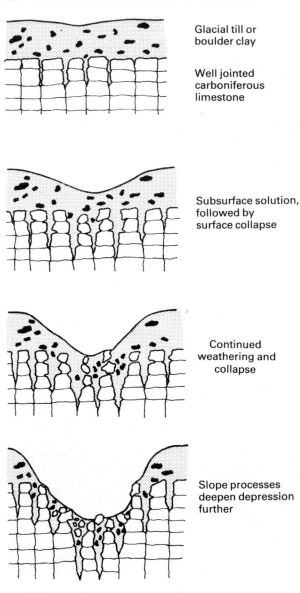

Glacial till or boulder clay

Well jointed carboniferous limestone

Subsurface solution, followed by surface collapse

Continued weathering and collapse

Slope processes deepen depression further

Fig 3.20 The development of a closed hollow such as a doline or shake hole.

faulting of their sides as to solution. In the poljes of the Burren, solution was probably aided by the lateral erosion of rivers when the water table was much higher, or even by glacial erosion in the case of the 60 metre deep Carran depression.

The limestone **gorge**, with its steep, unvegetated sides often littered with scree, is well exemplified in Britain at Cheddar, at Gordale Scar near Malham and at the Winnats Pass in Derbyshire. The traditional theories suggest that these result from the collapse of the roof of the underground caverns, the cavern needing to be located near to a sharp break in slope of the land as provided by the scarp edge of the Mendips plateau at Cheddar or the Middle Craven Fault at Gordale. However, many geomorphologists remain unconvinced by this hypothesis, looking to the lack of rubble from the collapsed roof, the sheer size of the gorges and the apparent existence of surface fluvial erosion features to support their objections. Many have

suggested that, for example, Gordale Scar is the result of the retreat of a waterfall which existed at the head of the gorge (as in Fig 3.21). Small postulates that the Vis gorge in the Grands Causses is entirely the result of surface erosion. In the case of Cheddar, most modern theories see the gorge as a vast dry valley cut by the rapid downcutting of a river when the water table was much higher than it is today and before the caves that currently transport the river were in existence. Whilst several of the gorges contain rivers, many are, for the most part, dry. Indeed, like most limestone areas, Karst scenery may support many dry valleys, some of which were considerably wetter in relatively recent times. The magnificent neo-Gothic painting of Malham Cove in the Tate Gallery shows a waterfall descending from the dry valley at the top. Is this first-hand observation or artistic licence? Other evidence tends to support the former.

Chalk

While Carboniferous limestone is hard, **chalk** is soft, if the former is grey the latter is white, while Karst scenery is angular then chalk's is gently rounded, and if the Carboniferous limestone derives its permeability from its regular joint system then chalk derives its mostly

Photo 3.14 Trow Gill, Ingleborough: looking down a Carboniferous limestone gorge.

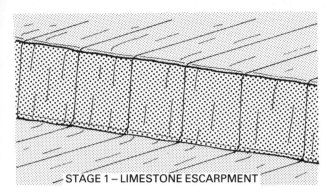
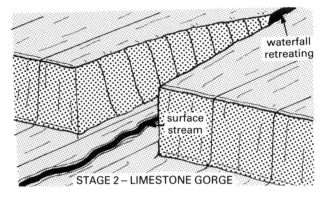

Fig 3.21 The development of a limestone gorge.

Photo 3.15 The South Downs near Fulking, East Sussex. Contrast the steep stark slope of the chalk escarpment with the gentler dip slope to the left of it.

from its pores. The chalk hills of southern and eastern England are best exemplified by the North and South Downs which provide many excellent examples of typical **scarpland**. As the massive Tertiary orogeny which produced the Alps buckled southern Europe, ripples were sent across northern Europe and led to the upfolding of much of southern England. The chalk hills re-main upstanding partly as a result of this, but also because their porosity has prevented the surface river erosion which has lowered the sandstones and the clays of the rest of the Weald. The shape of the chalk hills depends on the thickness of the chalk beds and their angle of dip – a direct consequence of the folding. An obvious contrast is provided by the symmetrical Hog's Back near Guildford with its steeply dipping beds, and the almost flat plateau of Salisbury Plain where the dip is negligible (see Fig 3.22).

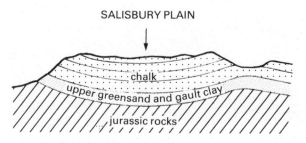
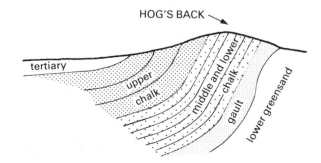

Fig 3.22 The effect of dip on the chalk hills (not to same scale).

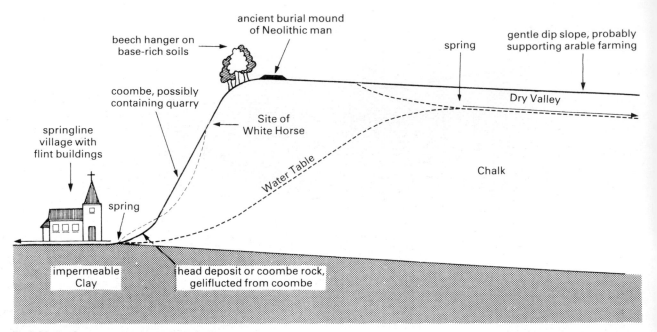

Fig 3.23   A schematic cross-section of a chalk cuesta.

The valleys between the hills may or may not contain a river and their sides characteristically have a well developed convex upper section and, on the whole, are quite steep. Although not exclusive to chalk, the **cuesta**, with its **escarpment** and **dip slope**, is often seen as a typical feature of a chalk landscape. Because they are usually thinly vegetated their prominent shape appears more unique than it in fact is. Their form is initially a response to the Alpine folding, but the present shape is due to an equilibrium attained between the undercutting river in the valley at the foot of the slope and the slope processes of weathering and mass wasting. Fig 3.23 needs careful study, but not all of the features shown are necessarily present in any one example.

Dry valleys, **bottoms** or **bournes**, which are often asymmetrical in cross-section but otherwise have many of the features of normal river valleys, are a common feature of chalk country. They are found on dip slopes, scarp slopes and on most chalk uplands. A simple explanation is that they originated when permanent surface drainage was present in the Pliocene when the water table was much higher. A slightly more complex theory suggests that they were formed in the tundra belt to the south of the retreating Pleistocene ice sheet. As the ground was subjected to permafrost it would be rendered impermeable and thus the dense network of powerful meltwater streams would be able to carve the dry valleys. The asymmetrical shape of the valleys is often explained by the differential frost weathering and **gelifluxion** during periglacial times caused by contrasts in aspect, but this theory is not wholly satisfactory in explaining the phenomenon in north-south trending valleys (see Chapter 10).

The **coombes** of chalk escarpments are large hollows which vary in shape from semi-circular to long and

linear, and must not be confused with glacial cwms or combes. Two processes have been put forward as an explanation for their existence. The first relies on the power of the spring which emerges where the water table surfaces on the escarpment. The chalk around the spring is constantly wet as throughflow, interflow and infiltration top up the groundwater. This weakens the chalk and allows spring sapping to erode it. This operates in various ways and, as it steepens the slope behind the spring, collapse will occur which hollows out the scarp face; as long as the stream continues to

Photo 3.16   Butser Hill, Hampshire: chalk dry valley – note the thinness of the soils on the slopes.

Photo 3.17 Chalk coombe in the escarpment near Westbury, Wiltshire.

remove the debris the hollowing out will proceed. Whether this process is powerful enough to form coombes of the size found on the South Downs is open to question, and the lack of any nearby stream or spring at 24 out of the 28 coombes between Treyford and Graffham in Sussex does seem to prevent the universal application of the hypothesis. An alternative theory relies once again on the periglacial period, this time for the lower temperatures and frost to have strengthened the gelifluxion process on the steep scarp slopes. The hollow remains after the gelifluected debris has been removed by meltwater, although some may remain behind as **head deposits** or **coombe rock,** and this in turn may act as supporting evidence for the theory.

As is the case with all limestones, local variations in composition will affect the precise form of all features. The regularity of the jointing in the chalk will vary from place to place and may control underground hydrology. **Flint nodules**, which are the chemically deposited remains of sea-dwelling radiolaria and sponges, appear as layers in the chalk. Their thickness and their frequency, indeed whether they are present at all, may affect the profile of a slope and may slow down forces of denudation.

More important, perhaps, is the thickness of the chalk beds, which may determine the height of the relief. Indeed, the three major chalk beds of Great Britain, the Upper, Middle and Lower, each have distinct characteristics and the form of the landscape may well depend upon which of the three is at the surface. The **Upper Chalk**, being on the whole more resistant to erosion than the two underlying layers, is thus more likely to form upstanding relief. The lower flinty layers of the Upper chalk are, in turn, more resistant than the upper layers. Also contained within the chalk are bands of conglomerate, known locally as Totternhoe Stone and Melbourn Rock, the former in the middle of the **Lower Chalk**, the latter at the base of the **Middle Chalk**. They are both capable of producing local variations in relief. Deposits of clay-with-flints and of glacial drift sometimes cap the chalk hills and alter the hydrology and vegetation and thus influence the process of denudation and the shape of the relief.

Solution features on chalk are less frequently discussed than their counterparts on Carboniferous limestone. They do exist, but large underground caves and tunnels are less likely both because the chalk is not strong enough to support such features, and also because the porosity of the chalk means that the solution is not so concentrated or joint controlled as it is in other limestones. Nevertheless, one can see quite deep **solution hollows** or **chimneys** on the cliffs at Seaford in Sussex, and **sink holes** do exist, as the appropriately named River Mole demonstrates in dry years when sections of its flow are underground.

Other British limestones

Having deliberately chosen Carboniferous limestone and chalk as the two most common and most contrasting limestones, it is possible to generalise by saying that most of the other examples lie somewhere in the spectrum of rock character and scenery between the two extremes.

Thus, **Jurassic** or **oolitic limestone** forms scarpland scenery and low hills, not unlike chalk but less smooth, with rock outcrops punctuating slopes and usually reaching greater altitude. Unlike the contemporaneous limestones of the Grands Causses, it is too soft to support Karst and contains few underground features, although still rather more than chalk. The steep scarp slope of the north-west-facing Cotswolds best demonstrates this, but it is also well exemplified at Rockingham in Northamptonshire and the Lincoln Edge south of Lincoln. The rock itself is composed of a mass of tiny, spherical grains resembling fish roe and these are an important determinant of its rate of weathering.

The **Durness limestone**, Cambrian in age and therefore the oldest British example, outcrops in north-west Scotland where it provides a Karst landscape on a miniature scale. Like chalk, the rock is both pervious and porous, but is very hard. Rivers disappear down sink holes, notably Allt Smoo which plunges 24 metres down a sink to appear in a cave in the sea cliff.

As an exception to the general, **magnesian limestone** has already been discussed. However, it has many similarities to other limestones despite its chemical differences, and it outcrops in a widening belt from Nottinghamshire to the Durham coast. Its effect on scenery in the Midlands is not striking but at Knaresborough in West Yorkshire it forms a prominent escarpment, and in Durham its influence is more noticeable for it allows little surface drainage and it supports a well developed network of underground solution caves which make use of the well jointed limestone.

Granite

On the whole, it cannot be said of **granite** that it controls landscape, for under different environmental conditions it can produce very different results. Even so, certain of its characteristics, notably its jointing pattern and its feldspar content, are vital controls in the interaction of landscape-forming factors, as the tors of Dartmoor demonstrate. As an igneous rock it provides a useful contrast with limestone. Like limestone there is a wide variety of granites in Britain, but they are not so easily divided into distinct classes such as chalk, oolitic and dolomite. Rather, they should be regarded as a continuum varying from each other in crystal size, colour, chemical composition and age.

Dartmoor is the best documented of all granite areas in Britain, and with its wild, rolling moorland about 400 metres above sea level it is, perhaps, the norm with which to contrast other granite areas. This enormous igneous intrusion is thought to be either the most easterly of a series of batholiths, **stocks** and **bosses** stretching west to the Scilly Isles via Bodmin Moor, or the largest of seven **cupolas** of one massive batholith which underlies most of south-west England. **Tors** surmount many Dartmoor summits. They are blocks of bare, dissected stone, five to ten metres high, surrounded by weathered material of all sizes from sand to boulders. They are by no means exclusive to Dartmoor, or indeed to granite, for they occur in the sandstone of the Valley of the Rocks and in the quartzite of the Stiperstones in Shropshire. The two most widely discussed theories for the Dartmoor tors both rely on more rapid weathering conditions from a climate less moderate than today's that exploited the differential jointing pattern of the granite. Linton postulated that the tors formed in embryo beneath the ground, and the existence of as yet unexposed examples in a quarry near Princetown on Dartmoor certainly lends support to his idea. In the warm, wet conditions of the tropical, late Tertiary climate deep chemical weathering occurred which reduced the rock to rubble where the joints were densest, but allowed spheroidal weathering to evolve corestones where the joints were more widely spaced. These corestones are the tors in embryo. Later erosion, including gelifluxion in periglacial times, removed the finest weathered material, the saprolite, and thus the embryo emerged from the ground.

Palmer and Neilson question the theory's reliance on chemical weathering, suggesting that its existence would have reduced rock waste to clay minerals and not to the quartz crystals and mica flakes of mechanical breakdown that most usually surround the tors, and which are present in too great a volume to be produced by present weathering. They point, therefore, to frost shattering in tundra conditions of the late Quaternary. Gelifluxion played a vital role, first in removing soil and exposing the granite on the summits to frost shattering, and second, once the frost action had responded to the differential jointing, in removing the finer waste material.

Whilst Dartmoor reaches summits of 600 metres, much of Rannoch Moor in Perthshire reaches no more than 300 metres. Indeed, in comparison with local

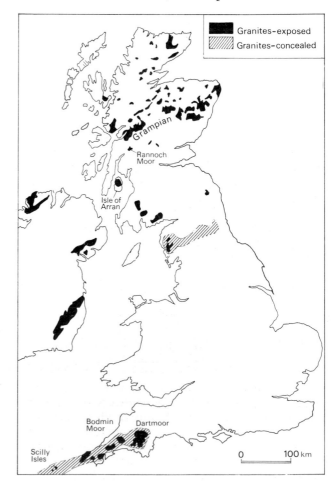

Fig 3.24 Granite outcrops in Britain.

igneous rocks. In Pleistocene times, frost shattering played havoc with the granite and, later, ice found a natural focus in the basin and deepened it, thus giving it the fairly featureless landscape that characterises it today.

A further series of quite different granite landscapes can be found in other parts of Scotland, where sharp ice-riven and frost-shattered peaks are typical, such as Ben Nevis and the 875 metre high peak of Goat Fell on the Isle of Arran. On Arran, the granite has produced two different sceneries. Where it is coarse grained, weathering has produced sharper, higher peaks, but where it is finer grained the rock has proved less resistant and gives more rounded and lower summits.

Age is the major reason why the granite of Mountsorrel in the Charnwood Forest forms such subdued scenery. Despite its relative hardness it forms part of a ridge which stands no more than 300 metres above the surrounding Midland Plain.

To identify a single granite scenery in Britain would therefore be misleading. Indeed, if one were to extend one's area of study one would discover tropical, humid locations where granite is considered a weak rock because of its rapid chemical decomposition in the local conditions.

Sandstone

If granite landscapes are an assorted variety then **sandstone** landscapes are a thoroughly mixed bag. Indeed, it

Photo 3.18   Houndstar, Dartmoor, Devon: the exposed corestones of the tor.

Photo 3.19   Goat Fell, Isle of Arran. The dramatic, frost-shattered summit of Goat Fell is seen in the distance.

relief it is really more a lowland than an upland, surrounded, as it is, by the Grampian Mountains. Surprisingly, similarly-aged, medium-grained granites form much higher land in the Cairngorms, and past geomorphological history must be sought as the explanation of the apparent weakness of the Rannoch granite. It probably once formed a shallow upland basin surrounded by more resistant metamorphic and

is often very difficult to distinguish rock type in a sandstone landscape without detailed study for it has few distinctive landforms, and those that do occur, such as the Bridestones, in the Valley of the Rocks, and the honeycombed inland cliffs of the Weald of Kent, are not common. This difficulty is compounded by the enormous variety of British sandstones. It is not easy to make any generalisations.

The imposing and towering relief of the Torridon Mountains, composed as they are of great thicknesses of feldspar-rich **Torridonian sandstones** which form frost-riven peaks of over 1000 metres, could not be more different from the gentle scarplands produced by the **Upper Greensand** in Kent and Sussex, which rarely reach 150 metres, or from the moorlands and plateaux of the Brecon Beacons and Exmoor.

If we take just one sandstone, the **Old Red Sandstone** of the Devonian era, we can see that it occurs in a wide variety of landscapes – in the Gower Peninsula it produces the sharp ridge of Cefn Bryn, some 200 metres high, near Corve Dale in Shropshire it produces undramatic, rolling scenery, leaving other rocks to form the landmarks, whilst the Black Mountains provide South Wales with some of its steepest, most dramatic slopes, rising to 600 metres. In the Mendips, Old Red Sandstone produces the highest point of Black Down, but it is, of course, the Carboniferous limestone which produces the striking features of this area. Thus there is no distinctive sandstone landscape.

This does not mean, however, that the character of sandstone is not relevant to the form of the land. Its degree of permeability, for example, is vital. Most sandstones, with the exception of the **greywackes** or **turbidites**, are permeable. Most are porous, but to what degree depends on grain size and shape which will vary enormously according to the origin of the material which composes the rock. Many sandstones are jointed, the Torridonian having a cuboidal pattern, the Old Red a dense, but irregular, distribution. The chemical composition is also a variable. All sandstones have

Photo 3.20 Ancient sandstone cliffs, Hastings, Sussex. These former sea cliffs were raised 30 metres above present sea level during the Alpine orogeny. Weathering processes are picking out the weaknesses in the sandstone.

Photo 3.21 Torridon Mountains at the head of Loch Torridon, north west Scotland.

a high silica content due to their high proportion of quartz, but the amount of feldspar and fragments of other rocks will also control their resistance. One of the reasons why the **Ordovician quartzite** forms the striking Stiperstones Ridge is that it not only contains a high degree of quartz but it is also cemented by a silica-rich **matrix**. In contrast, the **New Red Sandstone** of the Penrith area has a less strong **cement** and is correspondingly less resistant. Diversity without distinctiveness is the hallmark of the sandstone landscape.

It is not, therefore, possible to ignore the influence of lithology on landscape, but some of the sweeping statements made earlier in the century about rock controlling landform need to be corrected.

Questions

1 Refer to Fig 3.8 and answer the following questions:
(a) Is a negative or positive correlation suggested between the intensity of frost weathering and temperature?
(b) According to the graphs, how strong is a. frost weathering b. chemical weathering in Eastern England today?
(c) Suggest three ways in which the strength of chemical weathering could be assessed?
(d) Why does the intensity of chemical weathering increase towards the bottom left of diagram 3.8b?
(e) What aspects of rainfall besides mean annual total might also be determinants of the intensity of frost weathering?
(f) On a copy of Fig. 3.25, attempt to draw your own graph of the intensity of biological weathering in relation to rainfall and temperature.

2 Refer to Fig 3.26 which suggests a method of evolution for the formation of tors on Dartmoor.
(a) Of what rock are the Dartmoor tors made?
(b) What time scale would be involved between the beginning of Stage 1 and the emergence of the tors in Stage 3? Choose from *c* 10 000 years, *c* 500 000 years and *c* 10 000 000 years.
(c) What does the broken line, labelled BWF, indicate?
(d) Why might tors such as these be described as relict features?
(e) What characteristics of the rock encourage the formation of tors? Explain how each one that you mention contributes to the formation.
(f) What climatic conditions would be required for the course of events shown in Stages 1–3 to occur?

3 Refer to Ordnance Survey 1:50 000 sheet numbers 199 and 182, one of part of the South Downs, the other of an area of the Mendips. The former shows a chalk upland area between Eastbourne and the River Cuckmere, the latter an area of Carboniferous limestone to the north of Cheddar and Wells. For each map list the evidence that you can discern from the map that confirms the dominant rock type of the area. This evidence should be listed in two groups, conclusive and circumstantial. What extra evidence, other than a geological map, might aid you in this exercise?

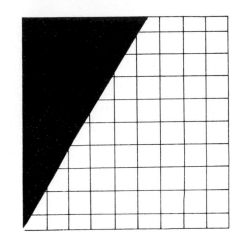

Fig 3.25

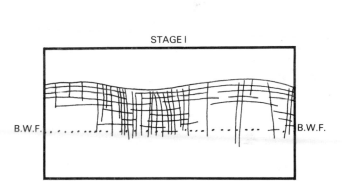

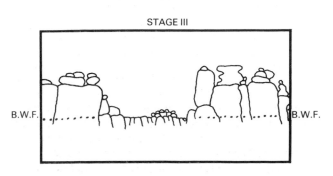

Fig 3.26 A theory of tor development.

Further Reading

The Earth's Changing Surface, M J Bradshaw, A J Abbott and A P Gelsthorpe (Hodder and Stoughton, 1978).

Slopes and Weathering, M Clark and R J Small (Cambridge, 1982).

The Origin of the Landforms of the Malham Area, K M Clayton, *Field Studies* 5, 389–424 (1981).

Mystery of the Dartmoor Tors, V Gerrard, *Geographical Magazine* 41, (1969).

Weathering and Landforms, C Ollier (Macmillan, 1974).

Weathering, C Ollier (Longman, 1984).

The Study of Landforms, R J Small (Cambridge, 1978).

Rocks and Relief, B W Sparks (Longman, 1971).

Field Observations of Limestone Weathering and Erosion in the Malham District, S T Trudgill, *Field Studies* 6, 201–236 (1985).

Weathering and Erosion, S T Trudgill (Butterworths, 1983)

Geology and Scenery in England and Wales, A E Trueman (Penguin, 1971).

Geology and Scenery in Scotland, J Whittow (Penguin, 1977).

Other References

The Disintegration and Exfoliation of Granite in Egypt, D C Barton, *Journal of Geology* 46, 109–111 (1938).

Notes on some Observed Rates of Weathering of Limestones, V G Goodchild, *Geological Magazine* 27 (1890).

The Problem of Tors, D L Linton, *Geographical Journal* 121 (1955).

The Origin of Granite Tors, Dartmoor, J Palmer and R A Neilson *Proceedings of the Yorkshire Geological Society* 33, 315–40, (1962).

The Geographic Cycle in Periglacial Regions as it is Related to Climatic Geomorphology, *Annals of the Association of American Geographers* 40, 214–36 (1950).

Some Factors in the Absolute Denudation of Limestone Terrain, M M Sweeting, *Erdkunde* 18, 92–5 (1964).

Slopes, A Young (Oliver and Boyd, 1972).

4

Slopes

Introduction

Slopes: a Classification of Landscape

At first sight it may seem unnecessary to devote an entire chapter to slopes, as they appear to a greater or lesser extent in every other chapter of the book. The reason why it is essential to study them in such depth is that they are the basic unit of every landscape. They represent an ideal method of classification, for every landscape can be broken down into a series of slopes of different sizes and shapes. Thus, a typical British river valley can be divided into the convex slopes at the top of the valley sides, the straight sections of the mid-slope, the concave sections of the lower slope and the flat or gently sloping segments of the flood plain (see Fig. 4.1). There is not a landscape in Britain, man-made or natural, that cannot be subdivided in this way, from the perpendicular 335 metre high cliffs of the Orkneys to the virtually horizontal plains of the Fens.

Slope Controls

Although they are a basic unit of all landscapes, slopes are not necessarily always well understood, largely because a slope's profile and plan are the result of so

many processes whose rate and capability are determined by so many factors. Fig 4.2 tries to identify the most important features of this interaction in an attempt to analyse the controls upon slope angle and profile. As the diagram reveals, influence is not necessarily direct. Climate, for instance, may exert a strong influence over soil thickness and character, which in turn will affect the type and character of vegetation that develops; in so doing, climate may have only an *indirect* effect on slope processes and profile. In other situations, climate may *directly* control the processes, but of course this gives it only an indirect influence on profile. It is usually the case, then, that the operating processes control the slope form, and they in turn depend on the local hydrology, geology, ecology and geomorphology.

Slope Processes: a Three-way Interaction

Before we proceed to examine each of the influences on slope form in detail, it is essential that we appreciate the interrelationship between the three sets of slope processes, **weathering**, **slope movements** and **slope-foot processes**. The movements of material on a slope may depend on the quantity of material or regolith to be moved, and that in turn is a direct result of weathering. However, slippage of regolith from the upper slope may not only reduce the thickness of the regolith there, but by exposing more bare rock to weathering may stimulate the supply of more weathered rock to the lower

Fig 4.1 Cross-section of the Welland Valley on the Leicestershire/Northamptonshire border: a river valley probably widened by a meltwater stream during the Pleistocene.

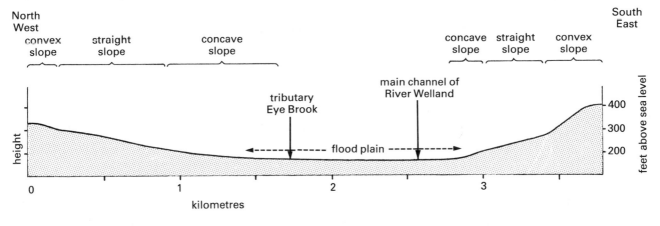

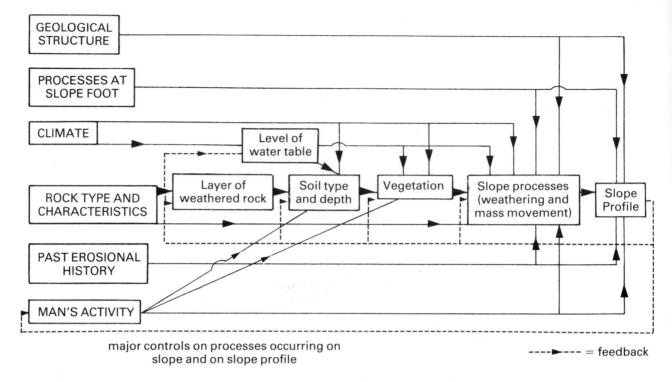

major controls on processes occurring on
slope and on slope profile

----▶---- = feedback

Fig 4.2 The inter-related factors that control slope form.

slope. A two-way relationship exists between these two slope processes, then: weathering stimulates slope movements, and slope movements stimulate weathering. As the mass movement conveys this weathered material down the slope it may cause it to build up, perhaps protecting the lower slope from further attack by weathering. To what extent this accumulation will be allowed to continue, however, depends on how active the slope-foot processes are, in which we may include erosion by sea waves, by a river, especially with an undercutting meander, or even by a glacier, as Fig 4.3 shows.

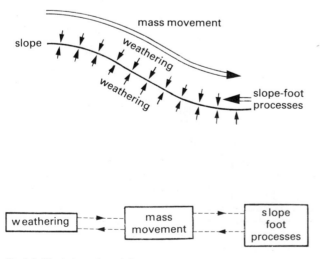

Fig 4.3 The interaction of slope processes.

If these processes are vigorously attacking the slope foot they will remove the material dumped by the slope processes and, by so steepening the slope, may encourage the continuation of the downslope movement; as we have already seen, this may stimulate weathering on the upper slope. In some circumstances however, the inability of these slope-foot processes to remove the accumulation of debris may slow down not just the slope processes but also the weathering that supplies them. There is a vital balance, or equilibrium, between the three sets of process. On most British slopes this equilibrium has been established and will cause the slope form to remain more or less the same, at least over the time scale of man's life span, although over longer time periods the balance may not be so stable.

Slope Control Factors

What, then, are the controls or factors that dictate how these slope processes operate? Obviously, it is not necessary to duplicate ideas in other chapters on weathering and slope-foot processes, although we may find that a certain amount of re-emphasis of some of these concepts occurs here.

Geological Structure

Like any of the other controls discussed here, this may or may not assume a dominant role. Fault-guided, almost vertical, inland cliffs such as Malham Cove exemplify geological structure operating in a dominant role. In a similar fashion, the steepness of a chalk slope in south-east England may well reflect the angle of dip of the beds which itself is a reflection of the asymmetry of the folding (see Fig 2.22). Even so, in both of these cases, the particular characteristics of the rock also contribute strongly to the form. Another structural influence akin to folding and faulting is vulcanicity. The steep scarps produced by the Great Whin Sill in certain areas of north-east England are very much a product of the angle of its dip and the thickness of its intrusion (Photo 4.1). One final facet of geological structure is the complexity of the bedding of the slope, for compound slopes, that is, those composed of a series of different rock layers, are often the most prone to major landslips.

Rock Type and Character

After the extensive treatment given to this topic in the previous chapter, very little needs to be added here. Its influence is often inextricable from that of geological structure in general, and this is hardly surprising as it is really an aspect of it.

Two questions must be asked about a rock. How vulnerable is it to weathering, for this will affect the nature and depth of the regolith, and to what extent is it able to resist the downslope forces which can cause mass movement? Resistance here is largely physical resistance, a property which clays such as the Gault and Weald of south-east England have in very small measure. Physically strong rocks such as granite and Carboniferous limestone may be prone to movement though, if regular vertical jointing provides a weakness from which the rock can pull away. Jointing is also an aspect of a rock's permeability which, in turn, is important as it determines how much water can seep into the rock. It is well established that saturated rocks are prone to slip.

Photo 4.1 Hadrian's Wall, Gt. Whin Sill, Northumberland. The steep craggy escarpment of the sill provided a naturally defensive location for the Roman Wall.

One obvious case where rock character may assert itself as a dominant controlling force over all others is on bare rock slopes, where any weakness or strength is likely to be sculpted by weathering into a feature of the slope's physiognomy.

Past Erosional and Climatic History

In interpreting any slope form it is essential to be aware of the past. An analysis of upland Britain's landscape is pointless for those not versed in a knowlege of glacial history, and as will be further revealed in Chapter 7, an analysis of any coastal slope is considerably hindered without a knowledge of past sea levels. Any previous climate can leave its imprint on a slope through the processes it allowed to operate, be they those of the tundra conditions of the late Pleistocene, the hot, humid conditions of the late Tertiary or the warm, temperate conditions of the later Pleistocene interglacials. Once again, though, the past erosional history need not prevail above all other factors, for example the steepness of the side slope of a glaciated valley, as shown in Photo 4.2, has been much modified by later processes, whose operation may have been interfered with by the vegetation and soil of today. Where a changing climate has caused a fall in the level of the water table, the effectiveness of springs may have been impaired with a consequent increase in the potential stability of a slope or a decrease in the amount of surface erosion.

Climate

Without doubt it is true that different climates encourage different processes, but this does not mean that slope profiles can be easily categorised into different climatic types. It may be true that certain generalisations can be made about slopes in arid areas (see Chapter 11), but slope form is so variable that climate can rarely predominate above all other factors. Its effect on various slope processes is unquestionable, however.

Photo 4.2 Scree slopes in the glaciated trough of Langdale, Cumbria: the operation of a series of processes on several different time scales.

Wetter climates, such as those of the humid tropics, stimulate soil and regolith development through increased chemical weathering, but at the same time invigorate the growth of vegetation which may act as a stabilising agent for the regolith. Field observations, especially those of Carson, indicate that an increase in the water input is often the stimulus that engenders a major mass movement, and not surprisingly therefore, major land slippages occur frequently in tropical rainy areas; but they are by no means exclusive to such regions. In extremely dry climates, weathering may be so slow that little debris masks the slopes anyway, but the intensity of the infrequent rainstorms, combined with the lack of vegetative protection, will permit surface wash to be of occasional importance, perhaps with associated mudflows. If large quantities of debris exist as a relic of a former climate, for instance in an alluvial fan, the latter process is particularly probable.

In humid temperate climates such as our own, surface wash will be severely restricted by the almost total cover of vegetation and by the relatively light nature of most of the precipitation which will prevent total saturation of the regolith. Soil creep is the most commonly observed process, but this does not mean that extreme climatic events such as a thunderstorm or snowmelt are not capable of producing more cataclysmic events of mass wasting. Tundra climates are too cold to allow a very full ground cover of vegetation, and for much of the year the ground may be so solid that very little change in it is able to occur. Summer melting permits gelifluxion and the various frost-induced processes of weathering and transport will act in support of it, impeded little by vegetation.

To summarise its impact, then, climate may stimulate or restrict the formation of the regolith and the vegetation cover, and each of these in turn may determine the degree of slope stability. More important than this, though, through the media of evaporation, precipitation, snowmelt and freeze-thaw it can control the hydrological cycle of a slope, and this of course is a vital aspect of the entire slope system.

Man's Activities

Evidence of this controlling factor is easy for all of us to observe. How often does the farmer pay for ploughing a slope by destabilizing it! The field in Photo 4.3 demonstrates the effectiveness of surface wash as a transporter of topsoil downslope in Northamptonshire during one winter. Landslides may be a useful device for the storywriter to introduce drama into a tale of the railroads of the wild west, but their presence is by no means fictitious. One has only to observe the speed of slope processes on a motorway embankment to appreciate this. By creating cuttings for a road or railway, man is setting up a slope on which all natural controls have been removed. The slope is so steep, and frequently so sparsely protected by vegetation, that weathering and mass movements will operate relatively fast in an attempt to re-establish a profile in equilibrium with the climate. What better location could one request than a motorway embankment for an individual study of slope process?

The Character of the Regolith

Climate, rock type and most of the other controlling factors will influence the character of the **regolith**, which in turn will help to determine slope form. Its unconsolidated nature makes regolith prone to downslope movement, and the extra weight of a deep regolith will increase the likelihood of instability. The passage of water, both from the surface and from upslope, needs to be effective and efficient if the regolith is

Photo 4.3   Soil erosion and gulleying on farmland near Southwick, Northamptonshire.

to maintain any stability. Regoliths rich in clay particles tend towards instability because of the clay's facility for water retention. A high percentage of clay particles will be found not only on slopes of clay bedrock but also in locations where chemical decay is rife, and the production of clay minerals is vigorous. Susceptibility to slope failure is reduced where the regolith has a high percentage of sand particles. This has been proved by So's analysis of landslips in Hong Kong which indicated the greater resistance of the well drained sandy weathered mantles of granite compared with the less sandy debris on volcanic rocks.

Soil is essentially a part of the regolith, and its crumb structure and grain texture will determine how much water it holds, and once again the presence of clay particles may play a very influential role. For example, a deep, clay-rich soil on a recently deforested slope in a tropical rain forest will offer little resistance.

Vegetation

As Fig 4.2 shows, both soil and vegetation are often mediating factors through which other controls exert their influence on a slope angle. It is doubtful whether vegetation can prevent or even slow down any of the larger scale movements, and as Photo 4.4 of the cliffs at Sheringham shows, even a dense grass cover will offer little resistance to movement on a steep slope on a potentially unstable rock.

It has even been shown by So in Hong Kong that vegetation can increase the chance of major landslips. He suggests that dense forest is likely to reduce surface wash, causing soil to build up between the trees thus deepening the mantle and increasing the potential for failure. However, vegetation can also do much to reduce the smaller scale movements of soil creep and sur-

Photo 4.4 The crescentic scar left by rotational slumping on the cliffs at Sheringham, Norfolk.

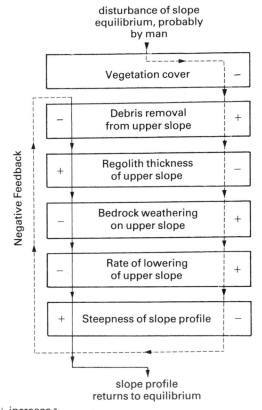

Fig 4.4 The operation of negative feedback to maintain slope equilibrium.

face wash, and it is for this reason that, for example, the steep valley sides of the Thirlmere Reservoir have been afforested, for sediment infilling is the greatest threat to the survival of any reservoir.

Time

If slopes evolve, and certainly it seems that they do, then it is vital that the stage of development is not omitted from an analysis. This is discussed more fully, later in the chapter (pp 89–91).

As a conclusion to this discussion of the controls on slope form, notice must be drawn to the feedback loops in Fig 4.2. These suggest that slope angle itself can act as a self-controlling mechanism. This is not difficult to understand, for a steep slope will, for example, increase the speed of downslope transport, the product of which may be to reduce the angle of the slope and so in time slow down the processes of movement. Such operation of negative feedback is demonstrated by a possible sequence of events in Fig 4.4.

Slope Form

It is all very well to analyse the main determinants of form, but what of the form itself?

Slope Materials

As a starting point we must realise that form includes not only shape but also the materials that make up the slope. Even brief experience of the British landscape can reveal that most slopes in a temperate climate reveal little bare rock. They are typically mantled in regolith, soil and vegetation and their surface form may well be very different from that of the underlying rock (Fig 4.5). These, of course, are the characteristics of valley side slopes in much of lowland Britain.

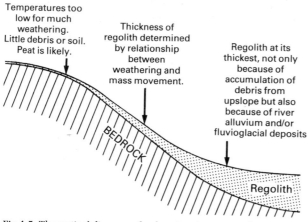

Fig 4.5 Theoretical diagram of a slope in a temperate climate.

As a contrast, Britain has some examples of bare rock slopes, as Photo 4.5 indicates, but they are largely confined to coastal cliffs and to the steep, frost-shattered upper slopes of the highland regions. Between the two extremes, a third type of slope exists, the debris slope, which is littered with fragments of unvegetated rock. In Britain this is best represented by the scree slopes which flank the walls of most glaciated valleys in the Lake District and Snowdonia.

Not all climates produce the same distribution as Britain. Less temperate climes, such as extremely cold or arid ones, may experience such minimal rates of weathering or be so detrimental to vegetation that bare rock and debris slopes predominate.

Slope Profile

Many attempts have been made to classify slope shape, and almost all of them resort to an initial splitting of the slope into units. As Fig 4.6 shows, these can be subdivided into **straight segments** and **curved elements**. Examples of segments are **rectilinear slopes** and **free faces**, whilst **convex** and **concave slopes** are both elements. Each of these may extend right across a slope, or may constitute just a tiny part of it. The free face, or cliff, is so called because it is so steep that any weathered debris will fall from it as soon as it is loose enough to do so. The rectilinear, or straight slope, varies enormously in both angle and extent. Convexity tends to be a characteristic of the upper slope.

Convexo-concave slopes

Observation of any landscape will quickly demonstrate that this series of slope units can be assembled into a

Fig 4.6 Classification of a slope into elements and segments.

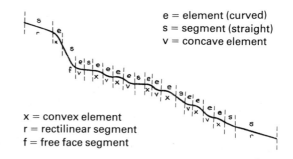

e = element (curved)
s = segment (straight)
v = concave element

x = convex element
r = rectilinear segment
f = free face segment

Photo 4.5 Am Basteir Ridge, Black Cuillins, Skye: unprotected slopes of the summit. Notice the impact of frost shattering in the foreground.

wide selection of different slope combinations. Theoretically the possibilities are almost infinite, particularly if one accepts that not only can the size and location of each segment on a slope vary, but also the number of times each occurs on an actual slope. However, in humid temperate environments such as Britain, the typical combination of units is in the **convexo-concave** and **convex-rectilinear-concave** slopes of Fig 4.7.

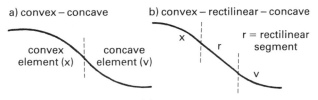

Fig 4.7 Two common types of slope.

Much heated discussion has assailed the ears of students and academics throughout the short history of geomorphology as to why these slopes are so common in such climates. It will suffice here to distil this into a few simple suggestions.

Convexity of the upper slope indicates increasing steepness downslope away from the summit. Soil creep being the most effective denuder of weathered material in this zone of the slope, it can be deduced that in-creased energy is required by the process to move the increased load of debris that accumulates downslope. This increased demand for energy is supplied by the steeper slope. However, as water moves downslope, either as surface flow or throughflow, its volume and speed increase, and with them the potential for surface wash. The need for a steep slope is thus reduced as the efficiency of the transporting medium has been increased, and so a gentler lower slope is adequate for the required load, and concavity is the consequence. In theory there should be a point of inflexion where the convex slope changes to a concave one. This, presumably, could reflect the point at which there is a balance between the demands made by the increase of load downslope and the supply of extra energy made available by the increased efficiency of transport. If this change of slope is extended to more than just a point, a rectilinear slope may develop across which the gradient is just steep enough to transport the amount of debris available, or, in other words, the efficiency of the transport processes is increasing at the same rate as the increased demands made upon them by the load.

Photo 4.6 Howgill Fells, Cumbria. A great variety of segments and elements makes up the compound slope, from the free face at the top through scree slope to the convexo-concave slopes nearer the river.

Photo 4.7 Gordale Scar, North Yorkshire: looking down a Carboniferous limestone gorge.

So much for the convexo-concave slopes that typify landforms in humid temperate areas, and are particularly well represented on many British chalk and limestone landscapes. What about all the other varieties of slope? Certainly some are really only variations on the convexo-concave theme, for instance where several series of convex-rectilinear-concave segments succeed each other down a slope. Each series may have been an adaptation to a particular base level of the river, and as the latter fell, a succeeding series of convex-rectilinear-concave segments developed downslope from its predecessor. On **compound** slopes, a particularly resistant rock band may disturb the pattern by interposing a steep, free face between two of the segments. Other disturbance to form may be brought about by a major landslip or mass movement on a much larger scale than the surface wash and soil creep that affect most convex-rectilinear-concave slopes.

Free faces

Not all British valleys are characterised by these convexo-concave slopes, however. If, for example, downcutting by the river has been too fast for the slope processes to keep up, as in the case of a gorge, the slopes may include extended **free face** segments and debris slopes. Photo 4.7 of Gordale Scar demonstrates how weathered fragments of limestone have built up at the foot of each free face and, unless they are moved by river erosion, may eventually mask the free face. Another type of valley slope which may include a well developed free face is that of a glaciated valley where overdeepening by the glacier has not yet been compensated for by the action of slope processes.

Scree slopes

Scree slopes differ from most other slopes in humid temperate landscapes in being depositional rather than erosional, a trait which they have in common with the slopes of moraines, drumlins, alluvial fans and sand dunes. Scree slopes are often concave in form, which may seem illogical at first as larger material is usually found at the base of the scree and this surely ought to have a steeper angle of rest than the finer material up-slope, and thus produce a convex slope. The explanation appears to be that whilst the upper part of a scree is at the expected angle of rest for the size of debris, the lower part is gentler than the expected angle. As larger fragments of debris break off from the free face above, their considerable velocities bounce them downslope and they fail to halt until an angle considerably lower than their expected angle of repose is reached, and their motion is checked (see Photo 4.8).

Photo 4.8 Base of a Carboniferous limestone scree in Dovedale, Derbyshire.

Micro-scale slopes

One final aspect of slope form is the smaller scale variations such as **terracettes**, **scars**, **gelifluxion lobes** and other irregularities. Some of these, as in Photo 4.9, can be explained only by reference to local peculiarities, perhaps of rock type or human influence, but many result from particular slope processes that will be dealt with in the following section.

Slope Processes

Classification

Frequent reference has already been made in this chapter to various processes of transport that occur on slopes. Many terms have been coined to describe them, the most popular of which is **mass movement**. Even this does not embrace all the processes, though, for it is hardly appropriate as a description of certain erosional processes of running water. The mass that is moved will be soil, or weathered rock, or solid rock, with or without a water flux, or a combination of more than one of these constituents. In size the movement can vary enormously, from massive rock slumps such as the one that transformed the profile of the Quiraing in Skye (Photo 4.10), to almost imperceptible creeps of soil grains.

Any classification of mass movements which attempts to assign different processes to distinct boxes or classes soon comes unstuck, for here we are dealing with transport of many different materials under a huge variety of conditions. In addition, many of the larger, faster movements so distort the initial mass that one can only hazard a guess as to what precisely has taken place. For these reasons a relatively flexible classification, such as that in Fig 4.8, is best adopted, in

Photo 4.9 Esk Valley, North Yorkshire. The apparently natural curves of the slope are remnants of 19th century excavation of the Cleveland Dyke.

Photo 4.10 The Quiraing, Skye. A massive landslip divorced the mass of ancient lavas on the right of the photograph from the crags on the left.

which the processes can be seen as part of a continuum. In this each term can be seen to occupy a zone of the triangle in which certain conditions prevail, rather than being a precisely located unit.

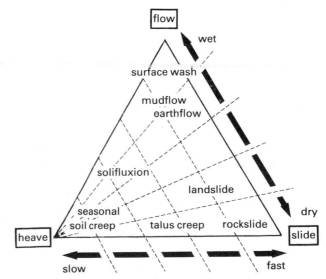

Fig 4.8 A classification of mass movements on slopes (after Carson and Kirkby).

Causes of Mass Movement

Mass movements will occur when the equilibrium which preserves a slope's stability is disturbed. To put this another way, the likelihood of a slope failing can be expressed by its **safety factor**, which is the ratio of resistance which the slope offers against movement to the force which is trying to enact that movement. Obviously, this ratio needs to be equal to at least one to preserve any stability at all, and for most slopes it will exceed that most of the time. As this is not a physics or engineering textbook the mathematics for calculating the safety factor will not be given here, but the bibliography includes several accessible sources for those interested.

a)

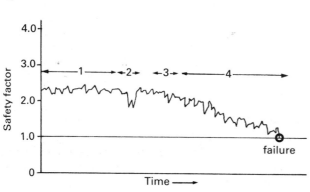

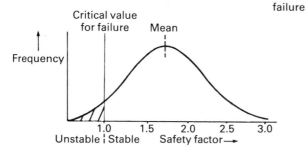

In this diagram, four conditions are represented:
1 Short term variations on an equilibrium slope
2 The impact of an extremely wet period
3 Seasonal changes which affect degree of saturation
4 Long term decline in shear resistance

b) For most of the time the safety factor remains well above failure

Fig 4.9 Variations of the safety factor over time on a hypothetical slope.

Over time the safety factor for a particular slope will vary (Fig 4.9a). In Britain, it can be expected to be lowest in winter. Over a longer period it may remain at much the same level, although man-induced changes on the slope can cause sudden fluctuations. The graph in Fig 4.9b indicates that if a sufficient number of measurements is made over time certain statements about probability of failure should be possible.

Fluctuations of the safety factor are caused either by a reduction in the internal resistance, or **shear strength**, of the slope, or an increase in **shear stress**, that is, the forces attempting to pull a mass downslope, or the simultaneous alteration of both.

Increases in shear stress can be caused by a multitude of factors. Steepening of a slope, as a result of the cutting of a new road, undercutting by the sea or a river or rapid incision by a river, are obvious causes. If a slope suddenly has to bear a greater weight than previously, because of the dumping of a mass of mining waste by man or by the natural addition of a mass of regolith or rock that has slid from higher up the slope, the same change will be effected. An increase in shear stress can also be brought about by vibrations, particularly from an earthquake, and by an increase in the volume of water contained in the slope. This, of course, could be the result of heavy or prolonged rain or snowmelt which may cause a rising of the water table or may simply saturate the surface layers from above. Its effect will be to increase the weight of any potentially mobile mass. By replacing the air in the pores of the regolith or rock the water will increase the pressure exerted on each grain, thus increasing the likelihood of movement.

It is a moot point whether the increase of water destabilises a slope just by increasing shear stress, for surely it will also simultaneously decrease shear strength or resistance. It can accomplish this by decreasing the cohesion of particles by saturation or by weakening the rock or regolith by various processes of weathering, such as hydration and solution. Not all of the effects of water need be brought about suddenly. Some of those described are progressive, such as the change in shear strength carried out by continuous percolation of water through a slope which may gradually carry away finer materials or wear away at minerals that are cementing the slope mass together.

Types of Mass Movement

Carson and Kirkby's division of mass movements identifies three different types of slope transport, the **flow**, the **slide** and the **heave**. To these is often added a fourth, the **fall**. Deeper understanding of Fig 4.8 will be gained if a moment is spent deciding whether falls can be added to Carson and Kirkby's diagram without destroying its unity.

Falls

We are all aware of the road signs which tell us to beware of **rock falls**, even though the method by which we are supposed to go about this may be beyond our ingenuity. They are characteristically found beneath steep, bare rock faces or free fall slopes from which fragments of rock can fall at any moment. Cliffs, such as the Jurassic sedimentary cliffs that extend for most of the coast between Scarborough and Ravenscar in North Yorkshire are so prone to such falls that all beachcombers are warned to stay clear.

All such falls are facilitated by joints and other linear weaknesses which reduce the slope's resistance, and are most commonly set off by freeze-thaw, an increase in water pressure or dilation as the result of a previous fall. Evidence from the chalk cliffs of the Isle of Thanet certainly confirms two of these statements at least (Fig 4.10).

If the fallen debris at the foot of the slope is not removed, it may gradually develop into a scree slope.

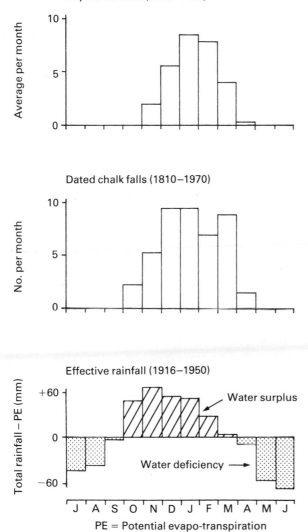

Fig 4.10 The effect of freeze-thaw and an increase in water pressure on the frequency of rock falls on the Isle of Thanet.

Slides

Slides happen quickly, although like most other slope processes the set of circumstances that causes them may build up gradually until suddenly a threshold of resistance is passed and the slide occurs. Solid rock and the overlying debris are both prone to such events, and as it occurs an entire mass will slide along a slip plane.

In Fig 4.8 two types of slide are identified. The first of these, the **rock slide**, is perhaps a massive version of a rock fall, on so large a scale that the whole slope may

slide. Quite often, slabs of rock of millions of cubic metres are involved, their slippage usually initiated by internal weakening of the rock mass by solution weathering. Even resistant rocks are susceptible.

The advantage of a flexible classification is apparent when one tries to differentiate in the field between a rock slide and a **landslide**. Theoretically the latter is the movement of any mass of material, rock or regolith along a slip plane, but whilst this may satisfy an armchair geographer, to the field observer the difference is not necessarily obvious.

For study of a landslide in the field, one is best advised to make use of coastal examples, for here undercutting by the sea may be so virulent and the cliffs so steep that landsliding will be a continuous, or at least a recent, process. The cliffs of north east Yorkshire provide a variety of different conditions. At Cayton Bay, near Scarborough, a chaotic landscape of hillocks and hollows has been created by the succession of slips of the Oxford Clay. Unstable, weaker rocks like this are particularly prone to landslides, a fact well exemplified further north at Robin Hood's and Runswick Bays in unconsolidated glacial drift cliffs. A bed of unstable rock can destabilise the entire cliff; on the northern side of Runswick Bay, the Wrack Hills are composed of a series of Jurassic sedimentaries. Slip planes develop in the Lias shales near the foot of the cliff, especially when the rock is saturated, and massive landslips occur which move the shale and the much stronger overlying Deltaic sandstones, too.

Whilst coastal landslips may be easy to observe because of their freshness, inland slides are often masked by soil and vegetation, especially if the movement is not a recent one. In Fig 4.11, the great semicircular embayment at Sutton Bank in the Hambleton Hills in the steep, 200 metre high western escarpment of the North York Moors has been partly created by a massive landslip of oolitic limestone overlying unstable Oxford Clay. On coming to rest the slipped mass so interfered with natural drainage from the escarpment that a lake formed. Rock falls continue to occur from the escarpment as the undercutting of the clay increases the slope's gradient. The only major rock slide of recent time was in 1755 and John Wesley, the Methodist preacher, was quick to assign it to the wrath of God.

Another example of an ancient landslip whose remains are now hidden beneath soil and vegetation is on the steep Jurassic escarpment near Rockingham in Northants, seen in Photo 4.11. The potentially unstable Lias clay which forms the escarpment is, at present, immobile, with no sign of any major slippage for the last three centuries. Indeed, measurements on the slope indicate that even in winter when the water table rises almost to the surface, the safety factor remains at or above one; even on the more exposed upper slope there is little indication of instability. For explanation of the series of slides, some of them quite deep-seated, we must resort to a tundra climate of the late Pleistocene when free drainage of the slope would have been impeded by permafrost, and freezing water in pores and

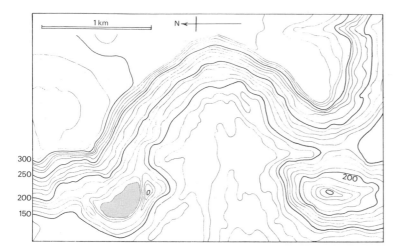

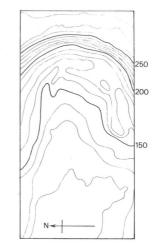

Fig 4.11 Two semi-circular embayments in the western escarpment of the North Yorkshire Moors, both caused by massive landslips.

Photo 4.11 Jurassic limestone escarpment, Rockingham, Northamptonshire. A series of embayments can be seen in the escarpment, each caused by an ancient landslide.

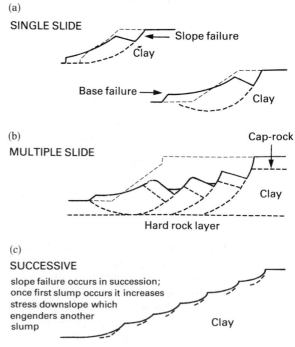

crevices could have increased pressure sufficiently for movement to begin.

What, then, have we learnt about slides? They occur in weak rocks, usually on steep slopes, often on compound ones, especially those that are actively undercut, and may be initiated by a change in the water regime of the slope or by very cold conditions. As the mass moves along the slip plane it tends to retain its shape and structure, and will often do so thousands of years after its occurrence, for few inland slides are recent.

Little has been said of the nature of **slip planes**. In some cases, the plane may be at the junction of two layers, for example on the Rockingham escarpment between the overlying boulder clay and the Lias clay, and in other cases a fault line, joint or bedding plane may provide it. Slopes composed of just one rock type also produce slides, and these will develop at a point beneath the surface where the shear stress becomes greater than the shear strength. Weak rocks such as clay have little shear strength to start with and are particularly vulnerable to the development of slip planes. The slip plane is typically a concave curve, and as the slide occurs the mass will be rotated backwards, hence many of these movements are referred to as

(a)
SINGLE SLIDE

(b)
MULTIPLE SLIDE

(c)
SUCCESSIVE

slope failure occurs in succession; once first slump occurs it increases stress downslope which engenders another slump

Fig 4.12 Types of rotational slide.

rotational slides. Three different occurrences are given in Fig 4.12. A series of massive steps or terraces is produced by the multiple slide, each one more steeply inclined than its predecessor. The character of the former hill top can be preserved in each slide, as the photograph of the movement at Overstrand shows (Photo 4.12). A feature of all three types of rotational movement is the scar which remains on the slope face, usually as a crescent shaped slash across the hillside.

Not all slides need be as deep-seated as most of the examples discussed so far. Some are much shallower, and move only soil or regolith. Certainly some of the smaller slides on the Rockingham escarpment are of this nature, but they still provide a series of terraces, such as in Fig 4.12b; the slip plane in Photo 4.4 is obviously not a deep one, either.

Neither need all the slides preserve the initial form of the mass. In a saturated mass many other processes may occur as the slip takes place, and flows of debris or unconsolidated rock may transform the slide into what is generally referred to as a **slump**.

Whether the mass that slid from the Wasatch Range of the Rocky Mountains in spring 1983 was primarily a slide, a slump or a flow is a question unlikely to concern the villagers of Thistle, Utah, for their village is now beneath the newly created lake which the moving mountainside dammed. Undoubtedly the movement has some features in common with a rotational slide – a 50 metre thick, 2400 metre long mass of weak, weathered clays and shales torn away from a deep scar on the hillside – but the sudden snowmelt that caused it transformed it into a train of sludge that took three weeks to slump to its final resting place in the valley below. Perhaps it was a slump, but few would argue with a villager from Thistle if he claimed that he had witnessed an earthflow, and not a slump or a slide.

Flows

This leads us very conveniently towards the apex of the triangle in Fig 4.8. One obvious contrast between a **flow** and a slide is that the former is more continuous, less jerky, than the latter and it is much more likely to contort the mass into a new form, although the preceding example will demonstrate how tenuous the division between the two is. Material composing the mass will be predominantly of small size, mostly no larger than sand, which means that debris, either soil or regolith, or perhaps pulverised rock, will be at risk. Deeply weathered clays in a semi-arid area would provide an example of the latter, so perhaps Thistle did suffer a flow after all.

A tip of mine waste provides another vulnerable environment; a measure of this was provided in October 1966 in South Wales. Abnormally high autumnal rainfall gradually increased the volume of water in the coal slag heap that towered over the village of Aberfan, raising the shear stress on the material to ominously high levels. Vigorous activity by springs within the tip increased the stress even further until a threshold was passed on the morning of 21st October, and the

Photo 4.12 A series of rotational slips in the boulder clay cliffs near Overstrand, Norfolk. The masonry is the remains of a former cliff-top house.

Photo 4..13 Aberfan, Mid-Glamorgan: the devastating flow of coal-mining waste of October 1966.

250 metre high tip could maintain its equilibrium no longer. The saturated slag debris took on the behaviour of a fluid, and so immediate was this liquefaction that the deadly torrent of coal waste that swept into the village engulfed a school, a terrace of cottages and a farm, giving the occupants virtually no chance of survival.

The speed of a flow is often the criterion used to differentiate between different types of flow. **Mudflows** cover the faster and more fluid end of the spectrum, although their consistency can vary greatly. **Earthflows** are thicker in consistency, and deeper, as they spew forth across a slope. A higher water content in the former will enable flow across gentler angles, and in Photo 7.4 of the boulder clay cliffs at Overstrand in Chapter 7, a mudflow can be seen superimposed upon an earthflow beneath.

Heave

In the left-hand corner of Fig 4.8 is a cluster of processes which could be termed **heave** or **creep**. Not only are these slower than the slides and flows, but they are more commonplace and, as such, tend to be on a smaller scale and far less catastrophic.

The impact of **soil creep** is not difficult to observe in humid temperate landscapes for it operates on slopes of only five degrees and is endemic on slopes of 35 degrees or more, even if they are vegetated. Tree trunks curving downslope and accumulations behind stone walls are evidence of past activity.

Creep occurs more readily in winter than in summer for its cause is localised expansion and contraction of the soil due to wetting and drying or freezing and thawing. As expansion occurs, for example as water swells up a clay particle or the pore water freezes, a grain is heaved up perpendicular to the slope, but with ensuing contraction gravity exerts an influence and the particle drops vertically to a downslope position. The reason why the process is also termed heave should, by now, be apparent. From surface rates averaging less than five millimetres a year in Britain, creep will decrease quickly with depth, but nevertheless it remains the most common slope process in environments where the more cataclysmic flows and slides are not usually present. In more extreme climates, creep may occur much faster, and readings measured in hundreds of millimetres per year have been recorded in tundra environments. On steeper slopes, soil may need no initiating mechanism of expansion to creep, for gravity may be sufficient to overcome the soil's shear resistance, and on others root growth, an animal burrowing or a man digging may be a sufficient impulse.

Controversy continues to reign over the origin of **terracettes**. Are these sequences of tiny steps which so commonly festoon our hillsides a product of soil creep, or are they animal tracks, trampled by generations of sheep and cattle? Again, they may well have a compound cause, begun by soil creep but emphasised by animals (see Photo 4.14).

Talus creep is just one of the ways in which fragments on a scree can move, for they are prone to rock falls and slides and even surface wash. The process here is akin to soil creep, being engendered by expansion due to frost heave or to solar heating. With so large a proportion of the scree's volume taken up by air, it is hardly surprising that water plays a much smaller role in this process.

The final process, of **solifluxion**, is more fully explained in Chapter 10 where some of the ambiguities which the term entails are ironed out. It will suffice to say here that it is a general term to describe the flow of saturated soil downslope. One particular variant is **gelifluxion**, by which surface materials are moved downslope due to summer melting in periglacial environments. In Britain, although mostly a process of the past, it may still conceivably be occuring in some locations.

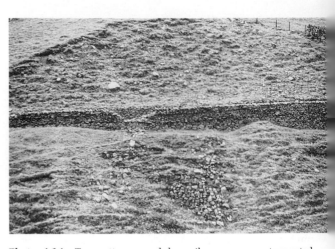

Photo 4.14 Terracettes caused by soil creep on a truncated solifluxion lobe, Kirkstone Pass, Cumbria. The steep slope was created by the construction of a road.

Effects of Running Water on Slopes

In some senses, perhaps, the washing away of surface material by running water on a slope is a mass movement, but its total dependence on water for transport provides a contrast that is sufficient for it to be considered separately. This is compounded by an additional contrast which is that movement is as individual particles rather than en masse.

Although relatively easy to envisage, **surface wash** is not easy to observe, in Britain at least. It is, after all, very rarely that one notices water trickling across hillslopes, except of course in the usual stream channels. Winter is the season in which the sight is most likely to be glimpsed, slithering across frozen or saturated ground, as the outcome of a prolonged or heavy downpour or the melting of snow. However, in climates which give less complete cover to their hillsides, such as arid and semi-arid, the process is more commonly observed for here the infrequent storms are intense. With little scope for percolation, the water can take only one path.

Surface wash, then, is an exit for surplus water from a hillslope, water that is unable to infiltrate because of saturated or impermeable rock or soil. Its degree of success in infiltrating a slope often depends on vegetation, for example grassland generates a good crumb structure in the soil which will aid efficient underground drainage. Vegetation, especially trees, intercepts rainfall and thus slows down the supply rate of water to the soil, enabling subsurface drainage to cope. When supply is too great for the capacity of the soil, surface flow begins, usually as **sheetwash** at the top of the slope but with gathering momentum and volume downslope it concentrates into **rills** and perhaps eventually into **gulleys**. In humid temperate landscapes its capabilities will be hampered by vegetation but on fallow fields considerable erosion can be inflicted. Footpaths, especially well used tracks across moorland slopes of national parks, provide man-made channels for surface water, and erosion here can be many times greater than for the rest of the hillside.

In the devastation of Exmoor hillsides, during the Lynmouth floods of 1952, sheetwash flowing from the shallow moorland peat of the summits was easily able to strip off soil and vegetation, leaving the weathered debris beneath open to gulleying which produced ravines in the hillsides up to six metres deep (Fig 4.13).

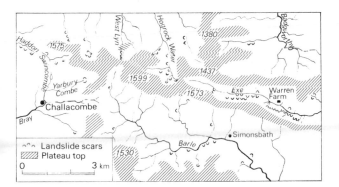

Fig 4.13 Landslides during the Exmoor floods of August 1952. In this central area of Exmoor, the thin soils were easily saturated by the intense storm, and over 75 slides were identified.

Such remarkable events are rare in Britain, and whilst sheetwash may be responsible for surface lowering of between two and five millimetres a year in the semi-arid areas of the south-west USA, rates of 0.01 millimetres per year are more typical for vegetated British slopes.

A similar contrast between vegetated and unvegetated slopes can be drawn for **rainsplash erosion**. Violent downpours of rain will have little difficulty in dislodging particles on a sand dune, but on a vegetated slope the cohesiveness of soils, even in the bare patches between the trees in, say, a beech wood, should prevent this. Having said that, however, droplets that build up on leaves after rainfall may be of sufficient size, when they eventually fall, to shift a soil grain. Sand grains have been seen to leap as much as a metre during rainstorms, landing with sufficient force to set other grains in motion.

One final process which is even more difficult to assess, but to which increasing weight is being

assigned, is **throughflow**; for as water moves downslope through soil its confinement to percolines, or natural pipes, appears to give it sufficient energy to transport material, and this, added to its solute load, may amount to a considerable volume.

Techniques of Slope Measurement

It is not just for a study of slopes that we need to know how to measure slope dimensions and processes, for an understanding of slopes may be an integral part of a project concerned with coasts, river valleys, the effects of glaciation or even the impact of rock type on relief.

Slope Profile

Before any analysis of cause or process can occur, we need to have a precise record of the slope profile. Most of us have experience of drawing cross-sections of valleys from OS maps, using the contours as a framework for our interpretation, but even the larger scale maps may not be sufficiently detailed for our purpose, and on slopes undergoing change their revision may not be sufficiently recent to be of use.

Availability of money, time and equipment will determine the practical method of slope assessment that one adopts. A range of methods is therefore suggested here. The crudest method, applicable for those not well endowed with resources, can employ home-made equipment. As Fig 4.14 shows, all that is needed is a semi-circular piece of card graduated like a protractor with a weighted string attached at the centre of the semi-circle. If the base of the card is aligned with the eye

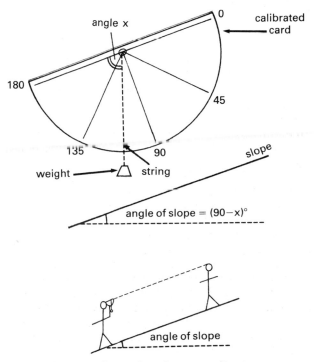

Fig 4.14 Measuring slope angle with improvised equipment.

Photo 4.15 A clinometer being used in a slope profiling exercise. The observer's right eye looks through the clinometer whilst the left eye is trained on the ranging pole.

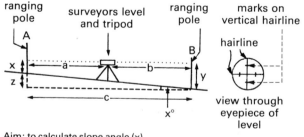

Aim: to calculate slope angle (x)
Method:

1 set up calibrated ranging poles at A and B
2 set up tripod between A and B and balance the level carefully by looking through the eyepiece of the level
3 take height readings x and y by looking through eyepiece of level:
   z = y−x
4 in addition to recording value where hairlines cross, also record heights on ranging poles of marks on vertical hairline of eyepiece. This should be done both for point A and point B
5 to calculate 'a' take the difference in height between two marks on vertical hairline and multiply by 100. Repeat for B to calculate b
6 c = a + b
7 $\frac{z}{c}$ = tan. x

Fig 4.15 Using a surveyor's level to measure slope angle.

of a helper, of similar height to the surveyor, standing up- or downslope, the angle of the slope can be recorded by subtracting it from 90 degrees. To increase accuracy, the card could be attached to a spirit level, and graduated poles could be used rather than relying on a partner's eyes being the same height above the ground as your own. The **Abney level** is a refined version of this crude equipment.

If funds are available, a **clinometer** may be used, as in Photo 4.15. No larger than a hand compass and as accurate as, but easier to use than, an Abney level, the method is very similar to that used in Fig 4.14. Graduated poles are carefully driven into the slope at equal distances or at points where the angle changes, and the horizontal line within the eyepiece is lined up with the same point on each pole. Without any calculation, the angle is then read off from the clinometer's scale either in degrees or as a percentage.

For more accurate measurement, and particularly useful therefore on gentle slopes, a **surveyor's level** and tripod can be employed, but one pays for accuracy, not just literally, but also in extra bulk and extra time of operation.

As Fig 4.15 demonstrates, graduated poles are set up in the same manner as previously. Accuracy of measurement is guaranteed by the series of spirit levels on the instrument. By focusing the viewfinder on A, three readings can be taken, as shown in Fig 4.15, the middle of the three representing the height x. The instrument has been so calibrated that by subtracting the top reading from the bottom one and multiplying the result by 100, the distance in metres of the tripod from A is obtained. After rotating the instrument through 180 degrees, the same readings can be taken to B. Thus, one now has the heights x and y and the distance c. To calculate the angle of the slope requires only the application of simple trigonometry.

Whichever of the three methods is used, a large quantity of data is generated which can be used either to plot an accurate curve of the slope profile or to produce a slope histogram, as in Fig 4.16. Whether curve or histogram, the diagrams are useful for comparison, either with the same slope over time or with other slopes on which different circumstances prevail. It is surprising how low many of the angles are. Scree slopes that look as precipitous as a cliff are usually about 35 degrees, and slopes that one needs the agility of a mountain goat to climb are rarely as steep as this.

For certain detailed analyses and comparisons of slope profiles, some measure of curvature may be required. Obviously, one will apply this only to curved elements; the method is simple and described in Fig 4.17. A negative answer indicates a concave curvature, and positive a convex one.

Slope Mapping

In order to achieve a more widespread spatial coverage of the slopes of a valley or a hill than a cross-sectional profile can give, there are various techniques of slope mapping that can be employed.

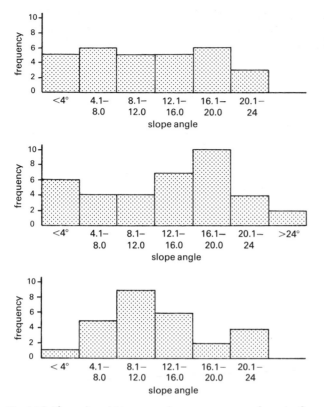

Fig 4.16 Three slope histograms of convexo-concave slopes in the Lammermuir Hills of southern Scotland.

In one sense, the simplest form of slope map is a contour map, for this ably demonstrates the shape, or **morphology**, of the landscape. For many purposes, however, it is too generalised, and more specific maps need to be produced.

One such map, based on grid squares and shown in Fig 4.18, can easily be produced by students from data collected in the field. The area to be mapped is first marked out by tapes. A series of parallel transects can then be made across the area, using 100-metre tapes, the direction of each maintained by use of a compass.

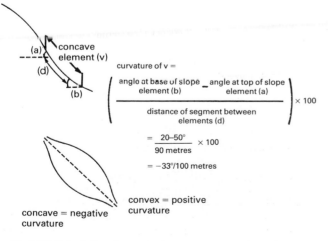

Fig 4.17 Calculating slope curvature.

At regular intervals along each one, say five or ten metres, the steepest angle downslope from that point, in whatever direction, is measured using a clinometer or similar device. A compass can indicate the deviation of this steepest slope from the line of the tape. This information can then be plotted in the manner shown in Fig 4.18. To increase the amount of information given here, the length of slope over which the steepest angle is maintained could be included by drawing the length of the arrow to scale.

Figure shown is angle in degrees

Arrow denotes steepest slope downhill from each grid intersection

Fig 4.18 Slope map of Moel Llyfnant, Gwynedd: method 1.

An alternative method, portrayed in Fig 4.19, is more subjective, but for some map users more effective. In this, areas across which slope angle and aspect are uniform are identified in the field, and then mapped. Whilst the overall impression may be more pleasing than that of the former, this method involves a certain amount of estimation by the cartographer, and different students could produce very different maps of the same area.

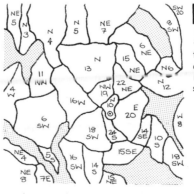

Areas which could not be said to be facing in any one direction

figures represent angle in degrees, compass bearing represents aspect of slope

Fig 4.19 Slope map of Moel Llyfnant, Gwynedd: method 2.

A third method, in Fig 4.20, uses some aspects of slope classification in order to reduce the complexity of the real world to a comprehensible form. Thus, symbols can be devised for different types of straight segment and curved element, for the surface material of the

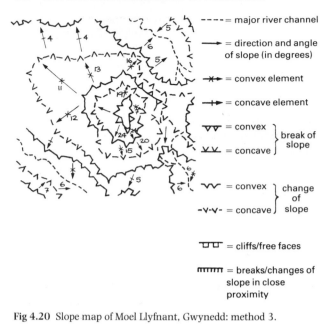

= major river channel

= direction and angle of slope (in degrees)

= convex element

= concave element

= convex ⎱
= concave ⎰ break of slope

= convex ⎱
= concave ⎰ change of slope

= cliffs/free faces

= breaks/changes of slope in close proximity

Fig 4.20 Slope map of Moel Llyfnant, Gwynedd: method 3.

slope, and for changes and breaks in angle of the slope, and these, combined with information about length and the angle of slopes can provide a very accurate representation of an area's slope morphology.

The three maps are each drawn for the same area, and it is worth pausing to evaluate each of the three methods of mapping. Criteria such as accuracy, breadth of coverage and visual impression might be used to make such a judgement. There is probably no best method – it is very much the perception of the individual. It would not be unreasonable for the reader to question the use and value of such maps. They are best seen as a preliminary description of an area's landscape before geomorphological explanation begins, although to the human geographer they may have many more uses in any analysis of the spatial distribution of human activity.

Slope Debris

In a study of scree slope on different sides of a valley or in different rock types, not only angle but also size of material may be a variable worthy of comparison. Any data collection on a scree slope is hazardous and one should proceed with care, but the results should make it worthwhile. A systematic or random sample of debris could be collected along a transect from top to bottom of the scree, perhaps using a quadrat to select stones at each of the sample points. A standarised measure of stone size must be adopted, perhaps the length of the longest axis. A simple test of correlation could be applied to test the strength of the relationship between particle size and variables such as distance from the top of the scree or angle of rest. For comparison of more than one scree, detailed comparison of histograms of stone size should be adequate, but a chi-squared test could also be employed.

Slope Processes

Any attempt to measure the rate of slope processes will quickly meet difficulties, but the challenge has been met with an ingenious array of improvisations. The difficulty is the very speed at which processes operate. Soil creep and surface wash are so slow that years may need to be devoted to any meaningful study, in the British landscape at least. The more cataclysmic processes are so unpredictable and often so fast that measurements can be made only after the event.

Soil creep

So commonplace a slope process has attracted many potential assessors. Good fortune may provide a wall or a building on the slope which can be dated precisely, and if so, a measurement of the depth of accumulation of soil against it may provide an indication of the amount of creep, but it will be of use only in comparison with other similar readings, for it will not tell us how quickly soil is moving downslope but merely indicate the significance of its effect. If one is fortunate enough to possess the correct implement, the age of a tree on a slope can be calculated by counting the rings in its trunk. The distance that the trunk has been curved downslope from its roots could then be divided by its age to give an approximation of creep.

Other methods rely less on a fortuitous obstacle on the slope, and actually attempt to measure the creep at first hand. The **Young pit**, shown in Fig 4.21 and named after its inventor, is one of the most widely used. A hole is dug in the soil, as deep as possible, and into one side is driven a series of small, durable rods placed in a vertical line. The face is photographed twice, once before the pit is filled in and then a few months or a year later when the hole has been carefully dug out again. With luck, the amount of soil creep should be recorded in the photographs. The experiment can be made or broken in the re-excavation stage, and one way of decreasing havoc caused by a wayward spade is to line the vital face of the pit with polythene.

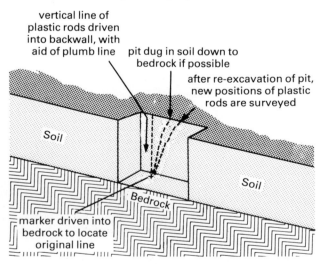

Fig 4.21 A Young pit for measuring soil creep.

A similar method, but involving only one pit excavation, could make use of a hole drilled by a soil auger. By filling the hollow with a column of brightly coloured balls or beads, and then carefully digging out a pit next to it after sufficient time has elapsed, rates of creep could be ascertained, but once again disaster might strike during re-excavation!

It would not be difficult to devise a series of simulated experiments, if all other methods fail. A box, about the size of a window box, in which one side has been replaced with glass, could be filled to just below the surface with soil, and beads or rods could be buried vertically so that they could be viewed through the glass. If one had the resources to prepare a number of such troughs, each could be adjusted to simulate different conditions. For example, variables such as slope angle, soil type, soil moisture content and vegetation cover could be altered to produce some useful relative rates of creep.

Talus creep may be easier to assess, with the possibility of planting painted stones horizontally across the scree slope and then observing their movement.

Surface wash

Estimates of surface wash can also be made from artificial structures in the landscape. Monuments, walls, telegraph poles or electricity pylons can often be dated precisely, and by measuring the depth of exposure of their foundations an approximation of surface erosion can be obtained, although one must appreciate that soil creep could be responsible for some of this.

A more direct approach would be to drive resistant steel pins into a slope so that they are anchored into the underlying bedrock. If washers are placed at the head of the pin, the effects of surface wash can be monitored as the washer slowly slides down the pin with the lowering of the surface, as shown in Fig 4.22.

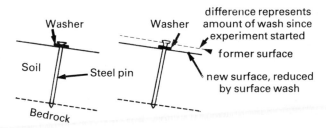

Fig 4.22 Measuring surface wash: steel pin and washer.

More ambitious and ingenious students might build themselves some sort of sediment-collecting tray or box that could be left on the hillside for some time. Constraints on design would be the need for cheapness yet durability of materials, sufficient strength to resist soil creep and sufficient protection from flooding by rain and from interference by animals and man. A design which complies with this brief is shown in Fig 4.23. A sequence of traps at different levels of the hillside might be adopted.

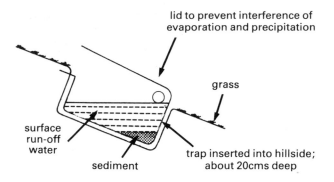

Fig 4.23 Measuring surface wash: sediment trap.

Slides, flows and falls

For the amateur, estimates of all of these will prove difficult. Comparison of early and modern maps or old and new aerial photographs can pay dividends if the movements are both large scale and frequent, but for the more ancient landslips of inland Britain there are fewer advantages.

Slow-moving flows, perhaps in boulder clay cliffs, could be monitored by observing the changes in a horizontal row of stakes across the slope, but some environments may be too volatile for such a method. Estimates of accumulation over time behind a barrier, such as man-made defences, could be attempted. To make any sense of such data, one has to face a problem common to most slope process estimates, which is calculating the surface area from which the slipped material has come. It is all very well to say that one metre of debris has accumulated in three months, but does that represent a metre's lowering across the whole slope or merely a few millimetres overall, and are certain parts of the slope more prone than others?

In common with many other geomorphological techniques, then, methods of slope process measurement are constantly being improved, but have not yet been perfected, and there is no reason why A-level geographers should not contribute to their refinement just as fully as professional geographers do.

Slope Evolution

It was stated earlier that in a person's lifetime the majority of slopes in a humid temperate landscape are likely to retain more or less the same form, as a response to an equilibrium being attained between all the controls on slope form. Over the longer term, on geological rather than human time scales, the form may well change. This is not to say that slopes do not experience change even in a few years, for if weathering, slope movements and slope-foot erosion can be measured, they must be effecting some sort of change to the slope. The point is that the shape of the slope is retained, even though an imperceptible amount of wearing back has taken place.

Since the inception of geomorphology in the mid-nineteenth century the debate about how slopes change over long periods has raged as persistently as the trade winds, and here only the briefest of outlines will be given, for it is difficult to justify how this scale of geomorphological change can be of much relevance to our ultimate goal of understanding the relationships between man and his environment.

Basically, there are three hypotheses, two of which explain how slope angle decreases over time and one which explains how certain slope angles are preserved.

Slope Decline

The **decline** of slope angles, according to one of geomorphology's most influential thinkers, W M Davis in 1899, begins after valley side slopes have become **graded**. As Fig 4.24 shows, initial downcutting by a river may be so fast that slope processes are unable to keep up and the slope profile becomes irregular and steep. Once river downcutting slows down or stops, however, the rate of weathering and transport on the slopes is enough to wear down and even out the irregularities until the slope is graded. In simple terms, this means that a balance has been achieved respectively between the weathering processes, the slope transport processes and the slope-foot erosion processes so that each is able to cope with the products of the former, thus maintaining the slope angle. Davis does not believe that this stage persists, however, for weathering and slope processes continue to wear down the slope. Processes active on the middle and lower slope need to be able to move not only the weathered debris produced in their areas, but also the material brought down from higher up the slope. Their inability to do so causes the areas upslope to wear down faster than areas downslope. As decline continues, the reduced angle of the lower slope is even less capable of coping with the required work and so its rate of retreat falls even further behind that of the upper slope.

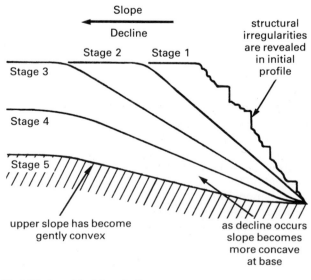

Fig 4.24 A model of slope decline.

The theory sounds feasible enough, but proving it is quite another matter without the aid of a geomorphological time traveller, for the time scale of decline is one of millions of years. If one were to compare slopes of similar geological structure in different localities within one area of today's landscape and their angles varied significantly, perhaps one would have found slopes at different stages of decline. One might thus produce factual evidence for Davis' ideas.

Slope Replacement

This second theory has much in common with the first, in terms of time scale, in that it explains why slope angle decreases over time and in that it stresses the relationship between the three types of process affecting a slope. The suggested mechanisms are, however, quite different.

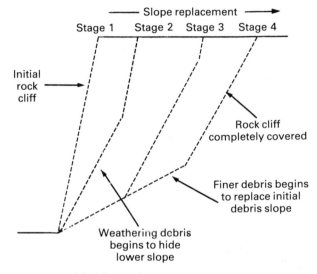

Fig 4.25 A model of slope replacement.

The founding father of this slope replacement theory was Walther Penck in 1924, and its major theme is that the slope will gradually be replaced by debris weathered from it which accumulates at a gentler angle on the retreating slope. The diagram in Fig 4.25 suggests how this might operate in a steep-sided river valley where river incision has ceased. Weathered material gradually builds up at the base of the receding slope, effectively protecting it from further weathering. The exposed upper slope, however, continues to wear back, in parallel, thus ensuring a concave slope. Whilst sounding feasible, it does of course assume that downcutting has ceased, which limits its applicability to the real world. Even so, in the case of a cliff now protected from marine attack it is a perfectly feasible suggestion, as it is where rapid frost action allows a scree to engulf a steep glaciated slope. Penck does consider the situation of a river continuing to cut down, and this, he suggests, will preserve the steepness of the slope, enabling the removal of all weathered debris and allowing the entire slope to retreat in parallel (see Fig 4.25).

Parallel Retreat

Supporting Penck's suggestions with concrete evidence is no easier than it is for Davis' theory. The **parallel retreat** of some slopes under certain circumstances also seems viable. King's suggestions for such an occurrence in semi-arid and arid areas are expanded upon in Chapter 11. For such a recession to occur, it is essential that the capacity of slope-foot processes is exactly balanced with the supply down the slope of weathered debris. If the capacity is greater than the supply the slope will be steepened by undercutting, and if it is less, debris will accumulate and reduce the angle.

Further investigation of slope profile may, in future, clarify the debate, for although in some environments we can be pretty sure about how slopes are evolving, in many it is still unclear. Meanwhile, the geographer will find more justification for his studies if he concentrates on those aspects of slope geomorphology that have a more significant impact on human activity.

Questions

Refer to Fig 4.26 which is based on Clark and Small's diagram of a slope system in a humid temperate climate.

1 What is meant by endogenetic and exogenetic factors?

2 Why does 'weathering' appear twice on the diagram?

3 There are two types of arrow shown; what does each represent?

4 Are there any major factors that you think have been omitted from this diagram? If so, name them and justify their addition to those already there.

5 Which of the following words and phrases characterise this system?

Open to energy and matter
Open to energy

Closed

Black box
White box
Grey box

Morphological
Process response
Cascading

6 Why could the pattern of soil and regolith in the diagram be said to be idealised?

7 A slope system may well maintain a steady state or equilibrium condition over the short term; this equilibrium may then be interrupted by a sudden change in the inputs. What possible causes are there of the change that could disturb British slopes? Give details.

8 Is it useful or relevant to look at a slope system such as this in isolation from other neighbouring systems? Justify your answer.

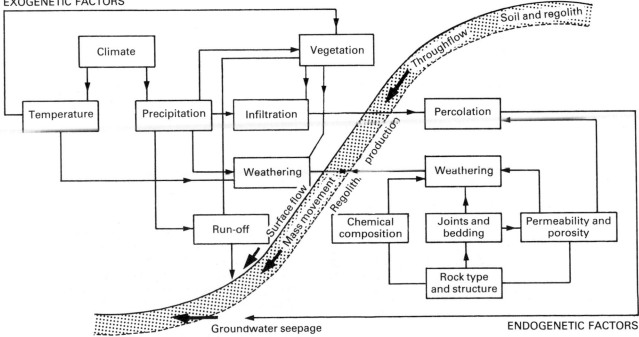

Fig 4.26 A slope in a humid temperate climate as a system.

Further Reading

Slopes and Weathering, M Clark and R J Small (Cambridge, 1982).

Process in Geomorphology, C Embleton and J Thornes (Arnold, 1979).

Face of North-East Yorkshire, S R Eyre and J Palmer (Dalesman, 1973).

Hillslope Analysis, B Finlayson and I Statham (Butterworths, 1980).

Techniques in Physical Geography, M D Newson and J Hanwell (Macmillan, 1973).

Modern Concepts in Geomorphology, P McCullagh (Oxford, 1978).

Disasters, J Whittow (Penguin, 1980).

Geology and Scenery in Scotland, J Whittow (Penguin, 1977).

Slope Development, A and D Young (Macmillan, 1974).

Other References

Models of Hillslope Development under Mass Fracture, M A Carson, *Geogr. Annaler* 1, 76–100 (1969).

Hillslope Form and Process, M A Carson and M J Kirkby (Cambridge, 1972).

The Geographical Cycle, W M Davis *Geographical Journal* 14 (1899).

A Theory of Bornhardts, L C King, *Geographical Journal* 112, 83–7 (1948).

Die Morphologie Analyse, W Penck (Stuttgart, 1924).

Mass movements associated with the rainstorm of June 1966 in Hong Kong, C L So, *Transactions of the Institute of British Geographers* 53 (1971).

The Role of Hydrology in the Landscape

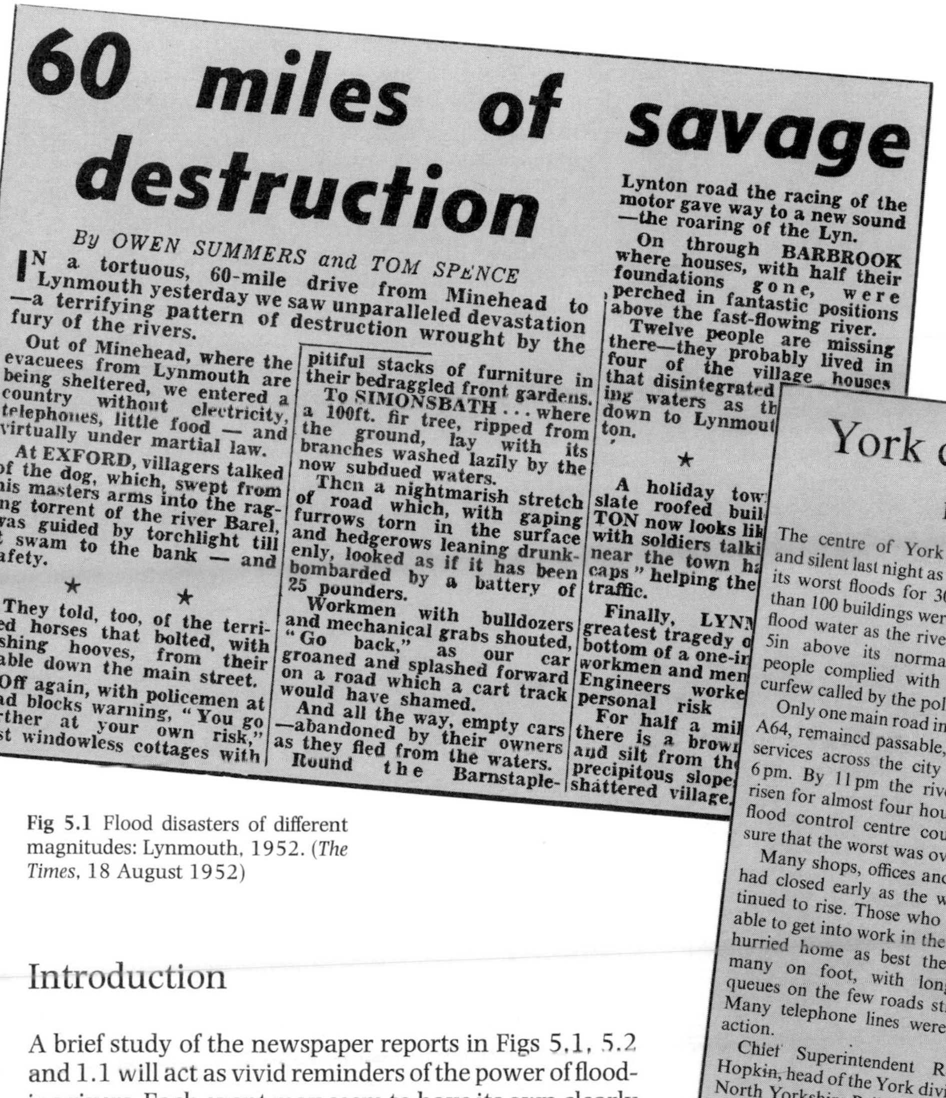

60 miles of savage destruction

By OWEN SUMMERS and TOM SPENCE

IN a tortuous, 60-mile drive from Minehead to Lynmouth yesterday we saw unparalleled devastation —a terrifying pattern of destruction wrought by the fury of the rivers.

Out of Minehead, where the evacuees from Lynmouth are being sheltered, we entered a country without electricity, telephones, little food — and virtually under martial law.

At EXFORD, villagers talked of the dog, which, swept from his masters arms into the raging torrent of the river Barel, was guided by torchlight till it swam to the bank — and safety.

★   ★

They told, too, of the terrified horses that bolted, with crashing hooves, from their stable down the main street.

Off again, with policemen at road blocks warning, "You go further at your own risk," past windowless cottages with pitiful stacks of furniture in their bedraggled front gardens.

To SIMONSBATH ... where a 100ft. fir tree, ripped from the ground, lay with its branches washed lazily by the now subdued waters.

Then a nightmarish stretch of road which, with gaping furrows torn in the surface and hedgerows leaning drunkenly, looked as if it has been bombarded by a battery of 25 pounders.

Workmen with bulldozers and mechanical grabs shouted, "Go back," as our car groaned and splashed forward on a road which a cart track would have shamed.

And all the way, empty cars —abandoned by their owners as they fled from the waters. Round the Barnstaple-

Lynton road the racing of the motor gave way to a new sound —the roaring of the Lyn.

On through BARBROOK where houses, with half their foundations gone, were perched in fantastic positions above the fast-flowing river.

Twelve people are missing there—they probably lived in four of the village houses that disintegrated [ ] ing waters as th[ ] down to Lynmout[ ] ton.

★

A holiday tow[ ] slate roofed buil[ ] TON now looks lik[ ] with soldiers talki[ ] near the town ha[ ] caps" helping the [ ] traffic.

Finally, LYNM[ ] greatest tragedy o[ ] bottom of a one-in[ ] workmen and men [ ] Engineers worke[ ] personal risk [ ]

For half a mil[ ] there is a brown[ ] and silt from the [ ] precipitous slope[ ] shattered village[ ]

Fig 5.1 Flood disasters of different magnitudes: Lynmouth, 1952. (*The Times*, 18 August 1952)

Fig 5.2 Flood disasters of different magnitudes: York, 1982. (*The Times*, January 1982)

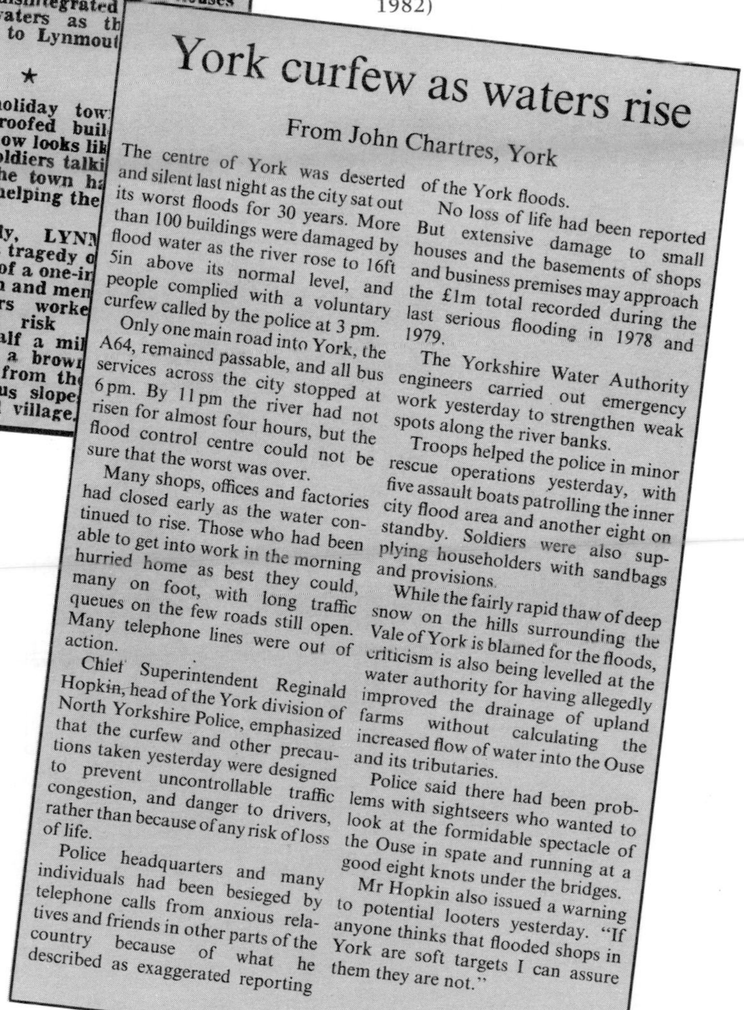

York curfew as waters rise

From John Chartres, York

The centre of York was deserted and silent last night as the city sat out its worst floods for 30 years. More than 100 buildings were damaged by flood water as the river rose to 16ft 5in above its normal level, and people complied with a voluntary curfew called by the police at 3 pm.

Only one main road into York, the A64, remained passable, and all bus services across the city stopped at 6 pm. By 11 pm the river had not risen for almost four hours, but the flood control centre could not be sure that the worst was over.

Many shops, offices and factories had closed early as the water continued to rise. Those who had been able to get into work in the morning hurried home as best they could, many on foot, with long traffic queues on the few roads still open. Many telephone lines were out of action.

Chief Superintendent Reginald Hopkin, head of the York division of North Yorkshire Police, emphasized that the curfew and other precautions taken yesterday were designed to prevent uncontrollable traffic congestion, and danger to drivers, rather than because of any risk of loss of life.

Police headquarters and many individuals had been besieged by telephone calls from anxious relatives and friends in other parts of the country because of what he described as exaggerated reporting

of the York floods.

No loss of life had been reported But extensive damage to small houses and the basements of shops and business premises may approach the £1m total recorded during the last serious flooding in 1978 and 1979.

The Yorkshire Water Authority engineers carried out emergency work yesterday to strengthen weak spots along the river banks.

Troops helped the police in minor rescue operations yesterday, with five assault boats patrolling the inner city flood area and another eight on standby. Soldiers were also supplying householders with sandbags and provisions.

While the fairly rapid thaw of deep snow on the hills surrounding the Vale of York is blamed for the floods, criticism is also being levelled at the water authority for having allegedly improved the drainage of upland farms without calculating the increased flow of water into the Ouse and its tributaries.

Police said there had been problems with sightseers who wanted to look at the Ouse in spate and running at a good eight knots under the bridges.

Mr Hopkin also issued a warning to potential looters yesterday. "If anyone thinks that flooded shops in York are soft targets I can assure them they are not."

Introduction

A brief study of the newspaper reports in Figs 5.1, 5.2 and 1.1 will act as vivid reminders of the power of flooding rivers. Each event may seem to have its own clearly apparent cause – the Lyn a summer storm, the Ouse a sudden snowmelt, the Arno an unprecedented deluge of rainfall within 24 hours, but further reflection will reveal that there was a whole range of contributory factors that contrived to create the floods. For example, the steepness of gradient of the Lyn's tributaries, the location of York at a junction of major rivers and the funnelling of the floodwaters through the narrow streets of Florence all exaggerated the effects of any sudden input of water.

Hydrological input   Hydrological output

Fig 5.3 The drainage basin as a black box system.

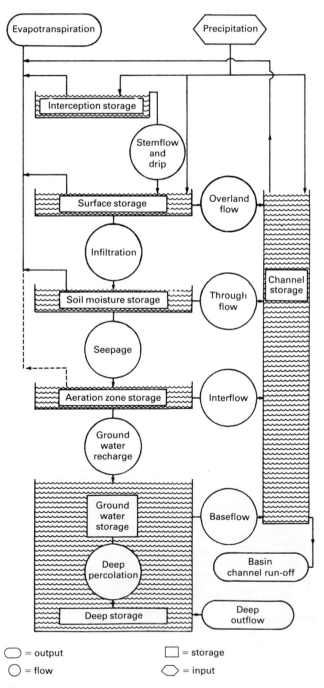

Fig 5.4 The drainage basin as a cascading system.

It is the aim of this chapter to explain not only how a precipitation droplet eventually becomes part of a river's flow but also how intricate is the pattern of inter-related factors which determine its route to the channel. An understanding of these variables will go a long way to explaining why some rivers respond to precipitation by flooding whilst others are able to cope with the changing inputs of water.

The Basin Hydrological System

No unit is better suited to the application of systems theory than the river basin and its **hydrological cycle**. Its boundaries are distinct, provided as they are by **watersheds** and the sea, its processes and transfers are a series of distinct inputs and outputs, and it is of an appropriate size for study.

At its simplest, it may be regarded as a black box system (Fig 5.3), the input of precipitation being transferred into outputs of **channel run-off, deep outflow** and **evapotranspiration**; the latter is the collective name given to all losses of water vapour whether from the earth's surface, the soil or vegetation. At its most complex it can be drawn as a computer program, not only with each input, variable, operating process, feedback and output being illuminated but also being quantified. An intermediate stage of clarification, perhaps a grey box system, is seen in Fig 5.4, although no attempt is made here to consider inputs and outputs of solar energy or the transfer of sediment through the basin.

Nevertheless, the diagram reveals the constituent parts of the hydrological system, each of which merits separate consideration here.

The Input

How effectively the system can cope with its input of precipitation depends on a wide range of variables in addition to the quantity of rainfall. The speed with which the heavy downpour of a summer thunderstorm can flood the streets indicates how important intensity is, for it will be far more difficult for the system to deal with this than the prolonged drizzle of an autumn day. Even so, continuous rainfall can provide problems, for the gradual accumulation of water could still exceed the system's capacity. It may well be important, therefore, how long it is since precipitation last occurred. The form of precipitation is also vital; snowfall delays the release of water until melting, which eventually may produce a much greater torrent than the equivalent amount of rainfall.

The Storages

Storages are a vital control on the operation of the system. Each one can be envisaged as a sponge, capable of absorbing and holding water as it travels through the system, but liable to begin to release it while it is filling with water, and eventually becoming so saturated that

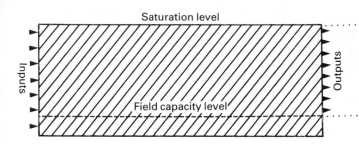

Total capacity: when filled to this level, output will become greater than input.

Filling to capacity: depending on facility of store to retain water, output gradually increases and eventually exceeds input.

Threshold level: water will not be released until this level is reached. Input is greater than output.

Fig 5.5 The soil as a water storage container.

it releases as much as it takes in. This leakage of water will not occur until a threshold level of water is reached, which is best exemplified by the **field capacity** of soil (see below). Fig 5.5 demonstrates the concept.

Interception storage

In the centre of a large city a significant percentage of precipitation will be intercepted by buildings before reaching the ground, but even in rural areas of temperate environments so little of the soil is exposed that **interception** will occur extensively whether in a wheat field or a woodland. Measurements from German beech forests suggest that as much as 43 per cent of precipitation may be intercepted in summer, although the figure is little more than half that in winter (Barry and Chorley).

The storage capacity of trees will vary enormously, from season to season for deciduous species and from place to place depending on tree density, leaf size, the size and shape of the canopy and the pattern of branching.

Surface storage

Surface storages occur in both natural areas of impeded drainage such as lakes and bogs, and artificial ones such as reservoirs, ponds, drainage ditches and canals. They are, again, most apparent in urban areas for here the flat, impervious surfaces of roof tops, pavements and playing fields provide excellent sites for puddles.

Channel storage

Despite being the medium through which water drains from the system, channels also act as stores. They receive their input indirectly through flows from other stores, and directly from precipitation that drops into them. In times of flood, when the channel may overflow and take in the entire breadth of the flood plain, **channel storage** will be a major constituent of the system.

Soil moisture storage

If a soil is dry it will absorb water from incoming precipitation and not release it until field capacity has been reached. This water is retained against gravity by the surface tension of each soil particle in the **capillary pores** that separate them. Before water can be released from the soil, therefore, these capillary pores must be filled or, expressed in another way, field capacity must be exceeded. In a finely textured soil, composed mainly of clays, the small capillary pores may be so numerous that field capacity will be considerable, much higher than in a freely draining sandy textured soil (see Fig 5.6).

As well as **texture**, storage is also affected by **soil structure** which is the pattern of crumb sizes in the soil and how the constituent grains are agglomerated. Water can be stored both within and between the crumbs, the development of which is partly controlled by the amount of decaying organic matter, or humus, in the soil.

Some soils may be permanently waterlogged, notably in areas of marsh or peat bog, in which case their storage is at saturation capacity most of the time. This means that not only capillary pores but all other air voids are full, too. The ability of some soils to absorb water may be affected by man's land use. Grassland has been seen to produce a well balanced crumb structure

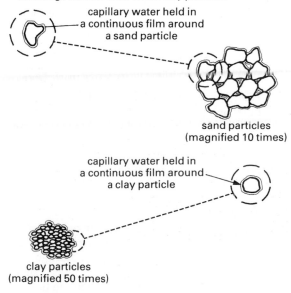

Note the gaps which appear in the sandy texture and the total large surface area of the clay particles

capillary water held in a continuous film around a sand particle

sand particles (magnified 10 times)

capillary water held in a continuous film around a clay particle

clay particles (magnified 50 times)

Fig 5.6 Capillary water and soil texture.

which enables drainage and retains moisture, whereas coniferous forests, with their associated **leaching** and acid humus, are liable to encourage **iron pans** or hard, impermeable layers beneath the surface that impede drainage. With so much interference with the structure and texture of agricultural land by actions such as deep ploughing, liming and underdraining, the soil moisture capacity may rely less and less on natural factors in the future.

Groundwater and aeration zone storage

Groundwater amounts to over 24 per cent of the earth's fresh water, and with a further 75 per cent frozen as ice and the tiny remainder making up all the rivers, lakes and soil moisture, groundwater can be seen to be the major supply of water for river flow and for man. Groundwater is stored beneath the **water table** in the joints, pores, cracks and fissures in the rock, which means that the amount of storage will vary according to the rock type.

At times, especially in low-lying areas such as valley bottoms, the store may become so full that the water table rises through the regolith and soil to the surface. The rising water, known as **vadose water** as opposed to the more permanent **phreatic water** below the water table, fills the voids in the rock that would otherwise be empty or aerated (see Fig 5.7). The **aeration zone** above the water table can thus also act as a storage area in the hydrological system and it will retain some of the vadose water even after the water table has receded again.

Deep storage

To estimate the actual depth to which groundwater extends is not easy, but in places it certainly extends down to 1000 metres below the surface, and even conservative estimates suggest that seven million cubic kilometres of groundwater may be in storage, excluding the ice caps. Water may stay in store for a matter of minutes or hours or for hundreds or even tens of thousands of years before being released.

The deeper layers of groundwater may play no part in the hydrological cycle and the water that seeps down to them can really be considered as an output of the system. Once below 1000 metres much of the water is saline and much is fossil water, the accumulation of which may have taken millenia. It is obviously vital that man does not come to rely on this source, particularly in the irrigation of the deserts, for to all intents and purposes it is a non-renewable resource.

The Flows

Linking the storages together is a system of flows which will begin to transfer water soon after rainfall begins and soon after water begins to enter a storage zone. Barring obstacles, these flows will be both vertical and lateral, depending for speed and movement on the slope of the land.

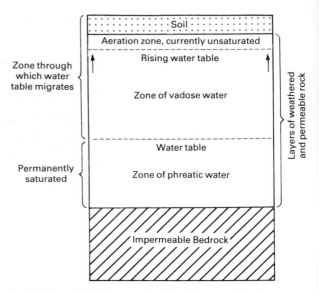

Fig 5.7 Theoretical diagram of levels within groundwater.

Stemflow and drip

Of the water that is intercepted by a tree, a considerable amount will eventually reach the ground by dripping from leaves or running down branches and trunk. In a town, the equivalent processes take place thanks to roof guttering, drainpipes and gargoyles, and the process here may be far more efficiently organised than in nature.

Infiltration and percolation

Most rainwater that reaches the ground infiltrates into the soil, from where some may percolate much deeper. The depth of penetration will depend on the requirements of the storages and the various barriers the water meets. A desiccated, trampled, unvegetated surface around a water hole in a semi-arid area may allow virtually no penetration at all, and if it does a hardpan or impermeable rock layer may halt progress. In more favourable circumstances water may penetrate as far as the water table or even to the deep storage below that. Every surface can therefore be said to have its own

Land use	Infiltration rate (mm/hr)
old permanent pasture	57
permanent pasture: moderately grazed	19
permanent pasture: heavily grazed	13
strip cropping	10
weeds or cereals	9
arable without weeds	7
bare ground – baked hard	6

Fig 5.8 Infiltration rates for a variety of agricultural land uses.

infiltration capacity and its own infiltration rate, some examples of which are given in Fig 5.8.

Overland flow

On tarmac roads or on hardpacked mud or clay, infiltration is so restricted that rainwater is forced to trickle across the surface and even on permeable surfaces the precipitation input may exceed the infiltration rate. In heavy storms the rate at which infiltration into the soil can occur may be insufficient to deal with the massive influx of water and so overland flow will begin long before underground storages are full. Tiny rills or even temporary streams may transfer the water across the surface, but when discharges are larger the flows may unite into sheets of water, especially when facilitated by an even, unvegetated surface such as a desert pediment. In rural areas of Britain overland flow is not an easy process to observe as vegetation obscures the tiny rills, but in a sudden melt after a heavy snowfall, or in an intense rainstorm, rivulets may be seen running across the frozen or saturated land.

Throughflow

As water percolates through the soil and regolith, its progress is liable to slow down as its possible routes through compacted soil and layers of rock become fewer. This may enable lateral flow, or throughflow, to occur. Such water will move downslope towards the stream, perhaps following natural pipes or percolines which often develop at the junction of two horizons of the soil or which are excavated from an earthworm's cast or along a root by the flowing water. Despite the difficulty of studying such flow, it is undoubtedly a vital contributor to the flow of all British river systems.

Baseflow and interflow

For water to flow from groundwater into the river channel, it is essential that the water table rises above the level of the river, for only that can provide the necessary hydraulic gradient. It is the baseflow which rivers depend upon when all other sources fail, and which allowed the Thames at Teddington to discharge 8–11 cubic metres per second despite negligible rainfall for several months in the drought summer of 1976. The difference between interflow and baseflow exists theoretically, but in reality is barely discernible, for it is not easy to tell whether water is discharging from beneath or above the water table.

Deep outflow

Not all flow from groundwater need be into the river channel, for it may be so deep that it can only discharge direct into the sea, a lake or another river basin downstream to which the particular river channel is a tributary, or, of course, to an even deeper storage zone. Deep outflow can thus be seen not only as a flow but also as an output.

The Outputs

Evapotranspiration

Water vapour represents a considerable loss of moisture from any drainage basin through the processes of evaporation and transpiration. One word, evapotranspiration, is used to summarise the loss because in so many cases it is impossible to separate the two processes, especially if the area is well vegetated. The essential difference is that evaporation occurs from waterbodies, the earth's surface and from within the soil, whereas transpiration releases water vapour through the pores of leaves.

Under some climatic conditions, evapotranspiration is so high that it may exceed the precipitation input, thus effectively cutting out river flow. It is for this reason that the terms potential and actual evapotranspiration have been devised. The former refers to the maximum possible that would take place under the climatic circumstances were there sufficient moisture available for it to do so. The latter is an indication of what actually takes place. If potential evapotranspiration is considerably in excess of precipitation it means that not only will the incoming rainfall be vaporised but also water from storage on the surface and in the soil and even regolith will be lost so that the channel's water supply will be severely depleted. Hot deserts experience such conditions almost permanently, but other more temperate areas such as Britain may be subjected to them for perhaps a month or a season, as the data in Fig 5.9 show for a small river in Somerset.

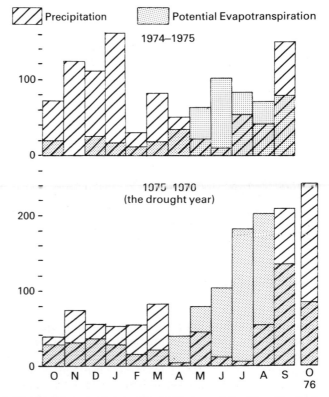

Fig 5.9 The water balance for a tributary of the River Doniford, Somerset.

Year	Q = Discharge	=	P Precipitation	−	(Potential evapotranspiration	± + −	(ET ± S) Change in storage)
1973–74 (Oct–Sep)	423.0	=	1137.9	−	(529.6 + 185.3)		
1974–75 (Oct–Sep)	445.7	=	897.7	−	(519.5 − 67.5)		
1975–76 (Oct–Sep) (the drought year)	95.9	=	685.7	−	(897.8 − 308.0)		

all readings are in millimetres

Fig 5.10 The annual water balance for a tributary of the River Doniford, Somerset (after Howcroft 1977). Note the enormous amount of water which needs to be released from storage in 1976 in order to maintain the river flow.

Streamflow

The final link that transfers water out of the system is the channel, and the efficiency with which it does so will be affected both by its size and shape and the intricacy of the network of which it is a part (see Chapter 6).

This system of hydrological inputs, outputs, storages and flows which makes up the drainage basin requires energy to operate. It derives this both from outside, using the energy provided by the sun, and from within, utilising the potential energy provided by the height of the land. A few moments' reflection on how this energy is used will further your understanding of the system.

The Precipitation-Discharge Relationship

Over Annual and Monthly Periods

The hydrological equation

In order to make comparison between different drainage basins or within a drainage basin at different times of the year, the inputs and outputs are often reduced to a simple mathematical equation. Thus,

$$Q = P - (ET \pm S)$$

where   Q is streamflow
P is precipitation
ET is evapotranspiration
S are changes in groundwater and
soil moisture storage over a given period,
say a month or a year.

Howcroft has used the equation in her study of part of the Doniford catchment, as Fig 5.10 shows.

From study of the equation it will be clear that if evapotranspiration does exceed precipitation then the river will have to rely on stored water for its discharge, assuming of course that there is some available. Most British rivers rely on the winter replenishment of their groundwater store to keep them going in summer, especially if there is any hint of drought as in 1976 and 1984.

The discharge ratio

A useful summary of the hydrological conditions of a basin, to be used in conjunction with the hydrological equation, is the **discharge ratio** which is obtained by expressing the annual **discharge** of a basin as a percentage of the total volume of precipitation. The impact of the 1976 drought is clearly seen in Howcroft's figures in Fig 5.10. A general impression of British hydrology can be gained from Fig 5.11, which shows the discharge ratio increasing towards the west and north. The lower the figure the greater are the losses likely to be from evapotranspiration and extractions for human activity.

Fig 5.11 The mean annual discharge ratio. For explanation see text.

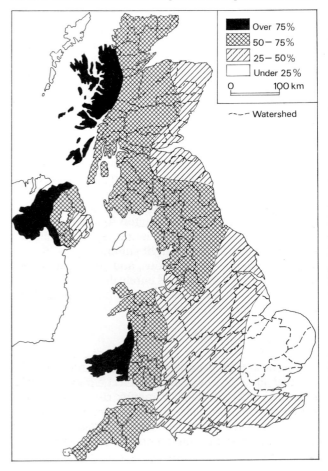

Average annual run-off

One further method of relating input to output is to compare precipitation and **run-off**. Run-off is the total amount of water that enters a river channel from the **catchment area** above a particular point over a given time period, usually a year. To be related to precipitation, run-off needs to be expressed in a similar form, namely as a depth per unit area. This can be carried out easily by taking the annual discharge of a drainage basin, measured as a volume, and dividing it by the basin's area, thus giving an annual average depth of water, or run-off, that each square unit (m², cm² or mm²) of the basin contributes to the river channel.

If run-off is expressed in millimetres it can be directly compared with precipitation, although both figures are likely to be averages that conceal considerable variation across the basin. The annual average run-off of the Spey is thus:

$$\frac{(55.86\,\text{m}^3) \times (60 \times 60 \times 24 \times 365)}{2650\,\text{km}^2 \times 1000 \times 1000} = 660\,\text{mm}$$

$$\frac{\left(\begin{array}{c}\text{average discharge}\\\text{per second}\end{array}\right) \times \left(\begin{array}{c}\text{number of}\\\text{seconds in a year}\end{array}\right)}{\text{area of basin in m}^2}$$

This compares with annual precipitation figures in the basin of between 650 and 1500 millimetres.

Over the Short Term

So far, all methods of comparing discharge and precipitation have been over a long time period, that is a year or a month. Whilst such information may be useful in the long-term planning of the water use of a basin, particularly in assessing how much water can be extracted for agriculture, industry or household use without depleting the resources, it is of limited use in attempting to understand the day-to-day variations in the water output of the channel. Even if the time period in these methods is reduced to a day, it is not particularly useful to a flood plain dweller or an irrigating farmer to know that, say, 15 per cent of an average day's rainfall becomes channel run-off. He will be much more interested in knowing how quickly the river is going to respond to rainfall, and for how long the river will keep flowing after the rain stops. Most of the methods of data analysis mentioned in this section have these more immediate aims in mind.

Lag time

By now it should be clear that storages delay the conversion of input to output, of precipitation to run-off. There could thus be said to be a **lag time** between the occurrence of the precipitation and the response of the river to that input. To be more precise, lag time is the time between the peak of a rainfall event and the corresponding peak of the river discharge. It is often most practical to measure this from the median point of the rainfall, as in Fig 5.12, although as one rainfall event

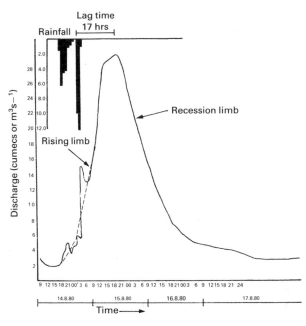

Fig 5.12 Storm hydrograph for an extreme summer event on the River Nene near Northampton.

may well merge into another, rather than being distinct, a fine definition of lag time may not be easy to apply.

Lag time for a particular river will depend partly on the characteristics of the storages but also on how full those storages are at the time of precipitation.

The storm hydrograph

For any specific rainfall event, it is instructive to compare the pattern of precipitation with that of discharge and this is usually done by means of a **storm hydrograph** as shown in Fig 5.12. Modification of the steepness and sharpness of the discharge peak is usually the aim of hydraulic engineers and others who work to reduce the flood hazard, and yet, ironically, the unintentional effect of man's other activities is often to steepen the curve in the first place. This is demonstrated in Fig 5.13, where three activities of man, urbanisation, drainage and afforestation, can be seen to alter the duration and height of the flood peak.

It would be misleading, however, to suggest that the shape of a storm hydrograph is exclusively the result of man's interference. Anything that delays the transfer of water to the channel will broaden and reduce the peak, be it a permeable bedrock such as chalk, gentle valley side slopes, dense vegetation or a deep and porous soil. This does not, of course, mean that one particular river will always respond in the same way, as the characteristics of the rainfall event will strongly influence the hydrograph, as the two contrasting storms in the Ise catchment demonstrate in Fig 5.14.

The steepness of the **rising limb**, then, depends on the speed of transfer of water; the quickest method of transfer is by overland flow, the slowest via groundwater

Fig 5.13 The impact of man on storm hydrographs.

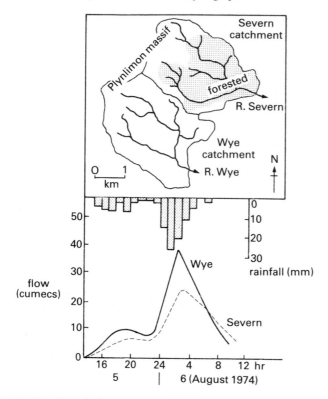

(a) The effect of afforestation on the hydrographs of two adjacent basins.

and baseflow. It seems logical, therefore, that we should be able to break down the river flow into constituent parts, as in Fig 5.15. Baseflow provides the reliable, more or less constant, element which responds very slowly to precipitation and experiences a long lag time. Overland flow, which is a relatively rare British occurrence, not only provides the peak of the hydrograph but causes it to occur in advance of either the throughflow or the baseflow peak. In gentler peaks overland flow may be absent altogether.

The gradient of the **recession limb** of the hydrograph is usually less steep than the rising limb as, although rainfall has stopped, the system of storage has been sufficiently well filled still to be discharging strongly and so reponse to the decline in input is much more gradual.

As Fig 5.32 shows, the precipitation can also be broken down into constituent parts, for a certain proportion will be required merely to recharge the soil moisture store before any run-off can occur.

The accumulation of a large number of storm hydrographs for different types of storm event in a drainage basin helps provide a most useful record from which it should be possible to predict how quickly and how high the river is going to rise under a particular set of conditions.

To facilitate this prediction a standardised graph, or **unit hydrograph**, can be drawn which uses the records of different types of storm event in a basin and shows the river's response. To allow comparison, each event must be standardised to a similar scale, say a unit of 25 millimetres of rainfall.

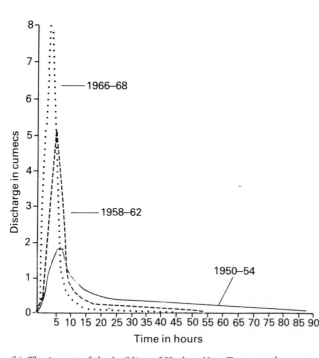

(b) The impact of the building of Harlow New Town on the mean unit hydrograph of Canon's Brook, Essex.

(c) The impact of the ditch excavation on a forested catchment at Coalburn, North Pennines.

a)

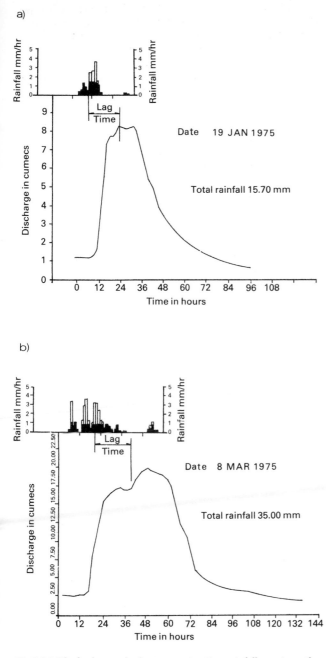

Fig 5.14 The hydrographs for two contrasting rainfall events on the River Ise, Northamptonshire.

Trends in Discharge

There are more than 1200 river gauging stations in Britain today, each one providing a continuous record of the discharge at that location. From the surfeit of generated statistics, three particularly useful modes of analysis are worthy of mention – **river regime graphs**, **flow duration curves** and **recurrence intervals**.

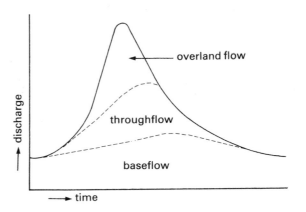

Fig 5.15 A theoretical hydrograph to demonstrate possible sources of flow.

River Regime Graphs

A river's regime reveals the fluctuations of its discharge over a year. As Fig 5.16 indicates, that may be for one particular year, such as the 1976 British drought year or 1982 when heavy winter snowfall brought particularly high discharges, or for an average year calculated from decades of records.

Fig 5.16 River regimes.

(a) The mean annual regime of the Volga, USSR – a regime affected by snowmelt.

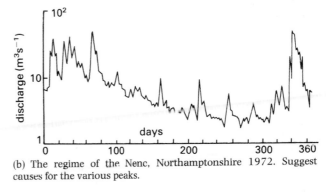

(b) The regime of the Nenc, Northamptonshire 1972. Suggest causes for the various peaks.

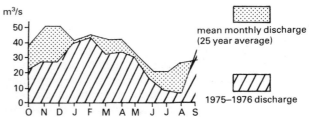

(c) The Dee, Woodend, Aberdeenshire: the drought year of 1975–6 compared with normal flow.

Seasonal patterns are often apparent, reflecting variations both in precipitation and temperature through evapotranspiration. Controls on the regime are less localised than those on the storm hydrographs, and to clarify this further, reference should be made to Question 1 at the end of this chapter.

Flow Duration Curves

One of the most useful pieces of information for the manager of any water utilisation scheme, a bridge engineer or a flood protection organiser, is how often flows of a certain magnitude can be relied upon to occur. Such information is not easily available, but careful analysis of past records, provided they are extensive, can provide some helpful clues.

How frequently a particular daily mean discharge has been exceeded or equalled in the past must first be calculated, and the data used to plot a cumulative frequency graph. Such graphs, known as flow duration curves, and exemplified in Fig 5.17, allow one to make certain statements about the levels of minimum and maximum flow and their frequency, which could be used as predictions. For instance, in Fig 5.17 one could state that the average discharge has never fallen below 0.5 cumecs (cubic metres per second) whilst for only five per cent of the time, one day in a hundred, has the discharge exceeded 15 cumecs. If one knows what magnitude of daily discharge is likely to be needed for the maintaining of a particular activity then one can see how frequently that level has been exceeded.

Danger can arise, of course, if one relies on the past being a perfect predictor of the future, for just because daily mean discharge has never exceeded a certain amount does not mean that it will not do so in future.

In order to straighten the curves, and ease comparison for the hydrologist, the graph is usually plotted on probability paper with a logarithmic scale on the Y axis.

If daily discharge varies a great deal, the line is likely to be very steep. This may reflect a very seasonal input of precipitation or output of evapotranspiration, or a low storage capacity which reduces lag time. With minimal variation of discharge, resulting from an even spread of precipitation or large storage capacity, the curve will be flatter, perhaps virtually horizontal. Most rivers will have more complex curves, as Fig 5.18 shows. It is worth pausing to consider what conditions of precipitation and storage are suggested by curves such as those of the Wharfe, the Ver and the Tees.

Recurrence Intervals

A more refined tool of prediction for the hydrologist, and especially for those interested in flood protection, is the recurrence interval of a discharge of a particular magnitude. Again, long records, preferably over a century or more, are required, from which maximum daily flows each year can be collated. With such knowledge one can calculate the probability of a particular

maximum flow being exceeded, and from this figure, the period of years before the occurrence of another similar flow, the recurrence interval, can be calculated. The formula is as follows:

$$\text{Recurrence interval of a} \atop \substack{\text{particular peak discharge} \\ \text{(in years)}} = \frac{(n+1)}{R}$$

Where n = no. of years records exist for
R = rank of particular peak discharge within entire record.

If these recurrence intervals are plotted on a graph, an invaluable visual aid for flood protection is provided.

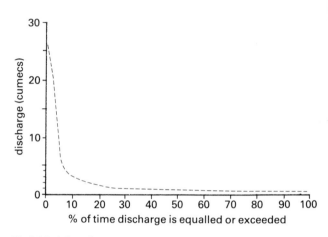

Fig 5.17 A flow duration curve.

Note the scales – logarithmic on the y axis and normal probability on the x axis

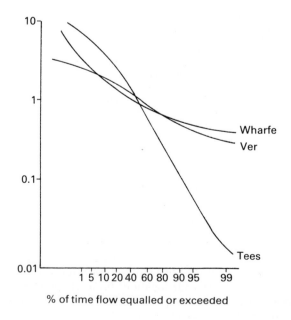

Fig 5.18 Selected flow duration curves.

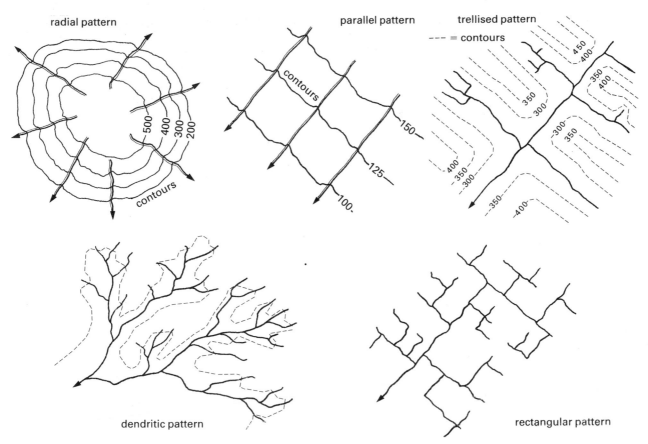

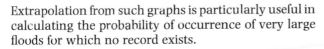

Fig 5.19 Descriptive terms for drainage patterns.

Extrapolation from such graphs is particularly useful in calculating the probability of occurrence of very large floods for which no record exists.

The Relationship between Drainage Basin Characteristics and Hydrology

By now it should be clear that the amount and speed of run-off is related to certain variables, namely, climate, geology and relief, man's activities, vegetation and soil. In addition, the idiosyncrasies of the drainage network and its basin also play an important role, for instance, if there are very few surface channels, lag time is obviously going to be longer than in an area of many channels. To identify the role that each aspect plays, characteristics of network and basin will be examined separately.

Drainage Network

Descriptive terms

Earlier in this century when geographers' work was epitomised more by the eloquence of its descriptions than by the rigour of its statistical analysis, drainage networks were described simply by the application of adjectives. Thus, terms such as radial, parallel, trellised, rectangular and dendritic were applied as shown in Fig 5.19.

However appropriate these terms were as descriptive tools, they failed to aid the geographer in his analysis of hydrological relationships, for who was to say whether trellised or radial, dendritic or rectangular produced faster lag times? Even as descriptive aids they were not foolproof, for how would the typical British drainage pattern in Fig 5.20 be described? The system allowed for too many exceptions and too much subjectivity; what is trellised to one person may be dendritic to another.

Drainage density

Objective methods of description have been evolved which have largely replaced these adjectives, and to them the name **morphometry** has been given. **Drainage density** is the most widely used, and this simply expresses the length of drainage channel per unit area of the basin's surface. Calculation is simple; the total length of channels is measured from a map and divided by the drainage basin area. Thus, in Fig 5.20a, the drainage density is $221/331 = 0.7$ kilometres per square kilometre.

This should mean that every drainage system on earth can be described, without exception, and

Fig 5.20 The Blyth drainage system, Northumberland.

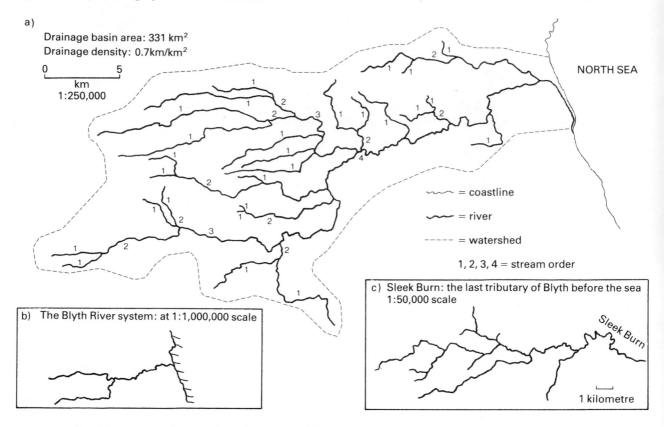

a)

Drainage basin area: 331 km²
Drainage density: 0.7km/km²

0 ———— 5
km
1:250,000

NORTH SEA

⌒⌒ = coastline
⌒⌒ = river
----- = watershed

1, 2, 3, 4 = stream order

b) The Blyth River system: at 1:1,000,000 scale

c) Sleek Burn: the last tributary of Blyth before the sea
1:50,000 scale

Sleek Burn

1 kilometre

everyone should agree on the results. This is a valid generalisation once certain difficulties are overcome.

For instance, suppose the scale of the map varies. The area remains the same but the detail alters. In Fig 5.20b only one tributary of the Blyth is shown; drainage density thus falls drastically compared to Fig 5.20a. At the larger scale in Fig 5.20c, six further tributaries appear from one minor tributary of the Blyth and the drainage density consequently increases.

At what season of the year was the map drawn? A winter network is likely to be much more extensive than a summer one, especially in a limestone area where winter bournes flow in the dry valleys. Should underground channels be included as part of the network? If so, how can they be traced? Should river width be considered? If not, the drainage density of the area of Fig 5.21a will be greater than that of Fig 5.21b. What about lakes, ponds, bogs, marshes and artificial drainage ditches? Are they part of a network?

Most of these difficulties are surmountable by applying a standard code of practice which should maintain

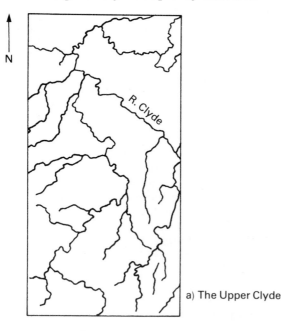

N

R. Clyde

a) The Upper Clyde

Fig 5.21 Two sections of the Clyde River system.

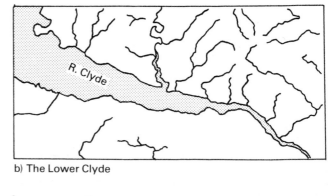

N

R. Clyde

b) The Lower Clyde

0 ———— 5
km

Location	Drainage Density (km/km²)
millstone grit of Forest of Bowland	1.96
granite of Dartmoor	1.04
old red sandstone of Brecon Beacons	1.00
igneous rocks of Ochil Hills	1.45

(all measurements from 1:50,000 O.S. maps)

Fig 5.22 Some examples of drainage density.

objectivity. Underground streams provide an obstacle. Perhaps dry surface channels should be included instead.

High drainage densities are likely to reduce lag time and sharpen hydrograph peaks. In turn, drainage density depends on an interaction of the usual hydrological controls, climate, rock type, relief, vegetation, soil and man. Typical figures for various British rock types are shown in Fig 5.22.

Stream ordering

A second method of morphometric analysis used to describe drainage networks is **stream ordering**. To each channel segment a number is given, dependent on its position in the drainage hierarchy. Thus, first order streams are those without tributaries stretching from the stream's source to its junction with another. Second order streams occur where two first order join, third order where two second order join, and so on. Careful study of the fourth order basin of the Blyth in Fig 5.20 should clarify this.

Not surprisingly, first order segments are most numerous and the higher order segments are much sparser. According to Smith and Lyle, Britain's highest order basins are no greater than five, but again the problems of scale which affect drainage density also apply here. If every tiny segment is included, orders of a much greater magnitude would be found; again, standardisation of method must be the rule.

It would be wrong to suggest that the order of a stream has *direct* effect on its lag time or storm hydrograph. Even so, in general terms it is probably true that lag times are longer for higher order streams, but this is because their catchment areas are much larger than lower order streams.

Certain interesting relationships have emerged between stream order and other basin variables, largely due to the pioneering work of Horton. When plotted on semi-logarithmic graph paper, stream order produces straight-line relationships with frequency of streams, stream gradient, stream length and drainage basin area. Thus, the higher the order, the fewer the streams, the lower their gradient, the greater their length and the larger the area they drain. These relationships can be easily tested by tracing and analysing networks from OS maps, and it is usually the case that the relationship is geometric rather than arithmetic, stream length, for example, increasing much faster than stream order.

Another morphometric index of a network is the **bifurcation ratio**. Bifurcation simply means forking, and this index is a measure of the amount of branching or forking that occurs in the network. It is the average ratio of the number of segments of one stream order to that of the one above. Thus, in Fig 5.20a the following can be recorded:

Stream order 1 = 27
Stream order 2 = 10
Stream order 3 = 2
Stream order 4 = 1

Therefore $Br = \left(\dfrac{27}{10} + \dfrac{10}{2} + \dfrac{2}{1}\right) \div 3 = 3.2$

The resultant figure will be low, less than 2.5, for very intricate patterns that resemble the branching of a tree, and high for simpler patterns where a large number of first order segments joins the main channel. In the former case, a sharply peaked hydrograph would be typical, especially if the basin is roughly circular, and in the latter a much gentler peak likely. It would be misleading to imply any direct relationship between bifurcation ratio and lag time, however.

Drainage Basin

Both size and shape of the drainage basin are important in determining the eventual run-off. Lag time is likely to be extended in a large catchment area because the possible sources of run-off are so scattered that water will take a considerable time to drain from them. The impact of drainage basin shape is less obvious. Certain relationships are suggested in Fig 5.23.

A circular basin, or a circular element in a basin such

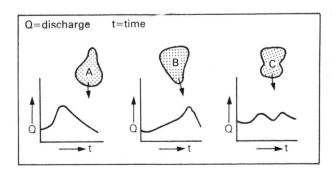

Fig 5.23 The influence of basin shape on the hydrograph.

as in A and B in the diagram, is prone to produce a sharp peak to a hydrograph as the distance that water has to flow to discharge from the basin is equal in all directions and water will arrive from all sources at roughly the same time. In an elongated basin, or an elongated element such as the top part of a basin A, the arrival of water will be much more staggered, for distance from source of water to the discharge point varies enormously. This will produce a much gentler slope to the hydrograph.

In order to facilitate analysis, these two elements, of elongation and circularity can also be assessed by the application of simple formulae.

The **circularity ratio** (c) =

$$\frac{\text{Basin area}}{\begin{array}{c}\text{Area of a circle with same}\\\text{basin perimeter}\end{array}}$$

Thus, a perfect circle is equal to one, and the less circular the basin the closer to zero is the ratio.

The **elongation ratio** (E or Re) =

$$\frac{\text{Diameter of circle of basin area}}{\text{Maximum length of basin.}}$$

Again, a perfect circle will produce an answer of one, and the more elongated the basin the closer the result will be to zero.

Hydrology as an Aid to Understanding Flooding

What have we learnt, then, about the likelihood of flooding? Certainly, streams that have intense, high volume inputs are prone, but their vulnerability is increased if valley side slopes are steep, if surfaces are impermeable, if the water table is high, if man has increased the speed of run-off, if vegetation is absent, if the network is dense in a circular basin or if the stream is of a high order.

A brief look at York's problems will support this analysis. Throughout its history the city has suffered from a series of inundations from the Ouse, notably in 1315, 1564, 1625, 1763, 1831 and 1947, and most recently in 1982. There has usually been one of two causes – sudden snowmelt or an intense summer storm. This simple increase in input is often aggravated, though, by soil frozen to impermeability, by a thaw accompanied by rain in winter or by a summer storm occurring when the soils are already saturated. Add to this the high water table in the flat, low Vale of York and the increasing amount of agricultural drainage in the Ouse catchment area, especially the cutting of the peat around the Pennine headwaters since the early part of the century, and the flood potential is increased. The potential danger increases still further thanks to the city's location (see Fig 5.24) on a river whose tributaries include the three major Pennine streams of the

Fig 5.24 The location of York.

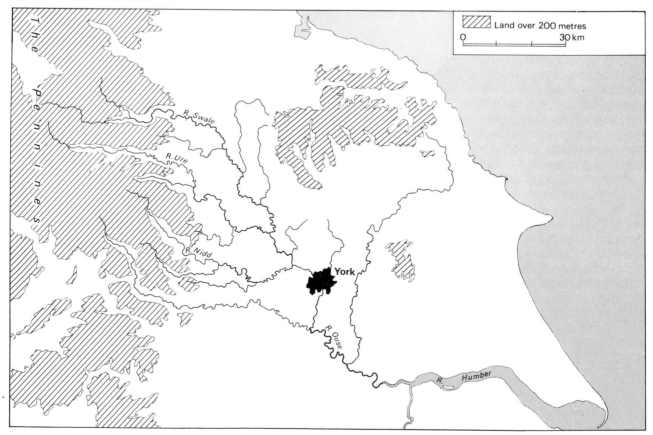

Swale, the Ure and the Nidd. When storm or snowmelt occurs in any of these, water is quickly funnelled down them towards York and the fourth order River Ouse. Wharves, a railway embankment, the great York Moraine and a very gentle river gradient of less than 1:10 000 constrict and aggravate the build-up of water still further and exacerbate the effects of the floods.

To extend our understanding of flooding, further study of the channel itself is essential, and for this reference must be made to the next chapter.

The Measurement of Hydrological Variables

The Precipitation Input

The measurement of precipitation by the standard **rain gauge** authorised by the Meteorological Office is described extensively in easily accessible sources and it will not be dealt with here. The problem for a hydrologist lies in obtaining a sufficient number of readings over the entire area of the drainage basin. Cheap, home-made alternatives to the official gauge may help provide a broader spread, but even so much interpretation from the readings will be needed to produce an average depth of input per area unit across the whole surface. A few moments' consideration of how you could best spread ten gauges over a small drainage basin known to you will exemplify the problems involved.

The Evapotranspiration Output

A similar difficulty will occur in averaging evapotranspiration output from the variety of surfaces. A much greater challenge, though, is to provide accurate evapotranspiration figures in the first place. To supply data for the hydrological equation, rates of actual evapotranspiration are required, but in fact these are more difficult to obtain than rates of potential evapotranspiration.

Data collection involves the measurement of either the two separate elements of evaporation and transpiration or the one combined process of evapotranspiration.

Evaporation pans, again of standard size, are open trays of water whose fluctuating level provides a good estimate of potential evaporation, once the input due to precipitation has been deducted. Evaporation from soil and other surfaces may be much lower than that from open water, however, and an alternative method will be needed here. Although the recommended dimensions are for a pan 1.8 metres square, the amateur can make do with smaller ones, provided that results are compared only with those from similar pans.

Rates of transpiration can be estimated using a **potometer**, shown in Fig 5.25, but a large number of different plants at different stages of their annual cycle will need to be considered to develop an overall picture.

Both the evaporation and transpiration figures de-

As the plant transpires, water is drawn along the calibrated tube AB. Air enters the tube and, as a bubble, gradually moves along the tube. The rate of transpiration over time can thus be assessed. Why do you suppose a store of water is needed in the funnel?

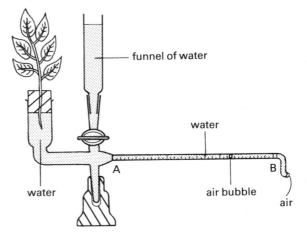

Fig 5.25 A potometer to measure transpiration.

rived here will be potential rates, for there is no shortage of water supply in either case.

Professional hydrologists may be able to afford a **lysimeter** to measure evapotranspiration direct. This is a sophisticated and expensive piece of apparatus which involves repeated weighing of a block of soil to gauge the changing inputs and outputs of water. Much simpler versions have been devised for the amateur, notably by Gregory and Walling (1973).

The **percolation gauge**, shown in Fig 5.26, shows four oil drums each of which enclose a carefully inserted block of soil. A pipe drains from the base of each drum to a well protected collecting area. If the input of precipitation is known and the output through percolation deducted from it, evapotranspiration should

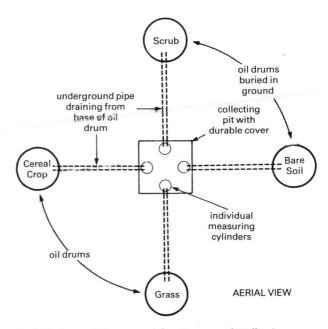

Fig 5.26 A percolation gauge (after Gregory and Walling).

equal the remainder. This assumes no change in soil storage over the data collection period. If the soil can be kept at field capacity throughout the experiment this problem will be in part controlled. By using three oil drums one can generate a series of comparable statistics. For instance, by leaving one drum free of vegetation, soil evaporation loss can be assessed; by planting three different types of vegetation, relative losses of evapotranspiration can be gauged; by maintaining one drum at field capacity but adding no extra water to another, a comparison of potential and actual rates of evapotranspiration should be possible, although this will need to be done over a sufficiently long period of time to overcome changes in soil storage.

If the application of such technology is not feasible, or if evapotranspiration rates for a forest are required, estimates can be made from formulae. Penman has produced a widely used index, but its equation employs meteorological variables that are not everywhere available, such as the mean daily wind speeds at a height of two metres, wet and dry bulb temperatures and the daily input of radiation.

Flows and Storages

In addition to the overall parameters of the hydrological equation of input and output, it may be desirable to measure some of the intervening hydrological variables of flow and storage. None of these is easy, even for the professional, and results obtained are best used for comparison with other areas rather than as definitive statements of the magnitude of a flow or store.

Interception, stemflow and drip

By positioning rain gauges beneath and beyond the perimeter of a tree, an appreciation of interception will be gained but readings will have to be taken continuously, perhaps at 15-minute intervals, to assess the lag time that interception clocks up. Leaf drip into the rain gauge will occur until well after rainfall has ceased, and measurements must continue accordingly. To obtain a fuller picture of the effect of vegetation, some estimate of stemflow is useful. A plastic gutter encircling the trunk or stem may give some indication of this, although comparison with rain gauge statistics will prove difficult. Interception by buildings should be easy to assess, in the short term at least. Comparison of rain gauge statistics from the roof of the building with the discharge from all external drainage pipes should give an indication of interception storage, although, as with vegetation interception, some of this will inevitably be lost as water vapour.

Infiltration and soil storage

To assess infiltration rates at different times on different surfaces simple equipment can be employed. A ring-pull can with both ends removed can be pushed lightly into the soil to the depth of a couple of centimetres. A

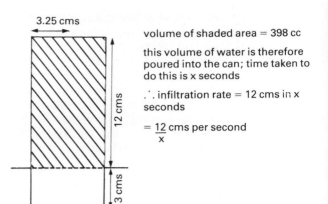

Fig 5.27 An improvised method to measure infiltration rate.

standard quantity of water can then be poured into the can and the time taken for it to infiltrate the ground recorded. Calculations will be simplified if the volume of water is equivalent to the volume of the can that appears above the surface, as Fig 5.27 shows.

The total infiltration capacity of the soil may be beyond our ability to assess but two simple experiments can provide us with data that can give us some indication.

1 To assess field capacity:
(a) take a specified volume of soil from a plot,
(b) dry it thoroughly in an oven and weigh it,
(c) take a measured quantity of water and pass it through the soil,
(d) reweigh the soil and deduct the weight of the dried soil,
(e) express the remainder, i.e. the retained water, as a percentage of the dry soil weight,
(f) This provides a field capacity useful in comparison with other soils.

2 To assess existing soil moisture conditions:
(a) take a specified volume of soil from the plot,
(b) weigh it,
(c) dry it thoroughly and weigh it again,
(d) express the moisture content as a percentage of the dry soil weight, and
(e) repeat at different stages during and after a storm.

It would be pleasing for the sake of completeness to include methods of assessing deeper percolation and groundwater levels for the amateur to undertake. However, as such techniques require the drilling of boreholes and wells into the bedrock, they are considerably outside the scope of this book.

Overland flow and throughflow

Neither of these flows is easy to measure due to their fluctuating nature over time and the intricacy of their paths of movement, but again general assessments are possible.

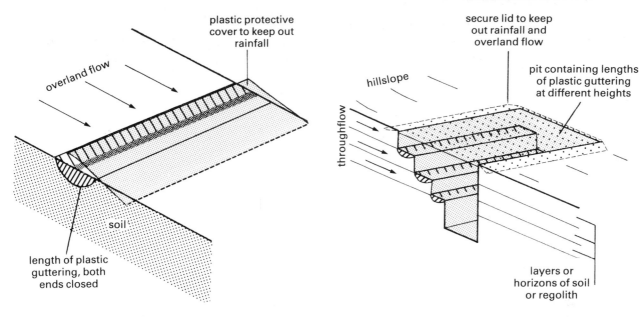

Fig 5.28 Measuring overland flow.

Fig 5.29 Measuring throughflow.

A metre length of plastic guttering, with both ends closed, entrenched into an isolated hillside and protected with a layer of plastic sheeting or corrugated iron is needed. It should be capable of avoiding interloping raindrops, animals and walkers. Continuous and regular collection of water will be essential to allow any accuracy in the readings. (See Fig 5.28.)

Throughflow measurements can be carried out nearby but this time the gutter will need to be at the bottom of a pit, which will once again need protection from the ravages of man and nature overground. If more detailed data are sought for deep soils, a series of gutters can be positioned down the stepped side of the pit, each collecting water from a different soil horizon (see Fig 5.29).

If the experiment is carried out on agricultural land that has artificial drainage, measurements of the discharge from the drainpipes into drainage ditches will provide interesting figures to compare with the experimental throughflow data. To standardise measurements of both types of flow, water should first be tipped into a measuring cylinder or flask.

For the amateur, interflow and baseflow are no less difficult to assess than groundwater storage, but streamflow is much more accessible and this will be described in the next chapter.

Regime Figures Refer to 1952

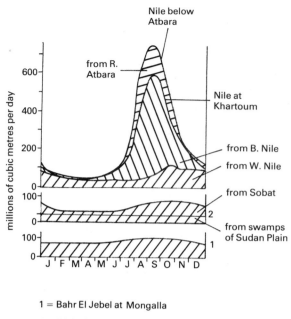

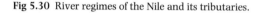

1 = Bahr El Jebel at Mongalla

2 = White Nile at Malakal

Fig 5.30 River regimes of the Nile and its tributaries.

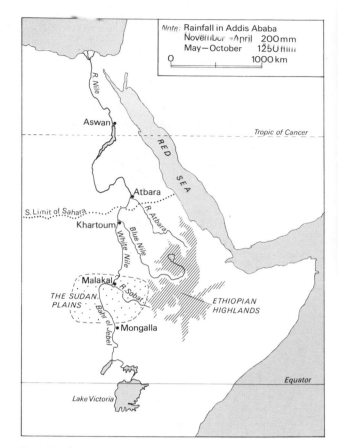

Fig 5.31 The Nile drainage basin.

Questions

1 Refer to the accompanying diagrams, Figs 5.30 and 5.31, of the Nile river basin and its regimes in 1952.

(a) What is the difference between a regime and a hydrograph?

(b) What two factors cause Mongalla's regime to be relatively even through the year? Explain how each one produces this result.

(c) What evidence is there, in the diagrams, that the discharge of the White Nile decreases between Mongalla and Malakal?

(d) Explain exactly why you think this happens.

(e) What measures could be taken to alter this state of affairs?

(f) What is the major determinant of the River Sobat's regime?

(g) Why does the discharge increase so slowly below Khartoum?

(h) These regimes refer to 1952; explain how and why you would expect the regime of the Nile below Atbara to differ today.

(i) What problems would the regimes of 1952 cause for the people of the Lower Nile?

2 Refer to Fig 5.32 which shows the suggested disposition of storm rainfall into its component parts.

(a) What forms does depression storage take?

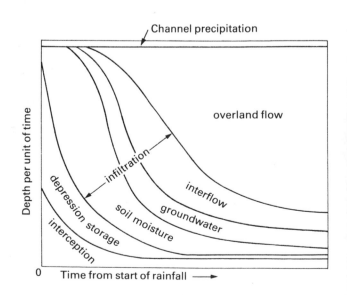

Fig 5.32 A possible disposition of storm rainfall.

(b) What is the difference between soil moisture and groundwater?

(c) Why does interception decrease with time and then remain constant?

(d) Every type of vegetation is likely to intercept rainfall. Detail the factors that will determine how much rainfall vegetation intercepts.

(e) What might cause the amount of channel precipitation to disagree with the diagram and vary over time?

(f) What soil characteristics will determine the speed and the amount of throughflow within the soil?

(g) In what ways might the building of a new town in the area cause changes in the diagram?

3 Refer to the diagram of Medicine Hat's soil moisture budget in Fig 5.33.

(a) Explain the meaning of each of the following terms:
   (i) soil moisture recharge
   (ii) soil moisture deficiency
   (iii) soil moisture utilisation

(b) What is the difference in the meaning of the terms actual evapotranspiration and potential evapotranspiration?

(c) Using information from the diagram only, attempt to describe the major characteristics of Medicine Hat's climate.

(d) Why is a knowledge of soil moisture deficiency of use to the farmer?

(e) To what other economic activities, besides agriculture, might a knowledge of the soil moisture budget be valuable?

Further Reading

Drainage Basin: Form and Process, K J Gregory and D E Walling (Arnold, 1973).

The River Basin, D Ingle Smith and P Stopp (Cambridge, 1978).

Elements of Geographical Hydrology, B Knapp (Unwin Hyman, 1979).

British Rivers, J Lewin (Unwin Hyman, 1981).

The Atlas of Drought in Britain, J C Doornkamp, K J Gregory and A S Burn (Institute of British Geographers, 1979).

Other References

Atmosphere, Weather and Climate, R G Barry and R J Chorley (Methuen, 1968).

Erosional Development of Streams and their Drainage Basins, R E Horton, *Bulletin of the Geological Society of America* 56, 275–370 (1945).

The Hydrology of a Small Catchment, H J Howcroft, *Field Studies* 4 (1977).

Distribution of Fresh Waters in Great Britain, I Smith and A Lyle (Institute of Terrestrial Ecology, 1979).

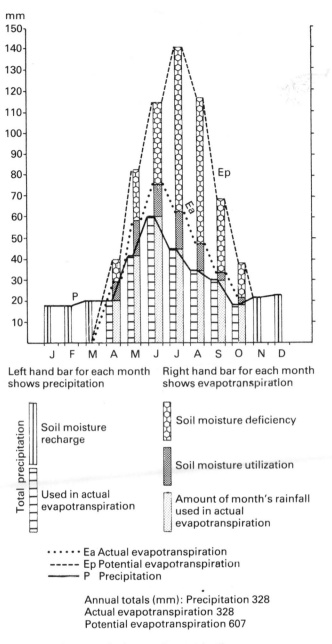

Left hand bar for each month shows precipitation

Right hand bar for each month shows evapotranspiration

Total precipitation

Soil moisture recharge

Used in actual evapotranspiration

Soil moisture deficiency

Soil moisture utilization

Amount of month's rainfall used in actual evapotranspiration

· · · · · · Ea Actual evapotranspiration
- - - - - Ep Potential evapotranspiration
———— P Precipitation

Annual totals (mm): Precipitation 328
Actual evapotranspiration 328
Potential evapotranspiration 607

Fig 5.33 Soil moisture budget, Medicine Hat, Alberta.

6

Rivers and their Landscapes

Introduction

It is hardly surprising that the river crops up so frequently in the imagery, mythology and poetry of the many cultures and civilisations of human history, for its influence upon daily life is surpassed by no other physical phenomenon, save perhaps the weather. Rivers excavate the surfaces which man inhabits, lay down many of the materials from which man derives a living and provide the water that may sustain or overcome him. For the geomorphologist they are a central feature of study, for many landscapes owe both their existence and their continued moulding to the work of rivers. No British landscape can be considered without reference to them, not even the glaciated uplands of northern Britain or the many varieties of coastal landscapes. Indeed, as will be seen in Chapter 11, few supposedly waterless desert landscapes are free from their influence.

The Long Profile and Sources of Energy

The Long Profile

By plotting a line graph of a river's height above base level against the distance from its source, as in Fig 6.1, one obtains an impression of a river's **long** or **longitudinal profile**. Those shown in Fig 6.1 are typical in

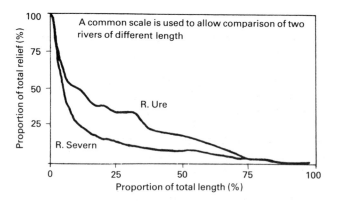

Fig 6.1 The longitudinal profiles of two British rivers.

being concave with a short, steep upper section to the curve succeeded by an elongated, gentle lower section. As rivers evolve through time they appear to work towards the achievement of a smooth, concave profile such as this, from which irregularities are gradually removed. As we shall see later, however, the aim is not always achieved.

River Energy

Rivers achieve their effects by using the energy available to them. The **potential energy**, or stored energy, that is available is proportional to the height above sea level. It may therefore be considerable in an upland stream that rises thousands of metres above sea level.

As water moves downslope, potential energy is converted to **kinetic energy** which is used to carry out the river's tasks. However, in the transfer from potential to kinetic most of the energy is lost as heat owing to friction encountered as the water moves. It has been estimated that 95 per cent of a river's energy is dissipated in this way, which leaves just 5 per cent to carry out the erosion and transportation of debris.

Energy and River Velocity

Kinetic energy is related directly to the **velocity of flow** and the mass of water, the former being the more important variable. Thus, in simple terms:

$$E = \frac{MV}{2}$$

$$\text{Kinetic energy} = \frac{(\text{mass}) \times (\text{velocity})}{2}$$

It can therefore be assumed that where velocities are greatest then so is the provision of kinetic energy. It could be further reasoned that the upper course of a river, where gradients are steepest, provides the greatest velocities and therefore maximises kinetic energy. Such a conclusion would be wrong, however, for it assumes that velocity is simply a function of gradient. Other factors intervene to complicate the relationship, for example the viscosity of the water, the

A–F are six different channel cross-sections

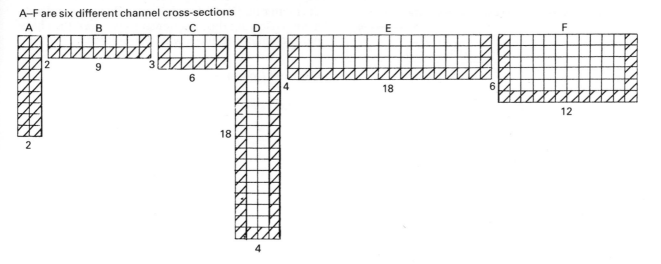

In the table below, certain dimensions of the above channels have been filled in. Fill in the missing figures. Channel G represents a semi-circular channel of 3.38 radius.

	A	B	C	D	E	F	G
Depth			3		4		3.38
Width			6		18		6.76
Cross-sectional area			18		72		
% of squares unshaded			44.4		66		

Study the results

(a) Which is the most efficient shape of channel, A, B or C? Why
(b) What do the results for A to F suggest about the relationship between efficiency and size of channel cross-section?
(c) Read about wetted perimeter and hydraulic radius in the text. Calculate each index for each of the seven channels. What conclusions can you draw about the relationship between each index and channel efficiency?
(d) Which channel shape is the most efficient?

Fig 6.2 The effect of channel cross-section on river velocity (after Land).

volume of water flowing at a particular time and various aspects of the river's channel.

The channel is particularly important as it creates the friction which dissipates the energy and reduces the velocity. This is clearly exemplified by an irregular bed containing large protruding grains or boulders, aquatic weeds or artificial obstructions such as bridge parapets or piers. A very sinuous course also provides obstructions to flow, and like an irregular bed creates turbulence which dissipates energy. No natural surface water flow, except in very particular circumstances, occurs without turbulence. The size and shape of a channel cross-section play an essential role in determining velocity, for the greater the percentage of water that is in contact with the channel bed the greater will friction loss be. A short exercise in Fig 6.2 will demonstrate this.

To express channel cross-section two terms are often referred to, the **wetted perimeter**, which should be self-explanatory, and the more useful **hydraulic radius**.

The hydraulic radius is the ratio of channel cross-sectional area to the wetted perimeter; the higher it is the less the interference with flow of the channel or the more efficient the channel will be as a conveyor of water. Semi-circular channels are the most efficient although they are very rare in nature; sometimes these are created in drainage and irrigation ditches or on straightened sections of rivers where flood prevention is paramount.

Velocity, then, is not simply a function of gradient, and it cannot be assumed that velocities are highest in the steepest, usually upland sections of a river's course. A brief review of the complicating factors above should show that most of them collaborate to provide the river with its least efficient course in upland stretches where a twisting, narrow, irregular channel burdened with obstacles dissipates a much greater proportion of the available energy than the more gently sinuous, larger, smoother channels of the lower course.

Experience may, however, cause you to question the logic of this argument. Surely the tumultuous torrents of upland Britain are flowing much faster than the slow and labouring lowland rivers such as the Thames in

These readings were taken by use of a flow meter, in metres per second.————— Downstream —————→

	ARM O'GRAIN	GRAINSGILL BECK	R.CALDEW at PODDY GHYLL	R.CALDEW by BOWSCALE TARN
14 April 1984	0.09	0.22	0.25	0.40
18 April 1986	0.58	0.60	0.72	0.74

Fig 6.3 Average velocity readings for the upper Caldew catchment, Cumbria.

London. The picture is deceptive. Upland torrents may possess one thread of rapidly flowing current, but when flows are measured throughout the cross-section an average velocity may result that is very low. Indeed, casual observation of an upland stream will reveal much of the sub-surface water and the surface water near the edges and near obstacles to be virtually stationary. Lowland rivers are interfered with much less and maintain a steady flow through much of their cross-section to produce average velocities sometimes higher than those of their upper course. The statistics in Fig 6.3 demonstrate this, although the increase downstream is usually very slight.

The Relationship between Long Profile and Energy

The conclusion from this discussion must be that the river in its lower course is a more efficient user of energy than in its upper course and, despite its far smaller potential energy, it is able to carry out far more work in the form of transportation and erosion. As velocity increase is only slight, the increased work output must also be attributed to the much larger volumes of water available there, for the kinetic energy which carries out the work is proportional not only to velocity but also to mass of water.

The concave long profile of a river must be seen as a reflection of the energy needs and uses of a river at different stages of its course. Steep gradients are needed in the upper course if the river is to overcome the massive energy loss to friction there, but far gentler gradients suffice downstream where energy use is more efficient.

It is also helpful to view the concave long profile as a model with which to compare particular rivers and to which rivers are attempting to adjust themselves through time.

The River Channel

Considerable reference has already been made to some of the characteristics of the river channel but further examination of its attributes is now pertinent. To do this two aspects of the channel will be looked at, first its dimensions and shape and second the characteristics of the matter passing through it, namely water and sediment. Following this, relationships between the channel and what it conveys will be examined.

Channel Geometry

The channel cross-section

As the channel cross-section in Fig 6.4 clearly indicates, channels of the upper course are usually irregular which may make measurement far from straightforward. To obtain an indication of cross-sectional area, water surface width is multiplied by average depth calculated from a series of depth readings at regular intervals, usually five per cent of the width. The difficulties of doing this in practice are exemplified in Photos 6.1a and 6.1b; should a channel split by a boulder be regarded as two separate channels, for instance?

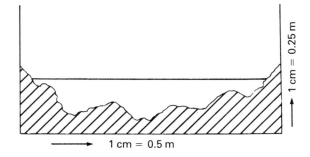

Fig 6.4 Cross-section of Grainsgill Beck, 14th April 1984.

Photos 6.1a and b Measuring the hydraulic geometry of upland streams. Neither the wetted nor the bankfull cross-section of such rivers is easy to define.

Description of Channel and Stream	Range of 'n'	Norm
1 Minor Streams (ie. bankfull width less than 33m)		
(a) Streams on a plain		
Clean, straight, bankfull, no riffles or deep pools	0.025 – 0.033	0.030
As above, with more stones and vegetation	0.030 – 0.040	0.035
Clean, sinuous, some pools and riffles	0.033 – 0.045	0.040
As above, with some vegetation and stones	0.035 – 0.050	0.045
Sinuous, lower stages, more stones	0.045 – 0.060	0.050
Sluggish reaches, weed, deep pools	0.050 – 0.080	0.070
(b) Mountain streams		
Clean, steep banks with vegetation submerged at bankfull, bed of gravel and cobbles	0.030 – 0.050	0.040
As above, but bed of larger stones	0.040 – 0.070	0.050
2 Major streams		
No boulders or brush	0.025 – 0.060	
Irregular and rough reach	0.035 – 0.10	

Fig 6.5 Manning's 'n' for various natural chananels.

In larger channels, especially those of the middle and lower course which are too deep for wading, other methods must be devised using plumb lines dropped from boats or even echo-sounding devices. To put the cross-sectional area readings into perspective and to make them useful for comparison, the vital statistics of wetted perimeter and hydraulic radius often supplement them.

Channel roughness

In order to facilitate the understanding of the relationship between velocity and channel geometry, an index of **channel roughness** has been devised, known as **Manning's 'n'**. This index was calculated from the observation of a large number of very different channels and it reflects the amount of friction that a particular cross-section is likely to offer to the flow of water. It therefore amalgamates the effects of particular materials that constitute bed and banks, of obstacles to flow in the river including vegetation, of channel sinuosity and of channel bed profile. For any particular stretch of river, Manning's 'n' needs to be calculated individually, but some indication of its scale can be discerned from Fig 6.5.

The relationship of channel roughness to velocity is expressed by the equation:

$$v = \frac{R^{\frac{2}{3}} S^{\frac{1}{2}}}{\text{'n'}}$$

where V is the average velocity, R is the hydraulic radius and S is channel slope. This once again confirms that river velocity is not simply a function of slope but also of channel characteristics.

Gradient and slope

To determine the average **gradient** of a river's bed along a particular stretch similar methods can be used to those for hillslope measurement, namely the clinometer and ranging poles, the Abney level and the surveyor's level (see Photo 6.2). However, in some cases, the interpretation of contours from a map may prove just as useful.

The angle of **slope** is more commonly used than

Photo 6.2 Using a surveyor's level to measure the slope of a river. The slope of the bank is measured, which is a convenient substitute for water surface slope.

	width m.	average depth	cross-section area m²	wetted perimeter m.	hydraulic radius	slope °
Arm O'Grain	1.7	0.09	0.15	3.8	0.004	9
Grainsgill Beck	3.1	0.15	0.46	4.8	0.009	6
R. Caldew	5.5	0.27	1.5	7.1	0.21	1

downstream

Fig 6.6 Channel geometry of an upland stream: readings for three points on upland tributaries of River Caldew, Cumbria.

gradient as it has the useful advantage of increasing in value with steepness. As Fig 6.6 indicates, actual field values, even in upland Britain, may be much less than expected.

Although slope has been seen to decrease steadily in accordance with a river's energy requirements from source to sea, local exceptions to this pattern are common. On a meso-scale, perhaps for stretches of several kilometres a change in the rock of the river bed, an obstacle created by tectonic activity, change in the coarseness of the bedload caused by man's activities or even the entry of a tributary can cause the slope to increase suddenly against the general trend.

On a much smaller scale, the bed can be seen to be very uneven, its slope punctuated by alternating gentle and steep reaches known as **pools** and **riffles** respectively. As Fig 6.7 shows, the steeper riffle sections are composed of coarser bed material than their gentler counterparts.

River plan

Straight channels in nature, even in short stretches, are extremely rare; it is only in the laboratory and as a result of man's interference that straightness can be maintained. The degree to which a river's plan deviates from a straight line varies enormously and to assess this variance a measure of **sinuosity** is often employed. By dividing the distance between two points along the course of a river by the straight-line distance between them, one derives the sinuosity ratio. As Fig 6.8 shows, this varies from values close to one to values two or three times as great for meandering courses. For upland streams, where banks are extremely irregular, sinuosity measurements in the field will prove a frustrating challenge, and measurements made from large scale maps may prove more helpful.

The Channel's Water and Load

Water flow

If river water moved in small, perfectly smooth, straight channels down extremely slight slopes, there is a strong chance that its flow would be laminar and it is certain that rivers would be much easier to study. As Fig 6.9 shows, **laminar flow** means that water moves in parallel layers with virtually no mixing. The fact that such flow occurs only in groundwater and occasionally in

Fig 6.7 Characteristic sequence of pools and riffles on stream bed.

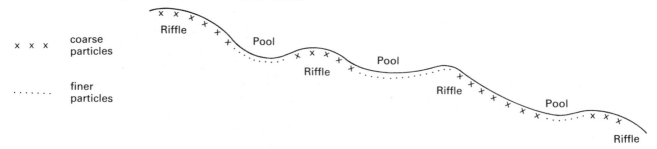

x x x coarse particles

.... finer particles

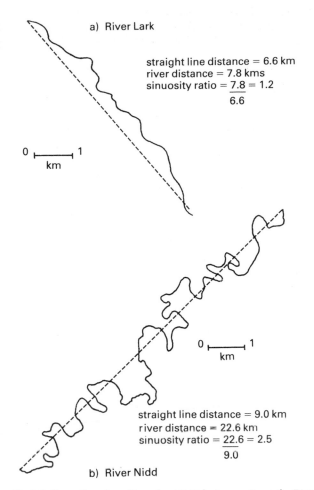

Fig 6.8 Sinuosity ratios of two short British river sections: the River Lark, Suffolk and the River Nidd, North Yorkshire.

surface rivers in the still conditions near beds and banks must indicate that river flow is usually much more turbulent and complex than this.

Flow becomes **turbulent** when a certain critical velocity is exceeded whose value depends on the viscosity of the water, its depth and the roughness of the bed and banks. For a shallow, irregular upland channel the critical velocity is very low, causing even very slow moving water to become turbulent.

In turbulent flow the water motion is chaotic, with particles moving backwards as well as forwards (see Fig 6.10). Extreme forms of turbulence, caused perhaps by a steep slope at a waterfall or rapids, or by a sudden increase in discharge, are known as **shooting flow**, under which conditions erosion is likely to be increased severely.

River velocity

Many of the determinants of a river's velocity and its variation through the long profile have already been explained. Local changes in velocity may occur, for example where changes in slope occur or where frictional losses are temporarily reduced, perhaps by the intervention of man.

Velocity also varies through the cross-section, in general increasing away from the slight movement recorded near bed and banks. Lines of equal velocity or **isovels** can be drawn, as shown in Fig 6.11. In irregular natural channels the line of fastest flowing water is usually easy to observe, pursuing a course as sinuous as that of the channel.

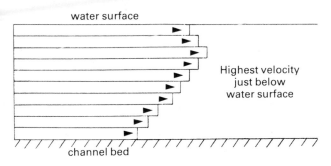

Fig 6.9 Laminar water flow.

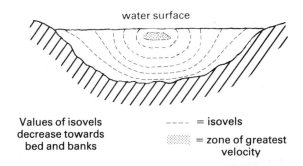

Fig 6.11 Theoretical distribution of isovels.

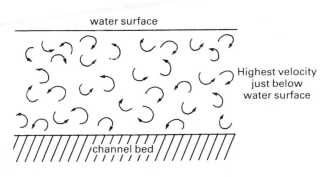

Fig 6.10 Turbulent water flow.

Measurement of velocity can be as easy or difficult as time and equipment allow. An interpretation of the game that Winnie the Pooh and friends played, dropping sticks from a bridge into the water beneath them, gives us the simplest method. In fact, sticks, being both difficult to spot and liable to interception, are not the most appropriate medium. Segments of orange peel, or better still holly berries, are much better implements, being bright of colour and biodegradable. By timing the passage of, say, ten berries along a measured stretch of channel, the velocity can be easily calculated by dividing distance by the average time. The problem, of

Photo 6.3 Using a flow meter to measure river discharge, River Caldew, Cumbria. The boy in the centre holds the flow meter which is attached to the digital counter held by the boy on the right.

course, is that the berry is likely to be sucked into the fastest current of water, and to achieve a realistic estimate of average velocity for the whole cross-section one needs to apply a correction factor, perhaps multiplying by 0.8.

More accurate results cost time and money, but the **flow meter** will certainly achieve them. The instrument, shown in Photo 6.3, consists of a calibrated pole with a foot to prevent it sinking into the streambed. To the pole is attached a propeller, from which a cable leads to a counter which records the number of revolutions of the propeller over a chosen time. Tables are consulted to convert the readings into velocities. The positioning of the flow meter is obviously vital and a wide number of readings is needed throughout the cross-section to ensure a representative average is obtained. Extensive field experience has shown that if

readings are made at regular intervals, (usually 5 per cent of the width), across the channel, there is no need to take more than one reading at each point, provided each reading is taken at 0.6 of the depth (see Fig 6.12). The readings are then averaged to produce a mean velocity for a particular station on the stream's course.

River discharge

A river's **discharge** is the volume of water that passes a point in a given time. It is measured in cumecs (cubic metres per second). To calculate it one needs to know the cross-sectional area and the velocity and then apply the simple equation:

$$Q = A.\bar{v}$$
$$\text{where A is cross-sectional area.}$$

OR

$$Q = w.\bar{d}.\bar{v}$$
Discharge = width × average depth × average velocity

To expedite calculation, though, discharge can be measured direct without individual measurement of velocity or channel geometry. This is easily done by

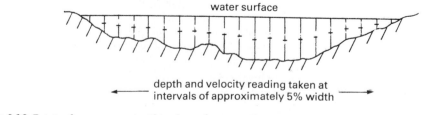

water surface

average velocity readings each taken at 0.6 depth at each point

depth and velocity reading taken at intervals of approximately 5% width

Fig 6.12 Points of measurement within channel cross-section.

measuring the speed at which an added quantity of salt disseminates itself through the water. To gain this information an **environmental multi-probe** is best employed. In order to assess the speed with which the salt is spread through the water, the conductivity of the water, or the ability to have electricity passed through it, must be measured. The guiding principle behind this is that the saltier the water the higher the conductivity. By establishing the conductivity prior to the introduction of salt, one can then observe the changing conductivity as the salted water passes the observation point. If the relationship between conductivity and salt concentration is known it is a relatively simple matter to convert conductivity readings into measurements of the changing salt concentrations over time and then into discharge readings. A detailed explanation of a field experiment follows:

1 Place probe of conductivity meter in river and record conductivity.
2 Pour measured quantity of salt, say 750 g, into stream a short distance upstream from probe.
3 Record conductivity every 15 seconds, as salt passes, until it returns to previous level.
4 Calculate average conductivity during the passage of the salt.
5 Convert this conductivity figure to a salt concentration by using a graph. This graph can be drawn by taking a series of conductivity readings from prepared concentrations of salt in stream water.
6 Substitute this concentration reading into the equation:

$$\text{Discharge} = \frac{\text{weight of salt (in grams)}}{\begin{array}{c}\text{average} \\ \text{concentration} \\ \text{of salt passing} \\ \text{point} \\ \text{(in gms/l)}\end{array} \times \begin{array}{c}\text{time taken for} \\ \text{salt to pass} \\ \text{measuring point} \\ \text{(in seconds)}\end{array}}$$

7 To convert this figure from litres per second into cumecs, divide by a thousand.

Although both methods of assessing discharge can be adapted for professional use, neither salt dilution nor the flow meter is really applicable to rivers of more than a couple of metres in depth, and other methods are usually employed. **Gauging stations** need to be able to achieve quick and accurate assessment of changing discharge, especially if they are involved in flood control or the management of water supply. Methods have been devised so that by one reading from a calibrated water depth or **stage board** the discharge can be rapidly calculated from a simple formula or graph. This is made possible by the construction of a weir or flume through which all the river water is funnelled. One of the more commonly used weirs is the **90° V-notch**, as shown in Fig 6.13a.

As the cross-sectional dimensions of the notch are known and flow velocities can be calculated in a laboratory from observation of the head of water flowing through a notch of such a shape, the discharge can be computed easily. Once a sufficient number of records has been accumulated the relationship between depth

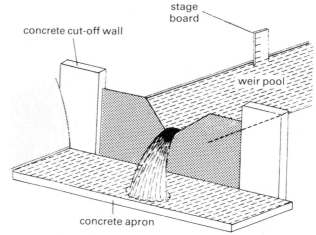

(a) The 90° v-notch weir.

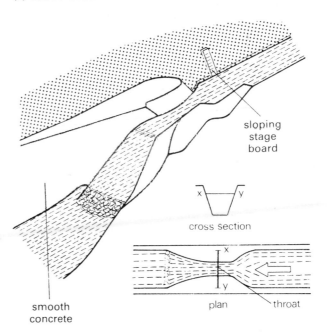

(b) The trapezoidal flume.

Fig 6.13 Structures to measure river discharge

of water, or stage, and discharge can be plotted as a graph (Fig 6.14) or expressed as a formula. All that needs to be done to record discharge after that is simply to read the stage board and refer to the graph or formula.

Flumes operate on a similar principle, except that the water is funnelled through a short channel of specific cross-sectional shape and area, as exemplified in Fig 6.13b. Their advantage over weirs is that they are less likely to become clogged with debris.

Energy at any point on a river's course is maximised when one particular discharge is achieved, **bankfull**. In other words, when the river is full to the top of its banks, but not yet overflowing, it is deemed to be bankfull. Examination of the channels in Fig 6.15 should quickly make clear why this is so. From Leopold's work it appears that the bankfull flood occurs once every 18

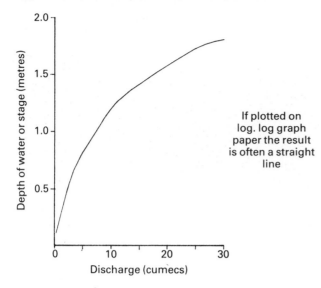

If plotted on log. log graph paper the result is often a straight line

Fig 6.14 A typical stage rating curve.

months on US rivers, and a study of British rivers suggests a return period of between one and three years. As we shall see in a later section the characteristics of a river at bankfull stage have been much studied. Measurement of bankfull discharge is by no means straightforward, not only because of its rare occurrence and torrential flow, but also because many channels are so irregular that it is not actually easy to tell when the bankfull stage has been reached.

Load

A river's **load** is the total quantity of sediments and solutes that it is carrying or moving at a particular time. Classification of the sedimentary load shown in Fig 6.16 can be applied to all particles in all environments, whether coastal, glacial, fluvioglacial, periglacial or aeolian.

Fig 6.16 Sediment classification by size of particle.

Cobbles
——60.0 mm——
Coarse gravel
——20.0 mm——
Medium gravel
——6.0 mm——
Fine gravel
——2.0 mm——
Coarse sand
——0.6 mm——
Medium sand
——0.2 mm——
Fine sand
——0.06 mm——
Coarse silt
——0.02 mm——
Medium silt
——0.006 mm——
Fine silt
——0.002 mm——
Clay

Fig 6.15 One channel at a series of different stages of discharge.

Note increase in hydraulic radius as discharge and channel efficiency increase.

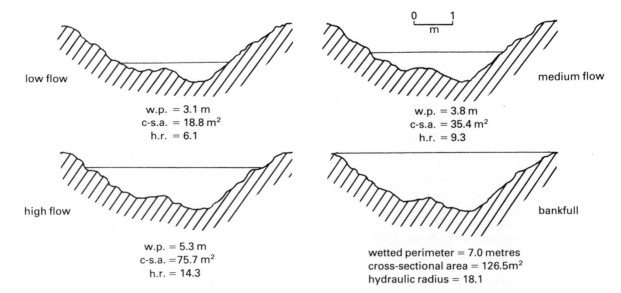

low flow

w.p. = 3.1 m
c-s.a. = 18.8 m²
h.r. = 6.1

medium flow

w.p. = 3.8 m
c-s.a. = 35.4 m²
h.r. = 9.3

high flow

w.p. = 5.3 m
c-s.a. = 75.7 m²
h.r. = 14.3

bankfull

wetted perimeter = 7.0 metres
cross-sectional area = 126.5m²
hydraulic radius = 18.1

Photo 6.4a and b The River Welland, Duddington, Northamptonshire. In the low flow of summer virtually no load is transported, but the snow-melt of spring increases the load, the discharge and size of the river.

It is a common practice to sub-divide river sediment into three categories, the **solute load** referring to particles that have been dissolved into the water, the **suspended load** referring to the particles held in suspension in the water, and the **bedload** which refers to the often larger particles of the river bed which the river is able to transport at one time or another.

Casual observation of any river gives some indication of the load it is transporting. The murky appearance of many rivers is usually an indication of the large suspended load that is being carried. Indeed, river names often reflect this, notably China's Yellow River and North Yorkshire's Murk Esk. To gain an accurate picture of the load, however, more objective methods need to be used.

Suspension load: Professional gauging stations measure suspension load by taking continuous, regular samples of known quantities of river water, filtering them and then recording the weight or volume of the residue. It is difficult for an amateur to compete with the effectiveness of this method, for random samples collected in, say, milk bottles give little indication of the total load and the infinitesimal amounts of sediment contained in them are extremely difficult to measure without very accurate balances. A simple method that

may be effective for the amateur is to use a white disc or plate. If this is submerged in the water until it can no longer be seen, its depth beneath the surface can be measured and compared to load conditions in different rivers or in the same river at different times.

Even the professional may find that his picture of total annual load is not a very accurate one, for most sediment is moved in times of flood, as Photos 6.4a and b clearly show, and he may not have a sufficient number of readings during the flood period to assess the quantity moved accurately. On rivers that flood frequently this problem is exacerbated.

Once samples have been collected, the professional may analyse the geochemistry of the load in order to trace its origins. Whilst possible with larger grains, the analysis of clay particles presents great difficulties, and researchers who wish to assess the origin of load have usually designed massive experiments that encompass the entire drainage basin, monitoring slopes, river banks and bluffs or river cliffs to assess their contribution to the river's sediment. For an estimate of total solid load including suspension and bedload, reservoir managers may be useful allies. When a Sheffield reservoir was drained in the 1950s its dredged sediment amounted to 85 000 cubic metres which, having accumulated in the 87 years since its construction, meant that the tributaries of its moorland catchment must have carried an average annual load of almost 1000 cubic metres of sediment.

Bedload: Although still beset by the problem of accurate assessment of the contribution of flood discharges during which the great percentage of bed-load is moved, this category of sediment is easier to estimate than suspended load for both professional and amateur.

An effective method in shallow rivers is provided by the **bedload trap**, simply a lined trench cut into the river bed into which load drops as it is transported (see Fig 6.17). Obviously, such traps are more easily excavated

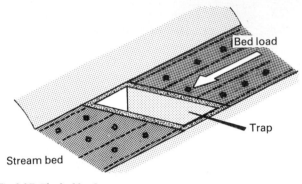

Fig 6.17   The bed load trap.

Photo 6.5   Using a quadrat to sample bedload.

by professionals as temporary river diversion may be needed whilst this is done, but there is no reason why a student should not construct one on a small stream, permission of course having first been obtained from the landowner! In deeper rivers suspended traps or baskets may need to be employed.

An alternative to the bedload trap for amateurs is the use of a **quadrat** to sample the sediment of the bed at different locations across and along the river. Measurement of the A-axis of larger grains and sieving of the smaller ones will produce useful comparative data, although one must bear in mind that not all bed deposits necessarily become load, and even if they do one has no indication from this method of the flow conditions and discharge when they do.

Solute load: For much the same reasons, solute load is as difficult for the amateur to measure as is suspended sediment, although a conductivity meter could be used to provide a general indication of total solute load. This operates on the same principle as it does when measuring added salt concentration to calculate discharge. To analyse the content of the load further, various tests are possible, for example to determine the quantity of some solutes such as calcium carbonate and sodium chloride, but for much of this analysis sophisticated equipment is required. Continuous, regular sampling by the professional, followed by laboratory analysis is essential to provide meaningful results, although for the student it is possible to design experiments to analyse the content of common solutes such as calcium carbonate and sodium chloride.

In urban areas and in intensive agricultural regions such as eastern England, the solute load is often a reflection of man's activities. As Fig 6.18 shows, nitrate levels are alarmingly high in some British rivers as a result of the massive applications of chemicals by farmers. Analysis of water in the Thames shows that it has increased its mean annual nitrate concentration from 2.5 milligrams per litre in 1928 to 8 milligrams in 1978 and, since then, to above 11.3, which is the recommended limit for a source of drinking water.

In upland areas the same may not be true, although in commercially forested areas fertiliser application may raise solute loads. On the rivers draining the western slopes of Plynlimon in central Wales, Lewin, Cryer and Harrison analysed solute loads of rainfall, overland flow and sub-surface flow and found that the fluctuating quantity of solute load in the river varied according to oscillation in the solute content of the rainfall. This suggests that, in this area, man's surface activities make only a small contribution. It is not impossible, though, in some areas, that man may contribute to the load of the rainfall, an idea that would certainly find support from those Scandinavians who attribute the acidification of their rivers and lakes to British pollution of their rainfall.

Hydraulic Geometry

Since the time of the great geomorphologists of the nineteenth century, such as G K Gilbert and W M Davis, many observations have been made about the relationships between different parameters of a river system. It is only in the past three or four decades, however, that sufficient methods have been devised to collect the data to classify and confirm many of these relationships. Much of this important research and analysis has been carried out by a series of American geologists and hydrologists such as Leopold, Maddock and Schumm, working in the river channels of North America. To the study of the various relationships within the internal workings of river channels has been given the name **hydraulic geometry**.

One river in particular, Brandywine Creek in Pennsylvania, has generated a great quantity of data. This river and many others have demonstrated relationships between width, depth, velocity and discharge which, when plotted on logarithmic graph paper, become straight-line relationships.

As one knows from the equations on page 118, at a particular station on a river's course, average depth, width and velocity are related to discharge. From Fig 6.19, however, we can see how width, depth and velocity vary in their downstream relationship to discharge, both during low flow and at times of flood. Width increases steadily but at about half the rate of increase of discharge, depth similarly but at a slightly slower rate of increase, and velocity virtually not at all, as we have already discussed . For the rate of increase of each variable to be identical to that of discharge downstream each curve would need to be at an angle of 45 degrees.

Total suspended sediment load increases at a rate almost as fast as that of discharge, whereas channel roughness decreases slightly, slope considerably and bed material size even more significantly.

A river's discharge, then, is related to a whole series of variables, but what is the significance of these relationships? We know some answers to this already. As a river flows downstream, its discharge increases and the efficiency of the channel shape, expressed by width and depth, also increases; thus the slope needed to maintain flow is reduced. But in addition, to sustain the increases in flow, the resistance to flow caused by channel roughness falls, and this is clearly linked also to the decrease in the size of bed material. The river system can thus be seen as a collaboration of variables, each one linked to the central component of discharge.

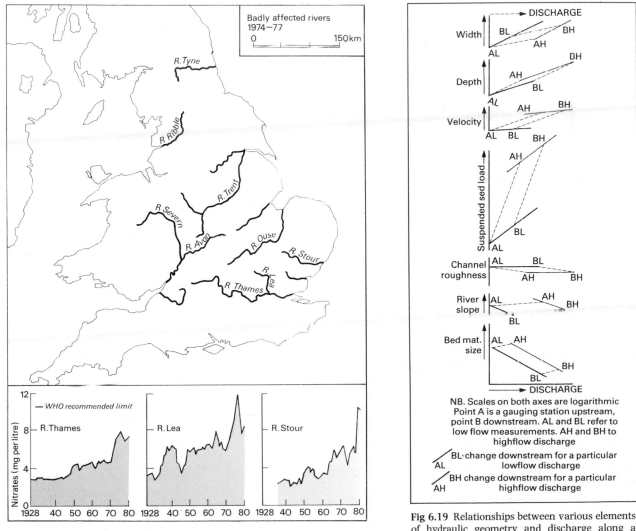

Fig 6.18 Nitrate concentrations in some British Rivers.

Fig 6.19 Relationships between various elements of hydraulic geometry and discharge along a river's course.

Much time has been devoted to further study of the link between discharge and channel morphology and most workers have concluded that the channel form is usually a reflection of the bankfull discharge rather than any other. Discharges lower than bankfull are likely to have a smaller proportion of excess energy to mould the channel, and evidence from the eastern USA and elsewhere suggests that although flood discharges may cause considerable damage and enlarge channels, their effects will be neutralised by the occurrence of bankfull conditions over the next few years.

Erosion, Transportation and Deposition

We may talk of links between discharge and other channel parameters, and of adjustments of a variable to a particular discharge, but such change is not automatic, processes are needed to effect it. The processes which allow slope, width, depth, bed sediment, load and roughness to adjust are **erosion**, **transportation** and **deposition**, processes which respond to the increase or decrease in energy which the discharge provides.

Erosion

By the process of erosion a river can deepen, widen or even lengthen its channel and thus adjust its efficiency to suit the workload to be done. Erosion is carried out by various processes.

A rock bed is worn down or abraded by **corrasion** as water drags particles of sediment across its surface, scratching it and smoothing it as it does so. This process is responsible for much of the downcutting that creates and deepens channels, and is likely to be most effective in upland channels in times of flood when the large angular fragments of bedload can be activated upon the exposed rock of the bed. Under these conditions one extreme form of **abrasion**, known as **potholing**, can occur in which fragments of load are whirled around in turbulent eddies to drill smooth depressions into the rock bed.

In the middle and lower courses of rivers where bedrock is less likely to be exposed to abrasion, the river is more likely to attack its channel, and in particular its banks, by **hydraulic action**. This is not to say that hydraulic action will not also occur in upper reaches, however. The sheer force of flowing water is sufficient to dislodge particles or fragments of unconsolidated material, which may eventually lead to bank collapse, especially on the outside of bends where the current collides with the banks. An exaggerated form of the process, known as **cavitation**, occurs where turbulence is extreme. Bank collapse results from shock waves generated by bursting air bubbles which derive from the decrease in water pressure associated with shooting flow at rapids and waterfalls.

A river can erode any part of its channel by **solution**, incorporating any element of soluble material into its flow. Limestone is especially susceptible, but many chemical compounds are soluble, especially in their weathered state, and thus a wide range of rocks may be vulnerable.

A fourth form of erosion that takes place in river channels attacks the load itself rather than the channel. **Attrition** of the suspension and bedloads, as fragments collide with each other in motion, causes particles not only to become rounded but also to decrease in size downstream. This, of course, has its impact on the efficiency of the channel downstream and helps to reduce the need for steep gradients in the lower course.

Whilst most of the river's erosion occurs within the channel, it will also undercut valley side slopes when it comes into contact with them, producing **river cliffs** or **bluffs**. Rivers can also lengthen their channels by extending upstream. This process of **headward erosion** may be carried out by **spring sapping**, described in Chapter 3. Gullies developing on hillsides after heavy rain may also join up with a river channel and effectively extend its course.

Transportation

The other aspect of a river's work is to transport the eroded material. This is carried in three forms, in suspension, in solution and as bedload. The **critical velocity** required to entrain a particle of sediment into suspension varies with the size of the particle, but the relationship is not a simple one as the **Hjulström Curve** in Fig 6.20 demonstrates.

The velocity required for erosion, shown by the dotted lines, is much higher for the smallest grains of clay than it is for sand-sized material, but as grain size increases above sand the critical velocity increases steadily. This apparent anomaly of high velocities for the smallest grains is explained by the fact that clay and silt particles readily stick to each other, bound by electrical bonding. It is also likely that a stream bed of fine particles will be so smooth that the water is not able to make use of the larger surface area offered to it by the protruding individual grains of a rougher channel of sand or gravel.

Figures of critical velocity such as those depicted on

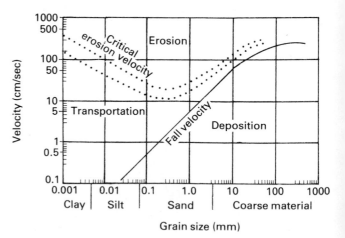

Fig 6.20 Hjulström's curve of erosion and deposition for uniform material.

this graph must be treated with great care, for they are based on the ideal conditions of laboratory experiments, and in any individual river local conditions may considerably alter the critical velocity. Hjulström made some allowance for this variation by denoting critical velocity with a band rather than a single line.

Once eroded, a particle will remain in suspension until the water velocity is reduced to the critical fall velocity, at which time deposition will occur. Careful study and consideration of Hjulström's curve is beneficial and further understanding will be achieved by answering the questions on it at the end of this chapter.

The maximum size of particle transported will also depend on the discharge, and **Hopkins' Sixth Power Law** suggests that whatever factor discharge multiplies by in time of flood, then the weight of the maximum load particle multiples by that factor to the power six. Thus, for example, if discharge trebles, it is capable of carrying a particle 3^6 or 729 times as heavy; if it quadruples, it can carry particles 4^6 or 4096 times as heavy, and so on. This gives a clear idea of the power of the river in flood. The maximum size of particle that can be carried at a particular time is known as the river's **competence**, and not only this but also its **capacity**, or total load, will increase greatly during flooding.

Both competence and capacity also increase steadily from source to mouth, and as load in suspension actually decreases inner water turbulence slightly, the efficient utilisation of energy can once again be seen to increase in a downstream direction.

There has been much discussion about which flood contributes most to the annual movement of load. Evidence from the River Creedy in south Devon, collected by Webb and Walling, confirms that it is not the high-magnitude, low-frequency floods that accomplish most of the long-term sediment and solute transport but the more frequent, lower-magnitude floods that are most effective (see Fig 6.21).

Little consideration has been given so far to the transport of bedload. The larger fragments that compose it are likely to be too heavy to be carried in suspension and so the river drags them along. Bedload movement is intermittent both in time and space, with individual grains being rolled or bounced along the bed. The bouncing motion, often described as **saltation**, is demonstrated in Fig 6.22.

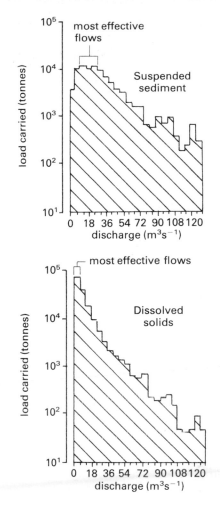

Fig 6.21 The relationship between discharge and sediment and solute load, River Creedy: the graphs record total weight of load carried by each discharge in a year.

Deposition

Once the river velocity drops below the critical fall value a particle will be dropped. As **fall velocity** is clearly related to size of particle, sediment is likely to be laid down in categories, which produces **sorting**, both laterally and vertically, of fluvial deposits (see Fig 6.23).

A local decrease in velocity could be caused by a change in any one of the variables which influence it. Thus, deposition may occur due to a sudden increase in friction when a river overflows its banks or when a slope suddenly decreases, for example below a waterfall or at the exit from a mountain zone into the lowlands.

Fig 6.22 The saltation of coarse particles on a riverbed.

Trajectories of individual particles

on landing, one particle may dislodge another and cause it to be entrained

Bed of stream

particle size decreasing

as velocity decreases, the size of particle transported will gradually be reduced until even the fine sediment is deposited

(a) Lateral sorting.

if a sharp decrease in velocity occurs, eg. on entering a lake, vertical layering of sediment may occur

particle size decreasing

(b) Vertical sorting.

two forms of sorting may occur simultaneously, eg. in a delta

(c) Lateral and vertical sorting.

Fig 6.23 Fluvial sorting of sediment.

A channel suddenly altering shape, perhaps becoming wide and shallow because of local rock conditions, could also encourage deposition. If a river leaves an artificially straightened efficient channel section or enters a lake, marsh, swamp or other vegetated water, velocity will fall and deposition may ensue. Many of us will have noticed deposition on the inside of bends where turbulence reduces velocity.

The Concept of Grade

We have established, then, that most of a river channel's variables are linked to discharge and any adjustment to the interrelationship between a variable and discharge is effected by the processes of erosion, transportation and deposition.

Thus, variations in flow over short periods of time can be compensated for by any one of a wide variety of possible alterations to channel geometry or long profile. For example, if a section of a river has an excess of energy to carry out its required work of transporting the load, it may seek to take up the surplus by reducing the velocity through a reduction in slope, which will be brought about by erosion and deposition, as in Fig 6.24. Alternatively, changes in channel plan, cross-section and roughness may be effected to adjust the resistance and absorb the surplus energy.

In the longer term, it is thought that rivers seek to establish an **equilibrium** or **graded long profile** in which the energy provision in any stretch is balanced against what is required to move the load through that section. It was originally thought that a river achieved this concept of grade or equilibrium only when a smooth, perfectly concave longitudinal profile had been reached. However, it appears that many irregular long profiles may have a graded or equilibrium profile,

their energy expenditure perfectly balanced with energy availability. This does not mean that once it is achieved change will cease. Changes in average annual discharge will continue as, for instance, man alters the basin's hydrological cycle by clearing vegetation or by urbanisation, or as climate changes or natural disasters, such as slope collapse or tectonic activity, occur. The achievement of grade may therefore be a state of quasi-equilibrium.

One of the difficulties with the concept of grade is identifying rivers with graded profiles in the field. Are the many rivers that are to be observed altering their channel geometry merely returning to the average or graded profile after an extreme event, or are they proving that the graded profile exists in theory rather than practice?

The Impact of Rivers on Landscape

Much of the discussion so far has been of the internal workings of the river. It is important to proceed to an examination of their impact on landscape if we are to justify the first paragraph of this chapter.

Valleys

Shape

Rivers ultimately create valleys, but they are not the only agent responsible. As Fig 6.25 shows, the river channel may be responsible for the excavation of only a fraction of the valley, especially where the valley is V-shaped.

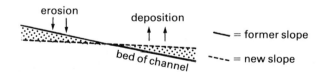

(a) Adjustment to excess of energy by reduction of slope.

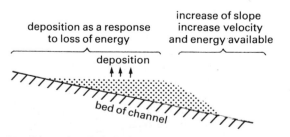

(b) Adjustment to bed of river to compensate for loss of energy.

Fig 6.24 Adjustments to channel slope.

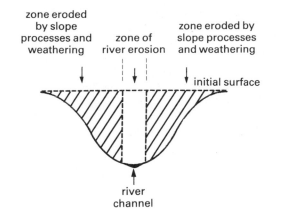

zone eroded by slope processes and weathering

zone of river erosion

zone eroded by slope processes and weathering

initial surface

river channel

(a) V-shaped valley.

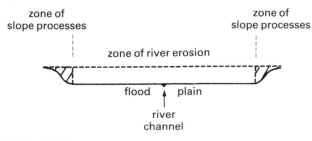

zone of slope processes

zone of river erosion

zone of slope processes

flood ↑ plain

river channel

(b) Broad valley.

Fig 6.25 The role of the river in valley erosion

V-shaped valleys are usually associated with the upper course of a river. This reflects the greater altitude of such areas which provides the potential energy to cut down. In the lower course of a river valley, where the height of the channel above the sea may be slight, there is little possibility of cutting a steep-sided valley as the river is not able to cut down below sea-level. The excess of energy available in the lower course, due to more efficient usage, will be utilised by the river in cutting sideways and producing a much wider valley bottom with side slopes well separated.

The precise shape of the 'V' will vary, depending, for example, on rock type, on the efficiency of slope processes, on the speed with which the river downcutting has occurred and on the aspect of the sides which may determine the rate of weathering. The interrelationship between river erosion and slope processes is also important, for if the river is able to remove the output of sediment from the slope, a steeper side wall will be retained than if it is not.

V-shaped valleys may, in certain circumstances, occur in the lower courses of rivers, especially in some highland areas where sufficient elevation is provided. This is especially likely where the coastal area has been relatively recently uplifted from the sea. The River Lyn in north Devon flows through a steep-sided valley to within a short distance of the coast. This probably reflects quite rapid cutting down by the river in response to marine erosion that removed the river's lower course and produced a much more local exit to the sea.

Gorges

A particularly steep-sided variant of the V-shaped valley is the **gorge**, which can result from a number of circumstances. Rivers flowing through a particularly resistant rock band may cut down more effectively than slope processes can wear away the sidewalls, and thus steepness may be retained. In other examples, notably the magnificent Avon Gorge which Bristol's Clifton Suspension Bridge spans, the river probably derived a large increase of energy from a major uplift of the area which enabled it to cut down through the Carboniferous limestone at a rate which slope processes have so far been unable to match.

As a waterfall retreats into an upland area, a gorge may also result, as in the case of Gordale Scar (see Chapter 3). They may also occur in the upper course of a river as a response to a long-term change in energy (see p 136).

Features of Deposition

Flood plains

On the broad valley bottom of its lower course a river may disgorge its contents in times of flood, hence the term **flood plain**. Such plains may be extensive in breadth; that of the Sussex Ouse is over one kilometre wide near the coast and the Cuckmere is about 750 metres. The Amazon stretches to several hundred kilometres in width.

Photo 6.6 The valley of the River Lyn, North Devon.

Photo 6.7   The Avon Gorge, Bristol.

Deposition within the river channel is responsible for flood plain formation. Indeed, in most cases this produces about 80 per cent of the sediment. As we shall discover in more detail below, sediment accumulates on the insides of meanders producing **point bars**, and as the meanders move downstream these bars may be incorporated into the flood plain (see Fig 6.26).

Each time a river floods it is likely to deposit a part of its load, for the vast breadth of the floodplain is effectively a very inefficient channel offering great resistance to flow. Layers of **alluvium** thus make up the flood plain, individual grains graded in size with larger sediment dumped closer to the channel in locations where resistance is felt first after flooding begins. Ridges of coarser particles left along the banks of the channel in such a way may produce natural **levees**, although these are not always easy to differentiate from man-made embankments.

When cores are extracted from flood plain deposits, sediment may be seen to extend considerably beneath present-day sea level, which means, of course, that the river in its current position could not be responsible for all of its deposition. In British flood plains in particular, exemplified in Fig 6.27, these deeper deposits are often fluvioglacial sands and gravels dumped by a turbulent and powerful meltwater stream that emptied into a shrunken sea during the Pleistocene Ice Age.

Deltas

Conditions of deposition

Deltas occur at the extremity of a drainage basin as sediment is discharged into the sea or at a point on a river's course where it enters a lake. Certain conditions

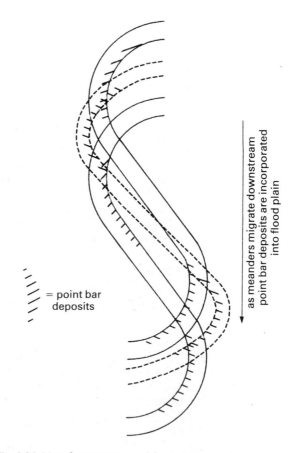

= point bar deposits

as meanders migrate downstream point bar deposits are incorporated into flood plain

Fig 6.26   Meander migration and flood plain formation.

Photo 6.8 The Nene Floodplain at Oundle, Northamptonshire.

are more favourable for delta formation than others. A powerful river discharge is necessary to overcome the waves and currents of the water body, although in a high energy wave environment or a zone of high tidal range this may not be enough to ensure sediment deposition. A high river sediment load is essential, a likely attribute for a river downcutting quickly in a newly uplifted area or eroding through an unconsolidated deposit such as loess or boulder clay. A gentle offshore gradient is a more feasible location for deposition than a steeply shelving shoreline, and if the climate favours rapid vegetation growth this may facilitate deposition by stabilising sediment.

Characteristics:

Deltas have virtually flat surfaces that may lie above, at, or below sea level. Although one major channel may discharge into the delta, many thousands of **distributaries** usually transfer the water into the sea. Distributary networks are extremely dense, rarely stable and consist of channels that branch out and may then join again, a characteristic known in its extreme form as **anastomosing**. Branching of channels occurs either because a mouth bar is deposited in midstream which divides the flow once the delta extends seaward from this point, or because a levee is cut through by a high discharge.

A particular characteristic of deltas is their dynamic nature, rarely stable in short or long term. Over short periods of time, a particularly high discharge may excavate distributary channels and may extend deposition seawards while, conversely, a low one may

Fig 6.27 Part of the floodplain of the River Forth.

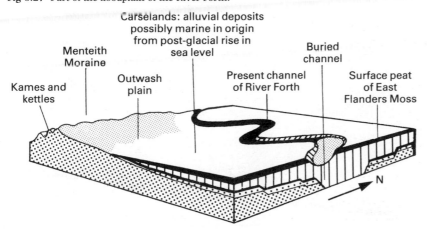

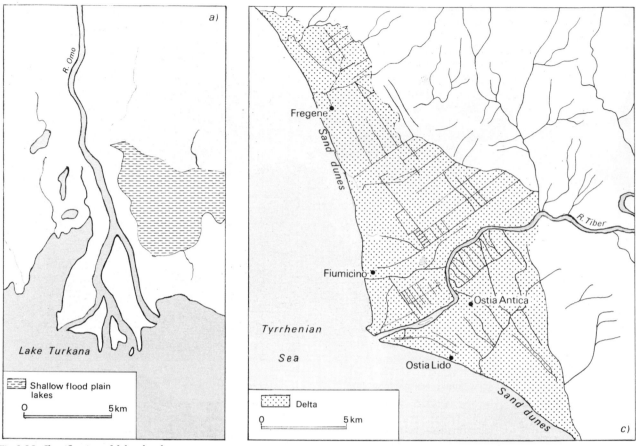

Fig 6.28 Classification of deltas by shape.
(a) Bird's foot: Omo Delta, Ethiopia.

(c) Cuspate: the Tiber, Italy. As the straight drainage channels suggest, much of the delta has been reclaimed for agriculture.

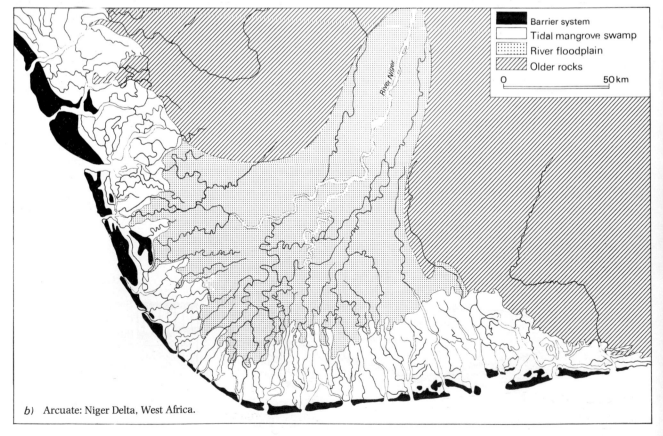

b) Arcuate: Niger Delta, West Africa.

aggrade channels and block them and fail to replace the sediment at the seaward end that marine erosion is removing. Over long periods, a rising sea level may restrict seaward extension, whilst a falling one may give the distributaries greater energy and allow a constant remoulding of the delta form as sediment is redistributed. When man has interfered with discharge or sediment load, as for example in the Aswan Dam Project on the Nile in Egypt where sediment discharge below the dam is severely reduced, the lack of replenishment of eroded sediment from the delta may lead to its contraction.

Although originally named after the Greek letter, the plan of a delta varies enormously, a traditional classification being **arcuate**, **birdsfoot** and **cuspate** (see Fig 6.28). Whilst useful for identification, this is not a genetic classification. A more useful method is to divide deltas according to the relative importance of the river and the sea in their development. Thus, deltas dominated by a powerful river action, as in the Mississippi, are differentiated from those where eroding waves restrict the delta's development, as in the case of the Sao Francisco in Brazil.

Formation:

Deltas form because the river loses energy as it enters the still conditions of a lake or encounters the opposing force of waves and currents. The way in which it does this will depend on the relative densities of the river water and the lake or sea water. If they are relatively similar, which is likely to be the case for a lake, the waters mix freely and deposition ensues. The coarsest particles are dropped first as the **foreset beds** (see Fig 6.29), with the finer material of the **bottom set** beyond them. Thus the delta gradually grows in a series of layers.

Top set beds surmount the foreset and are usually of finer material, often with a high organic content. If the influx of river water is less dense than the water body, due to either temperature or its load, mixing is delayed;

Photo 6.9 Woundale Beck, Cumbria. The river has well-developed meanders in its upper course within a kilometre of its source.

deposition will be similar but will spread out further on to the sea bed in layers at gentler inclination. When density is higher due to cold water or a heavy load, the water may sink rapidly and cause offshore deposition that will not necessarily produce a delta at all.

As a delta advances into the sea, its protruding distributaries line their channels with beds of sand, whilst waves and currents move the finer silt and clay into the stiller water between these fingers of coarser deposits. The traps of mud encourage vegetation to colonise and, in time, accrete to produce the marshy conditions of the delta plain. If deposition occurs within the distributaries and on their banks as levees, the channel may well stand out above the plain.

Alluvial Fans

Fans of sediment are also deposited on land at sudden changes of slope. In Britain the most likely location is at the base of a side slope in a U-shaped or fault-guided valley. However, they are most characteristic of semi-desert and desert areas and more comprehensive coverage is included in Chapter 11.

Meanders

Characteristics

Although usually a feature of the flood plain of the river's lower course, particular events in the geomorphological history of a river valley may see flood plains and **meanders** developing in the upper course, a fact that any visitor to the glaciated valleys of the Lake District could verify (see Photo 6.9).

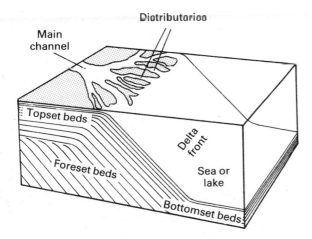

Fig 6.29 A river delta in cross-section.,

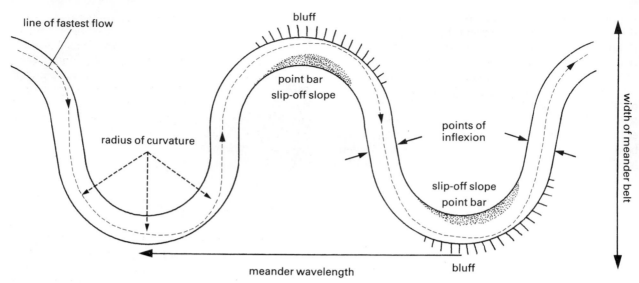

Fig 6.30 The features of a meandering stream.

A river is said to be meandering when its **sinuosity ratio** exceeds 1.5. Meanders are usually symmetrical, their form relatively consistent wherever they occur. Such consistency is supported by the mathematical relationships that have been shown to exist between their various dimensions (see Fig 6.30).

The **wavelength** of a fully developed meander is dependent on three major factors, channel width, discharge and the nature of the bed and banks. It is usually 7–10 times as great as channel width, and **points of inflexion** are usually 5–7 channel widths apart, measured along the channel. There has been much debate in the past about the particular discharge to which meander wavelength is related. Bankfull seems the most likely, with a suggested relationship between wavelength and the square root of bankfull discharge. Schumm's investigations have revealed that the lower the percentage of clay-silt in the bed and banks the greater meander wavelength is likely to be. But do any of these relationships tell us anything about meanders? They certainly do not provide an explanation, but we may find them of value in pursuing the causes of meanders.

Fig 6.31 The development of meanders through pools and riffles.

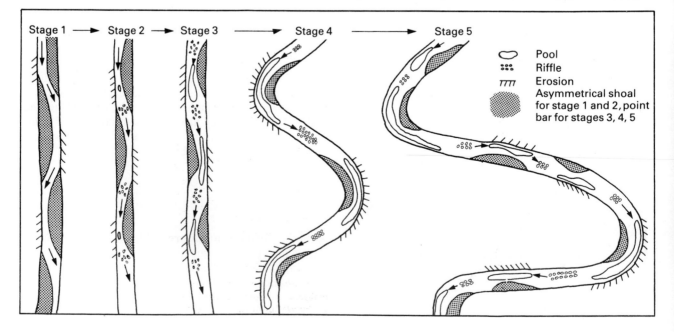

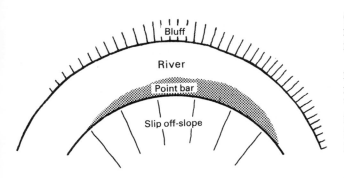

Fig 6.32 Features of a meander bend.

The link with pools and riffles

That meanders are inextricably linked with the development of pools and riffles in a channel bed is indisputable. Pools and riffles are the equally spaced irregularities of gradient that develop in both natural and artificial streams. Their development appears to be a response to the sinuous movement that occurs naturally in flowing water be it across a smooth metal plate, a sheet of ice or within a river channel. The widely accepted links between pools and riffles and meanders are shown in Fig 6.31.

The initial sinuosity of flow is emphasised by shoals of deposition which develop within the channel (Stage 1). Pools and riffles then develop, the coarse particles in the deposited riffles producing a steeper gradient than that of the eroded pool (Stage 2). Their development proceeds until the mean spacing along the channel is between 5 and 7 channel widths, the entire channel is becoming sinuous and shoals become point bars (Stage 3). The sinuosity increases as pools lengthen

(Stage 4), until eventually new sets of pools and riffles form in the straight sections between meanders which in time may spawn meanders of their own (Stage 5).

This appears to provide us with the rudiments of meander formation but, of course, many questions remain unanswered. Why is flow sinuous to start with? Why does the sinuosity of the channel, once initiated, increase until meanders are formed? What exactly is the rôle of the pools and riffles? None of these questions has an easy answer.

The rôle of helicoidal flow

The sinuosity of all natural flow probably reflects the frictional drag exerted on the water by the bed and banks. This causes lower layers of water to move both slowly and in a slightly sinuous pattern, and to interfere with and divert the upper layers into a more exaggerated pattern of sinuosity. Once the sinuous flow is established it will inevitably cause the current to collide with the banks, which is likely to lead to erosion and the creation of a bluff (see Fig 6.32).

From Fig 6.30 it can be seen that the **thalweg**, the line tracing the deepest water which also coincides with the line of highest velocity, swings from side to side of the channel, piling up water against the outside of the bend. On the inside of the bend, by contrast, velocity is reduced by the resistance of the coarser deposits on the point bar. The establishment of such velocity contrasts across the channel initiates an unequal pressure distribution so that water from the outside is drawn downward and towards the point bar as Fig 6.33 shows.

In three-dimensional view along the channel, therefore, the flow can be likened to a spiral or spring, which

Fig 6.33 Cross-section of the channel at a meander bend.

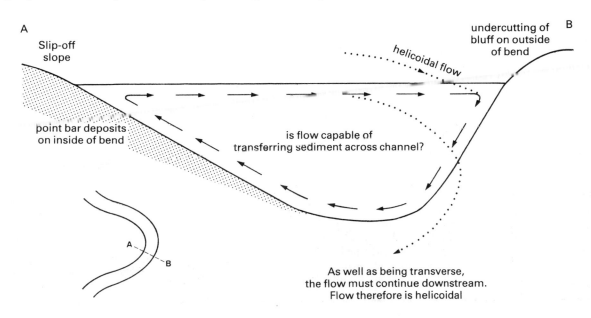

As well as being transverse,
the flow must continue downstream.
Flow therefore is helicoidal

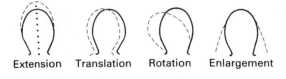
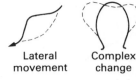

Extension   Translation   Rotation   Enlargement   Lateral movement   Complex change

meanders can move in many different ways

Fig 6.34 Meander movement.

gives it the name **helicoidal**. The ensuing turbulence on the inside of the bend is likely to cause eddying, with some water actually flowing upstream, a phenomenon easy to observe at most meanders. This dissipation of energy may well extend deposition on the point bar whose growth, combined with the erosion on the crest of the meander, effectively shifts the bend sideways, increasing the amplitude of the meander belt, (see Fig 6.34).

Some theories suggest that the helicoidal flow actually transports material across the river to the point bar, but modern research indicates that the flow is rarely strong enough for this, and point bars are more likely to be maintained by sediment from erosion of the bluff at the meander upstream on the same side of the channel. Helicoidal flow, though, seems to be an essential part of meander formation although the knotty problem of which came first, the meander or the helicoidal flow, the chicken or the egg, still remains.

Equalisation of energy expenditure

Once established, what stops the meanders from growing even larger? We have already suggested that their wavelength is linked to channel width, bankfull discharge and the silt-clay content of the channel perimeter, but Langbein and Leopold provide further explanation by suggesting that meanders represent the ultimate aim of a river to equalise its energy expenditure over a given stretch. In explaining how this operates, we should also illuminate the vital role of pools and riffles.

The link between pools and riffles and meanders seems unquestionable, not least because the spacing of meanders along the channel's course appears to be equivalent to that of pools and riffles (i.e. 5–7 channel widths). From Fig 6.35 we can see that more energy is expended over a riffle, where water is shallow and bedload coarse, than at the deeper channel of a pool. However, the curve that develops at the pool is likely to dissipate more energy than the straight reach where the riffle is located and therefore, as a result of meandering, the energy expenditure along a particular stretch is equalised. Perhaps, therefore, the stabilisation of meander growth occurs when the energy provided by the bankfull discharge can be equally expended along the stretch of river.

It is obviously vital that we view meanders in conjunction with the energy balance of a river. A river meanders in order to balance its energy with the load it needs to carry, presumably therefore in situations where it has insufficient bedload for its available energy. Meanders dissipate excess energy by reducing

slope and velocity over a given section. In this repect, then, channel pattern is just one of the variables which a river can adjust to achieve its energy equilibrium profile.

The effects of meandering channels

The meandering of a river helps create the flood plain, its constant oscillations having permitted the undercutting of valley side walls to widen the valley bottom. Even so, many British flood plains may have been created by the marauding meltwater rivers of the past rather than the misfit streams of today. Accretion at point bars is also a vital part of flood plain development

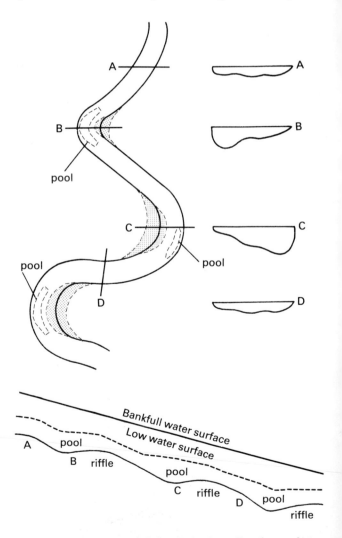

Fig 6.35 Cross-sections and longitudinal profile of meandering stream to explain energy expenditure over pools and riffles. (See text for explanation.)

for, as the river migrates, the bar is incorporated into the plain.

Meanders migrate downstream due to the erosion on their outer bends being concentrated just downstream from their apex. As they do so, imprints of the channel they abandon remain on the flood plain (see Fig 6.36). As migration occurs, it is possible that one particularly fast, eroding meander may catch up with one downstream, causing a major river diversion and the abandonment of the intervening meander as an **oxbow lake**. Such oxbows soon become the victim of infilling and can be easily detected only whilst their peculiar conditions allow a particular vegetation association to be maintained. The floodplain of the River Add in Strathclyde provides numerous examples.

Braiding

A **braided channel** consists of a mass of diverging and intertwining threads of water separated by ever-changing islands of sediment. Their deposition occurs when discharge falls, usually after a particular climatic event, and the river is forced to drop part of its load. Not all rivers respond to such changes by braiding, of course; particular circumstances seem to favour it.

Rivers with very variable discharges are particularly prone. This produces braids in rivers charged with snowmelt from highland areas, such as the Spey and the Findhorn in north-east Scotland, in rivers in desert areas of irregular rainfall or in rivers in monsoon areas, for example. Particularly heavy loads also stimulate braiding, such as in semi-arid and arid areas and glacial outwash zones. Incoherent banks may provide a large load too, and are also more likely to generate the shallow, wide, inefficient channels in which braiding usually occurs.

Photo 6.10 Braids in the River Spey, near Fochabers, north east Scotland.

One might ponder long upon the difficulties that one would encounter in trying to measure the discharge, channel cross-section and wetted perimeter of a braided stream. Should one consider it as a series of separate channels or one large one? The results will vary greatly, depending on the decision.

It is possible that the islands between 'braids' will become permanent, especially if vegetation is given time to colonise before the next high discharge. This is presumably more likely in a monsoon climate than an arid, tundra or even a temperate one. It is part of the tragedy of the Third World that in overcrowded valleys such as the Ganges in Bangladesh, the poor establish habitations on these seemingly permanent islands, only to find the river re-taking them.

Changes in a River's Energy

Causes

We have already considered that a river adjusts its various parameters to suit its supply of energy and in time may achieve a graded profile or reach a steady state. Suppose, however, that the energy supply were to change, significantly, in the long term, a change which is sometimes referred to as **rejuvenation**. How would the river system adjust and what evidence would we see of this in the landscape?

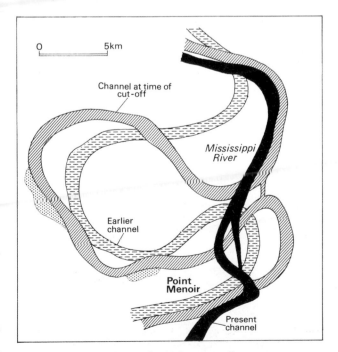

Fig 6.36 Formation of an ox-bow lake or cut-off.

First, we need to establish why and how the available energy could change. Potential energy is derived mostly from height above base level, which is usually sea level, but also from the weight of water flowing in the channel.

Elevation above base level can increase in the long term if the land is rising or sea is falling, perhaps due to isostatic readjustment following a glacial period, or to tectonic activity. It could decrease also due to land-sea readjustments, perhaps because of virulent marine erosion providing an onslaught on the shoreline.

A change to the river discharge that would alter the energy balance could be brought about by a gradual climatic change over centuries or millenia. Man's steady alteration of the environment could have a similar outcome, in either direction, for instance, via urbanisation, deforestation or drainage.

Effects

If energy can be either increased or decreased then it follows that the effects on the river can also be divided into two categories.

Effects of an increase in energy

As rivers can adjust to the energy input by altering a wide range of variables, a long-term increase could lead, for instance, to an increase of channel size, meander wavelength, load competence and capacity, bedload size, mean velocity, turbulence and roughness and the further excavation of the valley, both laterally and vertically.

Gorges: An increase in elevation is especially likely to see an impact on the valley for, if base level drops, the river will be able to cut deeper into its valley than previously. If the rate of tectonic uplift is faster than the speed at which the river can downcut, a **gorge** may develop, such as the Avon Gorge at Clifton.

Fig 6.37 A meander incised into a flood plain.

Incised meanders: If meanders exist they will entrench themselves to create **incised meanders** as shown in Fig 6.37. Incised meanders may be of several metres, depth cut into a flood plain or much deeper, gorge-like features such as those of the Lyn (see Photo 6.11).

The development of the Lyn valley provides an interesting example of a change in energy. Sissons suggests that the East and West Lyn rivers used to join the sea further west than their current exit at Lynmouth, but that continuous undercutting of the sandstone cliffs caused sufficient erosion for the sea to breach the Lyn valley and provide a new exit for it (see Fig 6.38). This caused its lower course to become dry, which partly explains the curious appearance of the Valley of the Rocks, and suddenly gave what was previously the middle course of the Lyn much greater potential energy. It used this to incise its valley and to produce

Photo 6.11 The incised meanders of the River Lyn, North Devon.

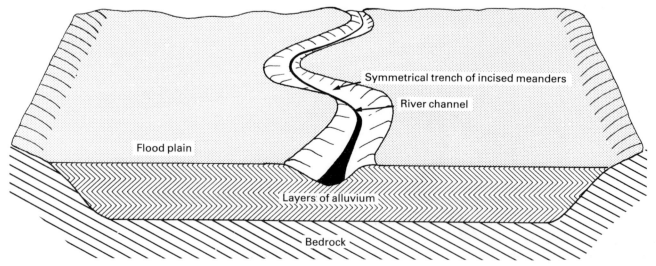

Photo 6.12 Ingrown meanders on the floodplain of Ashes Hollow, Church Stretton, Shropshire.

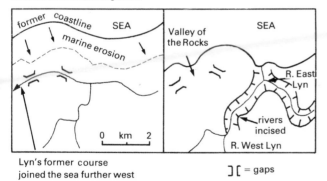

Fig 6.38 The evolution of the incised valley of the River Lyn (after Sissons).

the steep-sided valley that contributed so fiercely to the flood disaster of August 1952.

If uplift is slower than the rate of river downcutting, there is likely to be an element of lateral erosion by the river which will produce asymmetrical side slopes and **ingrown meanders**.

Knickpoints: A sudden increase in potential energy of the lower or middle course is a typical result of rapid uplift. The impact may therefore be focused in the lower course, at least initially, perhaps with the creation of a **knickpoint**, where the sudden increase in elevation produces a waterfall or rapids. Headward erosion

towards the upper course may see this waterfall recede up its valley and other knickpoints recede up all the tributaries as the long profile is gradually adjusted to a new energy equilibrium, see Fig 6.40. A gorge may develop downstream from each waterfall as it retreats. The Horseshoe Falls on the River Niagara in Canada have retreated over 300 metres in the last 300 years.

Knickpoints could also result from more local uplift in the river's course. Morisawa points to a small fault scarp in the alluvium of Cabin Creek, Montana, which

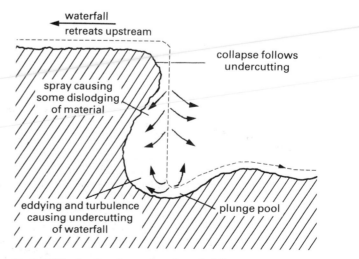

Fig 6.39 The headward recession of a waterfall.

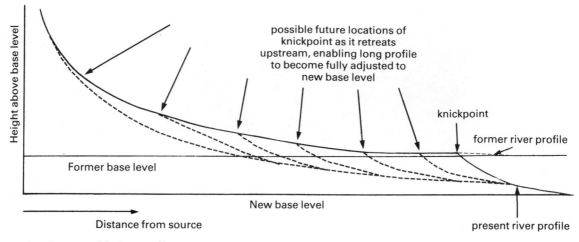

Fig 6.40 The adaptation of the long profile to an increase in energy.

produced a knickpoint which receded quickly to return the profile to one of equilibrium.

Terraces: These are usually remnants of a former flood plain which has been carved up by a rejuvenated river. An increase in energy has allowed downcutting and lateral erosion at meander bends, pushing back the limits of the new flood plain into the old. If successive changes in energy have occurred, perhaps as a result of the continuous alterations in relative levels of land and sea during and since the Pleistocene Ice Age, a series of

stepped terraces may ensue, best exemplified by those of the Thames. Walk from the Thames at Westminster two kilometres west to the vast expanse of the virtually level Hyde Park and you will have moved from the flood plain to the first, or Taplow, terrace some 15–20 metres above the river. Change direction and move a few kilometres north east and you will reach the Pentonville area on the second, or Boyn Hill, terrace at about 30 metres above the river. In south London, too, the terraces can be identified, Clapham Common surmounting the Boyn Hill and Putney the Taplow.

Simple cases are demonstrated in Fig 6.41 but in

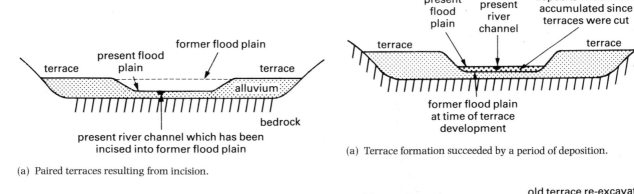

(a) Paired terraces resulting from incision.

(a) Terrace formation succeeded by a period of deposition.

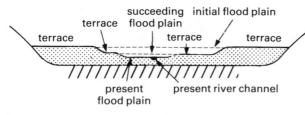

(b) Stepped terraces resulting from further incision.

Fig 6.41 Simple terrace development.

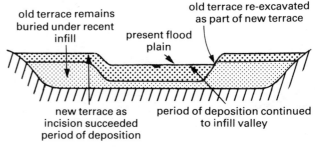

(b) New terraces cut into recent deposits.

Fig 6.42 Terraces resulting from a succession of periods of incision and deposition.

Photo 6.13   Terraces of the River Avon, Barford, Warwickshire.

reality the picture is much more complicated. A period of deposition may follow the development of the terrace, thus raising the new flood plain and reducing the effect of the terraces (Fig 6.42a). Aggradation may be succeeded by a further increase in energy and renewed terrace formation, perhaps re-excavating the initial terraces (Fig 6.42b).

Terraces of equivalent size and elevation need not occur on opposite sides of the river. In fact, many terraces are **unpaired**. If a river is cutting both vertically and laterally as it adjusts to uplift, this is especially likely. A meander slicing into the flood plain may find that by the time it has migrated across to the other side of the valley, sufficient uplift has occurred to lower the valley floor and enable the meander to incise the opposite terrace much deeper into the flood plain.

The terraces of several British rivers, notably the Trent and the Thames, provide ideal sites at which to study the stages of late glacial meltwater deposition, for the various layers of different ages have been exposed by the river's incision. Some of the best examples of river terraces are correspondingly found in these valleys. The terraces also provide some ideal settlement sites, for example the series of villages to the north east of Nottingham that sit on the gravel terrace of the Trent, notably Shelford, Gunthorpe and Bleasby.

Effects of a decrease in energy

A reduction in energy, however induced, is likely to be met with a response in some of the channel variables. Sedimentation in the channel is particularly likely as the amount of load is adjusted to cope with the decrease in energy. Observations downstream from dams certainly support this, for example in the River Tryweryn below the dam on Llyn Celyn in Gwynedd, and Park has shown that the channel of the River Tone is 54 per cent of its expected size below the Clatworthy Reservoir. At the same time deposition of some of the load may increase the slope, thus producing a greater velocity and partly counteracting the loss of energy (see Fig 6.24b).

If a change in relative levels of land and sea reduces the difference in height between source and mouth, it may involve the drowning of the lower part of the river valley to create a **ria**.

Fig 6.43 Terraces of a section of the River Severn. (Reproduced by permission of the Geological Society.)

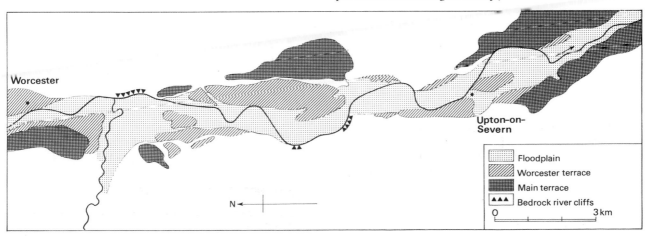

Photo 6.14 Gullying emphasised by footpath erosion, Hole of Horcum, North York Moors.

The Evolution of Drainage Patterns

In addition to the changes of channel and valley form and profile that occur due to energy changes, it is also quite conceivable that the drainage pattern will alter and evolve over time.

Gullying

At its simplest level and on the shortest time scale, the initiation and growth of **gullies** may take place to extend the drainage network. Envisage, for instance, an intense period of overgrazing or of deforestation, or the intensification of scarce rainstorms as an area's aridity increases. The speed, amount and virulence of the run-off will be increased sufficiently for the incision of gullies to take place into bare hillsides. These may, of course, be discontinuous and will probably contain streams only intermittently, especially in semi-arid areas, but in more humid climes where run-off is less sporadic gullies may become part of the permanent network. Load will increase as a direct result of gullying which in turn may cause aggradation at some point in the channel downstream.

River Capture

Over a longer time scale, drainage patterns may extend by **capturing** channels from other drainage systems. Headward erosion by a stream through the process of spring sapping (see Chapter 3) may allow it to cut back eventually to the headwaters of another river whose flow will then be diverted into the extending channel. This is particularly likely if the marauding **'pirate' stream** presents a steeper gradient than the **'victim' stream**. A small-scale example of this process is

Fig 6.44 An example of river capture: the headwaters of the Wey and the Slea, Hampshire.

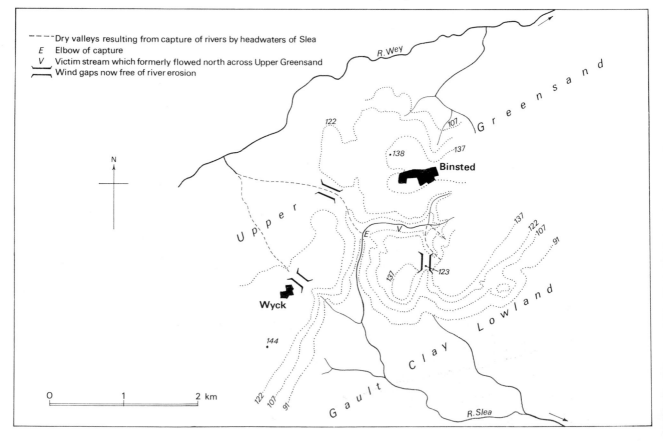

pinpointed by Small in the North Downs of Surrey, as Fig 6.44 shows. Here, the advantage given to the pirate stream by the soft Gault Clay, which facilitates headward erosion, and the difference in elevation of about 75 metres, is sufficient for capture to have taken place.

Many similar examples of river capture, usually on a larger scale than this, have been identified in the past throughout the chalk and greensand scarplands of south-east England and the Paris Basin. The Medway is a particularly potent marauder, having removed the headwaters of both the Darent to its west and the Stour to its east, enabling it to dominate the drainage of much of mid-Kent.

River capture occurs not only because of headward erosion, but also because of changes in the patterns of underground drainage that supply rivers allowing one river's catchment to be extended at the expense of another's.

However the process occurs, the results in the landscape may well be common. **Misfit** or **underfit streams** are typical, the victim river being left as a much reduced flow in a valley whose dimensions it could never have carved in its current form. The Darent, north of Sevenoaks, exemplifies this well as it shuffles across a valley bottom of more than a kilometre in width. **Wind**

gaps may also be a consequence of capture, as may dry valleys, both of them the remnants of former river valleys whose waters have been diverted from them. At the point where river capture occurs a sharp bend may develop where a river switches to its new course; such features are commonly known as **elbows of capture**. One further result of capture is likely to be the increased discharge of the pirate stream as its catchment area is now larger – this in turn may lead to any one of the adjustments mentioned in the previous section and may even engender rejuvenation.

It is not only the process of river capture that can lead to changes in river pattern over thousands of years. Climatic change may also be responsible, as may **glacial diversion of drainage** (see Chapter 7), tectonic movements or the accumulated effects of human activity.

Evolution over Geological Time

The development of accordant drainage patterns

If looked at over the longest time scale of all, that is, millions of years, or even across geological periods of time, the evolution of drainage patterns may be seen to be even more complex.

When a drainage pattern first develops it may be

Fig 6.45 Two possible patterns of consequent drainage.

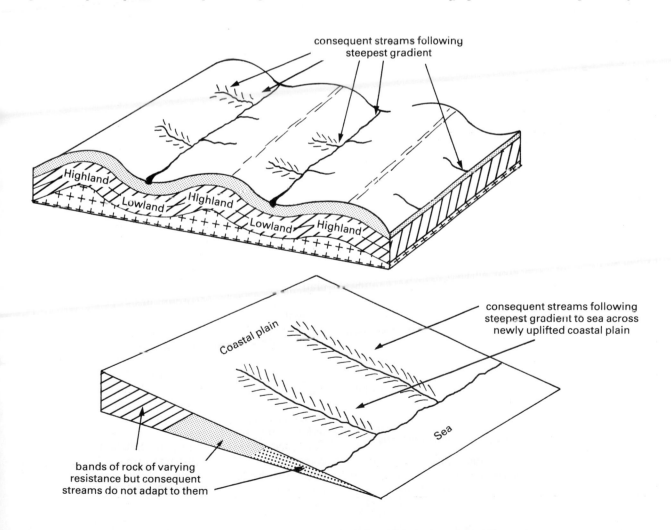

consequent streams following steepest gradient

Highland
Lowland   Highland
Lowland   Highland

consequent streams following steepest gradient to sea across newly uplifted coastal plain

Coastal plain

Sea

bands of rock of varying resistance but consequent streams do not adapt to them

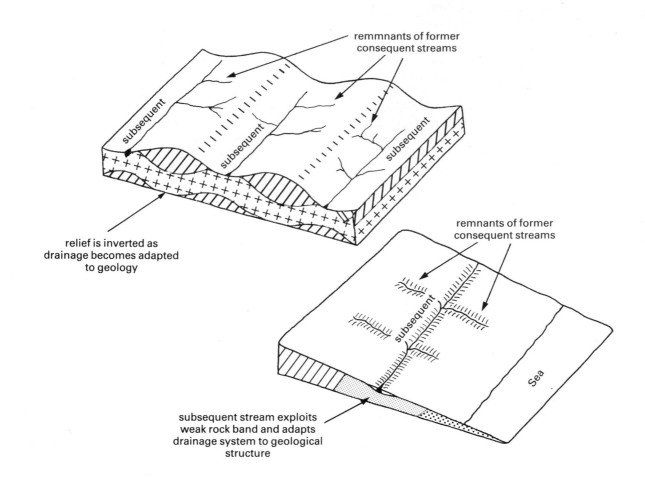

Fig 6.46 The development of subsequent drainage systems.

relatively simple, with major rivers following the steepest gradients to the sea. These **consequent streams** will depend on the nature of the land surface, two possible situations being shown in Fig 6.45. Such patterns remain fixed for a relatively short period of time, for rivers will soon begin to respond to the details of the geological structure of the land surface. Thus, **subsequent streams** develop as rivers cut into weaker rock bands, or anticlines are reduced to synclines. Eventually, the drainage system may become closely adjusted to the geological structure, a state of equilibrium which is often known as **accordance** and which is well exemplified by many of the rivers of lowland England. Such accordance may well remain until some large-scale event disturbs the balance, such as a major incursion of the sea, climatic change or tectonic disturbance.

When such a major cataclysm occurs, readjustment to structure will need to begin again, and in the intervening period the drainage may well be discordant with its structure.

The development of discordant drainage patterns

Two particular examples of **discordance** have been frequently identified by geomorphologists, one known as **superimposition** the other as **antecedence**. Super-

imposition, can best be likened to copper etching. When a design is etched into metal, the surface is first covered with a layer of wax into which the intricacies of the pattern are sculpted. When a satisfactory design has been achieved, acid is then allowed to penetrate the channels of the wax and to superimpose their pattern on to the metal beneath by corrosion. When the wax is removed the etching remains carved into the metal plate.

Imagine then, an accordant drainage pattern development on layers of sedimentary rock, let us say the radial pattern which drains the New Red Sandstone, Carboniferous limestone and chalk that once covered the dome of the Lake District. As the cover of sedimentaries, the wax, is removed over 30 million years during the Tertiary era, the radial pattern is superimposed, or etched, into the rocks beneath, rocks with which the radial drainage pattern is quite incompatible. Thus, today, the three parallel bands of Borrowdale Volcanics, Skiddaw Slates and Silurian rocks which compose the Lake District provide a geological structure discordant with the pattern of rivers and lakes which drain them (see Fig 6.47).

Fig 6.47 The discordant radial drainage system of the Lake District.

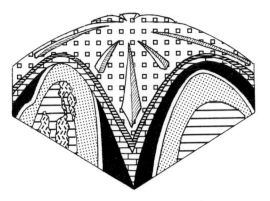

(a) Uplifted dome of sedimentary rocks on which radial pattern of drainage developed in late Cenozoic times.

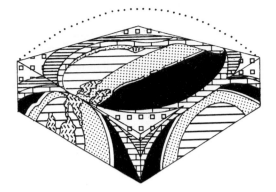

(b) Sedimentaries stripped off to reveal much older rocks onto which radial pattern of drainage was superimposed.

///// Igneous intrusions	≡ Skiddaw slates
⋯ Borrowdale volcanics	□ Coniston limestone
■ Silurian slates & shales	▫▫ New Red Sandstone
▥ Carboniferous limestone	▤ Coal measures

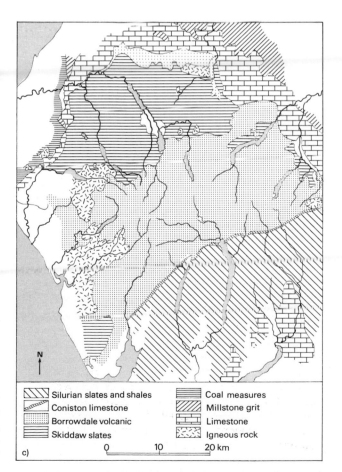

(c) Radial pattern of Lake District drainage.

Legend:
- Silurian slates and shales
- Coniston limestone
- Borrowdale volcanic
- Skiddaw slates
- Coal measures
- Millstone grit
- Limestone
- Igneous rock

0   10   20 km

A drainage pattern is described as being antecedent if it existed prior to recent tectonic uplift, but has maintained its course throughout. Thus, the Arun Gorge in the Himalayas has been cut as river incision has kept pace with isostatic recovery from the Pleistocene Ice Age, which has effectively increased the depth to which incision has been able to take place. The Nore Gorge near Kilkenny in southern Ireland provides another example of antecedence and of a river in discord with its structure.

Questions

1 Refer to Fig 6.20 of Hjulström's Curve.
   (a) Why are both scales logarithmic?
   (b) Why is erosion represented by a band rather than a single line?
   (c) Why do we have to be cautious about our interpretation of results from the Hjulström Curve?
   (d) If a particle of 0.5 millimetres were eroded by the river and the particle then moved into a reach of slower moving water, how low would the river velocity need to go in order for the particle to be dropped again?
   (e) Why does silt require a higher velocity than sand to be eroded from the river bed?
   (f) What do you suppose the title means by 'uniform' material?
   (g) Why does it make this specification?
   (h) How might the information derived from the graph help a geomorphologist to understand:
      (i) the distribution of material in a flood plain?
      (ii) the development of meanders?

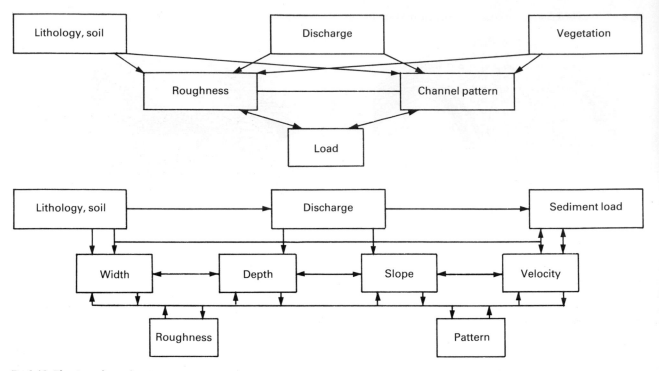

Fig 6.48 The river channel system.

2 Refer to the systems diagrams in Fig 6.48.
 (a) Give an example of each of the relationships and interrelationships shown.
 (b) List as many cases as you can of negative feedback operating within the river channel to maintain equilibrium after a change has occurred.
 (c) List as many cases as you can of positive feedback operating within a river system to allow a new equilibrium to be reached after a change in input has occurred.
 (d) What particular changes in the river system may lead to the operation of the positive feedback mechanism?

Further Reading

Drainage Basin: Form and Process, K J Gregory and D E Walling (Arnold, 1973).

The River Basin, D Ingle Smith and P Stopp (Cambridge, 1978).

The Meander Problem, A D Knighton, *Geography* 62, 106–111 (1977).

British Rivers, J Lewin (Unwin Hyman, 1981).

Rivers, M Morisawa (Longman, 1985).

Streams, M Morisawa (McGraw Hill, 1968).

Rivers, G E Petts (Butterworths, 1983).

Rivers and Landscape, G E Petts and I Foster (Arnold, 1985).

The Study of Landforms, R J Small (Cambridge, 1978).

Other References

River Meanders, L B Leopold and W B Langbein, *Scientific American* 15, 60–9 (1966).

Fluvial Processes in Geomorphology, L B Leopold, M G Wolman and J P Miller (Freeman, 1964).

Sources for Sediments and Solutes in mid-Wales, J Lewin, R Cryer and D I Harrison, *Transactions of the Institute of British Geographers*, Special Publication 6 (1974).

Man-Induced Changes in Stream Channel Capacity, C C Park in *River Channel Changes*, K J Gregory (Wiley, 1977).

Sinuosity of Alluvial Rivers of the Great Plains, S A Schumm, *Geological Society of America Bulletin* 74 (1963).

Devon Valley of Rugged Rocks, J B Sissons, *Geographical Magazine* 49, 711–4 (1977).

Effectiveness of different flow classes for sediment and solute transport, *Catena* 9, 9–23 (1982).

7

Coastal Processes and Landscape

Introduction

With coastal scenery and views of the sea being so important a source of recreation and inspiration for the British, it is not surprising that our geomorphologists have concentrated so much of their energies on trying to explain coastal landforms. Their attention may also have been grabbed by the severity of coastal erosion problems, for example at Seaford in Sussex where £10 million was set aside to stop the destruction of the shingle beach in 1985. Despite this interest, the understanding of certain aspects, particularly the relationships between waves and beaches, are only partially understood and an enormous amount of research still needs to be done.

In assessing the development of any coastline, there are certain important questions which one must answer. For example, what is the character of the land at our particular point of coastal study; is it highland or lowland, do its upland areas run perpendicular or parallel to the sea, is it geologically uniform? Is it the present sea level that formed the local features, or are past sea levels of more relevance? How important are the contributions of man, both unintentional and deliberate, and are they likely to change in importance in the future? How exposed is the coastline? Is the distance of fetch across which waves can be generated extensive? All of these questions, and more, should have been answered by the end of this chapter, but it is worthwhile to consider some of these in relation to a stretch of coastline known personally to you.

Scale

It is again essential that we bear in mind the scale of any process, factor or form that we are discussing and that we try to keep in perspective the importance of a particular issue to the coastline as a whole. Certainly, at the largest scale of coastline development, we need to refer to such factors as tectonic movement. As we saw in Chapter 2, offshore rift valleys and trenches may explain the massive indentations of the coast such as Cardigan Bay or the Bristol Channel. But if our brief is to explain the small-scale features of a beach we are likely to disregard such structural and geological factors in preference for patterns of sediment size and the localised characteristics of waves.

Similarly, we need to bear in mind the time scale at which processes are operating or at which landforms are created (see Fig 7.1). Some changes may be observable to the eye, such as mudflows of boulder clay cliffs, and changes in beach profile. These may be seen to come about very quickly if one happens to be present during a storm or at one of those times of year when the beach is undergoing transformation between its summer and winter forms. In the short term, too, one may just happen to be present when an arch collapses to form a stack, although here one is merely observing the passage through a threshold which the operating processes may have taken thousands of years to reach.

Time Scale	Coastal Process and Change
tens of years:	Slumping and other mass wasting of unstable cliffs; reworking of beach sediment; impact of man on beach plan and profile.
hundreds of years:	Development and growth of spits and barrier islands; diversion of river mouths; major landslides of cliffs; development of wavecut platforms; marsh development.
thousands of years:	Changing sea level after Ice Age; straightening of coastline by infilling of bays, erosion of headlands; development of arches and stacks; change of wind patterns.
millions of years:	Changes in relative positions of land and sea; inundation of land masses; opening up of new seas; continental drift.

Fig 7.1 The time scale of operation of coastal changes.

One exciting thing about the study of coasts is that, even when we are unravelling the mechanisms of very slowly operating processes, we may be able to notice change in form through the use of ancient maps from different centuries. At the largest time scales, where processes such as the relative change of levels of land and sea due to tectonic, isostatic or eustatic causes are occurring the alteration of the coastline may be less obvious but its importance should never be underestimated because of that.

Processes

Most of the processes that are described in detail here are those which cause relatively fast change and can bring about a transformation of a landform in as short a time as a matter of hours, months, years or, perhaps, decades. The reason for concentrating on these scales is that they are the processes most likely to have an impact on man and his activities and at the same time they are easiest for us to measure and to observe. Without doubt the most effective process operating on a coastline is the sea wave, and before we begin to understand how it affects the coastline it is essential that we look at its formation and movement in the open sea.

Waves

Formation

Waves are formed by the movement of wind across open water, and as they move across the surface of the sea they set up movements of water beneath them. It is easy to be misled into believing that the wave of water is actually travelling across the ocean, but of course this is an illusion, for the surface water remains relatively still in the horizontal plane as the wave passes. The wave in Fig 7.2 is an idealised one, for varying

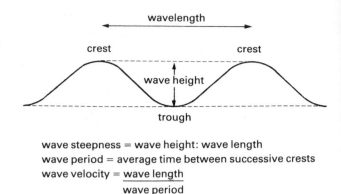

wave steepness = wave height : wave length
wave period = average time between successive crests
wave velocity = $\dfrac{\text{wave length}}{\text{wave period}}$

Fig 7.2 Wave parameters.

directions and strengths of wind during the wave's existence will forbid any such simple pattern. Nevertheless, it is useful to clarify the wave's basic parameters at this stage, and one of them, wave steepness, will emerge later with considerable significance.

As a wave travels across the ocean, it will gradually lose height and energy, a simple enough principle which is easily demonstrated in the bath. It is partly because of this that it is so difficult to predict how high a certain wave will be at any point. Wave size will depend on the interaction of a series of factors, which include how long and hard the wind has been blowing from a particular direction, what wind pattern preceded it, how large the ocean basin is and what waves generated from other sources are present.

One might bear in mind that waves of well over 20 metres in height have been recorded, although on British coasts waves of even a few metres are a rare occurrence. A commonly used division of waves is into the **swell** and storm varieties. The former are the everyday occurrence of waves generated in open sea by the prevailing wind and they tend to be low and flat with smooth crests. On the other hand, a **storm wave** produces a much rougher sea, often with a steeper form and white water on its broken crest.

Fig 7.3 The orbital movement of water within a wave.

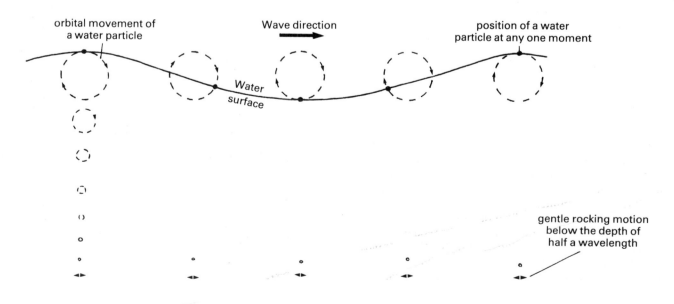

Water movement within the wave

As the wave moves, it generates an orbital movement of water beneath it, as Fig 7.3 reveals. The diameter of the orbit is equivalent to the wave height, and this diameter gradually decreases with depth until at a depth of half the wavelength the diameter is no more than one twentieth of its surface value. Depths greater than this may be enough to make the disturbance virtually insignificant, or at best a gentle rocking motion. It is for this reason that occupants of a submarine often find travel more comfortable once they have descended below the level of the waves and that underwater exploration films always portray the ocean bed as a place of such stillness. A further characteristic of this orbital movement, as Fig 7.3 shows, is that one orbit takes the same time as it does for one complete wave to move across the surface.

Waves in shallow water

What has all this discussion of waves in open sea, possibly thousands of kilometres from shore, to do with our study of the coastline? It is hoped that an understanding of wave genesis will aid the comprehension of the effects of waves on beaches and cliffs. As a wave approaches the shore, certain changes in its form begin to occur. As has already been said, if the generating force, the wind, has dropped the height will gradually decrease. In addition to that, important transformations occur as the wave reaches shallow water. It is here, when the sea bed is close enough to the surface of the wave to interfere with the orbital movements, that several changes occur. Wave height will steadily increase and wavelength will shorten, providing a steepening of the wave as it reaches the shore. This effect can be easily observed as waves, like folds in a rug being pushed up against a wall, build up one behind the other just before they break. As well as this, the orbital motion may become elliptical, as Fig 7.4 demonstrates, and the motion may be sufficient to begin to move material on the sea bed; this, of course, may be a vital geomorphological effect.

It is often considered that many of the most relevant changes to wave form occur when the depth of water is less than half the wavelength. Another rule of thumb is that waves will usually steepen until their sides have a gradient of about 15 per cent or the angle of their crest is about 120 degrees, at which point they are liable to break, and it is what occurs after breaking that is usually of most concern to geomorphologists.

It may seem pointless, or to a poet even sacrilegious, to attempt to classify such a highly diverse and inspirational a body as the foaming surf, but it may simplify our study if we do so. Galvin has tried to reduce breakers into four categories, and the best way of achieving a command of this classification is through observation either in the field or through film.

The essentials of the categories can be seen in Fig 7.5, ranging from the low and flat **surging breakers**, typical of steep beaches, to the high and short **spilling waves** of gentler beaches. Between the two extremes are collaps-

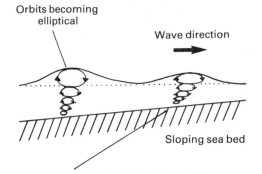

Fig 7.4 The changing orbital movement in shallow water.

ing and **plunging** waves and, as can be seen from the diagram, plunging and spilling breakers tend to break far more dramatically as they crash on to the beach than do the smoother collapsing and surging waves. The relevance of these wave types will be clarified later when we look at beaches. It will suffice to say here that, as waves break, water rushes up the beach as **swash** before returning, usually less dramatically, as **backwash**, and that both of these movements are capable of transporting material across the beach, although in opposite directions. The relative strength of swash and backwash is important in determining the amount of erosion of beach material of which the wave is capable. If the movement up the beach is stronger than the return flow the wave is more likely to be **constructive**, whereas if the opposite is true the wave will probably have a **destructive** effect on the beach.

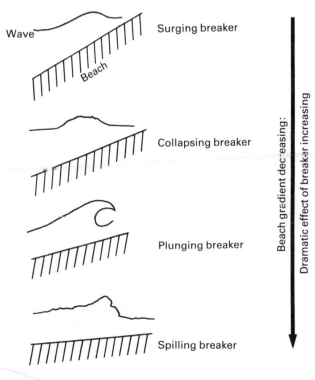

Fig 7.5 Types of breaker.

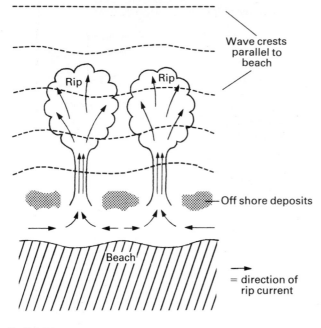

Fig 7.6 Rip currents.

The interaction between backwash and swash is one of the many complexities that cause so much difficulty to our understanding of the beach. As anyone who has stood gazing at breaking waves can confirm, the returning backwash interferes with the swash of the succeeding wave and often destroys what had promised to be a particularly dramatic breaker as it approached the beach. If waves are closely bunched together, that is if **wave period** is short, then this effect will be magnified.

In some cases the return of water to the sea down the beach may involve not only a straightforward downslope movement but may also include a **longshore** flow. This is demonstrated in Fig 7.6, in which rip currents can be seen to be responsible for a considerable amount of the return flow. As well as the transport of water they are also capable of shifting material and, as many bathers have found to their peril, of dragging people out from the shore.

Waves on headlands

Many of the transformations that occur in shallow water may not have the opportunity to take place on coastlines where the sea is deep, such as off a headland. Consequently the action of the waves is unlikely to be conducive to deposition and the full force of the wave will be used as an eroding force. The sheer hydraulic pressure of a crashing wave may be sufficient for this, especially in stormy conditions. The wave may also be aided by sand carried in suspension in the water which may act as an abrasive on the cliff, or by cracks and weaknesses in the cliff itself. The force with which the water enters such crevices may so increase the air pressure inside them that it weakens the crack further or even blasts the rock away.

Longshore drift

Another wave-induced process that operates on most coastlines is that of **longshore drift**, which is the movement of material along the coast parallel to the shoreline. Its occurrence depends upon the oblique approach of a wave to the shoreline, for, as Fig 7.7 shows, the wave may carry material up a beach at an angle approximately perpendicular to the wave crest, but gravity will cause the material and the backwash to take the steepest gradient seawards which in an oblique wave will be a different course from that taken by the swash.

Consequently, material may be seen to drift along a coastline, the effect being best demonstrated where accumulation has taken place against groynes, as in Photo 7.1, or any other man-made obstacle that juts out into the sea. It is often recognised that most British coasts experience this drift in one predominant direction, which is obviously determined by the predominant wind direction. Thus, north Norfolk is considered to have an east-west drift whilst east Norfolk and Suffolk have a north-south drift. However, such generalisations can easily obscure important detail, for drift may change direction several times a day. As Steers points out in his observations at Scolt Head Island in north Norfolk, after three days of north-easterly winds a westward drift of beach material of 5–10 metres occurred, whilst the two succeeding days brought stronger winds from the north west which effected an eastward drift of 4–10 metres. Even so, the orientation of the shingle ridges at both Blakeney Point and Scolt Head Island would suggest that movement is predominantly westward.

Wave refraction

The oblique angle of approach of waves required for longshore drift may be reduced, or even eradicated, by interference with the wave caused by the configuration of the coastline. This effect, known as **wave refraction**, is demonstrated in Fig 7.8 and occurs when the wave reaches shallow water and the orbital movement is

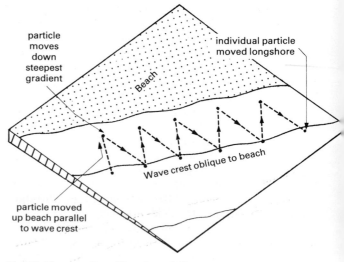

Fig 7.7 The operation of longshore drift.

Photo 7.1 Accumulation of sediment against the groynes on Sheringham beach, Norfolk. The direction of longshore drift is from right to left.

disturbed by the drag effect of the sea bed. It will cause certain parts of the wave to be slowed down and allow other sections to proceed on towards the shore unhindered. Thus, the wave crest may be contorted into a pattern which reflects the coastline's shape, and thus may often transform oblique waves into ones parallel to the shore.

Tides

It is not within the scope of this book to explain why **tides** occur, and it will suffice for our purposes to say that this regular upward and downward movement of the oceans is caused by the gravitational pull of the moon and the sun. A tide is best envisaged as a massive wave which, for any point on the coast, takes slightly over six hours to come in and the same time to go out again. High tide will occur once every 12 hours and 25 minutes. As Fig 7.9 shows, this massive wave will circulate round an enclosed basin in a movement easily simulated by taking a tub of water and moving your hands up and down and backwards and forward at the same time. In fact, in the North Sea, there are three such circulatory movements. It is this circulation which causes each location down the coast to have a slightly later high tide.

Tidal range

There are two aspects of tides of which we really need to be aware. The first is the **range** of height between high and low water. For any one place this can vary considerably from day to day. Nevertheless, we usually make use of the mean values and refer to the high water mark medium tide (HWMMT) and its low water

(a) Refraction on a hypothetical straight coastline.

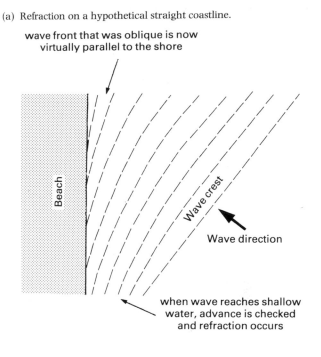

(b) Refraction on a coastline of headlands and bays.

Fig 7.8 Wave refraction.

equivalent. In actual practice, the levels may be exceeded, especially in storm conditions. Four times a month the tidal range may also deviate considerably from the mean. This reflects the two spring tides when

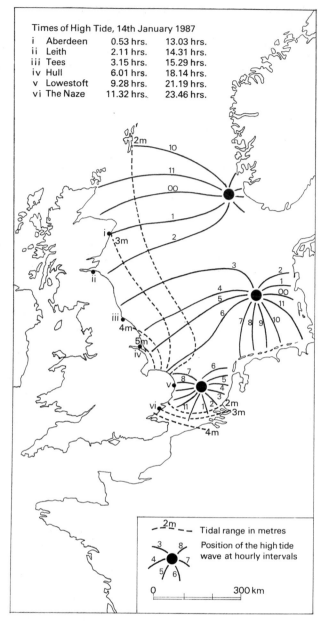

Times of High Tide, 14th January 1987

i	Aberdeen	0.53 hrs.	13.03 hrs.
ii	Leith	2.11 hrs.	14.31 hrs.
iii	Tees	3.15 hrs.	15.29 hrs.
iv	Hull	6.01 hrs.	18.14 hrs.
v	Lowestoft	9.28 hrs.	21.19 hrs.
vi	The Naze	11.32 hrs.	23.46 hrs.

Fig 7.9 The tidal circulation of the North Sea.

a cliff, this means that the zone of wave attack is moved up and down, and if the tidal range is slight the onslaught will be particularly concentrated. On a beach a large tidal range may be sufficient to cause a very wide zone to be exposed at low tide, although this will also depend on the angle of the beach gradient. As with cliffs, the stretching of the wave attack over so broad a front may reduce its effect.

Tidal currents

The second aspect of tides that we must consider is the occurrence of **tidal currents** and they are undoubtedly affected by tidal range for, on coasts where the variation in range is small, the currents are usually insignificant. These underwater currents reverse with the tide, moving water and material shorewards during the flood tide and vice versa during the ebb (see Fig 7.11). Their strength varies enormously. For example, on the shingle beach at Blakeney Point, Steers suggests they rarely have velocities greater than 1–2 knots and are able to move only sand and never shingle. However, in indentations of the coastline, such as bays and estuaries, or where the incoming tide is squeezed between islands, the range may be increased and so may the efficacy of the currents. It has therefore been estimated that such currents in the Mersey Estuary have dumped 68 million tonnes of marine deposits in

Fig. 7.10 Tidal ranges around the British coast showing coastlines with low tidal ranges which are also the coastlines on which most spits occur.

the high tide is much higher and the low much lower, and the two neap tides when the tidal range is much smaller than usual. Spring tides, which actually have nothing to do with the season, are particularly threatening if they combine with storm conditions, and many a flood warning has been given in recent years along the low-lying east coast when such a combination has been forecast. Local factors also cause the tidal range to vary considerably around the British coast and Fig 7.10 attempts to make some generalisations about this.

Tidal range is significant because it determines the levels at which waves can operate. In the simple case of

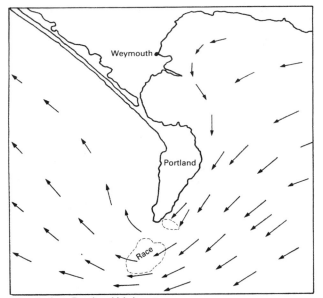

6 hrs before Portland highwater

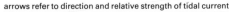

arrows refer to direction and relative strength of tidal current

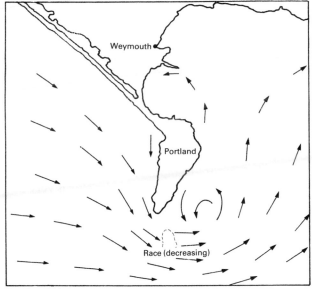

Portland highwater

Fig 7.11 The changing tidal current around the Isle of Portland, Dorset.

just 20 years. The most extreme case of an estuary increasing the tidal range in Britain is the Severn Estuary where the famous **tidal bore** can actually be seen as it moves up the inlet as a wave, often over a metre high and at speeds of up to 30 kilometres an hour. The flooding and associated erosion that this can cause are especially damaging when the bore is accompanied by a storm.

Weathering and Slope Processes

It is easy, when looking at coastal geomorphology, to forget that the normal processes of landscape denudation are occurring just as effectively as they are inland.

The cliff will behave in many respects like any other slope as weathering and mass movement slowly alter its profile. There is no need to go into all these processes again but it is worth contemplating whether any of these processes will be more effective in a marine environment.

Weathering

Without doubt, a cliff is the most likely location in Britain for the operation of salt weathering, and the porous chalk cliffs of Flamborough Head, the granular oolitic limestone cliffs of Purbeck, or the well-jointed Carboniferous limestone cliffs such as those of the Gower Peninsula are especially prone. It is into these cliffs that the salt-laden spray is most likely to find entry and where subsequent crystallisation will cause weakening. Alternate wetting and drying of the cliff face as tides ebb and flow may further increase the effect of the salt crystals and allow hydration to take place. Both solution weathering and frost action can be observed on cliffs, although in both cases it may be true that freshwater from the land is more effective than sea water. In the case of solution, sea water is normally saturated with calcium carbonate which would prevent much solution of limestone cliffs from occurring, and the effect of sea water as an agent of frost action has been questioned because of the comparatively soft ice that it forms. The solution of the chalk that has taken place in the cliffs at Seaford in Sussex (Photo 7.2) would certainly seem to rely on groundwater which has picked up acid from the humus of the soil before etching out the solution chimney down a master joint in the chalk.

Photo 7.2 Solution 'chimneys' in the chalk cliffs at Seaford, East Sussex.

Photo 7.3 Folkestone Warren, Kent: chalk slumping over unstable Gault clays.

It is not always as easy as this to identify the effects of a particular process of weathering as they may be obliterated or confused by the actions of erosion, especially in the lower parts of the cliff and on a wave-cut platform.

Slope movements

Every slope process typical of temperate climates can be observed operating somewhere on the cliffs of Britain, many of them providing headaches for the local town councils which try to provide recreational facilities on the cliff. Two extreme examples are focused on here, the first at Folkestone Warren in Kent in 1915. In one spectacular series of movements the whole cliff and foreshore changed along a stretch of 500–600 metres of the coast. Many thousands of tonnes of rock collapsed into the sea or onto the railway beneath, which at one location was moved nearly 50 metres seaward. One newly-built house just below the top of the cliff fell 15 metres, actually causing only minor injuries to its inhabitants and failing to break even one pane of glass. It is this last point that gives us a clue to the type of slope process, for it suggests a rotational slump as depicted in Fig 4.12. It was largely the geological and hydrological conditions of the cliff that caused the disaster, for unstable Gault clay underlies soft chalk, and saturation of both rocks, from prolonged or heavy rainfall, with the help of underground springs would seem to equate with the effects, which included the shifting of some massive chunks of chalk 400 metres into the sea. As can be seen in Photo 7.3, the landslips of Folkestone Warren today provide a much used recreational area and have much in common with the undercliff area at Lyme Regis in which the French Lieutenant's Woman seeks refuge in John Fowles' novel of the same name.

The second example is from a coastline on which devastating change continues to occur today, namely the boulder clay cliffs along the Norfolk coast between Mundesley and Overstrand. Like similar cliffs at Barton-on-Sea in Hampshire and Holderness in Yorkshire, the unconsolidated boulder clay is very unstable, especially when a winter of rainfall and freeze-thaw has weakened it even further. In the photograph it is possible to see the cumulative effect of many of these processes. The initial collapse is often due to a rotational slip, but the slumped mass in turn may then be subject to soil creep, to earthflows and even mudflows which, in Photo 7.4, were actually moving towards the photographer as the camera's shutter closed. Houses can be brought crashing to the seashore and retreat of the cliff top by several metres can occur in a few months, as it did during the period when these photographs were taken in 1973. Estimates suggest that these cliffs have averaged nearly one metre of retreat per year during this century.

The reasons why some cliffs are more prone to such processes than others are both geological and hydrological. It seems that certain combinations of permeable and unstable rock are susceptible and their vulnerability is then exploited by large amounts of water. Neither vegetation nor man seems to prevent the movements, and some processes may be compounded by the steepening of the cliff caused by undercutting by the sea. The fastest rates of cliff retreat normally occur where the debris of mass wasting is easily removed by the sea.

Wind

Coasts are one of the windiest environments in temperate regions, and the wind is responsible for a certain amount of landscape sculpture. Large expanses of dry sand are a sitting target for an onshore wind, and sand dunes are often a consequence of this action. Wind blasting on cliff faces may be effective, too, especially if the wind is invigorated by its load of sand.

Landforms Resulting Largely from Erosion

For the sake of simplicity, landforms will be divided into those that result primarily from erosion by the sea and those that are the consequence of deposition. Such a split is not wholly satisfactory as, for example, beaches and spits are subjected to erosional forces despite being included in the section on depositional features. This difficulty should be borne in mind as the following sections are studied.

Cliffs

Profile

A cliff is unlikely to be found on a gently sloping coastline such as where a coastal plain meets the sea. The cliff relies for its height, and indeed its existence, on the relief of the land which meets the coast. The reason for this is easily understood by studying Fig 7.12 which shows how cliffs gradually develop from wave attack on the land.

In the case illustrated, the height of the cliff is likely to increase as erosion continues, although in reality it is not always the case. At Seaford in Sussex the chalk cliffs are retreating towards a dry valley running parallel to the coast, and here, if erosion continues, the cliff will eventually lose height. The fluctuations of relief just along the coast at the Seven Sisters run perpendicular to the sea, and the cliff height varies accordingly, with some of the vales producing cliffs no higher than 12 metres, some 50 metres lower than those of the highest intervening hill crests (see Photo 7.11).

Geological control: The profile and shape of a cliff depends on the interplay of many forces and it is worth trying to isolate some of these here. One very relevant

Photo 7.4 Mudflow and earthflow in the boulder clay cliffs near Mundesley, Norfolk. The slumped boulder clay has been virtually liquified.

influence is the geology, and most especially the lithology of the cliff. Some rock types almost always form very similar profiles, notably chalk. The low physical resistance of the rock not only causes the lower part of the cliff to be susceptible to wave attack, but also prevents the cliff from being able to support an overhang. Collapse of the upper cliff is facilitated by the jointing of the chalk and, as the photograph of Flamborough Head shows, in some cases this can be very dense. The interaction of these characteristics usually leads to a vertical profile for chalk cliffs, which is maintained during the relatively fast retreat. For the Seven Sisters between 1973 and 1975 this has been estimated to be as great as 1.5 metres per annum.

Jointing may also determine cliff profile. Staffa, in the Inner Hebrides, has a remarkable series of cliffs composed of hexagonal columns; these owe their existence to the regular joint pattern of the basalt that forms

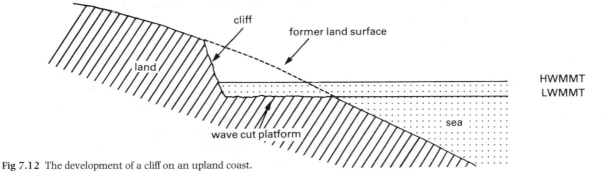

Fig 7.12 The development of a cliff on an upland coast.

Photo 7.5 Chalk Cliffs, Flamborough Head, North Humberside. Note the closely jointed rock.

Photo 7.6 The massively jointed Carboniferous limestone cliffs of Inishmore, Aran Islands, Ireland.

them. The regular, block joints of the Carboniferous limestone cliffs on the west coast of the Irish Aran Islands produce steep, vertical cliffs and the large debris blocks at the foot of the cliff in Photo 7.6 bear witness to this process. These limestone cliffs are in so strong a rock that considerable overhangs can be supported. Irregularities of profile here may also reflect the bedding of the rock, and the sharp protrusions at top and bottom of the distant headland in the photograph are probably the most resistant of the horizontal beds.

The angle of dip of the beds may be capable of controlling the angle of the cliff itself, for horizontal and vertical beds are more likely to produce vertical cliffs, whereas beds dipping seawards may produce an overhang and those dipping landward may cause a sloping cliff.

An interesting example of a profile whose shape has been affected by the structure of the bedding is at West Runton in north Norfolk where the resistant protrusion at the foot of the cliff is a bed of fossilised plant remains from an ancient forest, whose resistance contrasts starkly with the weak glacial deposits that make up most of the cliff.

Equilibrium of processes: As with any other slopes, the profile of a cliff also depends heavily on the relationship between the slope processes and the erosive processes at the slope foot. Is the sea able to remove all the debris which drops from the cliff? If not, slope replacement may gradually occur, or at least cliff foot protection, and the rate of retreat of the upper cliff may be much faster than that of the lower part. Where slope wasting is a particularly virulent process this is usually true, and the shape of the cliffs near Overstrand is much more a reflection of this than of marine influence. Thus, the ferocity of attack becomes an important factor and all the determinants of that, such as length of

predominant fetch, degree of exposure and amount of protection, come into play.

One particular form of protection from erosion is provided by the beach or rock platform at the cliff base. An unprotected headland will undergo much more continuous onslaught than a cliff at the head of a bay behind a wide, energy dissipating beach.

A different sort of protection is demonstrated by the two photographs of Lundy Island (Photo 7.7), which contrast the lithologically similar granite cliffs on each side of the island on the same day. The western cliffs of Lundy Island are at the end of an uninterrupted run up for the waves which stretches across the Atlantic, whilst the eastern cliffs face such serene seas that vegetation is able to colonise almost down to the water's edge.

It is easy to attribute some distorted cliff profiles to mass wasting where, in fact, the major disturbances have been caused by man. Much of the coast of North Yorkshire between Whitby and Middlesbrough has been ravaged by man's greed for minerals such as iron ore and alum, and what looks like a series of spectacular landslips at Sandsend is, in actuality, a confusion of scars and dumps left by alum miners.

Geomorphological history: The geomorphological history of the cliff may also affect its shape. Clark and Small describe a small cliff on the north coast of the Solent at whose base deposition is slowly taking place from east to west. The developing beach is providing protection from the sea so that the cliffs at the eastward end of the sequence are gradually being replaced by debris from slope processes, whilst the as-yet-unprotected western cliffs retain their vertical shape (see Fig 7.13).

A larger time scale needs to be used to explain the **slope-over-wall cliffs** which are common in Devon and Cornwall. As the series of profiles in Fig 7.14 displays,

Photo 7.7a The irregular coastline of western Lundy. Note the bare rock and isolated granite stacks.

Photo 7.7b The more regular coastline of eastern Lundy. Note the extension of vegetation almost down to sea level on these protected cliffs.

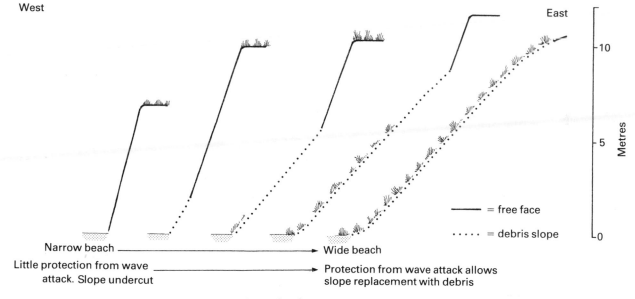

Fig 7.13 The response of a sequence of cliffs in Hampshire to beach deposition at their base (after Clark and Small).

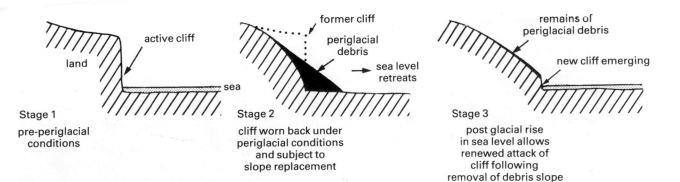

Fig 7.14 The evolution of slope-over-wall-cliffs.

many cliffs were left high and dry by dropping sea levels in Pleistocene times. Periglacial processes of frost action and gelifluxion were able to reduce the slope angle until rising sea levels once again produced a marine cliff, and the sea was able to excavate the debris and once again wear back the cliff base. The cliff lines of Lundy Island, referred to above, are both good examples of slope-over-wall cliffs, the larger upper section of the eastern cliff presumably a result of less rapid erosion of the cliff base there.

Plan

The plan of a cliffed coast will also be determined by many of the factors above. The relief and geology control form in a variety of ways. The outline of part of the Gower coast given in Fig 7.15 illustrates several of these. The large-scale pattern of anticlines and synclines has left two headlands of Carboniferous limestone, Oxwich Point and Pwlldu Head, separated by Oxwich Bay cut into the millstone grit. It is not that the millstone grit is any less resistant than the limestone as a rock, but that by being downfolded it provided less of an obstacle for the sea. Wave attack on a small cliff is bound to be more effective than that on a high cliff as the actual zone of attack is so limited by the tidal range. The neighbouring bay of Port Eynon seems to be developing for similar reasons. On a smaller scale on Gower, the series of small fault lines along the south-west coast also demonstrates the role of geology for their presence has produced a series of tiny inlets. The dramatic Peninnis Head on the Scilly Isles, part of which is

shown in Photo 7.8, shows how the joints have provided a weakness in the granite for weathering and waves to widen.

It is often the geological contrasts of a coastline that give it its most memorable features. The narrow incision of the Huntsman's Leap in Dyfed, some 140 metres

Fig 7.15 The geology of the Gower Peninsula, South Wales.

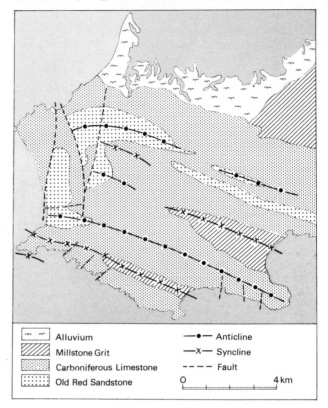

Symbol	Legend	Symbol	Legend
~ ~	Alluvium	—•—	Anticline
▨	Millstone Grit	—x—	Syncline
⠿	Carboniferous Limestone	– – –	Fault
⦂⦂⦂	Old Red Sandstone	0 4 km	

Photo 7.8 Peninnis Head, St Mary's, Isles of Scilly. The pattern of jointing has opened the granite headland to both weathering and erosion.

Photo 7.9 Fingal's Cave, Staffa, Hebrides. The cave has been etched from the basalt pillars which themselves result from the hexagonal jointing.

Fig 7.16 The geology of the Cornish coast. (Reproduced by permission of the Geological Society from Hendriks, 1937, *Quart. J. Geol. Soc. Lond.* 93)

deep but less than two wide, makes use of a master joint in the Carboniferous limestone, and the majority of coastal caves owe their initiation to a fault or joint. Such weaknesses encourage caves to develop by providing a focus for attack; as the hollow begins to deepen, the sea forces air into it with such vehemence that the rock is weakened by air pressure as much as by the pressure of the waves. The formation of **blow holes** is usually attributed to such a process as air, forced into the back of the cave, escapes up a vertical joint to the cliff top, weakening the rock as it does so. The blow hole develops as a funnel-shaped depression linking cliff top to cavern, and, in a rock such as limestone, solution from surface water may exaggerate the effect.

Some **geos**, as the narrow inlets such as Huntsman's Leap are known, probably form when the blow hole and cave extend to such a size that the cavern roof collapses.

The Cornish coast (Fig 7.16) provides examples of some of the most intricate cliff plans, and their idiosyncrasies can often be explained by the variation in rock resistance. Along the south and north coasts, a string of headlands and bays occurs reflecting, respectively, the hard igneous rocks such as the phyllite of Dodman Point and the softer Devonian sedimentaries of bays such as Kiberick Cove. Imposed upon this pattern is a smaller-scale series of inlets and promontories which have amplified the effect of igneous dykes and faults.

Although geological explanations loom large in any analysis of cliff profile and plan, it would be wrong to give the impression that their influence overrides all others. For any stretch of the coastline one must be prepared to examine the wave and tidal patterns, the movement of sediment, the influence of man, the effects of both vegetation and past sea levels before one plumps for an exclusively geological theory.

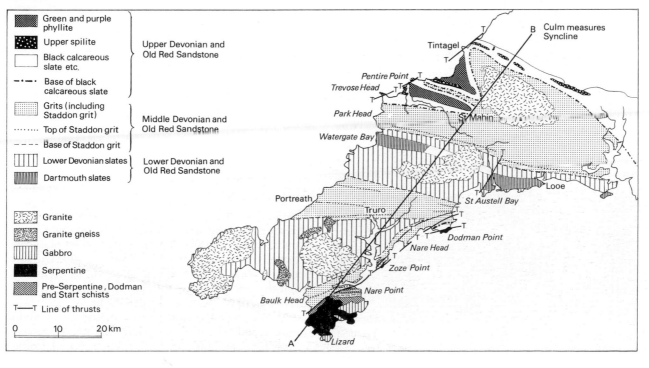

Photo 7.10(a) A coastal arch on Inishmore, Aran Islands, Ireland.

Photo 7.10(b) The Bow Fiddle, Portknockie, north east Scotland: a quartzite arch.

Stacks and Arches

Stacks and **arches** are common characteristics of cliff plan. The arch in Photo 7.10a is useful as an indication of both why the arches form and how they evolve. First, a headland, in the Aran case a small one, is needed so that waves can attack it from each side. The joints of the Carboniferous limestone have facilitated the process here. Caves form on each side and eventually cut through the headland to create a passage which is the basis of the arch. When this photograph was taken the arch had been in existence for some time, but notice the large joint-induced crack on the cliff top. Presumably, the arch would not need much more of a battering from the waves before the top would collapse into the sea to leave a stone column or stack.

There are few more difficult challenges for British climbers than the scaling of sea stacks, and in the past 20 years several successful conquests have been made of the imposing Old Man of Hoy in the Orkney Islands which stands, needle-like, 150 metres above the sea. In time the stack may succumb to wave attack, leaving only a submerged **reef** to trap an unwary mariner.

Photo 7.11 The wave-cut platform in the chalk cliffs at Cuckmere Haven, East Sussex. The Seven Sisters can be seen in the distance.

Platforms

Wave-cut platforms

As a cliff retreats, it leaves at its base a platform of rock. This may be revealed permanently, although it is more usually covered, at least at high tide. These platforms are often masked by sand and shingle in bays. The rock pools left beneath the cliffs, at the edge of the beach, when the tide goes out represent the only exposure of the **wave-cut platform** on many coasts.

Already we have made some assumptions about their method of formation which may not be correct, for are all such platforms wave 'cut', or could other processes be operating? Some geomorphologists certainly dismiss the term and adopt 'shore platforms' instead. Bird proceeds to identify three different types of platform, shown in Fig 7.17, the **inter-tidal**, the **high-tide** and the **low-tide**.

Inter-tidal platforms: These are the most familiar; they represent the gently sloping shelves which extend from high tide level to just beyond the low tide point, and result from wave attack on the cliff succeeded by wave abrasion on the platform itself. There is plenty of opportunity for the waves to wear down the rock, not only by using its load to abrade, but also to swirl it round to form potholes. This second process has been employed to good effect by flint nodules on the occasionally exposed chalk platform beneath the boulder clay cliffs near Overstrand. The breadth of a platform is determined by the rate of retreat of the cliff, the length of time that the sea has been at its present level, and the tidal range. The example in Photo 7.11, at the foot of chalk cliffs near Seaford is, of course, not just a wave-cut platform, for as has already been stated in this chapter the cliffs here are retreating due to both weathering and collapse, as well as wave action.

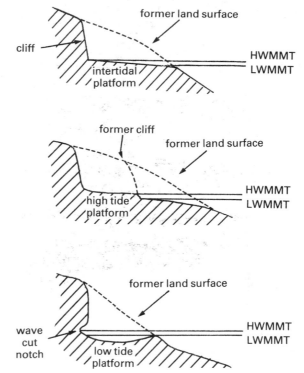

Fig 7.17 Types of shore platforms (after Bird).

Photo 7.12 The wave-cut platform at Robin Hoods Bay, North Yorkshire. Although the cliffs are predominantly of boulder clay, the platform is cut into the underlying Lower Lias. The inland-dipping beds have been picked out by erosion.

High-tide platforms: These could have several origins. Perhaps they form as a result of storm waves whose height can give increased power with which to crash down from above the normal high tide level. This is not an entirely satisfactory explanation, however, for storm waves arrive at a great variety of heights relative to tide and cliff and why should they, therefore, produce such horizontal platforms, eroded at just one level? Perhaps, then, they represent wave-cut platforms of a former, higher sea level. In some places this is probably true, but once again why are they horizontal when the usual inclination for a presently active wave-cut platform is seaward sloping? Because these theories are not wholly satisfactory, Bird suggests that it may not be the sea at all that is dominant, but the weathering of the cliffs. He proposes that salt weathering combined with alternate wetting and drying wears away the cliff as far as the level that is permanently saturated, that is, just above sea level. The sea therefore protects the lower parts of the cliff which remain whilst the rest of it retreats. The reason why the platform sometimes has a high rim at its seaward edge is possibly that it is kept saturated by breaking waves. Platforms formed in this way are likely to be more common in tropical environments where weathering operates more quickly, or in environments relatively free of constant attack from storm waves. It is probably because of this latter point that they have not been identified in Britain, but this is compensated for by the large number on the coast of south east Australia.

Low tide platforms: may be rarely, if ever, exposed. They are usually a feature of limestone coasts, which would seem to suggest the importance of solution in their formation. The problem remains of how lime-rich sea water can carry out this submarine process. The most likely explanation seems that night time cooling of sea water increases the capacity for water to dissolve carbon dioxide from the air, which then acidifies the water and enables the necessary processes of carbonation and solution to occur.

All of these platforms rely on the sea in some way, if only to remove the weathered debris or solutes. The surface of the platform is rarely even, which may reflect the process of formation or the fact that they may cut across a series of rock layers and mirror the idiosyncrasies of each.

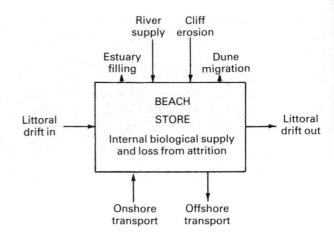

Fig 7.18 The beach as a sediment store.

Landforms Resulting Largely from Deposition

Beaches

Most of us have probably spent more time walking or sitting on beaches than on any other feature described in this book, and yet in this case familiarity does not necessarily mean understanding. The beach extends from the lowest level of low tide beyond the high tide marks to the upper point to which storm waves can fling material. Some experts would like to extend that definition to include the deposits beyond the low tide mark, for as we shall soon see, breaking waves set up movements of sediment that extend seawards. Whatever the definition, the beach can be viewed as an ever-changing store of sediment, with a series of inputs and outputs, as shown in Fig 7.18.

Beach profile

The profile of a beach varies considerably through time. On a micro time scale it may respond to one storm. Across a year it may show considerable variation between summer and winter, and in the longer term it may slowly be accumulating or disappearing. At which

ever of these scales we look, the same dominant controls must be examined, the **wave regime** and all the controls upon that, the type and size of beach sediment and, to a greater or lesser extent, the activities of man.

The relationship with waves: We have already seen that waves in which swash is stronger than backwash tend to build up the beach whilst in those where the backwash is superior the beach may be subject to destructive forces. However, this may itself be misleading for the destructive forces need not destroy the beach, they may merely alter its profile so that it is more in harmony with the prevailing wave conditions, and they may, in fact, widen and extend the beach seawards. This point is best exemplified by considering the effect of a steep wave, such as a spilling or plunging breaker, as it crashes down on the shoreline. It is likely to provide sufficient backwash to remove sediment back down the beach into the sea from the zone where it breaks. As Fig 7.19 shows, this will reduce the gradient of the beach. Further, the wave period in steep waves is often low, which means that the returning backwash will soon meet the swash of the succeeding breaker and thus in-

Fig 7.19 The impact of a steep wave on a sand beach.

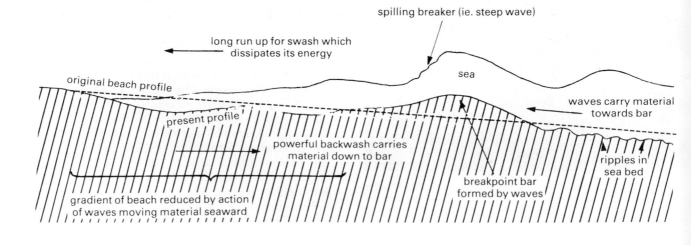

terfere with its ability to move material up the beach, thus compounding the effect of the first wave.

The opposite situation to this has the converse effect. As low, flat waves such as surging and collapsing breakers reach the beach, typically well spaced and with a long wave period, they push material up the beach in a swash that is barely interrupted by a far less effective backwash.

As storm waves are typically steep and most common in winter and swell waves are flatter and occur more widely in summer, it is possible on some beaches to observe a winter and a summer profile, as Fig 7.20 shows. The winter beach is characteristically flat and broad whilst the summer one is steeper, a reflection of the constructive waves. If this simple seasonal division holds true, there would be certain times of year when the beach is undergoing great change, presumably during autumn and spring. These times, especially the months of October and November, are often the most interesting in which to collect data for a beach project. However, like all simple classifications, the seasonal one is not always appropriate, for stormy seas may be a feature of a British summer, as the unlucky partici-

Photo 7.13 The Beach at Sandsend, North Yorkshire. This photograph was taken in October as the beach was being transformed from summer to winter profile.

Beach angle (°)	Mean sediment size (mm)
1.5	0.17
2	0.2
4	0.39
7	0.65

Fig 7.21 Evidence from Half Moon Bay, California of the relationship between beach angle and sediment size.

pators in the Fastnet yacht race of 1979 discovered to their cost, and beaches may alter accordingly.

Throughout the discussion so far it has been implied that the steepness of a wave determines the angle of the beach, with steep waves reducing the angle and gentle waves steepening it. This, however, is only part of the story, for beach gradient in turn will affect the steepness of the wave. Low gradient equates with shallow water and, as we saw earlier, this will usually produce an increase in wave steepness. Thus, spilling and plunging waves are associated with gentle beach gradients and surging and collapsing with steeper ones. The relationship between wave steepness and beach angle is, then, very much a two-way affair, with the two parts usually in equilibrium with each other. This equilibrium may well be disturbed by a storm, but adjustments will usually take place quite quickly to re-establish the balance.

Beach sediment: It would be wrong to reduce the question of beach profile to the simple harmonising

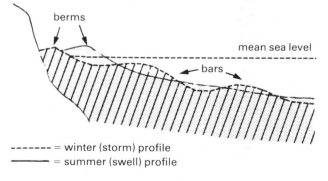

Fig 7.20 Summer and winter beach profiles.

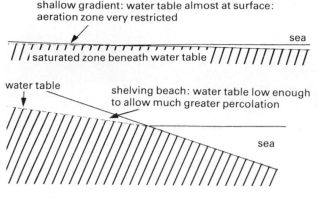

Fig 7.22 Effect of beach water table on percolation.

between gradient and wave type, for there are other complicating factors. Most important of these is the effect of beach sediment, for example sand will bring about a much gentler beach than shingle. The table in Fig 7.21 provides evidence of the impact of sediment size. In the case of shingle, this must be partly a reflection of the higher angle of rest associated with larger grain sizes, but this is only one small aspect. One of the ways in which sediment size can control beach profile is through its percolation rate. Shingle and other large material allows greater and faster percolation, thus as swash moves up a shingle beach its impact will be lessened and the resultant backwash reduced. Less effective backwash means less interference with the succeeding wave, and a wave in which swash is the stronger partner is more likely to induce construction. A sandy beach allows less percolation, not only because there is less volume between the grains to be filled with water, but also because the lower angle of the beach means the water table is nearer the surface (see Fig 7.22). The gentle angle of sandy beaches is therefore likely to be maintained by the destructive steep waves that it encourages. Once again, though, we must regard sediment as just one of the controls and not the only one.

Beach concavity: The reader cannot be blamed for having inferred from the previous explanations that beach angle and beach profile have the same meaning. This is not true, for an analysis of any profile should concern itself with the change of angles across it. Beaches are usually concave; that is, they get steeper as you move away from the sea. There are many reasons for this. The simplest is that the size of material increases up the beach. Large material on the upper beach may be partly the weathered remains of cliff falls, and there is plenty of evidence that sea-shore weathering is quite potent even below the chalk cliffs of Sussex, where for example, algae, limpets, mussels and winkles bring about both physical and biochemical weathering. The larger, and more rounded, material on the upper beach may alternatively have been flung there by storm waves at a spring high tide and are now out of the reach of everyday wave action. The general increase in sediment size may merely reflect the inequality of the swash and backwash with the strength of the former having greater competence than the latter (see page 125). The lower beach is rarely free from wave action except at extremely low spring tides, and this constant activity will produce attrition of beach material, which is another reason for the grading and the concavity of beach profile.

Beach landforms: Upon this profile a series of smaller-scale beach landforms may have been imposed, a selection, perhaps, of those shown in Fig 7.23. The **beach berm** is one of the most distinctive, the product of constructive waves building up a steep beach face. A low tidal range is a prerequisite of well developed berms, for this enables the moulding by the waves to be spatially concentrated and thus to construct a greater feature. As such conditions are not common on most British coasts, there is a paucity of fine examples of berms. The

Fig 7.23 Cross-section of an idealised beach of shingle and sand.

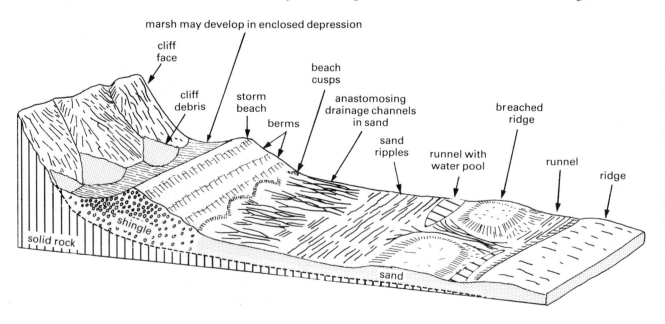

Photo 7.14 Shingle berm, Weybourne, Norfolk. This steep berm marks the limit of the high tide at least three metres above the present breaking waves.

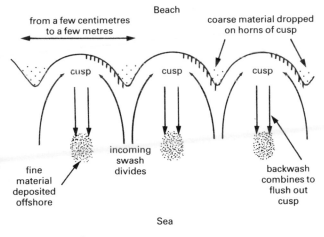

Fig 7.24 Cusp formation.

spreading out of the wave's work across a wider expanse of beach tends to produce a series of **ridges** and intervening depressions or **runnels**, which are particularly common on low, sandy beaches. It is the runnels which produce the shallow paddling pools of warm water on these beaches after the tide has gone out. On the seaward side of the berm a succession of smaller, superimposed ridges may exist. Each of these represents a level of the tide, the lowest at any one time reflecting the most recent high tide, as any ridges lower than this would have been destroyed. If waves that are primarily destructive replace the constructive ones, the berm will be slowly worn down, and if the new wave regime persists, the material will be moved seawards and redeposited just below the level of low tide as a **longshore bar** parallel to the shoreline.

The **cusps** are small embayments within the beach material, perhaps only a couple of metres across, the cause of which is not entirely clear. The most accepted theory envisages the splitting of the incoming swash into two separate flows, which reduces the power of the wave and causes the coarser material that the wave is carrying to be dropped in a form that eventually becomes the horns of the cusp (see Fig 7.24). As the two incoming flows join up again as the backwash, their energy increases and they not only move material from the head of the embayment seawards but also interfere with the incoming swash. Once established, the cusps may well continue to divide the flow and so reinforce the process of their formation. The circulation of water in these features is reminiscent of rip currents and they, on a larger scale, will also affect beach morphology. Their presence will normally entail the dissection of the longshore bar as the currents flow outward, but in some circumstances they may transform the bar into a chain of giant cusps, although these may not be visible except at very low tides.

Many sandy beaches have superimposed upon them a pattern of minute ridges and runnels referred to as **ripples**. They are usually only a few centimetres high at most, and result from movements of both waves and tidal currents across the beach. In cross-section they are often asymmetrical with the steeper side facing away from the oncoming flow of water. They can be seen to migrate across the beach with the fluctuations of the tide. After the tide has gone out a sandy beach may still support surface drainage in the form of tiny rills. The pattern of these **anastomosing channels** may be so intricate that some extremely high drainage densities can be recorded. If the power of their flow has sufficient strength, they may cut through not only ripples but also the larger sand ridges.

Beach plan

In order to simplify the study of beach plan some geomorphologists have used the subdivision of coasts into

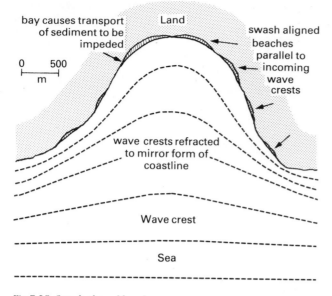

Fig 7.25 Swash aligned beaches.

those on which sediment transport is impeded and those on which it is free. Each will have a different effect on beach plan. The **impeded transport** coasts are those where protruding headlands trap material which may then accumulate in bays. Within these bays the wave crests are likely to be parallel to the shore line, especially if refraction is operating, and the beaches are referred to as being **swash aligned** (see Fig 7.25). Under **free transport** conditions, the coast is likely to be much straighter, and the associated oblique approach of the waves will induce drift along it. The beaches are thus **drift aligned** and if the coast changes direction suddenly, for example at a river estuary, the beach may well continue parallel to the drift and detached from the coastline. In this case they form **spits** (see Fig 7.26).

This two-way classification is so simple that it is bound to have some exceptions. One very obvious one is Chesil Beach in Dorset, which although swash

aligned, does not occur on a coastline of bays (Fig 7.27). There is also, presumably, the possibility that a coastline is not dominated solely by one group of waves, either oblique or parallel in approach, but experiences a mixture of both. One occurrence of such a combination is shown in Fig 7.28. Here the refraction caused by the configuration of the coastline produces swash-aligned beaches in the bays, but drift, which is predominantly northward, moves much of this material to the south side of the bay. The resultant beach is asymmetrical in plan, and is sometimes referred to as a **fish-hook beach**.

Virtually no aspect of beach form or process is free from interference by man's activities, and as we shall see in Chapter Twelve this can considerably alter the operation of all the processes described so far.

Spits

Although Britain's coasts display a selection of **spits** diverse in both shape and size, the features are not pre-

Fig 7.27 Chesil Beach, Dorset. A ridge of flint pebbles from Devon and Dorset coasts supplied from both east and west.

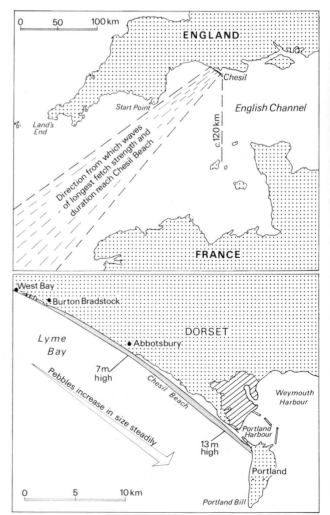

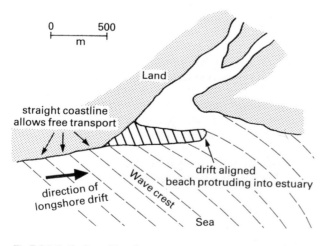

Fig 7.26 Drift aligned beach.

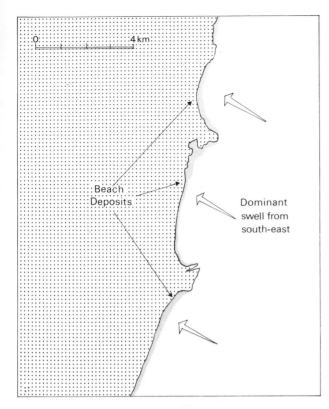

Fig 7.28 Fish-hook or zeta form beaches in New South Wales, Australia.

Fig 7.29 Some British examples of spits.

(a) Orford Ness, Suffolk.

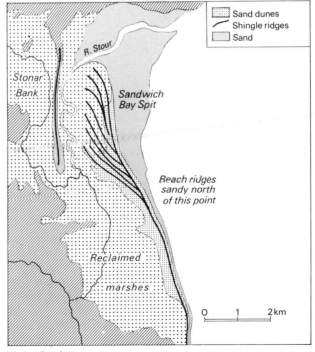

(b) Ro Wen, Mawddach Estuary, Gwynedd.

sent on every stretch of coastline. They are very much clustered in certain areas, the three greatest concentrations being along the coasts of East Anglia, of North Wales south of the Lleyn peninsula and along the southern coast of England between east Devon and the Isle of Wight. The characteristic that these sections of coast have in common is their small tidal range, usually below three metres, which seems to be a necessary environmental condition for spit development. Many spits are relatively recent in origin, some having grown significantly since mediaeval times. Despite the variety shown in Fig 7.29, we shall concentrate on just one spit here, at Blakeney Point in north Norfolk, to further our understanding.

Blakeney Point

Shingle provides us with the building material in this particular case, although sand can prove just as effective in spit construction, as the one at Borth in Dyfed demonstrates. The shingle ridge of Blakeney Point extends at a gentle angle some six kilometres from the old coastline and at its seaward end is about three kilometres north of it (Fig 7.30). It stands on a great submarine plain of sand, the ridge itself being visible above the sea even at high tide, although storm waves can occasionally submerge it. With the vast majority of the shingle being flint, some 97 per cent in fact, its source should be easy to trace. However, it is not as easy as it

(c) Sandwich Bay Spit, Kent.

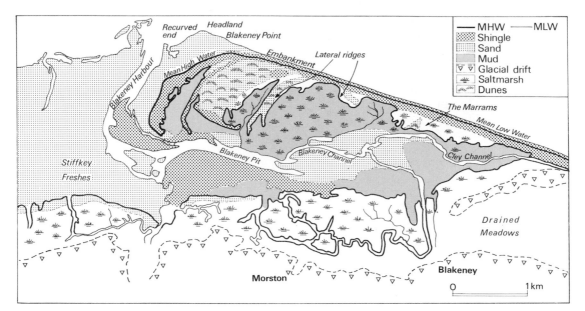

Fig 7.30 Blakeney Point, north Norfolk.

Photo 7.15 Blakeney Point, north Norfolk: view from the distal end.

may at first seem. It would be logical to assume that the flint derives from the chalk exposures in the cliffs to the east of the spit, near Sheringham, and that the predominantly westward drift brings it along to Blakeney. However, the vast quantity of material needed to sustain a spit of this size could hardly be supplied by so limited a source, and the coast to the east of Sheringham cannot supplement the supply for there is a sudden change in direction of drift east of here which takes material away from the required destination. An alternative supplier could perhaps be the chalk cliffs of Lincolnshire and Yorkshire to the north-west of the spit (Fig 7.31). Certainly the prevailing wind direction is north westerly at Blakeney, but the fetch is severely restricted and the associated waves could hardly be ex-

pected to move this much material, and even if they were able to, the spit does not appear to be aligned with north-westerly waves. The source may be correct, however, although a different process of transport is needed. It is thought that the erosive power of the great Pleistocene ice sheets may have scoured the Wolds of Lincolnshire and Yorkshire and dumped the remains in the North Sea in a convenient location for the north-easterly waves to bring them onshore.

In common with several other British examples Blakeney Point has a **recurved end**. This perpendicular change in orientation at the seaward end of the spit may simply be the result of the refraction of waves from the north east as they reach the end of the ridge. Or it may be a response to the frequent but less forceful north-westerly waves. Throughout its length, on the underbelly of the spit, a series of **lateral ridges** of shingle extends into the marshes each presumably representing former recurved ends and indicating stages in the spit's development.

It is not easy to discern whether Blakeney Point is continuing to extend into the sea. Merely to maintain its present size a vast input of shingle is needed, for the constant battering by waves allows attrition to produce a sizeable quantity of output. Observations of sediment movement have revealed that tidal currents as well as waves are active along the spit. They change direction with the flow of the tide, and can carry material of sand size each way along the beach. Their effect, though, would seem to be superficial rather than formative.

Double spits

Although Blakeney is a useful model by which to study other spits, it cannot demonstrate all their traits. It is, after all, a single example which may have particular local peculiarities. One quite contrasting type is the **double spit** such as the pairs that extend from each side of some river estuaries. Whether these are simply a response to variations in direction of longshore drift or are due to some more complex interaction of tidal currents, river outflow and drift is open to debate.

Cuspate forelands and tombolos

It may be that pairs of spits are also responsible for the development of **cuspate forelands**. These great triangular accretions of shingle that project into the sea may be formed on a coastline where waves of equal dominance approach from different directions. Two spits may thus grow from different points on the coast and eventually meet at their seaward or distal ends. For the largest of these forelands in Britain, at Dungeness, however, a different hypothesis has been forwarded. As Fig 7.32 shows, a shingle spit supplied from the west may once have grown out across a bay from Fairlight Head to Hythe. With a different sea level at the time of initiation, Fairlight Head would have been seaward of its present location. Breaching of the spit near to the point where it leaves the coastline led to the creation of an estuary here, the currents from which checked the continued supply of shingle from west to east. Waves from the south west were then able to transform its shape, and create a pronounced elbow within it. In time, continued accretion of shingle ridges and coastal attack from waves, from both south west and east, moved it to its present position. By this stage the spit was not just one but a whole series of parallel and perpendicular shingle ridges which today make up Dungeness. At an early stage of development the bay from Fairlight Head to Hythe was cut off from the sea and its shallow sediment has gradually evolved into Romney Marsh.

One other special case is the **tombolo**, where a spit joins an island to the mainland, such as the Chesil Beach link with the Isle of Portland or the bar which links St Agnes to the Gugh in the Scilly Isles.

Spits should not be seen as an isolated landform, for

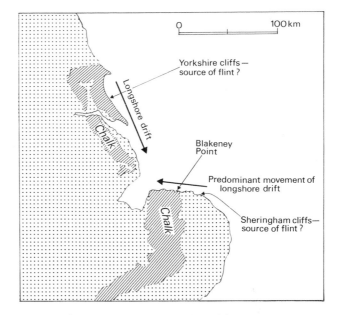

Fig 7.31 The problem of shingle supply at Blakeney Point.

they are very much an integral part of the whole environment around them. Their existence can often change the course of a river, as the examples in Fig 7.29 reveal. In addition, they frequently provide the sheltered conditions in which salt marshes develop, for example on the northern side of Hurst Castle Spit. They can also provide a base for sand dunes which, in turn, affect the landscape.

Barrier Islands

The term 'barrier' is an apt one to apply to the coastal features which it describes, for they often protect the land from the onslaught of the sea. **Barrier islands** differ from the longshore bar in that they are a distinct entity from the beach and the processes operating on it, and emerge above the sea even at high tide (see Fig 7.33). Their only similarity with a beach is that they take the

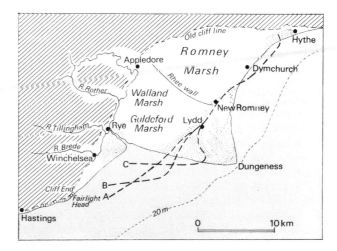

Fig 7.32 The foreland of Dungeness, Kent. The original spit followed line A and moved through positions B and C to present location between the mouth of the Rother and Dungeness.

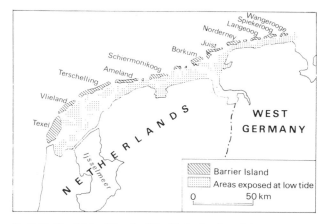

Fig 7.33 The Frisian Islands of The Netherlands and West Germany.

form of a ridge of deposits parallel to the shoreline. Like spits, they develop best on coastlines of low tidal range where tidal currents are too weak to hamper deposition.

There are almost as many theories of formation as there are different forms of barrier island. Three major hypotheses seem to emerge from the research and discussion, the first of which suggests that some islands may be former beach berms or ridges, or even sand dunes, that have been drowned by a rising sea level. A second theory also uses the post-glacial rise in sea level for an explanation, but looks to a later period for the actual deposition. Here the islands are seen to be deposited by the waves of the rising sea as glacial sediment is brought in from offshore. A third theory envisages a development not unlike that of a spit with longshore drift helping to deposit material parallel to the shore. Breaching of the spit by storm waves or even strong river currents may then divide it into a single or a series of islands.

In time the islands may be transformed into **barrier beaches** as they are pushed onshore by storm waves washing material from their seaward to their landward side. If such a beach seals the entrance to a bay, the sea water that it traps may gradually change into a **fresh-water lagoon**.

Sand Dunes

For **sand dunes** to develop along a coastline three prerequisites are essential. First, there must be a large store of easily accessible sand which is dry enough for the wind to pick up. At Blakeney this need is met by the extensive areas of sand at the end of the Point which are revealed at low tide. Shallow bays experiencing large tidal ranges, such as Morecambe Bay, and major river deposits offshore from estuaries, such as those of the Taw and Torridge in North Devon, are also useful suppliers, in the latter case the dunes of Braunton Burrows being the beneficiary.

The second requirement is a surface on which to build the dune, and almost any flattish area will suffice

whether at the top of a beach, beneath a cliff, on a saltmarsh, or, as at Blakeney, on a shingle ridge. Much to the chagrin of many a farmer the surface sometimes selected is agricultural land, and the British coast, as far apart as Culbin on the Moray Firth and the Gwithian Sands in Cornwall, is littered with examples of churches and even villages that have been engulfed by moving sand.

The third need is for a stabilising agent to control the shape of the dune once it begins to form. This is usually provided by vegetation and its role is absolutely essential. As the **embryo dune** first begins to form, perhaps in an environment that is quite salty, or even still occasionally covered by water at high tide, the colonisation of a plant such as sea twitch will aid its development. Much more commonly associated with dunes, however, is marram grass and this will take over as the larger **fore dunes** develop, in a less saline environment, in the lee of the embryo dune. Marram grass is well suited to perform its required role. Its seeds can be dispersed by the wind, they germinate quickly and, most importantly, they tolerate very poorly developed soils, if indeed wind-blown sand can be described as a soil at all. In addition, its extensive underground root systems help stabilise the dune and, because the grass is quick growing, the grass keeps pace with the dune's upward growth. Field observations have revealed that the plant stems produce a zone of zero wind velocity extending up to ten centimetres above the ground (see Fig. 7.34). This provides a sand trap.

In time, the decaying grass remains may provide sufficient humus and retain sufficient moisture for

Photo 7.16 Sand dunes, Formby, Lancashire. Notice the parallel ridges of dunes and the succession of vegetation moving inland.

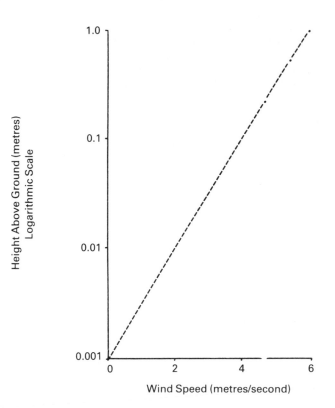

Below 0.001 metres from the ground air is still; when vegetation is present this zone of zero air speed extends up to 0.1 metres.

Fig 7.34 Graph to show decrease in wind speed near ground surface: measurements were taken on an open beach in south Lancashire.

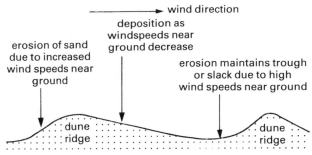

Fig 7.35 The development and maintaining of troughs between dune ridges.

other plants to colonise, but this is unlikely to happen if the wind continues to supply the dune with sand, for few plants other than marram will be able to tolerate such conditions. However, if further dunes develop in the lee of the fore dune, there may be sufficient shelter from both wind and sand for **plant succession** to proceed here and for marram to be replaced. Thus, a series of parallel dunes may represent a series of developmental stages in dune formation, those nearest the sea being at the embryonic stage and those farthest inland the most mature form of dune on which shrubs and small trees may well have become the dominant form of vegetation.

The dunes at Blakeney form the highest point on the entire landform, and they are arranged in a sequence of ridges perpendicular to the prevailing north-westerly wind which has to blow across the widest part of the sand flat on its way to the dunes. A variety of ages of dune is represented, from the isolated hummocks of embryos with their sand couch grass and sea holly, through the fore dunes where marram grass predominates, but where sand is constantly mobile, to the highest dunes, some of which have become fixed, cut off from fresh supplies of sand and held down by carpets of moss which separate the now isolated clumps of grass. Separating each of these ridges are depressions, or **slacks**, a common feature of dune areas. These lows may reach down to the water table and may even retain salinity from occasional inundation, and as such have their own distinctive vegetation. As Fig 7.35 demonstrates, they form as wind accelerates down the lee of the preceding ridge, eroding the sand as it does so.

Salt Marshes

Like sand dunes, the development of **salt marshes** is encouraged by the presence of certain environments. Sheltered water is often considered to be one of them, such as in estuaries, bays or in the lee of spits such as Blakeney Point. However, Steers points out that total protection, although helpful, is not essential and cites the unprotected but extensive Stiffkey Marshes to the west of Blakeney. Shallow water is, however, present here and this would seem to be necessary for the deposition to begin. A large and continuous supply of fine material is a further requirement, which could be river-borne alluvial deposits if the marsh is in an estuary or, if it is not, could simply be mud and silt which the waves have brought onshore. The sand flats at Blakeney have provided an ideal base for a marsh to form, and as can be seen in Fig 7.30, it has formed not only on the underside of the spit but also along the old coastline below the now relict cliffs. Despite its name, such a sand 'flat' is unlikely to be perfectly level, which will mean that mud can accrete in its hollows and depressions. With wave power being so depleted, tidal currents will take over as the major force of transport and erosion, but their limited energy will restrict the size of material moved. To be deposited, the mud which is suspended in the water will require the velocity of the current to fall to almost zero. Knowledge derived from Hjulström's Curve in Chapter 6 will be useful here, for tiny particles are so fine that they will stick together and the velocity needed to pick them up again will be considerably higher than the settling velocity at which they were dropped. Once deposition has begun, therefore, it has a certain amount of protection against erosion. It needs far more than this, though, if the mud is to become a marsh and not just a mud flat.

The next vital requirement is the colonisation by vegetation, and this can start as soon as plant seeds are dropped into the pools of mud. **Halophytes**, or salt-loving plants, are the only ones likely to tolerate these early stages, their seeds having been transported here in the plumage of birds, on the feet of man, or by wind or water. Amongst the earliest arrivals may be eel grass and marsh samphire, and these pioneers will quickly begin to cause accretion around their roots and stems causing clumps of vegetated mud to appear at low tide. As these clumps enlarge, and as their tops are less frequently covered by the tide, other plants such as the sea aster and sea lavenders will move in. As the clumps get bigger, so the tide begins to be directed between them and upward accumulation of mud may now reach a peak, perhaps as much as a centimetre a year.

Channels between the expanding areas of marsh now funnel the tide until eventually the water is confined only to the system of **creeks** which drain the marsh after high tide. The marsh may now be inundated less and less, especially if mud continues to be deposited when the tide does encroach upon it. The landward areas will be particularly free from salt water, and vegetation here may undergo several stages of plant succession, proceeding first to the series of grasses which make up **saltings**, a type of coastal meadow, and later even further through the hierarchy towards **climatic climax**. Many marshes, and those at Blakeney are no exception, exhibit spatial zoning of vegetation, reflecting the past stages of the marsh development. Thus, in the most seaward reaches, where daily inundation occurs, the early colonising plants are still found, and as the frequency and extent of inundation decreases landward so the components of the plant community vary.

The creeks of salt marshes have been much studied, not least because they represent miniature models of drainage systems in terms of morphometry. However, the similarity does not extend to behaviour for their flows of water have very different properties from rivers. The sinuous high-density channels of creeks can be seen in Photo 7.17, and so long as their banks are vegetated their form will remain relatively stable unless, of course, some event as catastrophic as a spring tide does something to alter it. A feature of most marshes is the **salt pan**, that is, a small enclosure within the marsh on which little will grow because of the saline soil. They may represent areas that have been cut off from the tide as the marsh grew or, more probably, the upper sections of creeks that have been isolated due to a bank collapse downstream. Once isolated the water may gradually evaporate or may remain stagnant, as it is in those shown in the photograph of Culbin Sands (Photo 7.18).

Much of the pattern and evolution of marshes that has been detailed here has been disturbed, indeed simplified, in the past century. This is due to the invasion of a remarkably fast-growing, tolerant and therefore enormously competitive plant, known as rice or cord grass. Since it was first introduced into Southampton Water to accrete mud and keep the shipping channels clear, it has spread to almost every coastal marsh in Britain and is so successful that it has been fought vigorously by the managers of the nature reserves at Blakeney who wish to preserve the complexity of the natural ecosystem.

Photo 7.17 Creeks in the salt marsh behind Blakeney Point, Norfolk.

Photo 7.18 The salt marsh at Culbin, Moray Firth, north east Scotland. In the foreground a series of cut-offs can be seen; as these dry out they will become salt pans.

Changes in Sea Level

No consideration of the British or any other coastline can ignore the impact of sea levels of the past. To develop this theme fully, we should start many hundreds of millions of years ago, for the geological history of the British Isles cannot be understood unless one looks back into the periods such as the Cretaceous, which saw much of these islands submerged beneath a sea into which great deposits of chalk were laid down. But our purpose here does not necessitate so large a time scale, and we need concern ourselves only with the transgressions of the sea associated with recent geological time, from the beginning of the Pleistocene Ice Age through the two million years to the present. The impact of the changes which the Ice Age engendered can still be felt today, as Fig 7.36 shows. The southern parts of Britain are actually sinking relative to the level of the sea, a fact which made the building of the Thames Barrage all the more urgent. To counterbalance this the northern parts of the country are gaining on the sea, by as much as nine millimetres a year in the Fort William area, and the nation could be said to be pivoted about a line drawn approximately from North Yorkshire to south Cornwall, via Glamorgan.

Causes of Changing Sea Level

Pleistocene Ice Age

Undoubtedly the most profound cause of change in sea level is the onset and the demise of an ice age. The onset of an ice age means that an increasing percentage of precipitation is in the form of snow, and temperatures are so low that little melting is likely to occur. Run-off into rivers and the sea will be so restricted that the latter will become depleted. As a source of water for precipitation the sea will still be tapped but the source will not be fully replenished. So the level of the oceans falls, and the more widespread the ice distribution becomes the lower it goes. Melting ice, as the glacial period ends, has the opposite effect. A continued melting of the world's present volume of ice would raise the average sea level by between 40 and 60 metres, enough to engulf most of the world's major cities. The fluctuation of sea levels is not as simple as it may seem, however, for it rose and fell for every advance of the ice and for much of Britain this meant three major advances and four interglacials, if we include the present as one of them.

Each time the ice came and went different extents of glaciation were reached so that each time, the volume and level of the sea were different. Thus, the Pleistocene and the succeeding Holocene period, have given us many different coastlines, fragments of each of which may exist in various parts of the country. These ice-induced fluctuations are referred to as **eustatic changes** in sea level.

Regrettably, the pattern we have described so far is only part of the story, for we have not yet explained why the land appears to be moving as well as the sea in

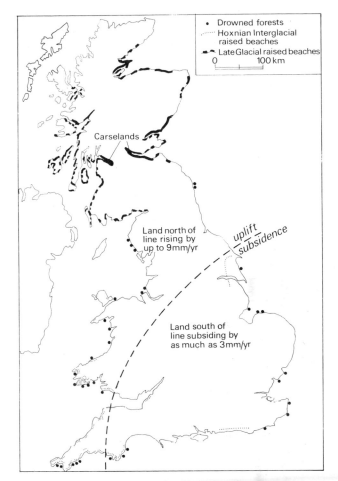

Fig 7.36 Some aspects of changing sea levels.

Fig 7.36. Ice sheets are not only immensely thick but also immensely heavy, so heavy that their presence literally weighs down the land and slowly depresses it. Thus, during an ice age the land as well as the sea falls. The relief of the ice being removed causes the land to 'breathe out' and it effectively rises, a form of **isostatic adjustment** (see Chapter 2). Thus, in an interglacial or post-glacial period the land and the sea are both rising. If the rising were at the same rate in these two movements the effects would be nil. However, land does not respond as quickly as sea to these changes, and there is thus a lag time. Imagine, then, a situation after the ice has melted in which the sea is rising but the land has not yet done so. Coastal features may have time to adapt to the new sea level, only later to be raised above the level of the sea by the rising of the land. Thus a raised beach perched 15 metres above today's sea level may not simply represent a sea level at some time in the past 15 metres higher than today's, but a complex interaction between the changing levels of land and sea over thousands of years.

Tectonic movements

It would be wrong to leave the impression that all sea level changes are a response to fluctuations in the world distribution of ice. One other major cause is tectonic movement. Imagine the impact, for example, of ocean floor spreading as it enlarges ocean basins, or, conversely, the effect of plate subduction as it reduces them. Submarine vulcanicity will also have its impact, even if on only a local scale such as the emergence of Surtsey in 1963. The faulting of a coastline may also alter levels of land and sea relative to each other.

Effects of Changing Sea Levels

It would need a text the length of this entire book to interpret the effects on the British coast of all of the changes of sea level that occurred during the Pleistocene Ice Age. We shall, therefore, limit our studies to a smaller time scale, approximately 130 000 years, for this time span is long enough to include glacial and

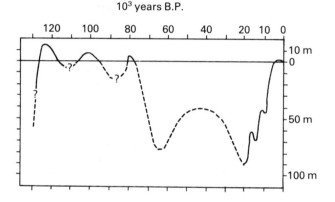

10^3 years B.P.

Fig 7.37 The possible sequence of sea-level changes over the last 130,000 years.

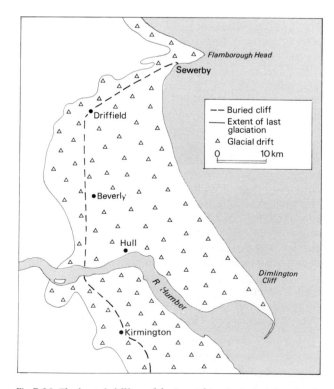

Fig 7.38 The buried cliff line of the Ipswichian interglacial sea level.

interglacial periods and to provide us with a sufficient understanding of the principles and effects of sea level change. The graph in Fig 7.37 uses field evidence to construct the possible fluctuations of sea level over this period. A brief review of the changes will suit our purposes here.

Sea level was, on average, about 15 metres higher than at present around British shores during the last major interglacial, the Ipswichian. Evidence of this is fragmentary, but **raised beaches** on the Gower Peninsula date from this time, as does the old cliff line shown in Fig 7.38 which extends from Sewerby in Yorkshire southwards into Lincolnshire. For much of its course the cliff is buried by deposits from the ensuing glaciation, but near Sewerby chalk boulders and animal remains appropriate to the warmer temperatures of the interglacial are discernible in the form of a raised beach. Dating of the sediments on the terrace of the Thames on which Trafalgar Square stands shows them to be of this age, too, which means that this would have been the flood plain of the river at this time.

The final advance of the ice was not an extensive one, but sufficient to reduce the sea level. This would have exposed sand flats to erosion and have generated sand dunes, but perhaps more importantly, it would have led to the development of slope-over-wall cliffs. Cliff lines would have been left high and dry as the sea receded, exposing them eventually to the full force of periglacial attack. Their bases would become protected by the weathered debris whilst their tops would be shattered and worn back by the activities of frost and gelifluxion, as Fig 7.14 demonstrates. In some areas pre-existing cliffs were totally submerged by the head deposits of gelifluxion. Many rivers would have been present in Britain at this time, and their erosive power probably increased by meltwater discharge. This, combined with the lower sea level would have enabled greater downcutting to perhaps 30 metres below present sea levels.

Many other shoreline features would also have developed during this glacial period, but the major rise of sea level of up to 40 metres since then will have relegated them to a location on the continental shelf. In Scotland, however, this may not be so, for here the ice was thickest in the final glacial advance and therefore isostatic recovery has been great. This has allowed an abundance of raised beaches to exist, as Fig 7.36 shows. Traditionally, it was thought that these raised beaches could be identified at three levels and they became known as the 25, 50 and 100 foot beaches. More recent work has shown that it is infinitely more complex than this, with varying rates of post-glacial eustatic and isostatic change producing a coastal landscape of many different levels. It has also produced the **carselands** or raised mud banks which flank parts of the River Forth.

Post-glacial advance of the sea has meant that many former interglacial cliff lines have once again resumed their role as coastal boundaries, and the sea, in the case of slope-over-wall cliffs, is gradually reshaping them. In other areas there are thick glacial deposits to be re-

Photo 7.19   Kingsbridge Ria, Devon: looking across the drowned river mouth, or ria, towards Salcombe.

Photo 7.20   The remains of the ancient drowned forest at Borth, Dyfed.

moved before the former cliff is reached. In the case of the Seven Sisters the sea has not only resumed its former level but has vigorously worn back from its interglacial position. The downcut river channels of glacial times have been infilled and in some cases their valleys drowned to form **rias**, if they were V-shaped, and wider flatter **cstuaries** if the flood plain has been inundated. Three particular stretches of coastline are known for their rias—south Devon, for example at Kingsbridge (Photo 7.19), south-west Ireland, for example Bantry Bay, and west Wales, for example Milford Haven. In Scotland the drowning of glaciated valleys has produced **fjords** such as Loch Torridon (Fig 7.39).

In some coastal areas forests were able to develop in the improving climatic conditions of post-glacial times, only to be submerged as the sea level rose (Photo 7.20).

The impact on man's activities of sea level change is considerable. From the cliff-top fortifications in Rye or Winchelsea in Sussex one can look out over the few kilometres of salt marsh, knowing that when the castles were built one would have been looking directly out over the sea. The economic function of ports can thus be changed. On the other hand, natural ports such as Milford Haven and Loch Long have been created by the drowning of valleys. On lowland coasts, effects are particularly significant, for a larger area of land stands to be gained or lost than on a highland one. In the Scilly Isles, raised beaches provide flat level areas for daffodil farms, whilst in other areas they provide recreational facilities such as car parks or even golf courses.

Coastal Measurement Techniques

The familiarity and appeal of coastal environments may encourage many a student to embark upon an investigation of processes and landforms. Whilst there are many possible areas of study, there are also many pitfalls and careful preparation is essential. One possible project might be to investigate the processes operating on a beach to evaluate any change that is occurring.

Beach Techniques

It is essential that one first establishes the time scale over which one is working, for to establish any significant pattern one really needs to carry out a project of this nature across several years or at least across one whole year. If such time is unavailable, short cuts can be made, but accuracy may be sacrificed. There are two ways in which one could derive maximum results from a short time period. One of these is to compare

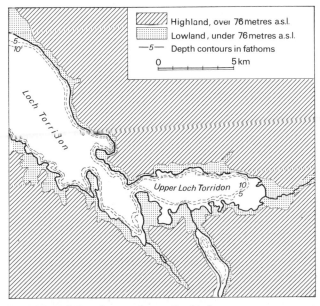

Fig 7.39 Loch Torridon, north west Scotland.

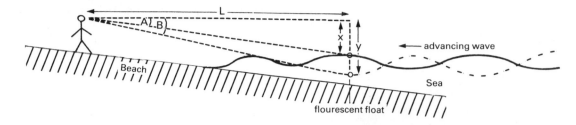

1 Use clinometer to measure angle A to wave crest, and angle B to wave trough
2 Estimate or measure distance (L) between observer and wave
3 Calculate x and y using trigonometry
   x = (tan. A).L
   y = (tan. B).L
4 Wave height = y − x

Fig 7.40 Measuring wave height.

observations made before and after a storm, so that normal and extreme conditions and effects could be contrasted. An alternative is to concentrate one's data collection around the period of maximum change on a beach as it alters from its summer to its winter profile.

Whichever of these is chosen, precise timing will still be difficult. What, then, should we measure?

Beach material

By analysing beach material we are able to evaluate the degree of sorting on a beach. On swash-aligned beaches this is likely to be graded across the beach, whereas drift-aligned beaches may well show grading along them. A sampling method is essential, preferably along a series of transects. On sandy beaches each small sample should be dried and sieved, as described in Chapter 9, to establish the mean grain size at each point. Each sample of shingle can be analysed by measuring, say, the length of the longest axis, and thereafter by calculating the mean for each location.

Beach angle

There are many ways of measuring beach slope angle, most of them described in Chapter 4. For slopes as gentle as beaches accurate measurement is obviously useful, and a surveyor's level is ideal.

Waves

These can provide a real challenge to professionals let alone amateurs. Wave height could be measured by using a fluorescent float and a clinometer as in Fig 7.40 or by observing the rise and fall of crest and low against a breakwater or harbour wall. Similarly, wavelength could be estimated against a premeasured distance, particularly if one is able to stand on a groyne or harbour wall and look down on the waves. From estimates of length and height, wave steepness can be easily calculated, and this is a useful indicator of a wave's energy.

Assessing the relative effectiveness of swash and backwash is difficult. By timing the average period between successive wave crests, one can gain some insight into the likely interference of backwash with swash. A refinement of this statistic, called **phase difference**, is even more useful. Phase difference is the ratio of the time of a wave's run-up to its wave period. The run-up begins as a wave breaks and ends at the furthest point up the beach that the swash reaches. Different types of breaker have varied phase differences. The longer wave period of low, flat, constructive waves reduces the calculated value of phase difference, whilst steeper spilling waves may have long run-up times which last for several wave periods and therefore increase the value of the phase difference (see Fig 7.41).

If one's time scale is restricted it will be difficult to make any definite conclusions about predominant wave direction. Nevertheless, it is useful to record this at the time of one's observations as it will have a bearing on longshore drift. If no better method is available, a plank of wood aligned with the beach could be placed in the swash zone and another plank placed next to it parallel to the wave crest. The intervening angle could then be measured. For a longer-term appreciation of

Fig 7.41 Phase difference.

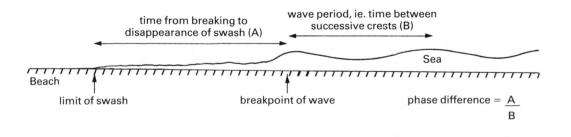

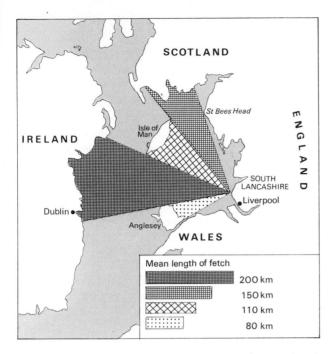

Fig 7.42 The length of fetch of waves approaching the coast of south Lancashire.

wave direction, local meteorological or RAF stations will usually provide data on wind strength and direction from which wave data could be extrapolated. This should then be matched up with possible fetches, as in Fig 7.42, to give a fuller picture of the impact of waves from various directions.

Longshore drift

The impact of longshore drift on a beach is much more straightforward to assess on shingle than on sand. A line of pebbles sprayed with fluorescent paint across the beach can be left, hopefully to be undisturbed by people, but to be distorted by the ensuing drift. Very frequent checks on the line will be needed if the drift is not predominantly in one direction. A similar method cannot be used on sand as individual, painted particles will be impossible to identify later. Accumulation against groynes and other obstacles could be measured if these are present, or pieces of lightweight brick could be substituted for the sand, large enough to be seen but light enough to be drifted as easily as sand.

Tides

The tidal range may be interpreted from beach jetsam or by the levels of berms, although of course the upper limit is much easier to judge than the lower.

Tidal currents provide a greater challenge, for they are very variable and operate on the sea bed. What is needed is something which is light, but visible, and which will stay on the sea bed and not float. These criteria are met by the **Woodhead seabed drifter**, which is a fluorescent plastic saucer with holes in it to allow

the current to move it along. To keep it on the bottom tiny copper weights are attached, but not too heavy to check its flow. Even so, the tracking of the drifter is not necessarily easy.

Using the above methods at the suggested times, a general picture of the scale and detail of changes in beach morphology should be discernible.

Cliff Retreat

If rate of cliff retreat is one's objective, then time is probably too short to carry out many field observations except perhaps some measurement of slope processes as suggested in Chapter 4. Instead one must resort to the study of old maps and documents, if they are available. Evidence of former coastal villages such as Eccles in north Norfolk can certainly be traced. For cliff retreat as fast as that at Barton-on-Sea the various editions of large-scale OS maps will suffice.

Vegetation Analysis

Maps across a much longer period will help us with an analysis of spit growth, as they have at Orford Ness in Suffolk, and also possibly of marsh development. Field observations of marsh growth are beyond our scope, but vegetation analysis both here and on sand dunes will provide useful insight into the role of vegetation in landform development.

As with all vegetation analysis, sampling is essential, and once again the use of transects is ideal. A quadrat can be used for the actual sampling of types and quantities of different plants. Once a sampling point on the transect has been selected, the quadrat should be randomly thrown and its contents analysed. Rough estimates of percentages of each type of plant in the square can be made, or more precise a method can be adopted using a 100 square grid within the frame. Any book of British flora will aid identification, but the survey will need to be done in summer for the flowers to be used for this. Associated surveys of soil moisture, acidity and nutrients could accompany the survey.

Conclusion

It is, then, undoubtedly true to say that coastlines are one of the most dynamic landscapes in Britain. Change is occuring continuously, and on some of them drastic alterations take place within a human lifetime. In some areas this may mean that bays are gradually succumbing to sedimentation, and as the intervening headlands retreat, the whole coastline is straightening out. In others, however, an equilibrium has been reached between form and process so that present features are preserved. In such a manner, beach angle and wave steepness may be balanced against each other, or the supply and removal of sediment from a salt marsh, from a spit or from a beach may just equate with each other.

Man's activities frequently disturb such an equilibrium, often having unforeseen consequences many kilometres from their point of occurrence. Several modern barrage schemes, across the Wash and Morecambe Bay for instance, have at present been rejected and perhaps it is just as well, for until more research is done it is almost impossible to predict the havoc that such a change to tidal and longshore currents, wave patterns and sediment movement could cause. This is one of the themes that will be explored more fully in the final chapter.

Questions

In order to answer most of these questions, reference has to be made to a specific page of the chapter.

1 Give some examples and detailed explanations of how some landforms undergo both deposition and erosion. (**page 153**).
2 Explain why the larger upper section of the eastern cliff of Lundy Island implies less rapid erosion of the cliff base than on the western cliff. (**page 156**).
3 Explain in detail why a small cliff provides less of an obstacle for wave attack than a larger one. (**page 156**).
4 Explain each of the three factors given which determine the width of a wave-cut platform. Can you think of any more? (**page 159**).
5 Explain precisely how the sea can protect a cliff. (**page 159**).
6 Explain in your own words why wave period is important in determining the movement of sediment up and down a beach. (**pp 160–61**).
7 Explain what adjustments might take place after a storm to re-establish the beach equilibrium, and how they might operate. (**page 161**).
8 Explain how asymmetry of swash and backwash can cause beach concavity. (**page 162**).
9 Why do you think a low tidal range encourages spit formation? (**page 165**).
10 Suggest the various possible sources of material that waves deposit on a beach. Are there any other sources besides those that come from the sea? (**page 165**).
11 How does a zone of zero wind velocity act as a sand trap? (**page 168**).
12 Suggest as many ways as you can in which the processes in marshland creeks differ from those in rivers. (**page 170**).
13 Why would an equal rate of rising of land and sea make the effect on coastal landscapes easier to interpret? (**page 171**).
14 Does sea floor spreading in an ocean basin produce a rise or a fall in sea level? (**page 172**).
15 Using the information in this chapter, try to draw a systems diagram of a beach, in which inputs and outputs are identified as well as the variables and processes that determine how inputs are transformed into outputs.

Further Reading

Coasts, E C F Bird (Blackwell, 1984).
Geographical Variation in Coastline Development, J L Davies (Longman, 1980).
An Introduction to Coastal Geomorphology, J Pethick (Arnold, 1984).
The Study of Landforms, R J Small (Cambridge, 1978).
The Coast of England and Wales in Pictures, J A Steers (Cambridge, 1960).

Other References

Slopes and Weathering, M Clark and R J Small (Cambridge, 1982).
Breaker Type Classification on Three Laboratory Beaches, C J Galvin, *Journal of Geographical Research* 73:12, 3651–9 (1968).
Blakeney Point and Scott Head Island, J A Steers (National Trust, 1964).

8

Glacial Processes and Landscape

Introduction

It is probably no exaggeration to say that the Pleistocene glaciation of the British Isles has left a greater impact on the present landscape than any other climatic event of the past. This is partly due to the magnitude of the event and the profound effects of glacial processes, but more important than that is the fact that, in geological time, the last **Ice Age** has only just finished. Undoubtedly, there were many world glaciations prior to the Pleistocene, the Ordovician being prominent amongst them, but effects of these early ice ages have, in many areas, long since been overcome by succeeding geomorphological events and even faint traces are difficult to discern.

Dating of deposits and sediments suggests that the Pleistocene began about two million years ago. With the age of the earth estimated at about 4500 million years this makes these events very recent. Indeed, if the entire history of the earth were to be compressed into the twentieth century, this is the equivalent of the Pleistocene beginning some two weeks ago and ending only one and a half hours ago.

Glaciations begin as temperatures gradually fall over a long period of time. Precipitation takes the form of snow rather than rain and temperatures remain sufficiently low to prevent excessive melting so that permanent snow cover, succeeded by ice cover, ensues. Why the temperatures fall is open to much debate. Some research suggests that a decrease in the amount of incoming solar energy is responsible, with emission of heat from the sun varying according to cycles of various lengths. A more widely accepted theory points to slight oscillations in the orbit of the earth around the sun, making the globe more remote from the source of heat. An extensive period of vulcanicity could inject sufficient dust into the atmosphere to reduce incoming solar radiation, and we are all aware of a similar result being possible from a major intercontinental exchange of nuclear warheads; a nuclear winter could become a nuclear ice age. Changes in the earth's surface caused by plate tectonics could also engender a temperature change. Realignment of land and ocean could interfere with the amount of solar energy normally reflected or radiated, and newly folded mountain ranges could

sufficiently interfere with global wind circulation to bring about considerable changes to world climate patterns. (See Fig 8.1.)

The Glacial History of Britain

It takes only a short series of extreme winters in northwest Europe or North America for the broadcasting and publishing media to home in on an alleged expert who is able confidently to interpret these events as the coming of a new ice age. It is difficult to take such opportunists seriously, for so short are the records that the cold spell is more likely to be a minor fluctuation in average temperatures than any long-term climatic deterioration. Even so, short-term glaciations can occur, as evidenced by the **Little Ice Age** in Europe which began in Tudor times and extended for four centuries until the mid-nineteenth century. It was epitomised by long hard winters, and by the Seine and the Thames freezing over; it was captured in art by Dutch and Flemish painters, Bruegel being a noted example of the latter.

Reconstructing the sequence of events during the Pleistocene is as fascinating and as frustrating a task as any great murder mystery, for evidence is fragmentary and often circumstantial. Hardly surprisingly, therefore, the available evidence, usually in the form of inaccessible sediments, can be interpreted in different ways. There is certainly agreement that the Ice Age was not just one long uninterrupted period of low temperatures, but that it was punctuated by a series of warmer **interglacials**, temperatures during some of which may have risen up to 3°C higher than those experienced in Britain's present climate. There is disagreement, however, over the number of interglacials that took place, with some recent research suggesting as many as 21 periods of glaciation within the Pleistocene. The most widely accepted, and much simpler, scheme of events involves only three major and one minor advance of the ice. As Fig 8.2 shows, these three great advances of the ice during the Pleistocene were the Anglian, the Wolstonian and the Devensian, followed, on a limited scale, by a fourth, the Loch Lomond re-advance. An attempt to attribute a spatial dimension to these events has been made in Fig 8.3, which shows that southern

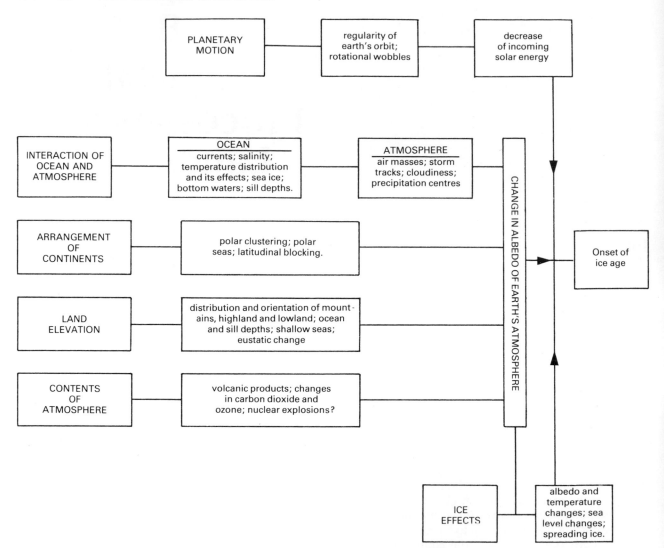

Fig 8.1 Causes of Ice Ages.

England was probably never glaciated. It is not easy to uncover evidence of the Wolstonian in Britain, but it is usually assumed to have reached a similar latitude to the Anglian. Its existence is confirmed by parallel glaciations in other parts of Europe and by ocean bed deposits. The fourth and minor advance of the ice affected only the uplands of Britain with, for example, corrie glaciers advancing only as far as the headward reaches of the great glacial troughs of Snowdonia and the Lake District. The table in Fig 8.2 gives some indication of the length of an interglacial; it can be seen that the period of time since the end of the Pleistocene is considerably less than an interglacial. Does this mean that we may still be in an interglacial? We cannot be certain, although the majority opinion is that we are.

Ice

Its Extent

It is one of those amazing, but true, facts that about three-quarters of the fresh water on the planet is in the form of ice. Hardly surprising, therefore, that arid, but rich Middle-Eastern states have looked to Antarctica and its icebergs for a source of water. During the Pleistocene the glacial periods saw an even greater proportion of the water as ice, for there was nearly three times as much ice on the continents then as now (see Fig 8.4). About 85 per cent of today's continental ice is in Antarctica, and with another 12 per cent in Greenland the tiny amounts still present in Europe could be seen as insignificant. They should not be, however, for many of the world's most magnificent glaciers are found in the French and Swiss Alps, part of the 3000 square kilometres of ice in the Alpine region in all. Britain today has no permanent ice although the north and north-eastern facing slopes of some of the higher Scottish mountains may retain patches of snow from the preceding winter even in midsummer.

During the Pleistocene the situation was quite different. As temperatures fell, ice advanced not only from the North Pole to cover much of continental Europe, the USSR and North America as far south as Illinois and Indiana in the USA, but also advanced from highland areas where the permanent snow line slid slowly down the hillsides. Thus, Cumbria would have faced an onslaught of ice from Scotland in the north and from its own Lakeland fells.

The area of land covered in ice has decreased in the late twentieth century at least as far as most northern hemisphere ice masses are concerned. Many Alpine glaciers have lost up to 33 per cent of their area in the last century, having extended during the Little Ice Age, and the Athabasca Glacier of northern Canada has retreated by over 1.5 kilometres since the 1870s. There are, of course, exceptions to this. In August 1986 the Hubbard Glacier in Alaska was advancing at a rate of over 12 metres a day as it surged forward across an 8-kilometre front, cutting off the upper end of a fjord as it did so.

Fig 8.2 The climatic changes of the Pleistocene: the precise pattern of interglacials during the middle Pleistocene is open to much debate.

Its Properties

One really needs to rid one's mind of the idea of glacial ice being akin to that formed in the freezer compartment of a refrigerator. Not only is it much less pure, but it is also not simply water that has been frozen. The best way to simulate glacial ice is to make a snowball, or iceball, which is effectively what one creates by the moulding and squeezing of snow in one's hands. In other words, glacial ice is compacted and pressurised snow from which much of the air has been removed.

When snow first falls it appears to accumulate quickly, but much of the thickness is usually given by the pockets of air trapped between the snowflakes rather than by the snow itself. The density of newly fallen snow is probably no more than 0.06–0.08, that is, over 90 per cent air and less than 10 per cent snow. Its nature will soon change, even without human feet to compress it, for natural compression will probably have increased the density to 0.2 within a couple of days. If temperatures permit the snow to remain, the

Time scale	Era	Stage	Climate	
10,000 B.P.		Late Devensian	Cold, includes Loch Lomond Readvance (2000 years)	C
12,500				C
26,000	Upper Pleistocene	Late Devensian	Glaciation	
115,000		Early and Middle Devensian	Cold	C
128,000		Ipswichian	Temperate interglacial	W
		?	Cold	C
		Ilfordian	Temperate interglacial	W
	Middle Pleistocene	Wolstonian	Glaciation	C
		Hoxnian	Temperate interglacial	W
320,000		Anglian	Glaciation	C
		Cromerian	Temperate interglacial	W
550,000		Beestonian	Cold, periglacial	C
		Pastonian	Temperate interglacial	W
690,000				
	Early Pleistocene			
2,000,000			C=COLD W=WARM	

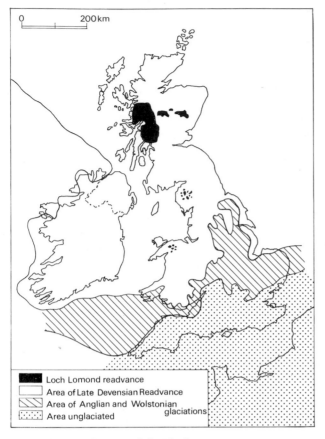

Fig 8.3 The spatial pattern of glacial advances.

	Maximum during Pleistocene (millions km²)	Present extent (millions km²)	% Decrease
Antarctica	13.8	12.5	9.4
Greenland	2.3	1.7	26.1
Canada	13.4	0.15	98.9
N. Europe	6.7	0.003	99.5
USA	2.6	0.08	96.9
Asia	4.0	0.12	97.0
Alps	0.04	0.003	92.5
S. America	0.87	0.03	96.6
Australasia	0.03	0.001	96.7
Total	43.7	14.6	66.6

Fig 8.4 Comparison of present distribution of ice with maximum extent during Pleistocene.

continuing natural process may cause the density to rise as high as 0.5 after just one winter and by this stage an intermediate compound has been formed known as **firn** or **névé**. The majority of snowballs are most likely firn balls, a fact for which few participators in a snowball fight tend to spare a thought! Whether the years of contortion and pressure ever rid the ice of all its air is unlikely, and densities of above 0.8 or 0.9 may take decades or centuries to reach.

Its Forms

Reference has already been made to different spatial forms of glacial ice and it is important that these are borne clearly in mind throughout this chapter. At the largest scale is the **ice sheet**, capable of covering entire continents and of being over 3000 metres thick. It is well exemplified by the sheets of Antarctica and Greenland and by the feature which covered northern Europe during the Pleistocene. At a smaller, but nonetheless significant, scale is the **ice cap**, which is referred to as a **jokull** in Iceland and which may sit across a mountain range, such as the impressive Vatnajokull and Hofsjokull. In both sheets and caps, ice flow may occur, usually from the thick dome of the centre out towards the edges.

The **glacier** is the most common, the smallest scale and the most familiar ice form; nevertheless, it requires some definition. A glacier is a flowing stream of ice often restricted in width by surrounding relief. Even so, it can have considerable dimensions. The Beardmore Glacier of Antarctica extends over 200 kilometres and in places is over 20 kilometres wide. Like most natural features, their students have been quick to classify them.

Valley glaciers are the most familiar to inhabitants of the British landscape, having once clothed most Lake District valleys, for example. They often follow pre-existing river valleys, originating in an ice collection centre in the uplands, perhaps at a corrie. **Corrie glaciers** themselves are less extensive, filling their distinctively shaped upland basins but not venturing far from them. **Piedmont glaciers** may well constitute the lower reaches of a valley glacier. The ice is much broader and shallower as it spreads out on to a lowland beyond the confining restraints of an upland valley. Finally, there are **outlet glaciers**. These are literally the outlet for ice flow from ice sheets, protruding out from the edges of, for example, the Antarctic ice mass towards the sea; a notable example is the Beardmore Glacier.

Glaciers

Being easier to study and to understand, glaciers have traditionally been the ice mass to which most attention has been paid, and with the majority of accessible research concentrating on glaciers this text is bound to repeat the emphasis of its predecessors.

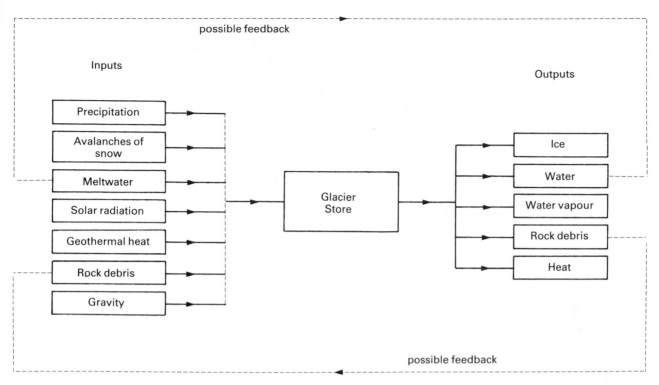

Fig 8.5 The glacier as a black box system.

Glaciers as Systems

Once again, it is helpful to our understanding if we conceive of glaciers as systems open to inputs and outputs of energy and matter. This is reflected in Fig 8.5 which indicates that glaciers are constantly processing a variety of inputs into a series of outputs. Rock debris, for example, can enter the glacier in many different forms, as scree cascading down from the hillsides, as clay and silt dumped upon or within the ice by meltwater streams or in fragments of all sizes picked up by the glacier itself. Although primarily derived from snowfall, glacier ice may have other inputs, for example from snow avalanching from above or from meltwater freezing onto the ice. A considerable proportion of the input of solar radiation may be reflected by the glacier's glassy surface, but that which does get through is important, not only in providing meltwater but also in warming the ice and thus altering certain of its properties. Warmth penetrating the glacier from beneath, that is, geothermal heat, may have similar effects, particularly in determining the temperature of the base of the glacier.

Outputs are just as varied. Moraines and meltwater deposits are as varied in shape and size of sediment as the debris inputs. Evaporation of meltwater provides only part of the water vapour output, the rest being supplied by sublimation as ice transforms to a vapour without passing through the intermediate stage of a liquid. More important processes in reducing the ice volume, however, are melting, whether within, beneath or on the surface of the ice, calving, as lumps of ice break away on entering a lake or a sea, and wind erosion of the surface, particularly if the wind is laden with ice crystals. In summer months air temperature is not necessarily the most important factor in surface melting; the amount of rainfall is also vital.

It would be an easy conclusion to reach that the inputs and outputs are all spatially distinct, with inputs occurring in the upper reaches of the glacier and outputs in the lower. This, of course, is not so, for snow can fall throughout the glacier's course and melting can occur quite readily in the afternoon sun in even the highest altitudes. However, it is valid to say that in the upper part of the glacier over a year the inputs will probably exceed the outputs whilst the reverse is true in the lower part. There is therefore, presumably, a theoretical point along the glacier's course where the two processes are approximately equal. This point, as Fig 8.6 indicates, is known as the equilibrium line and it separates the **accumulation zone** from the **ablation zone**, ablation being the general term given to all the processes by which ice wastes away.

If net accumulation occurs above this point and net ablation below it, surely it follows that the glacier is becoming top heavy, for its head is expanding and its lower reaches are contracting. This would be true if flow were not occurring, but the transfer of ice from head to toe maintains the equilibrium of the entire glacier.

As well as this spatial variation of input and output, there is also variation over time. Winter is likely to see greater inputs of snow, less of meltwater and far less ablation, whereas all these characteristics will be reversed in summer. The balance between the two is unlikely to be exact in any particular year, but over a decade or so an equilibrium of input and output should be established, as Fig 8.7 suggests.

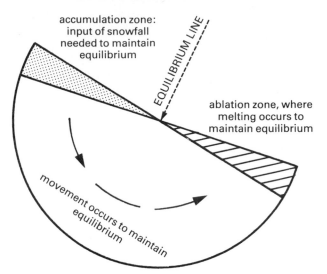

Fig 8.6 Schematic long profile of a glacier to explain balance of accumulation and ablation.

Such an equilibrium could not be expected to hold if the glacier is in the stage of **retreating** or **advancing**. Most Alpine glaciers would certainly not show a net balance of ice mass over the past century as they have gradually adapted to the warmer conditions following the Little Ice Age. These variations in ice mass over time are referred to as the **regime** of the glacier. Although akin to river regimes, they are not identical. Whereas a river regime is concerned with the annual variations in total discharge, the glacial regime is concerned with the deficit or surplus of annual accumulation against annual ablation. Alpine glaciers such as the Rhône could therefore be said to have a negative regime, as annual accumulation has rarely equalled ablation since that glacier's retreat from the village of Gletsch in the 1920s.

Ice Movement

Although giving the appearance of being just a straightforward downslope movement, glacial flow is a highly complex mechanism composed of many different types of motion. As we shall see, it comprises not

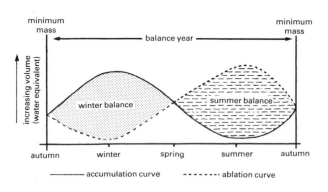

Fig 8.7 The annual balance of ice mass within a glacier.

only flow downhill but also movement of ice down through the glacier towards the base and movement upwards to the surface.

Types of flow

As far as the downslope flow is concerned, there are two basic processes which may or may not occur simultaneously, **internal deformation** and **basal sliding**. To understand the difference, a simple parallel can be drawn with the motion of another solid body downhill. Imagine a hillwalker has lost his footing as he climbs a slope and begins to slide down it. Two things will happen: first, he will slide down the slope perhaps on the seat of his trousers, thus maintaining his form even though it is in motion. Second, deformation of his body may begin to occur – his limbs may get twisted beneath him and perhaps fracture. In short, his body will become contorted.

Now transfer those two processes to a glacier. First there is basal sliding, in which whole blocks of ice are set in motion from beneath because the ice can no longer resist the stresses put upon it. Like the climber, the block of ice may well retain its form as flow occurs. Stress will have built up for a number of reasons: the steepness of the slope, meltwater providing sub-glacial lubrication or a build-up of pressure from ice accumulating behind an obstacle such as a protruding rock barrier. The flow will tend not to be continuous, but to proceed in a series of jumps responding to the climaxes of the stress.

Internal deformation of the ice body is much more complex and involves both creep and fracture. The downslope pull of gravity or the sheer weight of ice upstream can exert sufficient stress on ice crystals for them to respond by sliding over each other or by transforming their own shape. Thus, they creep downhill. If these tensions are strong enough, the crystals may fracture and slippage may occur along the resultant slip planes. By both methods the form of the ice body changes from within.

The speed of both forms of flow may depend on similar factors, such as the gradient, the thickness of the ice and its temperature. A particularly important parameter for basal sliding is the temperature of the base of the glacier for, in cold glaciers where above-zero temperatures may never be recorded, the ice may be permanently frozen to the rock and, with no meltwater to lubricate it, basal sliding may not be possible at all.

Variations in rates of flow

Along the course of the glacier: with so large a range of variables affecting their form and size, it is to be expected that rates of flow along the course of a glacier will vary. As has already been stated, the gradient and the thickness of the ice may be the two most important variables in determining this. However, the effects of the increase or decrease in speed that is thus engendered may be quite complicated. As the ice speeds up, perhaps because of an increase in ice thickness caused

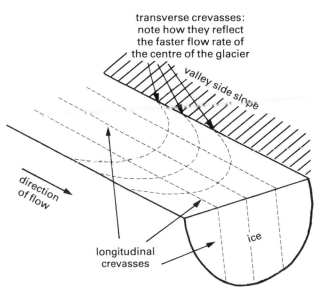

Fig 8.8 Extending and compressive flow. (For explanation see text.)

compression and may trap debris brought up from the glacier's base by the rising ice. Parallel bands of dirt may thus be embedded in the ice. Careful study of Fig 8.8 should help to clarify these points.

Across the surface of the glacier: the **transverse crevasses** that result from extending flow normally curve upstream. Differential rates of movement across the surface of the ice may soon straighten them or even reverse their curvature. This is because frictional drag where the glacier is in contact with the valley walls

by constriction of the channel or by the joining of a tributary glacier, or because the glacier is flowing over a steep bedrock barrier, it will thin out. This phenomenon is known as **extending flow** as the ice is stretched or extended in response to the acceleration. The tension created by the stretching will create crevasses across the surface of the ice and from them slip planes will extend down into the ice to its base. An important component of extending flow is that ice from the surface slides down these slip planes towards the base, a process that is occurring simultaneously with the general flow downslope. When ice decelerates, at the bottom of a slope for instance, compression rather than tension will occur and the method of flow will be quite different. Here, **compressive flow** takes place. The ice thickens as a response to loss of speed, and sliding of ice along the slip planes created upstream will be upward from the base. Crevasses close up due to the

may cause the sides of the glacier to move much more slowly than the centre. Measurements of flow in the Saskatchewan Glacier in Canada indicate that ice velocities in the centre of the ice stream may be five times that of the sides. Where contrasts such as this occur they may not only be capable of transforming the transverse crevasses but also of creating **longitudinal crevasses** parallel to flow.

Within the glacier: for similar reasons of frictional drag, but this time with the bed rather than the channel sides, rates of flow are likely to decrease towards the base of the ice. This can be verified by inserting a column of ball bearings into a borehole in the ice and observing the column's distortion over time in a method not dissimilar to methods of measurement of

Photo 8.1 Extending flow in a glacier on Mt. Ollivier, New Zealand.

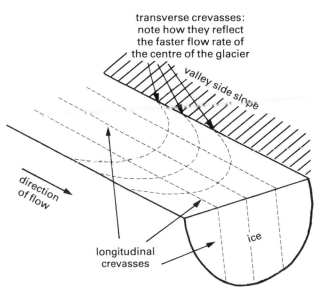

Fig 8.9 Cross-section of a glacier to show two types of crevasse.

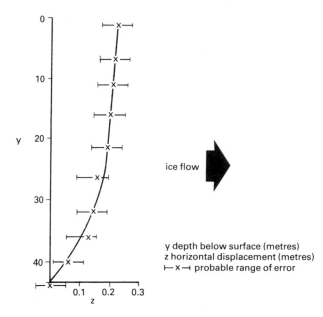

Fig 8.10 The flow velocity profile within the Saskatchewan Glacier.

soil creep described in Chapter 4. As Fig 8.10 demonstrates, this may reveal that the differential between surface and base rates is sufficient to create slip planes within the ice along which parallel blocks of ice slide. If not, it will certainly reveal that rates of internal deformation vary considerably through the ice. Isovels joining points of equal velocity can be drawn for glacier cross-sections in the same way as for river cross-sections, and a fine example of a typical pattern is shown in Fig 8.11.

Over time: the majority of glaciers rarely experience flow rates, even at their surface, of a metre a day and at certain times of the year even a few centimetres may not be achieved. This is quite a contrast to river speeds where a metre per second, or over 85 kilometres a day, is quite conceivable. Such slow rates of glacial flow mean that the body of an unfortunate climber trapped down a crevasse maybe a century ago could still be locked in the ice, having not yet been conveyed to the **glacier snout**.

Variations of flow through time occur in both the short and long term. One could argue that the fastest speeds should be recorded in summer, particularly in the ablation zone, when meltwater lubrication will be at its greatest. On the other hand, surely the reduced ice mass of these zones in this season will effectively reduce speed, whereas the high winter mass of the accumulation zone will produce maximum rates there. In fact, the highest velocities are usually recorded in the ablation zone in summer, although occasional localised peaks will be reached in the accumulation zone in winter.

It has already been mentioned that glaciers will respond to longer periods of temperature change such as the Little Ice Age, perhaps causing an advance of the

glacier snout. Temperature change may also be one of the causes for what are known as **surges**, in which glaciers become unusually active, such as the incredible 75 metres a day that was achieved by the Black Rapids Glacier of Alaska in 1937. Complete understanding of why these waves of ice should roll down a glacier has not yet been reached, but fluctuation in the input of snowfall and even earth tremors have been considered as possible causes. It certainly appears feasible that increased snowfall could put greater stress on the glacier which, in turn, could lead to sufficient subglacial melting to reduce resistance further and to cause the glacier to respond by surging forward.

Much shorter-term and more localised surges may occur in parts of the glacier's course following the surmounting of an obstacle or rock barrier. The ice behind such a barrier will have been temporarily delayed and had time to gather its strength to push forward.

Glacial Erosion

Few readers of this book would question the fact that the great valleys of the Lake District such as Borrowdale and Langdale were carved by glaciers, and yet it was not until the mid-nineteenth century that this theory became recognised, let alone accepted. This followed the pioneering work of such men as Louis Agassiz and the Reverend Professor Buckland who realised the similarity between the landscape of British uplands and that of the currently glaciated Swiss Alps. Glacial erosion, then, is accepted as a powerful tool, although, as we shall see, certain authorities are now beginning to question its efficacy, suggesting that too much reliance has been placed on it at the expense of meltwater action. Perhaps such controversy is to be expected, for although the evidence of glacial erosion may seem glaringly apparent, it is really only circumstantial; it is difficult, if not impossible, actually to measure or observe the erosion processes taking place.

Methods of Erosion

A simple division of erosion processes into **abrasion** and **plucking** is, nowadays, thought to be too simplistic, and the traditional theory of ice being able to pluck pieces of solid rock from the ground seems dubious. The classification adopted here will, therefore, be more comprehensive.

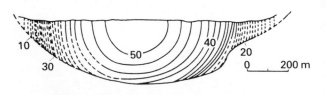

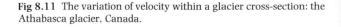

velocities are in metres per year

Fig 8.11 The variation of velocity within a glacier cross-section: the Athabasca glacier, Canada.

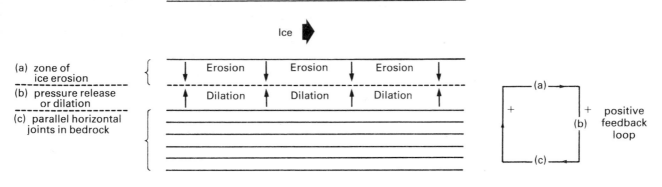

Fig 8.12 The link between glacial erosion and horizontal bedding.

Abrasion

Anyone who has experience of carpentry can easily envisage this process. A sand-papered desk top has much in common with an abraded rock surface. It appears smooth to the touch and yet, in effect, is covered with a multitude of microscopic scratches, each one grooved into it by a grain or particle of rock. The weight of the moving ice provides the equivalent pressure to the carpenter's arm. The abrasive tools are pieces of rock of all sizes from **rock flour** to boulders that protrude from the glacier base and are held rigid by the ice. As the rock is worn down, a layer of debris builds up beneath the ice which, when held together by frozen meltwater, may itself act as an effective abrading agent.

The sandpaper analogy can be extended further to a consideration of the factors determining the effectiveness of the abrasion. The following questions can best be answered if one bears in mind the parallel question for the effectiveness of sandpaper. Does rapid basal sliding increase abrasion, or, by moving the tools so quickly over the surface, reduce it? Does the presence of meltwater act as a lubricating film and thus increase basal sliding and abrasion, or does its presence buoy up the glacier so that the abrasive tools are out of reach of the rock surface? What shapes and sizes of fragment will be most effective? Do these fragments need to be harder than the bedrock, or vice versa for greatest erosion? Does the rock flour which the erosion produces help or hinder further abrasion? What happens if the fragments wear out and lose their angularity; does abrasion cease?

Most of the answers should be logical, but one final point is useful. Abrasion relies on its tools, and unless its worn ones are replaced it cannot continue. Fragments of scree, or the dropped glove of a climber come to that, gradually move down through the ice as snow accumulates on top of them and sub-glacial meltwater removes ice from beneath them; thus, provided the worn tools are removed, say by meltwater, there should be a guaranteed constant supply of fresh fragments.

Erosion of rock fragments

Whilst the ripping out of lumps of solid rock, or plucking, does not seem feasible, the **entrainment of loose rock** seems perfectly viable. Ice is capable of freezing around even massive boulders and embodying them into the flow. Meltwater may aid this process. A large rock obstacle in the path of the glacier may interfere with flow to such an extent that pressure builds up behind the rock from the accumulating ice. If such pressure leads to melting, the rock may be enveloped in a film of meltwater which, with release of pressure, may refreeze, or **regelate** around it, and the rock will become part of the glacier.

For any fragment to be picked up by ice, it will obviously help if it has been loosened previously. Joints will add to this weakening, allowing something more like the original plucking to take place. But not all joints will permit this, for they will need to have been widened by weathering to lower the resistance sufficiently. Such weathering may have been extreme in pre-glacial times, for as temperatures gradually fell frost shattering would have been rampant in the valley, allowing not only expansion of joints, but also providing a large quantity of loose debris for entrainment.

Glacial erosion may also take advantage of horizontal joints. As layers of rock are removed and replaced by ice the weight on the underlying rock may be reduced thus allowing it to relax, to dilatate, and produce further parallel or horizontal joints which themselves can encourage further erosion; a fine example of the operation of positive feedback, as Fig 8.12 shows.

Rock fracture

A third, although far less significant, method of erosion results from the sheer force of ice ramming rigid fragments of frozen rock into the bedrock, but this time the analogy is with the brute force of a chisel rather than the gentler motion of sand-papering. The results are manifold: the rock may crack in response to the pressure, it may be grooved or, like a chisel being forced across a dining table, it may be punctuated by a series of chatter marks.

Rate of Erosion

Being difficult to simulate in a laboratory, and the base of glaciers being so inaccessible except through perilous sub-glacial tunnels, there are few available statistics

Location	Average abrasion rates mm yr^{-1}*		Ice thickness (m)	Ice velocity (m yr^{-1})	
	Marble plate	Basalt plate			
Breiðamerkurjökull	3	1	40	9.6	plates flush with bedrock surface
Breiðamerkurjökull	3.4	0.9	15	19.5	
Breiðamerkurjökull	3.75	–	32	15.4	
Glacier d'Argentière	up to 36	–	100	250	plates project above bedrock

* estimate of measurement error = 0.3 mm

Fig 8.13 Some experimental measurements of glacial abrasion.

which indicate the rate of erosion. Some estimates are given in Fig 8.13, however.

Analysis of controlling factors is much easier to carry out, and Fig 8.14 summarises the most important ones. It is vital that one considers not only the ability of the ice to erode but also the susceptibility of the bedrock to erosion (see Question 1 at the end of this chapter).

Effects of Erosion

Glacial erosion wears down, it carves, it moulds, it smooths, it sharpens; in short, it reshapes the landscape on a scale that marine and fluvial erosion are only rarely capable of. Even so, its effects may also be seen at very local scales.

Small Scale Effects

The smooth and polished surface of a boulder or rock outcrop on an upland valley may be its inheritance from abrasion hundreds of thousands of years ago. To preserve such a surface it would need to have been buried for much of that time because weathering could otherwise have disfigured it. The same is true for scratches or **striations** that are preserved in rocks, for they are a natural focus for any modern weathering process. Striations can be of any length from millimetres to metres, or even kilometres in a few extreme cases, and can be found on any surface, vertical or horizontal, that was once exposed to moving ice. As the product of abrasion they may be present in their millions, if small and indiscernible to the human eye. Distinctive individual examples may result from one large abrading fragment, their shape and size depending on

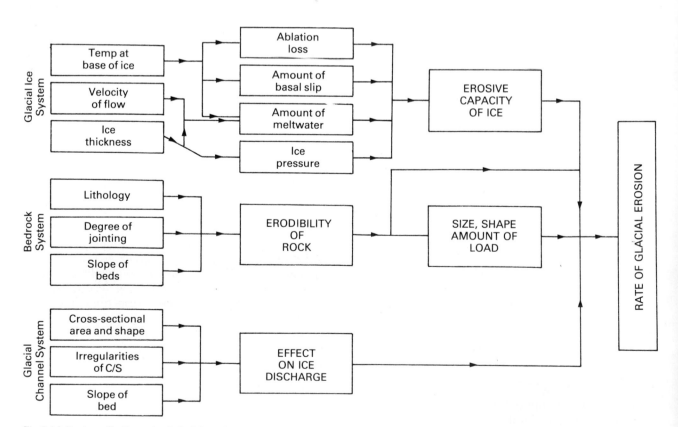

Fig 8.14 Factors affecting rate of glacial erosion.

the relative hardness of tool and bedrock and the pressure exerted from the ice. A fragment of chalk is likely to make little impression on a surface of granite, for example, and a brittle rock like obsidian may well crack rather than take kindly to etching.

A similar, although less common, small-scale feature are the **chatter marks** and **grooves** that rock fracturing may leave behind. Often crescent-like in shape, the chatter marks are likely to occur in series.

Larger Scale Features

Ice erodes upland and lowland alike, but its most distinctive features are undoubtedly left in the highlands and it is to these that we shall turn our attention first.

The glacial trough

It might seem incredible to a modern student that in the early days of Victorian tourism, the towering scenery of glaciated valleys such as the upper parts of Borrowdale in Cumbria were considered too frightening for ladies to see lest they should succumb to fainting fits. Fortunately, such attitudes have long since disappeared and the glories of Loch Ness, Great Langdale and Glencoe are appreciated by all.

The **glaciated valley**, with its characteristic 'U', or more accurately parabolic, shape is well known to all students of geomorphology, most of whom would hold that it owes its existence to a glacier which once flowed down it, deepening, widening and straightening the former river valley that it followed. The mere mention of the term conjures up an image of perhaps the Lauterbrünnen valley of Switzerland or the Nant Ffrancon in north Wales as the perfect example. But a little investigation would show that not all glaciated troughs exactly replicate this perfect image; they are in fact a highly diverse form.

The first reason for this is that most glaciated valleys, in Britain at least, have been subject to changes during the last 10 000 years. As the climate improved in post-glacial times, lakes and rivers of meltwater may have dumped layers of sediment in their bottoms. Further sedimentation could have occurred as temporary lakes became infilled. In the Nant Ffrancon valley, bores have shown that the bedrock is some metres below the present-day surface. Gradual increases in temperature would also have permitted rapid frost action on the valley walls, gradually replacing the bare rock slopes with debris (see Fig 8.15). Riggindale, shown in Photo 8.2, is certainly not a perfect parabola.

The size and the erosive power of the glacier are a vital control of form. A true parabola tends to occur in those valleys where several glaciers have amalgamated. The Kirkstone Valley, in Photo 8.3, being near the source of the ice at over 500 metres above sea level, tends to have much more of a V-shape than the more classic valleys further from the ice collection centres. Some researchers have suggested that V-shaped glaciated valleys are more likely to occur where the gradient is steeper, but this point need not, of course,

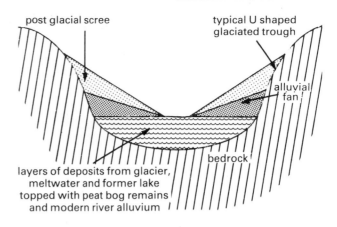

Fig 8.15 Diagrammatic cross-section of a glaciated valley.

contradict the former. A glacier's erosive power is likely to reflect its input of snowfall, and if Pleistocene totals were proportional to today's Scottish totals then it is hardly surprising that the deepest glaciated troughs are in the western highlands and islands where precipitation totals are the highest. One must not forget that the more powerful the glacier, the more debris or moraine it is likely to carry, and the deposition of this in great quantities may also produce considerable modifications to form.

Characteristics of the rock which composes the valley are a third determining variable. The contrasting character of the Borrowdale Volcanics and the Skiddaw Slates in the northern part of the Lake District is reflected in the detail of their glacial landforms. Angularity of the watersheds and valley side slopes of the former, as exemplified by Wasdale or Great Langdale, is a result of the varying resistance of the many fine layers

Photo 8.2 Riggindale, Haweswater, Cumbria: the trough of a tributary glacier to the main Haweswater valley beyond.

Photo 8.3 Looking down the V-shaped glaciated valley of Kirkstone to the U-shaped trough of Brotherswater. The glacier of the former valley joined other tributary glaciers to form the deeper wider valley beyond.

often used, and there are many fine Cumbrian examples, notably the valleys of Wasdale and Borrowdale. **Icelandic troughs**, on the other hand, result from glaciers that issue from ice caps, usually on upland plateaux such as the south-east Grampians to the south of Balmoral where Glens Doll, Clova, Muick, Mark and Lee provide good examples. Other than their different origins, which are largely a result of local topography, Icelandic and alpine are not necessarily easy to differentiate between.

Further variation in form could have been caused by the modifying effects of advances and retreats of the ice. Those valleys which saw ice creep into their upper regions at the time of the Loch Lomond re-advance may have been left with a large number of dead ice hummocks, which remain today as a series of carbunkles on their flat floor. It is an important point to remember that the shape of a glaciated valley depends not only on the vagaries of the erosional processes but also on the quirks of deposition.

Even man's activities can cause the mental image to be out of line with reality. Raising the water level of the lakes in the Haweswater and Thirlmere valleys to increase Manchester's water supply has produced troughs whose flooded bottoms look very different from those of the more natural Ullswater which lies between them.

Erosional features of the glacial trough

Contrast of form may also be produced by the presence or absence of particular erosional features, and some of

that compose the Borrowdale Volcanics to the frost shattering that took place above the glacier's surface. Corresponding smoothness of the Skiddaw area is a reflection of the much more uniform nature of the rock, which has allowed few weaknesses to be exaggerated by weathering. The Jaws of Borrowdale is the graphic name for the narrow waist of a major English glacial trough caused by a band of rock crossing the valley at this point. Its resistance, probably the result of local metamorphism, would have proved too great for the glacier to widen the valley any further (see Fig 8.16).

Lithological contrasts are not the only aspect of geology to leave their mark on the form of glacial troughs. Many glaciers have utilised the weakness provided by a fault line to produce extremely straight vales, such as Strath Conon to the north east of Inverness. Moffatdale, as seen in Photo 2.2, is another extreme example, and the fact that hanging valleys such as the Grey Mare's Tail are suspended some 200 metres above the floor of the major trough add further to the effect (see Photo 8.4). Without the advantage of a fault the tributary valleys could not possibly have cut down so deeply. The glacier that once flowed off the Cumbrian hill of Blencathra down the Glenderamackin Valley completely changed direction because of the fault line which crossed its path; this has produced a distinct elbow in the valley, as Fig 8.17 shows.

A fifth reason for the diversity of form may be the different types of ice collection centre from which the glacier emerges. Where glaciers form from the merging of a series of smaller corrie glaciers, the term **alpine** is

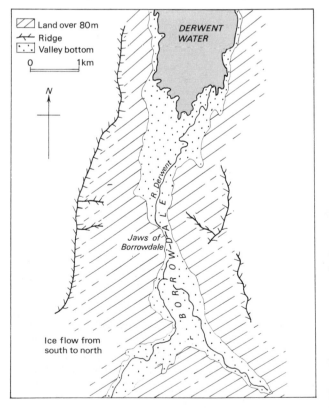

Fig 8.16 Borrowdale showing ice constriction at the jaws.

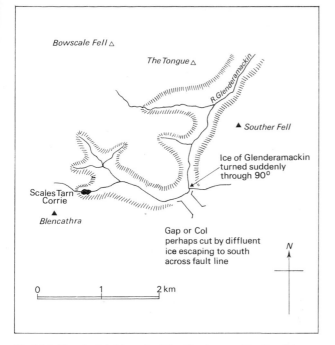

Fig 8.17 The glaciated trough of the Glenderamackin, Cumbria.

Photo 8.4 Moffatdale from the Grey Mare's Tail: a view from the hanging valley into the glaciated valley which runs across the photograph.

these are sufficiently distinctive to be dealt with separately.

The deepest part of a glaciated valley may well be its upper reaches, which must imply that glaciers may need to traverse gentle uphill gradients to reach their snouts. This **overdeepening** of the upper course may well be a response to the erosive action of extending flow as ice plunges over the trough end of the valley. Such steep trough ends develop in alpine valleys at the confluence of many smaller corrie glaciers, or in Icelandic valleys where ice drops into its valley from the plateau top. Overdeepening produces rock basins within the long profile; the **rock barriers** which terminate them may also act as dams to present-day drainage, a feature which gives the characteristic lakes and lochs of upland Cumbria and the Scottish Highlands.

Spectacular ice falls occur on the course of a glacier where it surmounts rock barriers. If the glacier is a powerful one it will wear down such obstacles and little trace of them may remain in post-glacial landscapes. Where they do survive they may produce **rock steps** which are usually the sites of waterfalls and probably represent the outcrop of a resistant band of rock that happens to traverse the valley at that point. In other locations, if they appear below the confluence with a tributary valley, they mark the point where the ice was able to cut down deeper due to its increased erosive capability. A more controversial theory suggests that rock steps may mark a halting place of the glacier during its retreat, and today's step reaches down to the level to which meltwater issuing from the stationary glacier could erode. The glacier could thus be said to

have had a protective role as the bedrock beneath it was not worn down in the same way as the rock downstream. This theory is feasible in certain locations, but if the step shows distinct signs of abrasion on its upstream side and a quarried, irregular downstream face it is surely the product of glacial, not meltwater, erosion.

This contrast between different parts of a rock out-

Photo 8.5 Roches moutonneés in Easedale. Ice motion was from left to right in the photograph.

Photo 8.6 Stirling Falls, New Zealand: a hanging valley, tributary to a fjord.

Photo 8.7 Glencoyne, Ullswater, Cumbria. The alluvial fan in the foreground provides the farm with its highest quality land. Glacial melt-water from the impressive hanging valley behind the farm was responsible for depositing the fan.

crop is also true of **roches moutonnées**, which are seen in Photo 8.5. Once again, these are protrusions of bedrock which the ice has not been able to eradicate. When the rock is overridden by ice, its back is polished and striated as it is worn down by abrasion. Blocks may then be pulled from its downstream side if jointing or some comparable weakness has loosened them. They may reach a considerable size; in the small valley of Greenburn Bottom in the Lake District one example towers some 15 metres above the valley floor. Because they often occur in clusters, some geomorphologists have suggested that they do not merely represent resistant outcrops which the ice cannot overcome, but are actually a product of the selective method by which ice erodes.

Little more needs to be added about **hanging valleys**. The former tributary glaciers which they represent probably followed a tributary river valley that existed before the ice came. A spectacular example is included in Photo 8.6. In Britain hanging valleys are rarely so grand, although striking waterfalls may issue from them, such as the Lodore Falls of Borrowdale, which may be currently depositing **alluvial fans** on the floor of the major trough. Some of these, though, may have been created by a gushing flow of meltwater as the glacial period ended. A particularly fine series of fans occurs on the north side of Ullswater, notably the Glencoyne fan which provides much needed lowland meadow for the sheep farm (see Photo 8.7).

Glaciers are far less sinuous than rivers, as their inflexibility and lack of manoeuvrability mean they are far more prone to cut corners and reduce their angle. In time they may completely remove the bends in the valley to create the efficient, straight channels for which they are noted. In so doing they may obliterate interloc-

king valley spurs, to leave as their only relic **truncated spurs** such as those on the southern side of Blencathra, pictured in Photo 8.9.

High on the side walls of some glacial troughs natural processes have provided gaps through which modern communication routes can pass. Such **gaps** or **cols**, well represented in Cumbria by the Blea Tarn Gap on the site of Great Langdale and in the Irish Lake District around Killarney by Moll's Gap, have been created by **diffluent ice**. Such streams of ice are thought to have broken away from the main glacier by taking advantage of a weakness on the side wall. It is quite likely that ice from the Glenderamackin Valley did this, using the fault line to divert southward away from the main direction of flow (see Fig 8.17).

Cwms, corries, or cirques

These rounded upland hollows, which look as if a giant ice-cream scoop has scraped a portion from a hillside, are sufficiently common for most languages to recognise their existence. Thus the French cirque, the German kar, the Cumbrian combe, the Irish coire, the Welsh cwm and the Scottish **corrie** all refer to the same feature. They are often likened to armchairs, because of their steep back wall and side walls and open front, but it is really only the modern bucket armchair which can support this analogy.

Corries, as we shall call them, act as the collecting ground or source for many valley glaciers, but it is important that we remember that not all such glaciers emanate from such sources. From the rose diagram in Fig 8.18, it can be seen that most of the corries of the Lake District face north or north east. This simple fact should tell us that their origin must be linked with low

temperatures, for in this northern hemisphere location the sun's energy never comes in from these directions, allowing the snow to accumulate more readily, as summer wastage is less likely. Shelter from prevailing westerly winds may also aid the process.

Corries, then, originate with the accumulation of snow. As patches of snow develop, perhaps on uneven ground or in hollows, and harden to firn or even ice, processes take place, collectively referred to as **nivation**,

Photo 8.9   The distant mountain of Blencathra reveals truncated spurs, the effect of a glacier moving from left to right across the photograph.

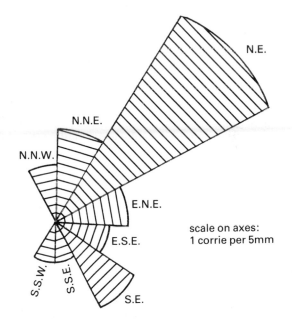

Fig 8.18   Corrie orientation in the Lake District.

Photo 8.8   Alluvial fan in the Hooker Valley, New Zealand. In this recently active glacial environment the fan has resulted from fluvioglacial deposition.

which deepen the hollow. Nivation is not fully understood, because it is so difficult to study at first hand, but it is thought to involve frost action beneath the snow, meltwater erosion and perhaps chemical action too. When sufficient deepening has taken place the ice begins to flow away from the back wall, probably in a method not dissimilar from extending flow described earlier. By a rotational movement ice slides across the developing corrie and, in so doing, deepens it further. Compressive flow compacts the ice as it reaches the lip of the corrie, and its erosive ability is reduced, thus explaining why the **rock barrier** or **threshold** is not

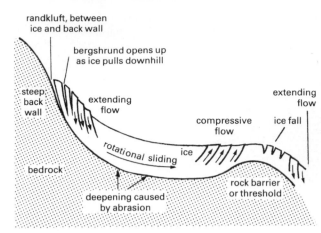

Fig 8.19 The development of a corrie.

Photo 8.10 Blea Water, Cumbria. Notice the sheer back wall and precipitous scree slope of this classic corrie.

broken through by the ice. The back wall itself is gradually steepened during this time, as water penetrating the **bergshrund** and the **randkluft** seeps into the rock, and, on freezing, shatters it. The fragments broken off can then be used as tools of abrasion.

During the final brief re-advance of the ice, many corrie glaciers once again came into existence but most would not have advanced far beyond the limit of the corrie. Dumps of moraines may well surmount the threshold, therefore, and the two barriers may combine to hold back a small lake in the corrie.

From a wide-ranging sample of observations it has been concluded that corrie shape is relatively consistent under many different geological conditions, and it has been suggested that the ratio of length to height is of the order of 3:1. Such relative figures cover a wide range of different scales from the huge 16 kilometre wide Walcott Corrie in Antarctica to a more typical British example, Blea Water in Cumbria, whose back wall plunges almost 400 metres from the arête of High Street to the bottom of a 65 metre deep lake (see Photo 8.10).

Despite a certain uniformity of shape, local idiosyncrasies of geology, topography and climate are bound to produce slight variations. Once again the Skiddaw Slates and the Borrowdale Volcanics provide us with a contrast; the homogeneity of the former produces much more rounded, indeed far less striking examples, despite the notable exception of Scales Tarn (see Photo 8.11), whilst the latter produces amphitheatres with stark and angular walls.

Arêtes and horns

Corries are rarely isolated features; they usually occur in groups, perhaps, as in the case of Snowdon, encircling the mountain peak (see Fig 8.20). In such a situation, the peak may protrude above them as a jagged pinnacle known either as a **horn**, notably the Matterhorn, or as a **pyramidal peak**. Not all mountains that support corries will develop such features: their summits

Photo 8.11 Scales Tarn, Cumbria. A corrie on the Skiddaw Slates: looking down the steep side wall towards the threshold or lip.

may be too flat or rounded, or the mountain too large for the peak to be picked out in this way. Despite well developed corries in its northern and eastern faces, and far less well developed ones to the south and south west, there is no way one could describe the dome of Ben Nevis as a peak.

Where corries cut back into a ridge against each other, the intervening apex may be sharpened into an **arête**. A fine example, Sharp Edge, runs along the side of Scales Tarn, its rigid teeth honed by frost shattering of both the present and the past. In late glacial times such attack would have been merciless, for horns and arêtes would have stood out above the glaciers quite unprotected.

Fjords

Fjords are essentially glaciated troughs that have been drowned by a post-glacial rise in sea level. With steep side walls and trough end, and with their upper reaches overdeepened by glacial action, it is hardly surprising that they are so widely used as sheltered bases for shipping, notably the deep-water oil terminal at Finnart in Loch Long north of the Clyde, and the nuclear submarine base at Faslane in nearby Gare Loch.

As the longitudinal section in Fig 8.21 demonstrates, fjords usually have a distinctive rock bar or. **threshold** near their mouths. This may reflect the point at which the valley glacier met the sea, began to float and thus became less capable of downcutting, or it may simply be that the glacier began to thin out at this point, released from the restrictions of a narrow trough. Alternatively, in pre-glacial times, this seaward zone may have suffered less frost shattering than the inner part of

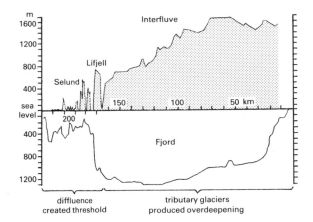

Fig 8.21 Longitudinal profile of Sognefjord, western Norway. The peculiarly irregular profile of the interfluve is explained by the difference in scales. The vertical is over forty times that of the horizontal.

the valley due to the moderating effect of the ocean and thus was able to withstand glacial erosion more successfully than the rest of the valley.

Fjords punctuate the coast of western Scotland, particularly fine examples being Lochs Torridon and Hourn, but they are more usually associated with western Norway where such fjords as Hardanger and Sogne provide magnificent incisions into the coastline.

Lowland features of glacial erosion

It may seem unjust that, after giving so much attention to features of upland glacial erosion, only a small section is devoted to lowland features. The prime reason for this is that the lowland features of Britain are less distinctive and, as a consequence of that, tend to be hidden beneath covers of drift, alluvium and soil through which their outline does not emerge. However, in formerly glaciated regions where the climate has not improved to the same degree as Britain's, such as the Canadian Shield and exposed parts of Greenland, lowland glacial landscapes may still be seen in their raw state.

Smooth, streamlined hillocks and depressions are the hallmarks of such landscapes, whether carved by glaciers in lowland valleys or by ice sheets. The hillocks may vary greatly in size from lengths of a few metres to kilometres, and may occur in several different forms, notably **whalebacks**, **rock drumlins** and roches moutonnées. Abrasion gives all of them a polished, striated surface, but it is their shape that differentiates them. That of the whaleback should be self-evident from its name, whilst the rock drumlin's is very similar to the depositional drumlin's described earlier, although, of course, it is composed of solid rock.

It is the plucked and angular downstream face of the roche moutonnée which distinguishes it from the other

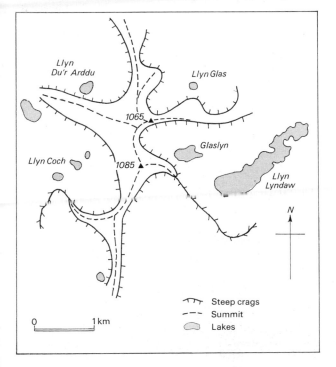

Fig 8.20 The summit of Snowdon: corries or former ice hollows cut into the mountain from every direction.

Photo 8.12   South Harris, Outer Hebrides: a glacially scoured lowland landscape.

two features. Scattered between these clusters or lines of hillocks are depressions which may vary enormously in profile and dimension. They may be grooves parallel to ice flow, or irregularly shaped rock basins defined by patterns of joints which allowed the ice to overdeepen the pre-glacial landscape. To remove rock from joint-weakened or fault-fractured zones such as these, the full interplay of glacial processes would be required – freeze-thaw, abrasion, block removal and the entrainment of loose debris. These bleak lowland landscapes of glacial scouring are sometimes termed **knock and lochan**, and Photo 8.12 exemplifies them. On this small scale, they are more likely the product of a lowland glacier than an ice sheet, they are present in parts of Scotland where local climatic and geological conditions are not convivial to soil and vegetation. One such denuded landscape is impressed upon the gneiss of the coastal platform of north-west Sutherland where open water, bog and bare rock conspire to produce one of Britain's most inhospitable scenes.

But what of the rest of lowland Britain? How did the erosive action of the ice sheet affect it? Many of the irregularities mentioned above may well be etched into the bedrock of these areas too, but most are buried beneath deep layers of glacial and post-glacial deposition. Undoubtedly, a general reduction of relief also took place, with the interfluves being both smoothed and lowered by the immense thickness of ice.

The Glacial Erosion Controversy

Other than an occasional hint of dissent, the discussion so far has suggested that ice is a very virulent medium of erosion and since the pioneering work of Agassiz in the 1840s this view has seen off most challenges. In order to achieve a proper perspective, however, it is important that we pay some attention to the challenges that have been made.

After so impressive an array of major edifices of the landscape described already in this chapter, is it really feasible to challenge glacial erosion? The answer is yes, but only under certain circumstances, when there is doubt about how the mechanisms of erosion operate. We might question, for instance, how a cold-based glacier actually erodes when, for much of the time, its base, at −10°C or below, is frozen to the bedrock. It is difficult for it to move, let alone erode. Yet, apparently, it can and does erode, and we cannot resort to sub-glacial meltwater for an explanation, for presumably temperatures do not permit it. One possible explanation is that in some cold-based glaciers, warmer ice which is capable of deformation exists above it and it is this which moves. Abrasive implements held by this layer could thus penetrate the basal ice and carry out their work. But even so, where are these implements coming from, for they certainly do not originate from sub-glacial erosion? The only conceivable answer is that they originate as supra-glacial debris that drops on to the glacier from frost-shattered side walls and then sinks through the ice. But this is not a complete explanation, for some glaciers are too cold even for these occurrences. We might also be indicating that, under some conditions, freeze-thaw is responsible for far more denudation than it is usually accredited with.

A second question we might ask is, just how important a contribution does sub-glacial meltwater make to glacial erosion? If it is capable of creating gorges as impressive as that at Newtondale (see Chapter 9), surely in any glacial valley its role cannot be ignored. Small cites further evidence from Norway to support this where a gorge over 200 metres deep has been carved by sub-glacial meltwater near the upper end of Hardanger Fjord. If the theory of rock step formation, which suggests that retreating glaciers protect whilst escaping meltwater erodes, can be verified then we must indeed assign a very important role to meltwater.

A further set of questions surrounds the corrie, that distinctive landform which to many is the epitome of glacial erosion. How exactly does nivation create hollows beneath patches of snow? Woolly explanations which suggest it is primarily a function of freeze-thaw fall apart when one measures temperatures beneath the snow patch, which, according to some Californian observations, never fall below 0.5°C. Snow, it must be remembered, is an insulator. Icelandic studies have provided different, and yet no more supportive evidence, for observations here have shown that even in the warmest months, temperatures of the subsoil may remain below 0°C. For freeze-thaw to occur, temperatures must fluctuate above and below zero and not remain on one or other side of it. To confuse matters further, however, evidence from Queen Maud Land in Antarctica suggests that snow can melt in temperatures as low as − 17°C, as long as it is bathed in sunshine. Would these be sufficient grounds to support the theory that nivation occurs by freeze-thaw beneath the snow, with tiny streams of meltwater removing the shattered debris? Perhaps so, but what about chemical weathering beneath the snow? Given van't Hoff's rule (see Chapter 3), surely at such temperatures chemical activity is stifled? This is true for all except carbonation, for ice-cold water can hold more carbon dioxide than much warmer water and thus may be quite active beneath the snow patch.

A second related question challenges the premise that the steep back wall of the corrie is a product of frost shattering at the base of the bergshrund or down the randkluft. How can meltwater, seeping down such gaps, freeze if the insulating ice is preventing temperatures from fluctuating sufficiently for it to do so?

A third difficulty besets the explanation of the corrie's rock threshold. There is a danger of confusing cause with effect. Compressive flow and rotational slip may maintain the threshold once it has formed, but how do these processes occur in the first place unless the threshold has already formed. The threshold is the chicken – or is it the egg?

The point of questioning the efficacy of glacial erosion is not to doubt its significance, but to demonstrate that the evolution of glacial landscapes is not an open and shut case. Many truths still wait to be discovered.

Glacial Transport

By now it should be only too apparent from where a glacier derives its load, but a synthesis of ideas at this juncture will help.

Ice picks up its load, and erodes it, gravity drops it down from overhanging frost-shattered slopes, streams of meltwater fill crevasses with it or strew it across the surface, and regelating meltwater beneath the ice incorporates it into the frozen mass. Thus the ice has a **sub-glacial load** (beneath it), **a supra-glacial load** (on top of it) and an **englacial one** (within it). The presence of debris may stain one's pure white image of a glacier to give a more realistic picture, streaked with greys and browns. In the ablation zone, in fact, the white, or even blue, ice may be quite submerged beneath great mounds of dirt and debris (see Photo 8.13).

Glacial Deposition

Simply by placing deposition into a different category from erosion we have created a division where, perhaps, there should not be one. Erosion and deposition are continuous processes, – as a glacier erodes so it deposits, often in close proximity. The reason why we do separate them is that in post-glacial landscapes the relics of erosion and deposition tend to dominate quite separate locations. A simple division might suggest that upland landscapes are relics of glacial erosion with just a superficial covering of deposits, whilst lowlands are primarily depositional areas in which the effects of erosion have been largely covered up. Of course, such a designation contains many exceptions, but for post-glacial landscapes it may be less so, not least because of the conveyor-belt properties of a glacier, processing debris, entraining it, eroding with it, dumping it and re-entraining it. Thus, zones of erosion and deposition are not necessarily distinct.

Glacial deposits often fare badly in studies of geomorphology. Their forms are less inspiring and undramatic – Wordsworth's romance with the Lake District was more a product of its erosional forms than its depositional! They are less easy to classify: categories merge with each other and deposits spread over one another. We must not be deterred, though; there is much to learn about the impact of deposition on British scenery.

Why does Deposition Occur?

Glacial deposition occurs because ice melts, and ice melts due to pressure-generated heat, geothermal heat, daytime warming of the surface, or due to the warmer temperatures of lower altitudes into which the ice moves. The controls on most of these sources of heat need little elucidation, except perhaps for pressure-generated heat which will depend on such variables as ice thickness, the roughness of the bed, the speed of the ice and the internal deformation of it.

Where does Deposition Occur?

The location of glacial deposition is largely linked to the reasons for it occurring. It can occur on the surface of the ice, at any point beneath it, on the sides of a valley, where ice enters a lake or the sea, behind an obstacle and immediately around the outward limits of the ice.

What is Deposited?

Ice can deposit anything that it has picked up or transported, although it may well have changed its form since joining the ice. It can dump blocks that are larger than houses, pebbles, fragments of rock, sand, fine material that abrasion has powered into rock flour, clays and silts. Chaotic mixing is typical of a glacial deposit; a jumble of material that juxtaposes clay with boulders. No fluvial sorting will be found here, for when ice drops material that which is nearest the base is dropped first, regardless of size; the fine material will not be suspended as it is in a river. The only semblance of organisation may be that some of the elongated particles have a similar orientation, their longest (A) axis parallel to the direction of ice flow, a characteristic inherited from their mode of transport. Fragments will be angular, possibly smoothed by abrasion, but not with the rounding-off of edges equivalent to the attrition of a river.

Although glacial deposits are unconsolidated in post-glacial landscapes, during the glacial period they may well have been frozen into a solid mass for short or long periods of lower temperatures. Thus, as ice continued to move over them or pushed them forward, their rigidity may have caused them to shear and sliding along shear planes to occur. A similar result may also occur, not because the debris was frozen to rigidity, but because the sheer weight of ice above it had squeezed out any meltwater and caused it to behave as a solid. Such layering of the deposits along sheer planes may well survive deglaciation and still be discernible.

Glacial debris is termed **till**, and various types of till have been recognised according to the location of their deposition. Thus, there are the major categories of **lodgement** and **ablation till**, the first referring to material which is laid down beneath moving ice, due to pressure melting and frictional drag, and the second referring to the dumping of supraglacial and englacial material as ice wastes away beneath it, perhaps during summer ablation or near the glacier snout or ice sheet periphery. Further subdivisions are possible, but not necessarily helpful.

To embark upon any classification of glacial deposits is a risky business, for the overlaps are even more apparent than in other branches of geomorphology. Confusion is not helped by the tendency for deposits to be heaped upon each other in no particular order, often inter-bedded with meltwater deposits. Indeed, the original deposits may have been completely reworked or deformed by an advance of the ice, by meltwater streams or by sub-glacial or supra-glacial flow, whereby the till itself may flow, soon after its deposition, across bedrock or across the surface of the ice. Add to this alteration by post-glacial rivers, wind action, weathering and slope processes and one has a melée for which classification is a most daunting prospect. If this is further complicated by deposits from a previous glaciation also being present, the task may well be impossible.

Nevertheless, certain distinct landforms of glacial

Photo 8.13   The Lower Arolla Glacier, Switzerland. This shows the snout of an active glacier currently advancing. Note the push moraine on the ice surface.

deposition have been identified even if field recognition does demand more than just a cursory glance.

Moraines

If till is the debris which ice deposits, then **moraine** refers to the landforms which glacial deposits or till create. Some forms are much more temporary than others. Medial moraines, for instance, are rarely found in post-glacial landscapes such as Snowdonia or the Lake District; they need to be studied in currently active glacial areas before they are destroyed.

Photo 8.14   Thornythwaite Farm, Seathwaite, Cumbria. The ridge on the nearside of the farmhouse is the remains of the terminal moraine. The glacier would have been moving away from the viewer towards the farmhouse.

End moraines

End, or **terminal moraines,** are ridges transverse to ice flow, composed of debris dumped at the snout of a glacier or at the periphery of an ice sheet. Their size will vary according to the ice mass and their age – in a Lake District valley the remains of such features are rarely greater than ten metres high, the ridge upon which stands Thornythwaite Farm at the entrance to Seathwaite being a fine example (see Photo 8.14). Yet in Pleistocene times the moraine which terminated the Ullswater glacier was probably nearly 300 metres high and at the snout of New Zealand's Franz Josef Glacier today the moraine reaches 430 metres. The Cromer Ridge in north Norfolk which marks the southerly limit of the late-Devensian, the third major glaciation, is now not even 100 metres high but in scenery as subdued as this it is, nonetheless, a noticeable landmark.

The deposition of end moraines is a combination of many processes including dumping of supra-glacial and englacial debris, as ice melted, and saturated lodgement till either being squeezed from beneath the ice margin or being transported by sub-glacial flow. Indeed, many may also include layers of fluvioglacially deposited debris.

As transverse deposits, they are sitting targets for remoulding, especially by meltwater streams which may alter both plan and profile. The impact on the landscape of an end moraine depends principally on its size, but it may also depend on its capability as a dam. At less than 10 metres above sea level, Loch Lomond would undoubtedly be a fjord were it not for the terminal moraines to the south of the lake in the Leven valley that have held back the water. Without an end moraine, many a Cumbrian corrie would lack the tarns that are characteristic today.

End moraines commonly occur as a series of ridges rather than a distinct individual feature, perhaps reflecting the various methods of deposition or the fluctuating edge of the ice. If a major re-advance of ice occurs after a stationary period, moraines may be bulldozed forward to create **push moraines** as chaotic as their predecessors and subjected to thrusting along shear planes as the frozen moraine shivers forward. In the British landscape, such features are rarely distinguishable, but in Iceland and on various islands of the Arctic Ocean distinctive examples can be seen today. When ice pauses for long periods during the retreat from its limits, **recessional or stadial moraines** may mark each station, comparable in form to the end moraines but usually of a smaller dimension.

Lateral and medial moraines

Most of the material in a **lateral moraine** is derived from periglacial activity on valley side walls causing loosened debris to drop onto the sides of the glacier. As ice wastes away beneath it during deglaciation, the inner part of the moraine may be carried away, but the outer part should be lowered gently onto the valley side from which position it may settle by sliding downslope. Particles of debris tend to retain their angularity for, unlike the englacial and basal debris of a terminal moraine, there is little chance for rounding off edges on the moving surface of the glacier. Where scree, gelifluxion or vegetation have not buried them, lateral moraines can be discerned on the walls of some Scottish and Cumbrian valleys, but without detailed sediment analysis they may be easily confused with kame terraces (see Chapter 9). Such analysis could, for example, decide if the linear protrusion on the western flank of the Ullswater valley above Brotherswater near the junction with Dovedale were a lateral moraine or not.

Medial moraines may well lose all form during their emplacement on valley floors. They owe their existence to the coalescence of two lateral moraines where one glacier joins another. They are the most vulnerable of deposits in a post-glacial landscape and may be absorbed into the spread of ground moraine soon after the ice melts. As relics of a former climate in Britain, traces sometimes persist, most likely on craggy spur ends above the devastating ravages of valley floor meltwater such as the junction of Dovedale and the Kirkstone valley mentioned above.

Transverse parallel moraines

There are as many names as there are theories of formation for this type of moraine in which till has been moulded into parallel ridges and depressions. It is described variously as **transverse-fluted, ribbed, washboard, corrugated** or **Rogen moraine,** the latter after a particularly well studied area of its occurrence in Sweden. Different scales of occurrence have tended to produce different names from the 20–30 metre ridges of Rogen moraine to the much smaller washboard. Two groups of theories have been expounded, those for the smaller scale which suggest it is formed at the ice-

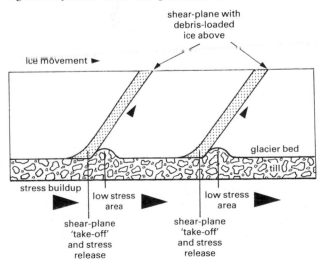

Fig 8.22 A possible method of Rogen moraine formation.

Photo 8.15 Drumlin, Healaugh, Swaledale, North Yorkshire.

front as seasonal fluctuations of the ice push forward and cause the till to be wrinkled, and those for the larger scale which suggest it is a sub-glacial feature produced in areas of compressive flow. In such conditions the ridges may develop immediately downstream from the shear planes where stress may suddenly be considerably reduced (see Fig 8.22).

Drumlins

A far more familiar form is the egg-shaped **drumlin**, swarms of which cluster in the Ribble valley of Lancashire, the Central Plain of Ireland, for example around Athlone, and in the Eden valley of Cumbria around Penrith. These sub-glacial, ellipsoid, streamlined moraines may form small hillocks, perhaps 50 metres high on these lowland plains, but in more upland zones such as the Greta Valley between Keswick and Penrith they are much smaller, rising no more than 5–10 metres above the surrounding area. In many cases, these mounds of till vary enormously from the perfect half-egg, although all have their axis aligned to glacial flow.

Their blunt (stoss) end points upstream and their shape has been likened to that of aircraft wings (see Fig

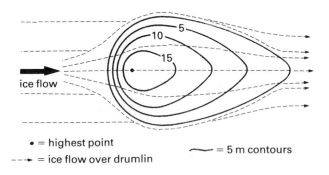

• = highest point
- - -→ = ice flow over drumlin
⌒ = 5 m contours

Fig 8.23 Ice flow around and over a drumlin.

8.23). This suggests that their streamlined form is moulded to create minimum resistance to the moving ice around them. This principle does not, however, supply us with a method of formation.

Perhaps the drumlins are deposited by ice sheets through whose base debris is unevenly distributed spatially; where it is concentrated and the material is dislodged it gradually builds into a mound which is moulded and streamlined by the clean ice which is easily able to deform around the embryonic drumlin. It may be that obstacles generate this process by providing friction with the heavily-laden patches of ice and causing deposition. Obstacles may be lumps of bedrock, but as most drumlins contain no such hard core, it may be that cores of frozen till would be a sufficient blockage to initiate deposition. Quite a contrasting theory purports that drumlins are an erosional form, sculpted from the underlying till by the moving ice.

Whether the result of deposition or erosion, the speed of the overlying ice will modify the drumlin's form, with faster speeds causing elongation. Fluted moraine, with crests parallel to ice flow, may well be an extreme form of this.

Ground moraine and till plains

From most glaciers and ice sheets a layer of **ground** moraine consisting primarily of lodgement till may be deposited. It is this which may be sculpted into drumlins and it is upon this that many of the distinct forms above may be laid down. Ground moraine subdues relief at all scales – at the smallest it may fill hollows and depressions, at the largest it may fill in valleys. At one time it probably blocked the Jaws of Borrowdale, damming a lake in the upper valley. Few parts of the lowlands of central and eastern England are free of it. Spurs may be capped by it or vales coated with it, and many local drainage problems of a rugby field or a farmer's land may be exacerbated by it. When present across extensive lowland areas it may be a major constituent of till plains.

As the largest of all glacial deposits, **till plains** consist of both lodgement and ablation till. East Anglia's low relief has been blanketed by such a sheet of till which is often 30–45 metres thick and in places up to 100 metres. it can be particularly well studied where it is exposed on the coast, as it is in north-east Norfolk. Its stratification is enormously complex, and although the constituents and structure of the ablation till may differ from the lodgement till which underlies it, it may not be easy to distinguish one from another.

On a larger scale, it may be possible to distinguish the three major glacial advances and even the interbedded layers of interglacial deposits. Within East Anglia there is great variation in the composition of the till; one of its more distinctive features is the area of chalky boulder clay where chalk fragments from the wolds of Lincolnshire and Yorkshire are a major constituent (see Fig 8.24).

It is within East Anglia that much of the analysis of

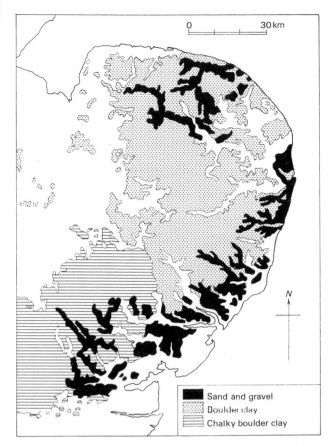

Fig 8.24 Glacial deposits of East Anglia: the imprint of post-glacial rivers can be easily seen. In some cases eroding the deposits, in others covering them with alluvium.

deposits has been done that has enabled researchers to build up a history of British Pleistocene glaciation. Hardly surprising, therefore, that East Anglian place-names such as Gipping, Cromer, Lowestoft and Hoxne feature prominently in the names of the various glacial and interglacial periods (see Fig 8.25).

A till plain produces scenery with few dramatic landmarks and reduces in prominence those that preceded its deposition. Although many valleys of eastern England were plugged by the till, a considerable number of modern drainage lines appears to be re-excavating pre-glacial river valleys, so the landscape cannot be said to have been totally obliterated.

Dead ice topography

Dead ice is ice that becomes detached from its life-blood, broken off from the active ice upstream during deglaciation. Such isolation usually results from local topography; in the Cumbrian example in Fig 8.26, for instance, a protruding rock barrier has stretched the thinning ice until eventually the downstream section is ruptured. The dead ice may well be protected from ablation by the insulating affects of a thick cover of moraine, which, as ice upstream continues to melt, may in turn be protected from meltwater erosion thanks to its position on top of the ice mound. When the dead ice finally melts, its cover of moraine may then be dumped as a **hummock**, a chaotic collection of which is

	Stage	Evidence
Upper	DEVENSIAN	
	IPSWICHIAN	interglacial lake deposits at Bobbitshole, Ipswich
Middle	ILFORDIAN	terrace at Ilford, Essex
	WOLSTONIAN	formerly known incorrectly as the Gipping (Suffolk) Glaciation
	HOXNIAN	interglacial lake deposits at Hoxne, Ipswich
	ANGLIAN	glacial deposits on Suffolk coast at Corton
	CROMERIAN	lake deposits at West Runton, Norfolk
	BEESTONIAN	silts and fluviatile gravels at Beeston, Norfolk
	PASTONIAN	tidal deposits at Paston, Norfolk
Lower	BAVENTIAN	marine sands and silts on Suffolk coast at Easton Bavents
	ANTIAN	
	THURNIAN	
	LUDHAMIAN	marine deposits at Ludham, Norfolk
	WALTONIAN	crag at Walton-on-the-Naze, Essex

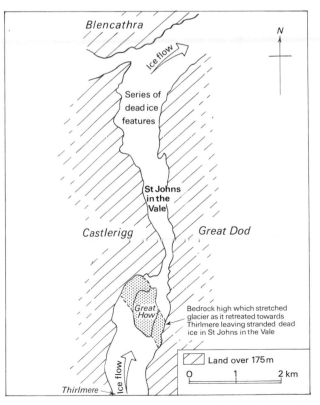

Fig 8.26 Explanation of dead ice features in St John's in the Vale, Cumbria.

Fig 8.25 (*left*) Evidence of Pleistocene deposition from East Anglia.

Photo 8.16 Dead ice hummocks at the foot of the Kirkstone Valley, Cumbria. The ice approached from behind the viewer. Note how easily the river is cutting down into the unconsolidated glacial deposits.

seen in Photo 8.16. Frequently, dead ice hummocks are both more numerous and fresher than any other morainic deposit in upland British valleys. This is mostly a reflection of their young age, for most are the relics of the Loch Lomond re-advance of some valley glaciers, which means that the hummocks are most commonly located on the rims of corries or in the upper reaches of a trough.

In areas which have been very recently deglaciated, such as those areas where retreat has followed the Little Ice Age, another feature, the **kettle hole**, may be found interspersed with the hummocks. These represent similar masses of dead ice that were buried beneath moraine, so that on melting the ice allowed the moraine to collapse into its vacant hollow, leaving a surface depression. Many of the British examples which undoubtedly existed 10 000 years ago have been infilled or drained but some remain, notably the series of meres around Ellesmere in Shropshire which are dammed by dead ice hummocks and kames (Fig 8.27).

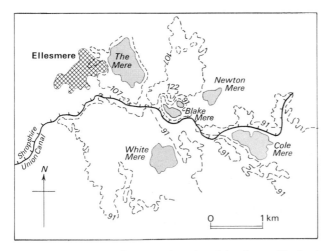

Fig 8.27 The Meres of Ellesmere, Shropshire: lakes dammed by dead ice hummocks and kames.

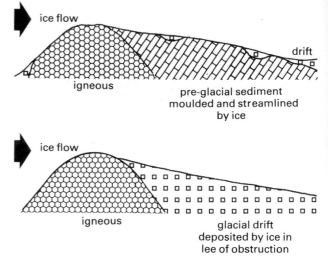

Fig 8.28 The formation of a crag and tail.

Crags and tails

Edinburgh Castle stands magnificently upon the core of an ancient volcano, and from it the Royal Mile stretches majestically downhill to the south west towards Holyrood House. As aware as they may be of the history of the area, few tourists who follow that route appreciate its glacial history. As ice sheets moved southwards over the site of modern Edinburgh, a tail of deposition was dumped behind the protruding obstacle of Castle Crag. Continued ice movement streamlined the deposit, as Fig 8.28 shows, and left it as the major British example of what is known as a **crag and tail**.

The Impact of Glaciation on Drainage Patterns

A review of this chapter would quickly confirm how strong an impact glaciation has had on the British landscape. Most of the effects detailed so far have been direct influences, but there are also indirect effects, of which the alteration of drainage patterns is probably the most significant. Glaciation cannot help but interfere with pre-existing drainage when one considers just the straightforward impact of a glacier on a valley, for by deepening it it may change its base level and gradient, and by straightening and widening it it can completely alter its course. Similarly, the array of mounds and hummocks left in a valley bottom can completely disorganise drainage patterns, creating lakes and bogs and forcing diversions. Most attention, however, has been given to less straightforward, but often more striking effects of glacial interference.

The Effect of Diffluent and Transfluent Ice

When the flow of ice in a valley is impeded because of the presence of other ice or because its rapid accumu-

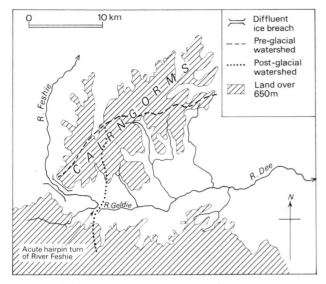

Fig 8.29 The diversion of the Feshie due to diffluent ice.

lation is not being discharged quickly, some of it may break through a weak point in the valley walls to escape as **diffluent ice** from the major flow. Once established, the escape route will expand into a col which may become so deep and wide that post-glacial rivers become diverted through it. Such an occurrence appears to have interfered with the upper course of the River Feshie in the Cairngorms which undertakes an acute hairpin turn to flow towards the Moray Firth rather than a more logical course via the Geldie and Dee to the North Sea (see Fig 8.29). Ice flowing down

the upper Feshie valley in Pleistocene times was probably blocked by larger glaciers flowing into the Geldie trough from north and south, thus forcing it to excavate a breach to the east. This steeper course has proved a much more natural line of drainage to the modern Feshie than the Geldie valley, and so the Spey river system has been extended to the detriment of that of the Dee.

Where such glacial breaching occurs on a regional rather than local scale, the term glacial **transfluence** is used to describe it, and the most noteworthy British example is the breaching of the western Scottish highlands. The ice cap which straddled Scotland had its divide to the east of the pre-glacial north-south watershed, which meant that the ice flowing westward was forced to breach it in many places. Today, more than 30 major passages through the watershed exist, as shown in Fig 8.30, the effect of which is that the upper courses of many rivers that would otherwise have flowed eastwards now drain to the west coast. The effective north-south watershed has thus been shifted significantly eastwards; a particular example is shown in Fig 8.31.

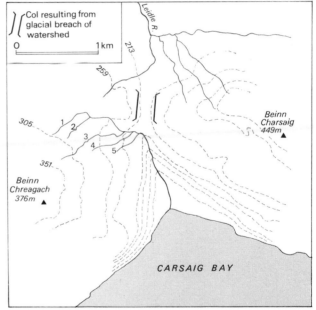

Fig 8.31 Glacial breach of watershed, near Carsaig, Island of Mull: the breach, which has caused tributaries 1–5 to join a south flowing river rather than the north flowing Leidle, also allows a road to cross the highland of the Ross of Mull.

Fig 8.30 The glacial breaches of Scotland's major watershed.

The Effect of Advancing Ice

It is likely that the Thames in pre-glacial times followed a course many kilometres to the north of its current one, flowing along the Vale of St Albans to reach the sea eventually on the Suffolk or Essex coast. Its gradual displacement southward, as Fig 8.32 shows, occurred as the ice advanced, forcing it to divert around its margins.

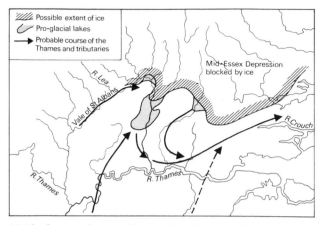

(a) The first ice advance of the Anglian Glaciation blocked the mid-Essex Depression and forced the Thames south through a pro-glacial lake, from which it escaped across the Hampstead–Epping Ridge.

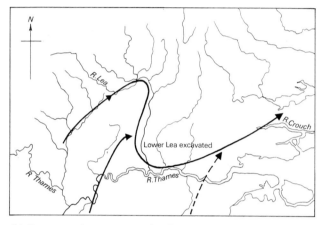

(b) Temporary ice retreat saw the Thames continuing to use its new route, in the process excavating the course of the Lower Lea.

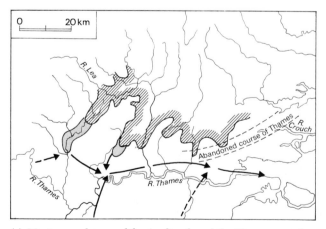

(c) Maximum advance of the Anglian forced the Thames even further south. Meltwater from pro-glacial lakes added to its discharge via spillways to the west of present-day London.

Fig 8.32 The diversion of the Lower Thames. The pre-glacial course of the Thames probably lay well to the north of its current path, through the Vale of St. Albans and into East Anglia.

The Effect of Glacial Deposition

Glacial deposits may completely submerge former river valleys and channels, especially in lowland regions, and they may or may not be re-excavated by post-glacial streams. In other areas they may merely divert modern drainage lines. Such an occurrence appears in Fig 8.33 where drumlins have forced the upper waters of the Aire flowing from the western Pennines to be diverted westward to join the Ribble and so become part of the Irish Sea's catchment rather than the North Sea's.

Ice Direction

Throughout this chapter, reference has been made to upstream and downstream as if it is always easy to tell the direction of ice flow. In a present-day glacier, it is, of course, but in many British landscapes the ice advance has to be discerned from fragments of evidence, both circumstantial and absolute. Even in an upland valley, ice direction may not be obvious, for ice can breach watersheds, and flow within ice caps and sheets need not respect drainage lines.

A general picture may be gained from linear features, be they parallel, such as lateral moraines, or transverse, such as terminal moraines. A refined view may be derived from four features in particular.

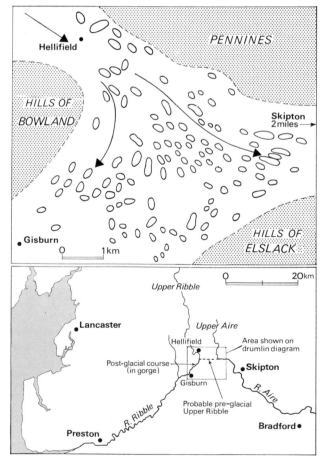

Fig 8.33 The diversion of the Upper Ribble.

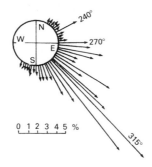

Fig 8.34 A rose diagram of striations in the Tampere area of southern Finland.

Erratics

First, one can use **erratics**. An erratic is any fragment of glaciated debris that is composed of a rock different from the local bedrock. One has only to trace its origin to determine the direction of advance of the glacier which conveyed it. This task may provide many difficulties, however, for glacial deposits are a chaotic jumble of many different fragments, not easy to isolate and which may have travelled long distances from their origin, perhaps hundreds of kilometres. One relies, therefore, on large erratic boulders of rocks whose origins are easy to identify. Shap granite, with its distinctive pink crystals, outcrops in one particular locality in the eastern Lake District; and yet its erratics are scattered across a wide part of northern England. One notable concentration occurs in the North York Moors, which indicates that ice must have travelled up the Eden Valley and crossed the Pennines in the area of Stainmore Forest on its journey to the east coast.

Striations

If they occur in sufficient numbers, striations can be used. Being linear, they can of course indicate only that the ice followed one of two opposing directions. Interpretation is not necessarily easy, for confusion with cleavage lines, joints and fault lines and even an etched-out mineral vein may cloud one's studies. Crossed striations may also bewilder the unwary, but are explicable if each limb of the cross represents a different glacial advance. Equipped with compass for orientation and ruler for dimension, the amateur can make a useful study of striations and perhaps produce results as significant as those in Fig 8.34.

Drumlins

Drumlins are a third source of evidence. As their longest axes are parallel to the direction of ice flow, a swarm of them can provide a welter of information. In addition, it is believed that their individual shape reflects the speed of the ice – the faster the flow the more elongated the mound. In Fig 8.35, elongation ratios have been plotted for each drumlin to indicate the varying speeds of flow. This is calculated by dividing the long (A) axis by the maximum width or B axis of each drumlin. Thus, a drumlin that is 25 metres long and 10 metres at its widest point has an elongation ratio of 2.5.

Stone Orientation

The fourth method of deriving evidence from glacial features makes use of deposits by studying the **orientation** of fragments of till, drawing on the principle that the majority of larger fragments are transported with their long axis parallel to ice flow. To carry out such an analysis of the till's fabric is relatively straightforward for the amateur. First, a suitable site needs to be selected. Unless one has a mechanical earth digger available to excavate the till and penetrate beneath the weathered surface layer, it is usual to use a till face that has recently been exposed, perhaps by a new farm track or a meandering, downcutting river. Even so, slope processes may have interfered with the initial deposit. A sample of 50–100 pebbles must then be measured, a delicate job, for the protruding pebbles should not be disturbed from their resting place in the exposed face. The longest axis of each one must be determined and its orientation recorded from a compass measurement.

The angle of dip of each stone may also be recorded, using a clinometer or Abney level, for it is essential to determine whether the fragment was moving towards or away from the observer. This can be easily concluded from the angle of dip (see Fig 8.36).

If the site has been selected correctly, then one should find that the majority of fragments are aligned in a similar way, as the rose diagram in Fig 8.37

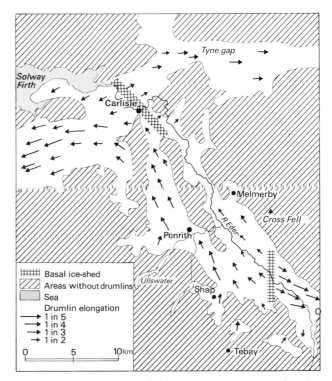

Fig 8.35 The distribution and elongation of drumlins in the Eden Valley and Solway Lowlands.

(a) aerial view.

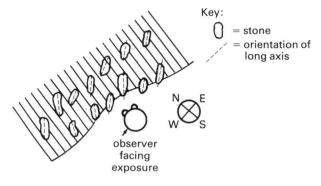

(b) cross-section of exposure.

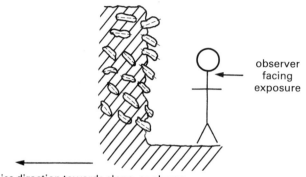

ice direction towards slope, as shown
by orientation of majority of stones

Fig 8.36 Stone orientation in an exposure of glacial till.

in this case the ice movement was, presumably,
predominantly from the south west

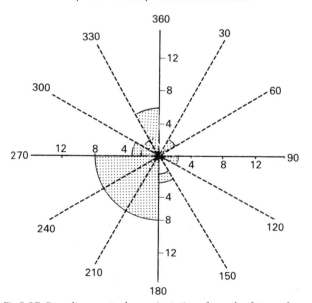

Fig 8.37 Rose diagram to show orientation of sample of stones from
an exposure of boulder clay in the Glenderamackin Valley, Cumbria.

indicates. It should not be too difficult to discern at least
the general direction of ice movement. If no such pattern emerges, it is likely that the till has been disturbed
by gelifluxion, river erosion, man or modern slope processes and weathering.

Photo 8.17 The Glenderamackin Valley, Cumbria: looking up the
valley towards the ice collection centres.

A Case Study

The disadvantage of dividing glacial action into
categories is that it implies that each process is operating in isolation. In reality, one landform may not just be
subjected to both erosional and depositional processes,
but may experience them simultaneously. For this reason, one particular upland valley is included in Photo
8.17, to show all the influences operating upon its
form. The glacier that carved it probably utilised a preexisting river valley which itself may have used a fault
line on the eastern slopes of Blencathra. Ice emanated
from many small collection centres, the largest and
most striking being the corrie of Scales Tarn (see
Fig 8.38).

Particular features of the valley to note are the profusion of dead ice hummocks in the upper valley, many of
them probably marking the farthest limit of the ice from
the corries during the Loch Lomond re-advance.

Both sides of the valley are masked by great
quantities of scree, pre-glacial, glacial and post-glacial
in origin. Gelifluxion lobes produce the ripples along
each valley slope. Active in immediate post-glacial
times, they transferred glacial and weathered material
down the slopes.

Towards the river the valley side slopes steepen to a
sharp 'V', suggesting considerable fluvial incision, (see
Fig 8.39). This was probably started by a much larger
meltwater-fed predecessor of today's stream, cutting
down into unconsolidated ground moraine in the valley bottom. The river of today has probably continued
this process as it adjusts itself to the post-glacial base
level.

Bracken and nardus grass largely protect the

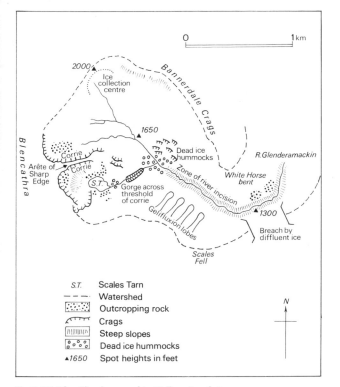

Fig 8.38 The Glenderamackin Valley, Cumbria.

Questions

Refer to Fig 8.14 and answer these questions.

1 Ice thickness is mentioned as a control factor. What, in turn, will ice thickness depend on?

2 What aspects of lithology will affect susceptibility to (a) abrasion, and (b) other forms of erosion?

3 How is bedding attitude of relevance to rock erodibility?

4 Suggest ways in which roughness may manifest itself.

5 Could any of man's activities affect any of the factors in a presently active area? Explain how.

6 What similarities and differences are there between these factors and those affecting the rate of river erosion?

Further Reading
Sediments, D Briggs (Butterworths, 1977).
Glacial and Periglacial Geomorphology, C Embleton and C A M King (Arnold, 1968).
Glaciation, C A M King (Macmillan, 1984).
Glacial and Fluvioglacial Landforms, R J Price (Longman, 1973).
Scotland, J B Sissons (Methuen, 1976).
The Ice Age in Britain, B W Sparks and R G West (Methuen, 1972).
Glaciers and Landscape, D E Sugden and B S John (Arnold, 1976).

Other References
Glaciers: do they really erode?, R J Small, *Geography* 67, 9–14 (1982).
The Study of Landforms, R J Small (Cambridge, 1978).

hillsides from weathering and major slope processes, but in exposed areas both processes still modify the screes and the rugged outcrops such as Sharp Edge and Scales Tarn. Vegetation cannot prevent soil creep from maintaining terracettes on the solifluxion lobes. Sheep and tourists are probably even more active, though, with expanding footpaths becoming a more distinctive feature of the valley each year.

Fig 8.39 Incision of a post-glacial river and creation of V-shaped valley in floor of trough.

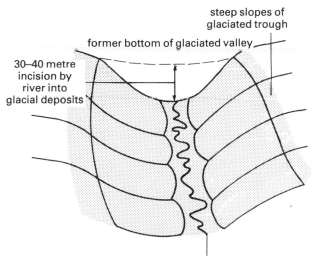

steep slopes of glaciated trough

former bottom of glaciated valley

30–40 metre incision by river into glacial deposits

meandering River Glendermackin

9
Fluvioglacial Processes and Landscape

Introduction

Anyone who has seen a glacier in the field or on film will appreciate that parts of its environment are as much 'fluvial' as 'glacial', with numerous flows of meltwater interwoven with the streams of ice (see Photo 9.1). These flows of water may well have their own specific effects, and it is for this reason that we apply the term **fluvioglacial** to those landscapes, landforms and processes which are the product of glacial meltwater.

It may seem strange to divorce their study from that of purely glacial features by devoting a separate chapter to them, but the point of this is to emphasise their importance, for they are too easily overshadowed by the more distinctive products and actions of ice. However, it would be wrong to assume from this that ice and meltwater operate in isolation, for they frequently act in concert. This is hardly surprising when one considers where the meltwater is operating, on top of, within and beneath the ice, for its activities are inextricably bound up with those of the ice. Indeed, the meltwater system could perhaps be regarded as a subsystem of the entire glacial system (see Fig 9.1).

By holding such a view, one may merely regard meltwater erosion as being a further weapon in the

Photo 9.1   Gross Glockner Glacier, Austria: a moulin on the surface of a glacier into which a meltwater stream sinks.

Fig 9.1 The glacial meltwater sub-system.

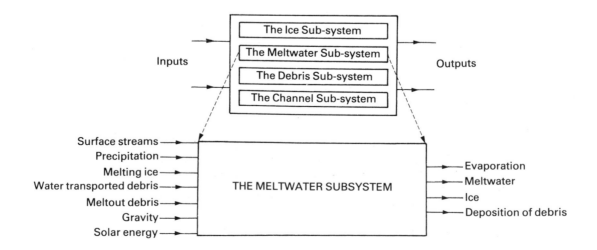

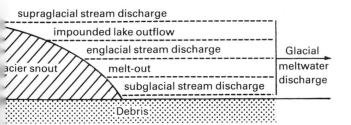

Fig 9.2 Sources of glacial meltwater.

erosional armoury of the glacier. Certainly, the increasing emphasis being given by certain geomorphologists to sub-glacial meltwater in the formation of glacial troughs might support such a view.

However, the advantage of studying fluvioglacial activity separately is that it gives us the opportunity of looking at the entire range of meltwater processes together, and of considering the vast fluvioglacial landscapes that exist beyond the limits of the ice. Such areas occur in both formerly and presently glaciated regions, as Photo 9.2 shows, and within them glacial processes play only a small part.

Meltwater

Variations in Flow

To observe and measure the characteristics of meltwater one must choose one's location and time very prudently, for flows are notoriously 'flashy', easily capable of washing away an unsuspecting encampment of glaciologists. As Fig 9.2 shows, the discharge from a glacial snout will be the amalgamation of many sources of meltwater derived from various parts of the glacier.

Peaks of flow are likely to be related to peaks of air temperature which bring about melting, thus making the afternoon's discharges much greater than the night-time's, and summer's much greater than winter's. The correlation is by no means perfect, however, for there is likely to be a lag time between the melting and the stream flow. During the day the output from a stream discharging from the glacier snout will gradually respond to the arrival of meltwater from all parts of the glacial system, perhaps reaching a peak in the late afternoon or early evening, by which time the meltwater has re-excavated the network of supra-, sub- and englacial channels which may have been closed by ice movement, freezing or debris during the night. In the same way, in Fig 9.3, daytime meltwater peaks may be seen to increase steadily from early summer to an early autumn climax, for by the end of the season the network will have increased its efficiency and water will be most easily conducted through it. Although melting may continue in winter, flows will be much reduced, with most of the water derived exclusively from sub-glacial melting. Diurnal variation may thus

be negligible, for the violent fluctuations caused by summer melting will not occur.

Variations in rates of meltwater flow, within and beneath the glacier, will depend on many factors besides air temperature. Rate of ice flow, which in turn may depend on ice thickness, the occurrence of obstacles or the gradient of the slope, will be an important influence. Most importantly, it will determine the friction and the pressure that help to melt the ice. The amount of precipitation, especially in summer, is also relevant, as might be the sudden draining of ice-dammed lakes within the glacial system.

For the amateur geomorphologist, the measurement of any glacial discharge stream may be too risky, for as well as their unpredictability, their discharge peaks may be too great for any of the conventional methods described in Chapter 6. Greater success may be achieved in a study of supra-glacial streams, although here the added obstacles of crevasses and **moulins,** the rushing mill races of water plunging down crevasses, may prove insurmountable.

A Comparison with Rivers of Temperate Environments

In many ways meltwater streams can be treated as rivers, with their equivalent processes of transportation, erosion and deposition. There are contrasts, however, as has already been seen in the extreme oscillations of discharge, matched elsewhere in few but desert rivers. The acute apexes of velocity which result are capable of greatly exaggerated feats of erosion, with speeds of 50 metres a second providing a force of water sufficient to undermine any unconsolidated bank or to drill sediment violently into the stream bed. Hydraulic

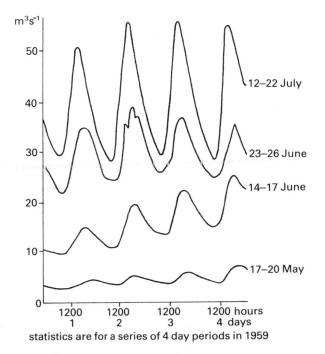

Fig 9.3 The diurnal fluctuation in discharge of the meltwater fed Matter-Vispa River.

action, cavitation and potholing are thus frequently experienced methods of meltwater erosion.

Another contrast is in the meltwater stream's channel, for it may well be carved into ice. In such a situation, excavation occurs, due not only to the erosion of a solid but also to melting resulting from the temperature of the water as well as its force. Streams within the glacier may be able to carve tunnels which, in times of peak flow, may confine and concentrate the rush of water, and in times of low flow may become blocked with sediment.

In meltwater streams, sediment load is as high as in any floodwater discharge, boosted not only by high velocities but also by high quantities of available and unconsolidated material. The high concentration of suspended load gives the water a murky or even milky appearance, and the correspondingly prolific bedload will permit much corrasion of the channel.

Much lower temperatures in meltwater compared to rivers in, say, a cool temperate environment, mean that carbon dioxide is more readily soluble, which allows carbonation to become a more active denudational process.

One final contrast is that the highly variable discharges of glacial outflow streams, combined with the great expanses of unconsolidated deposits, frequently produce braided channels. Indeed, some of the most complex and ever-changing examples of **anastomosing drainage** are to be found today beyond the limits of such great glaciers as the Athabasca and the Black Rapids of Alaska (see Photo 9.2).

Features of Fluvioglacial Erosion

Perhaps all glacial erosion features are in part also fluvioglacially eroded, for undoubtedly meltwater plays a rôle in the etching of nivation hollows, in the rotational slip of ice which helps form corries and in the erosion of glacial troughs. Here, however, we turn our attention to features which are almost exclusively meltwater products.

Meltwater Channels

The most prominent feature is the meltwater channel, and as Photo 9.3 of Newtondale suggests, its imprint on the landscape can be almost as dramatic as that of the glacial trough. This does not mean that their origin is distinct, however, and controversy has raged over their precise formation since their identification and study in Spitzbergen by glaciologists of the late nineteenth century.

Characteristics

Before proceeding to explanation it will be useful to decide what characterises a meltwater channel. First, one must accept that, although valley-like in size, they are essentially channels, which means that at some time they were probably bankfull with water. Unlike

Photo 9.2   The Jomosom Valley, Nepal. The fluvioglacial stream with its seasonal discharge of meltwater braids freely across the outwash deposits of the glacier.

Photo 9.3   Newtondale, North Yorkshire. It is easy to forget that this dale represents a meltwater *channel* not a valley.

valleys they are often discontinuous features, extending perhaps a kilometre or two before disappearing beneath drift or being blocked by an intervening spur or hill. Then they reappear for another short stretch. Meltwater channels may take little notice of pre-existing relief, crossing drainage divides as they carve their courses across hillsides. As a result they are often quite dry in the post-glacial landscapes of upland Britain, although in other circumstances they can provide the route for a modern drainage line. They tend not to widen downstream, normally retaining the steep sides and flat bottom of their cross-section with no increase in size.

Overflow channels

Meltwater is present in greatest quantities during periods of deglaciation when ice masses are depleting and retreating. It is for this reason that, in the early part of the century, meltwater channels were often seen as escape routes for water from ice-dammed lakes which were pounded against glacier snout, valley side walls and a transverse moraine. As water built up in the lake shown in Fig 9.4, channels of escape would have been cut through the valley walls and across the drainage divide which would have eventually provided new drainage lines through which the lake of meltwater emptied. One of the major proponents of such an occurrence was Kendall, and it is his work on North Yorkshire which provides some excellent examples.

As Fig 9.5 shows, Kendall envisaged a series of **pro-glacial lakes** existing in various valleys of the North York Moors as ice retreated in late-Pleistocene times. As can be seen from the map, meltwater and local river water were trapped by ice fronts and hillsides in Eskdale and its tributary valleys such as Wheeldale, and to the east in Harwood Dale and Hackness.

Kendall's suggestion for Eskdale was that various isolated upland valleys of today were in fact part of a network of **overflow channels** which were formed by meltwater draining from the 100 metre deep Lake Eskdale into Lake Pickering to the south. Thus, as the examples in Fig 9.6 demonstrate, meltwater carved channels such as Lady Bridge Slack and the Randy Mire Valley across drainage divides as water drained from Eskdale into Wheeldale and eventually into the massive master channel of Newtondale

As Photo 9.4 indicates, such channels are easy to discern today, the one shown here being about 80 metres deep, 800 metres long and 40 metres wide. Some of these channels were merely overflows from the lake, others were cut as escaping water moved around

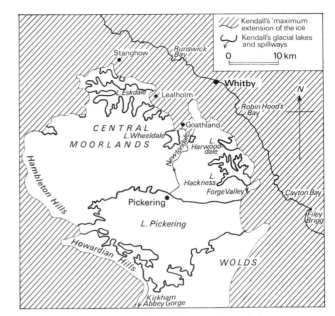

Fig 9.5 The pro-glacial lakes of the North Yorkshire Moors as envisaged by Kendall.

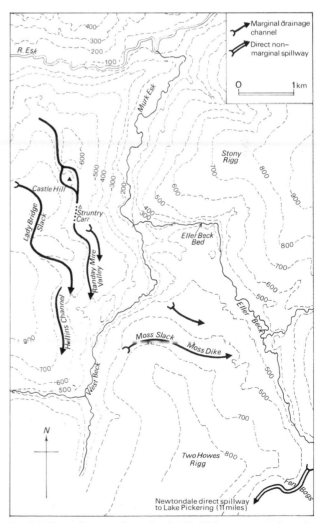

Fig 9.6 The meltwater channels of Wheeldale Moor, North Yorkshire.

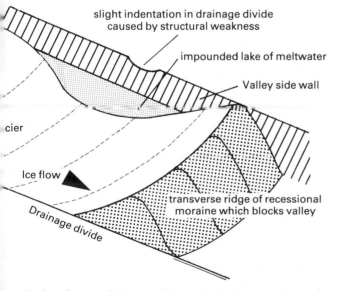

Fig 9.4 Theoretical diagram of impounded meltwater lake: as lake level rises, it eventually escapes through small indentation and carves it into a meltwater channel.

Photo 9.4 Marginal meltwater channels on Wheeldale Moor, North Yorkshire. These form part of the network that linked Eskdale and Newtondale.

the margins of the damming ice to pursue its destination to the south.

However attractive and complete this theory sounds, it is not as widely accepted today as it was earlier this century. Gregory, amongst others, questions whether a lake ever existed in Eskdale, and if it did, suggests it was one of much smaller dimensions. He challenges all of Kendall's evidence, pointing out, for example, that many of the overflow channels are not high enough above the valley floor to have drained the lake, Ewe Crag Slack, for example, being only 20 metres above it. Other channels, he suggests, are beyond the limits of the lake's possible shoreline so could not possibly have drained it. In yet more channels he finds evidence of dead ice deposits which would have been removed if the channel had been carved by the torrential flows of escaping meltwater.

Marginal meltwater channels

What alternative thesis, then, could explain these meltwater channels? It is certainly possible that some of them were cut by water flowing along the margins of the ice, not necessarily as part of the escape route from a pro-glacial lake but as meltwater streams along the

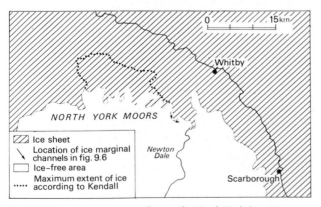

Fig 9.7 The maximum extent of ice on the North Yorkshire Moors, as Gregory proposes.

margins of active or stagnant ice. To allow for such a possibility, ice cover would have been much more extensive than Kendall envisaged, as Fig 9.7 shows.

Marginal meltwater channels are thought to be developed by streams flowing either along the margins of the glacier, or in sub-glacial tunnels close to the margin (see Fig 9.8). Schytt has observed them on present-day glaciers in Greenland and Sissons has identified an extensive network in Strathallan in Perthshire. In such post-glacial landscapes many may have been lost for they are often etched into drift or other superficial deposits and do not survive the final throes of **deglaciation**. If Gregory's limits of ice as shown in Fig 9.7 are correct, then the channels of Lady Bridge and Randy Mire could certainly have been marginal.

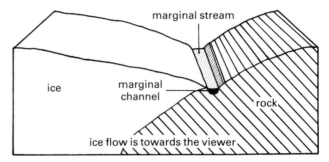

Fig 9.8 A meltwater channel carved by a stream marginal to the ice.

Pro-glacial meltwater channels

Gregory also disputes Kendall's suggestion that Newtondale, the spectacular 22 kilometre long gorge which provides the only major north-south entrenchment across the North York Moors, is merely an overflow channel between the northern lakes and Lake Pickering. He agrees that meltwater carved it, but suggests that this was from the northern ice impounded against the unglaciated central block of the North York Moors, its only route of escape being southward.

If this is the remains of a channel, then its maximum dimensions of 100 metres deep by 250 metres wide must have given it a bankfull discharge as high as 10000 cubic metres per second, which is many times greater than the Thames experiences today even when in flood. Although such discharges would rarely have been achieved, flows were probably great enough for Newtondale to have been cut in a very short period, perhaps in less than 100 years. Discharges were undoubtedly great, for knowledge of Hjulström's Curve and Hopkins' Sixth Power Law allow us to analyse the sediment in the delta at Newtondale's southern end and predict the likely flows of water that transported them there. The town of Pickering today surmounts the delta, the parish church positioned at its apex.

Sub-glacial channels

Three possible theories of meltwater channel formation have emerged, then, the overflow channel, the ice-marginal and the **pro-glacial**, that is, those in the area in advance of the ice, such as Newtondale. A fourth type of channel, the **sub-glacial**, also exists, and Gregory suggests that the largest of Kendall's overflow channels, between Lakes Kildale and Eskdale, had such an origin. Water confined in a sub-glacial tunnel assumes increased force due to hydrostatic pressure which not only allows it to carve a channel but is also perhaps the reason why some sub-glacial meltwater streams are able to flow uphill. This idiosyncrasy shows up in the up-down longitudinal profiles common to many sub-glacial meltwater channels, such as those which Price identified near West Linton in Peeblesshire. However, not all sub-glacial meltwater channels are so apparent in today's landscape. Some, such as certain East Anglian examples, for instance the one beneath the valley of the Cam near Saffron Walden, have been completely buried by later deposits of fluvioglacial, glacial and fluvial origin.

Lake Strandlines

Whether or not we believe that Eskdale ever contained a pro-glacial lake depends on the relative strength of Kendall's and Gregory's evidence, but in other British valleys the existence of such lakes is less disputed. It is widely accepted, for example, that Glen Roy in the Western Highlands of Scotland, just south of Loch Ness, once contained a lake 16 kilometres long and up to 200 metres deep. As Fig 9.9 indicates, glaciers advancing from several directions in the Loch Lomond re-advance, 10,000 years ago, entered the glen and blocked the normal exit for its rivers. Drainage became impeded, and in common with several other local valleys, Glen Roy was gradually engulfed by a lake. There is plenty of evidence for such lakes, and much stronger than that put forward for Kendall's Eskdale. **Deltas**, such as the one in Photo 9.5a, represent deposits of streams discharging into the lake from surrounding uplands. Finely-layered beds of clay and sand, so typical of present-day pro-glacial lake beds, occur where sections have been exposed by the excavation of the road along the glen (Photo 9.5b).

The water level of each lake was determined by the height of the surrounding relief, and cols cut in previous glacial periods were used as escape routes for meltwater, often being enlarged to form overflow channels. Thus, Glen Roy's lake water never lapped higher than 350 metres as this was the height of its lowest col, at its northern end, which led into the Spey catchment area. A lake of this size would have allowed the generation of waves of considerable dimension and these would have been able to erode notches into the hillside. Today these are represented by the parallel roads of Glen Roy, a series of horizontal **strandlines** or shorelines of 6-7 metres width, high on the valley sides, as shown in Photo 9.6.

Three distinct roads can be identified, each the product of a different lake level, for water was able to escape as the ice gradually retreated. A col, identifiable today at about 325 metres above sea level, would have allowed some of the water to escape to the east into

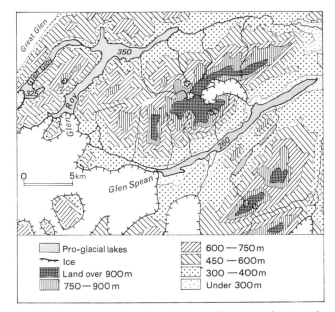

Fig 9.9 The creation of pro-glacial lakes in Glen Roy and surrounding valleys during the Loch Lomond readvance.

Photo 9.5(a)   The remains of a delta in the former lake of Glen Roy, northern Scotland. A post-glacial river has dissected the delta but the flat top can still be seen on both left and right of the photograph. The view looks up a tributary of the glen.

Photo 9.5(b)   The finely-layered sediments exposed on the former lake floor of Glen Roy. A map is included for scale.

Photo 9.6   The Parallel Roads of Glen Roy. The former lake levels of 350 m, 325 m and 260 m can be picked out clearly on the hillsides.

Glen Spean once the ice had receded. Thus, the second strandline or road would have developed, to be succeeded by a third once the lake in Glen Roy had been connected to the 260-metre level of the even larger Spean Lake to the east. The dropping of the lake from one level to the next probably represented a quite catastrophic event at the time, with water suddenly able to breach one of its dams, perhaps overflowing the ice or escaping through a sub-glacial tunnel towards the col. There is certainly plenty of local evidence to suggest that the final drainage of the lakes took place sub-glacially. The River Gloy, for instance, as Fig 9.10 indicates, flows through a deep gorge, probably cut beneath the ice as Glen Gloy's lake suddenly emptied in a torrent of floodwater. It seems strange that the river does not follow its former valley to the south west rather than this north-western route to Loch Lochy. This sudden sub-glacial outburst could certainly explain the anomaly, as could a similar occurrence account for the larger Spean Gorge to the west

Small Scale Meltwater Erosion Features

Many meltwater channels can, of course, be very small scale, the tiny rivulets that carved them capable of little more than scratching the surface for a few metres. On the larger channels, however, which may have been sculpted in solid rock, a variety of additional small scale features may be discernible.

Pot holes similar to those in the beds of some upland rivers are particularly likely given the high velocities of flow. In association with them one often finds **sichel-**

wannen which are smooth, crescentic depressions, again carved by the turbulent hydraulic action of meltwater into the walls and bed of the channel (see Fig 9.11).

Although they may be more than ten metres across and several metres deep in some extreme cases, they are not easily discovered in the meltwater channels of England. In Newtondale, for example, the bare rock bed is for the main part hidden beneath deposits of the past 10 000 years, sometimes up to a depth of ten metres, and the walls have been disturbed by rock falls, soil formation and afforestation.

Features of Fluvioglacial Deposition

Characteristics and Classification

Once again, the problem of classifying the infinite variety of the natural environment occurs, and the academic literature is littered with a myriad of gallant

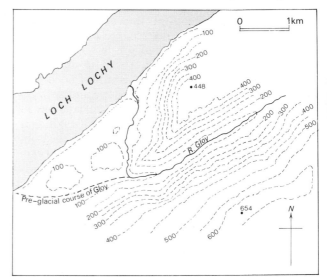

Fig 9.10   The present and former courses of the River Gloy. (See text for explanation.)

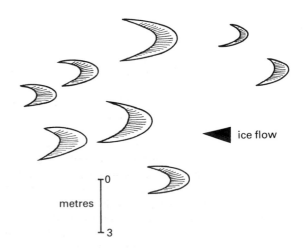

Fig 9.11   A possible pattern of sichelwannen on a rock surface.

attempts to produce the definitive glossary of fluvioglacial deposits.

Fluvioglacial deposits are distinct from their glacial counterparts in that, by being transported by water, the individual grains tend to be more rounded. In so fluid a medium as water it is also conceivable that sediment transport over larger distances than is likely in ice will occur; this is particularly true for the fine sand and clay-sized sediment. Fluvially-deposited material will also be laid down in a more ordered manner than glacially-dumped material. Sorting will occur, both vertically and laterally, as water gradually loses energy and with it its ability to carry the larger particles. Some sources even suggest that the mean grain size of meltwater deposits is smaller than that of ice deposits, given the attrition in turbulent water. So firm a statement may be misleading, though, except for a comparison of very local deposits, for varying dimensions of glacier and meltwater flow, different types of parent material and different histories of erosion and deposition may be far more important in determining sediment size than how it was last deposited.

Despite these theoretical differences between glacial and fluvioglacial deposits, in the field the contrasts are easily obscured. This is not just because the two may be deposited together within the same landform, but because both media, meltwater and ice, are working and re-working material from similar origins. Fluvioglacial deposits are thus a mixture of sediment derived from glacial erosion, meltwater erosion, frost-shattered detritus dumped on to the glacier, and former deposits. It may be difficult, therefore, to accept any clear distinction between glacial and fluvioglacial deposits, let alone between different individual fluvioglacial deposits. Indeed, faced with a moraine and kame, or even an esker and a kame, in a valley bottom, it may well prove impossible even for the expert to retain any clear picture of their difference.

Nevertheless, detailed analysis of sediment, location and mode of deposition can provide us with clear boundaries by which to delimit the various characteristic fluvioglacial landforms. Their location with regard to the ice provides such a clear boundary. Those deposited beyond it are termed **pro-glacial**, and should be exclusively meltwater deposited, with little or no direct glacial influence. Those deposited by meltwater within, on top of, beneath or marginal to the ice are termed **ice-contact**, for in their deposition the role of the ice is far more critical (see Fig 9.12).

Another clear reason for classification is the mode of deposition, whether it occurred in the turbulent environment of a meltwater stream or the relative calm of a meltwater lake. Both occur in pro-glacial and ice-contact locations, and in both cases the reason for deposition is much the same as in any fluvial environment – a loss of energy. This energy loss may be caused by the sudden drop in discharge so typical of meltwater flow at certain times of day, by a flow encountering an obstacle of sediment such as rock or ice within an ice tunnel or a supra-glacial channel, or by the stream entering a lake impounded on the glacial margin or in a

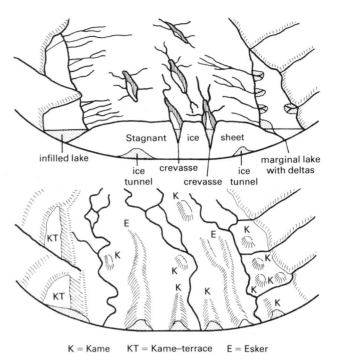

Fig 9.12 Some of the fluvioglacial deposits associated with a stagnant or retreating ice mass.

pro-glacial location. Energy reduction will also occur on the sudden loss of channel restriction as water disgorges from a confined ice tunnel onto the valley floor at the glacial snout. Sudden changes in gradient also cause energy loss, perhaps as an englacial stream, after plunging down a crevasse, reaches a local base level within the ice. Finally, energy can be reduced by a stream splitting into several smaller, less efficient channels or even by prolonged daytime evaporation from a supra-glacial stream or lake.

Ice-Contact Features

The two major ice-contact features both rely on Celtic origins for their names, the esker and the kame.

Photo 9.7   Carstairs, Scotland. The ridge from left to right across the photograph is an esker. Although not very high, its effect on this lowland relief is quite profound.

Photo 9.8 The floor of Greenburn Valley, Cumbria. The lighter coloured linear ridge, perpendicular to the moraine on the left of the photograph, is an esker.

Eskers

Eskers are an obvious feature of a few British landscapes, occurring most prominently on the lowlands that flank the Moray Firth, for example around Croy, Dornoch and Brora. As Photo 9.8 shows, they may also occur in the bottoms of glaciated valleys such as this one in Greenburn in the Lake District.

Eskers are long, sinuous ridges of cobbles, gravel and sand that usually snake across gently sloping, low relief often undulating with the rises and falls of the landscape.

As in Photo 9.8 they may be no more than a few metres long, but in the glaciated lowlands of northern Canada and Scandinavia, where they provide many an excellent foundation for a Finnish routeway, they are represented by particularly prominent examples, such as the 400 kilometre long Munro Esker in Canada. Their height and width are proportional to their length, the Munro's width measurable in kilometres and its height in tens of metres. Like drumlins, they rarely occur in isolation, perhaps linked together in a network as intricate as any drainage pattern.

The most accepted theory for their origin is that they were moulded in sub-glacial tunnels in which meltwater streams gradually accumulated bed deposits which, on the wasting away of the ice, were left as upstanding ridges. Like most fluvioglacial deposits, the esker may derive some protection against erosion in the very violent deglaciation period by being frozen together. Even so, slumping of its sides and some erosion would occur once removed from the restraining influence of the tunnel. The hydrostatic pressure that allows some sub-glacial meltwater channels to have up-down profiles also enables eskers to traverse local fluctuations in relief.

In common with so many theories in this book, however, there are many alternatives. Could the larger eskers, for instance, really be formed by tunnels hundreds of kilometres in length? It is conceivable, but only as the tunnel extends backwards and the ice front retreats during deglaciation.

Research by Price in Alaska and Iceland suggests that eskers can also be superimposed on the sub-glacial surface from the bed deposits of supra- and englacial streams. This process will be facilitated by the downwasting of the ice, as Fig 9.13 shows, but it may be so precarious that it seems unlikely to explain the most extensive Finnish and Canadian examples.

Some authors reject all theories of ice-contact tunnels and adopt a pro-glacial theory, suggesting that the ridges merely represent the distributaries of a former delta that extended from the ice front as meltwater streams discharged from it. As usual, there is probably no need to reject any of the theories, but to accept them all, and more. There is no reason why eskers should not have a variety of origins.

Beaded eskers are a particular variant of the form, resembling a necklace of beads, the ridge linking together broader bulges of sediment. Perhaps each bead reflects a summer period of melting when more

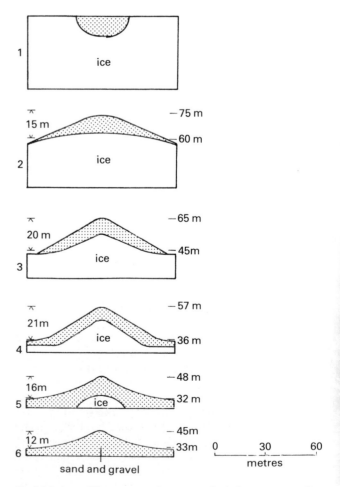

Fig 9.13 A possible sequence of events in which downwasting of ice allows the deposits in a supraglacial stream to be lowered on to the valley floor as an esker.

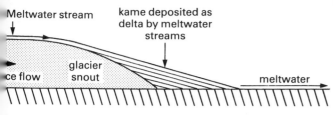

Fig 9.14 Kame formation at the glacier snout.

material was transported and deposited, with the linking chain representing deposition in intervening cooler periods. This sequence seems particularly credible if the ice front was retreating during formation so that the bead formed as a delta as the water emerged from its tunnel at the ice front.

Kames

In theory, **kames** are easy to separate from eskers, for they are steep-sided mounds of fluvioglacial material of various shapes and sizes. In reality, there may be more of an overlap, especially if the kame takes a linear form. Kames may abound in a deglaciated valley bottom or lowland such as Glen Roy although, like eskers, they are sitting targets for meltwater escaping from the retreating glacier.

They may also have a number of forms of origin, although essentially they are dumps of sediment which meltwater has left within, or on top of, the ice, their final deposition relying on the downwasting of the glacier. Meltwater streams may fill a crevasse, an internal cavity within a tunnel or a supra-glacial depression with finely sorted sands and gravels. As Fig 9.14 shows, they may even be dumped by meltwater as its gradient is reduced on flowing across the snout of the glacier. The eventual form of the kame may be much modified by slumping of its sides after deposition. In some cases, especially if deposition is occurring in an ice-contact lake, probably at the ice margins, a delta may develop, in which case the feature becomes a **delta kame**.

Kame-terraces such as the one in Photo 9.9 are linear shelves deposited on valley sides or any other higher ground which the ice brushes up against, and they represent the bed deposits of channels or lakes that existed along the margins of a glacier. They are as prone to post-glacial denudation as are lateral and medial moraines.

As they are most commonly formed in the ablation zone of the glacial mass, kames may be interspersed with kettle holes, the remains of dead ice (see Chapter 8), and are well represented in the Ellesmere area of Fig 8.27.

Pro-Glacial Features

Sandar

The area beyond an ice front is subjected to so many changes over time that it is likely to provide a considerable challenge to analysis. As ice advances, the area is subjected to a deluge of melting water and load, but all its erosional and depositional consequences will later be reworked and submerged beneath the onslaught of the meltwater of deglaciation. The thick deposits which characterise the zone have been termed **sandar** (singular = sandur), or **outwash plains**. A sandur may be restricted by valley walls in the case of a valley glacier or may spread out uninterrupted across a plain. Drainage patterns in such areas tend to be very disorganised and very dynamic, their braiding lattice of channels dumping sediment as it responds to variations in the availability of meltwater. Patterns of sediment deposition vary, but many are fan-like as streams split into smaller channels that splay out across the chaotic surface. Fans amalgamate into each other in a similar way to the alluvial fans of desert and semi-desert regions. Despite the seeming disorder of sandar, there is some sorting of material, with larger sediment being dropped near the ice front. This may give the

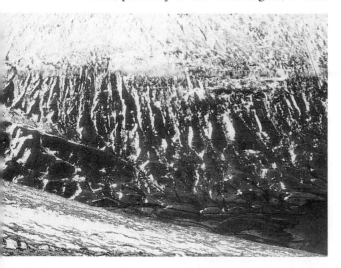

Photo 9.9 Hayeswater, Cumbria. The platform, half way up the valley side on the left, is probably a kame terrace.

Photo 9.10 Sandur, Katmai, Alaska: This sandur, although confined by valley walls, is 4 kilometres wide in the foreground. Anastomosing channels flow from the glaciers behind the photographer into the distance.

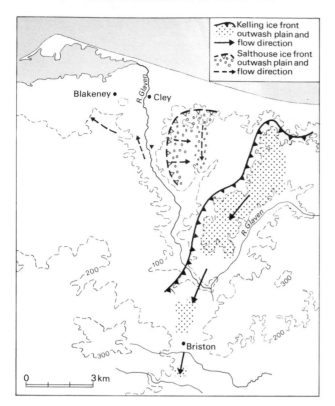

Fig 9.15 Outwash plains of north Norfolk.

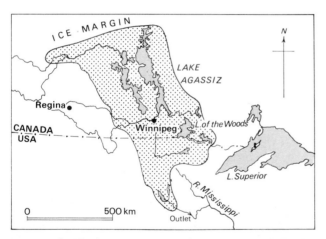

Fig 9.16 The Pleistocene pro-glacial Lake Agassiz, named after the nineteenth century pioneer of glaciology. The much smaller lakes of today's landscape are also shown.

sandur a considerable gradient, perhaps as great as 1:30.

The extent and size of the feature will largely depend on the size of the glacial basin from which it receives its sediment, for the sandur represents its major output of deposition. In Iceland some fine active examples can be seen beyond the massive Vatnajokull, and in the western part of the Jutland peninsula the outwash deposits of the Pleistocene glaciation have provided the Danish Heath Society with the massive task of reclaiming the sandy soils for cultivation. In Britain most sandar have long since been interfered with either by man or by

post-glacial denudation. None is as well developed as the magnificent examples of the North German Plain or Poland, but Kelling and Salthouse Heaths in north Norfolk are both traceable in today's landscape. The two successive locations of their retreating ice front can be seen in Fig 9.15. Escaping outwash deposited a sandur of perhaps ten square kilometres at Kelling, its gradient a gentle 1:500 as it grades from gravel to sand.

Outwash deposits in Britain are also represented in highland valleys where they are usually referred to as **valley trains**, and in lowland valleys, such as the Thames and the Trent, where they have been exposed in terraces by the downcutting rivers of today.

A particular variant of the sandur is the **pitted** or **kettled sandur**, which is really not exclusively pro-glacial or ice-contact in origin. They are thought to develop in the snout zone of the ice mass, as discharging meltwater begins its deposition of the sandur on top of sections of ice. As these lumps of dead ice become detached they are insulated by the sandur and, on melting, leave a pitted surface of collapsed hillocks and mounds, often crossed by the anastomosing channels of meltwater streams. They may merge into the true sandur or form a distinct feature, perhaps separated from the sandur by a terminal moraine

Pro-glacial lake deposits

Meltwater discharging from an ice mass has many possible obstacles to dam it, both solid and unconsolidated. It is not surprising, therefore, that **pro-glacial lakes** often develop. The lacustrine (lake) environment is very different from that of an active channel and the features that compose it may be easily distinguished. **Lake beds**, or **lake plains**, can be extensive landforms, notably the massive Lake Agassiz which stretched across the US/Canadian border near Winnipeg (Fig 9.16). Here, meltwater from the retreating continental ice sheet was trapped between the ice margin to the north and the hills of Dakota and Minnesota to the south, submerging an area of over half a million square kilometres.

Lake-bed deposits are very distinctive, and have been well studied in the valley scars exposed by the downcutting River Severn at Preston Montford in Shropshire. Thin layers of sediment, perhaps only millimetres thick, called **varves**, can be analysed to date such lakes, each varve consisting of two layers distinguishable in colour and grain size. As Fig 9.17 shows, in winter the lake's frozen surface may well restrict the entry of meltwater, permitting only the settling out of fine, suspended, darker-coloured silt, which in summer will be veneered with a thicker layer of coarser, lighter sand, the output of meltwater. If unexposed, such varves may be blue-grey in colour, having not been bared to the oxidising effect of the atmosphere. It was the occurrence of such deposits in the quarries in Danby in Eskdale that first led Canon Atkinson in 1891 to propose the existence of the lake there.

A particular feature of lacustrine deposits is the delta, a common landform of the former lakes of the Glen Roy area. Beaches, too, may remain in the unexposed reaches of some examples.

It is the profusion of irregularities in the bed of Lake Eskdale that composes part of Gregory's evidence against Kendall (see pp 210–211). He identifies eskers and **crevasse infillings** one of which is ten metres high, which not only means that the lake plain is remarkably uneven but that ice, rather than a lake, probably extended across this area in late-glacial times.

Interference with Drainage Patterns

By now it must be quite apparent that meltwater interferes with, and sometimes determines, modern drainage patterns. Indeed, this probably occurs to almost as great a degree as glacial interference. Diversion of the rivers Gloy and Spean in the Scottish Highlands has already been referred to, where meltwater channels are utilised by today's rivers. When one considers how often meltwater channels disregard relief by breaking through drainage divides, and how they are capable of flowing uphill, it is hardly surprising that they play havoc with modern patterns of drainage.

Since Kendall's pioneering work in Eskdale, numerous other pro-glacial lakes have been identified, some theories holding water rather more effectively than others. These lakes are important because they often provide the mechanism by which meltwater can divert drainage, namely the overflow channel.

The headwaters of the River Derwent are in the eastern part of the North York Moors, and the river drains southward into the great east-west trench of the Vale of Pickering. However, rather than follow the logical, and its former, eastern course to the sea near Scarborough, only eight kilometres away, the Derwent swings west along the vale and then south through the Howardian Hills and Yorkshire wolds to join the sea eventually via the Humber. This more than 100 kilometre diversion is

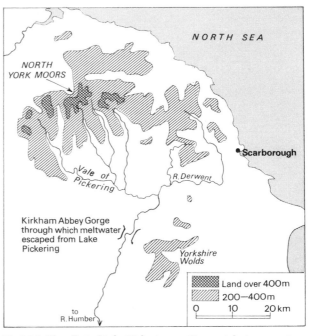

Fig 9.18 The effect of Lake Pickering on Derwent drainage system, North Yorkshire Moors.

believed to have been caused by the blocking of the Vale of Pickering by ice, as Fig 9.18 indicates, and the impounding of meltwater in the enormous Lake Pickering. Overflowing water from the lake escaped southward cutting the Kirkham Abbey Gorge, seen in Photo 9.11. In post-glacial times the rivers that drain into the Vale of Pickering from the North York Moors continue to use this passage to the sea.

Like Kendall's Lake Eskdale, the existence of all such lakes is now challenged, not least because close examination of the overflow channels often reveals an up-down profile which seems inconsistent with escaping meltwater. In addition, certain authors, notably Sissons, have questioned whether ice is a capable dam,

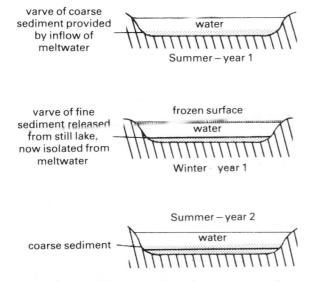

Fig 9.17 Theoretical diagram to show the varves in a meltwater lake: the thickness of the varves has been exaggerated for the purposes of this diagram.

Photo 9.11 Kirkham Abbey Gorge, North Yorkshire. The Derwent, flowing left to right in the foreground, flows through a gorge cut through the Howardian Hills as meltwater escaped from Lake Pickering.

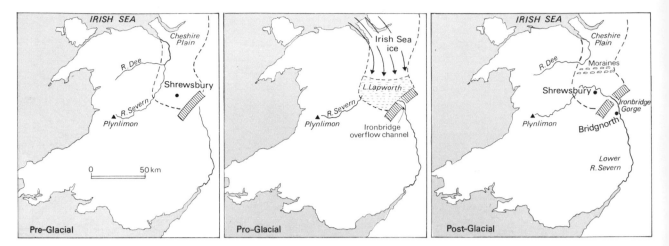

Fig 9.19 Lapworth's theory of explanation for the diversion of the River Severn and the creation of the Ironbridge gorge.

especially in times of deglaciation when it is likely to be as leakproof as a sponge. Thus, early theories have been re-evaluated; a case in point is the diversion of the Severn in its upper course on the Welsh border. It is widely believed that the river was once a tributary of the Dee, flowing north across the Cheshire Plain. As Fig 9.19 shows, Charles Lapworth, a contemporary of Kendall, postulated that waters of a pro-glacial lake, trapped between ice and the hills of Shropshire, escaped through an overflow channel and excavated the Ironbridge Gorge, through which the Severn has since been diverted. Although the belief is still held that the diversion of the Severn took place, it is now thought unlikely that the lake existed, at least to this extent. The gorge is thought, instead, to have formed as a sub-glacial channel with the meltwater's effectiveness increased by being pressurised in its confined tunnel.

Examples of diversion abound, such as the Teme and the Lugg in Herefordshire, the Warwickshire Avon and some of the tributaries of the Wear in County Durham. It remains to be proved whether pro-glacial overflow or sub-glacial channels were the major culprit.

A rather different imprint on drainage resulting from meltwater can be seen in some parts of the East Midlands. Valleys such as the Nene or Welland now contain river channels quite incapable of having carved them, for, as Photo 9.12 shows, the valley bottom is well over 600 metres wide and yet the channel is no wider than six metres. Add to their capacity late glacial meltwater, and their meandering channels could well have been responsible, although these ancient channels are now most likely buried beneath a blanket of deposits.

Techniques of Analysis

Methods for the Amateur

Sorting analysis

Certain methods of analysis for glacial deposits have already been mentioned in Chapter 8, but there are various other techniques which are relevant to both fluvioglacial and glacial sediments. **Sorting analysis** is

Photo 9.12 The Welland Valley, Harringworth, Rutland: a vast flood plain cut by a river charged with glacial meltwater.

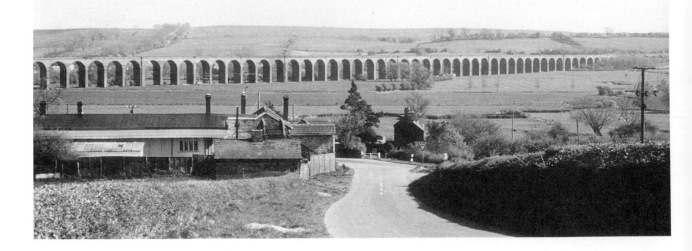

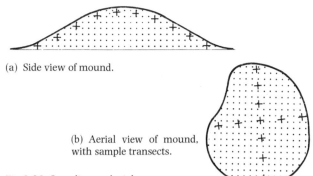

(a) Side view of mound.

(b) Aerial view of mound, with sample transects.

Fig 9.20 Sampling a glacial or fluvioglacial deposit.

Photo 9.13 Using an auger to sample sediment.

essential in any assessment of a landscape of deposition, for by determining how well sorted is the deposit one can make some definite conclusions about its origins.

Suppose, for example, that one wished to make a comparison between two neighbouring depositional mounds in a valley bottom, such as that in Photo 9.9, to compare their relative degrees of sorting and perhaps decide if one had been more influenced by fluvioglacial action than the other. A systematic sample could first be made of each mound using transects, as shown in Fig 9.20. At each point a trowel full of sediment could

be collected or an auger could be used if preferred, as in Photo 9.13.

Whichever technique is used, the sample must be taken from below the soil layer, and, if possible, from sufficient depth to avoid the slumped and weathered surface layers of the mound. Drying in a laboratory, followed by pounding with a pestle and mortar into the original constituent sediments should then be undertaken. Each sample would then be shaken through a series of sieves, each decreasing in size, and the weight of material in each size category determined.

Obviously, in a sorted deposit, one would expect most of the sample to be of a particular size, and one could decide upon its origin of deposition simply by gauging how concentrated is the sediment in one size category. Another rule of thumb is that the size distribution of sediment from a glacial deposit tends to be bimodal, as in Fig 9.21, whereas in a fluvioglacial deposit it is often unimodal. This is because the finer clay and silt size material, so typical of a till, may well have been completely washed out from a fluvioglacial deposit.

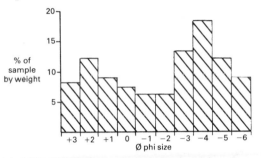

(a) A bimodal distribution typical of a glacial deposit.

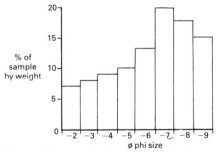

Note: Higher negative values of Ø size indicate larger sediment

(b) A unimodal distribution typical of a fluvio-glacial deposit.

Fig 9.21 A comparison of the distribution of material by size in a glacial and fluvioglacial deposit.

More sophisticated techniques of analysis are available; below is an example of exactly how to establish the degree of sorting of glacial or fluvioglacial sediment.

Method:

1 Once sediment has been sieved, the amount in each size category should be weighed. The results from a sample in the Glenderamackin Valley, Cumbria are shown below.

2 Draw a cumulative frequency graph of ϕ size and weight on arithmetic probability paper (Fig 9.22).

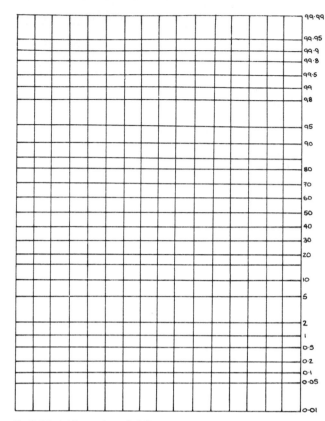

Fig 9.22 Arithemetic probability paper.

Table of results:

0 size (phi)	diameter (mm)	weight	weight as a percentage of total	weight as a cumulative percentage
$-6 \to -7$	64–128	0	0	0
$-5 \to -6$	32–64	0	0	0
$-4 \to -5$	16–32	28	8.7	8.7
$-3 \to -4$	8–16	64	19.5	28.2
$-2 \to -3$	4–8	22	6.8	35.0
$-1.24 \to -2$	2.36–4	12	3.8	38.8
$-0.22 \to -1.24$	1.18–2.36	56	17.5	56.3
$+0.7 \to -0.22$	0.6–1.18	58	18.0	74.3
$+1.75 \to +0.7$	0.3–0.6	40	12.4	86.7
$+2.7 \to +1.75$	0.15–0.3	24	7.5	94.2
$+3.7 \to +2.7$	0.075–0.15	12	3.8	98.0
>3.7	<0.075	6	1.9	99.9
Total:		322	100%	99.9%

ϕ (phi) size refers to a commonly used negative logarithmic scale of sediment size.

3 Read off ϕ size values for 84 per cent and 16 per cent of cumulative weight. Substitute figures into the sorting equation:

$$\frac{\phi 84 - \phi 16}{2}$$

4 Interpret the answer as follows:

<0.35	very well sorted
0.35–0.5	well sorted
0.5–0.7	moderately well sorted
0.7–1.0	moderately sorted
1.0–2.0	poorly sorted
2.0–4.0	very poorly sorted
>4.0	extremely poorly sorted

Photo 9.14   Measuring the radius of curvature of the most acute angle on the stone's AB plane.

In our particular example, this process would have to be repeated for each sample taken to produce conclusive results. All results are likely to be relative rather than absolute; no deposit that has been laid down in a turbulent meltwater channel is going to be perfectly sorted, but relative to a glacial deposit it will show some sign of it. Much clearer sorting would be expected in a delta from a pro-glacial lake and even greater clarity from a lake-bed deposit.

If one considers the degree of error that may enter such an experiment, especially in the sample-collecting stage, such a technique may be considered too refined for your particular exercise. In that case one may merely take a series of systematic samples either vertically through a deposit, or horizontally across, say, a suspected outwash plain. These samples can then be processed in a similar way to that described above, except that one would merely record the mean grain size for each sample and then graph them to see if there is any indication of increase with depth, or decrease with distance, from the suspected ice front.

Analysis of roundness

No sorting analysis is ever easy, and results from experiments may prove inconclusive. The degree of roundness of the larger individual fragments may instead be measured to determine whether or not the sediment was water-borne. A simple method to carry this out would take the most acute angle of the AB plane of each fragment in one's sample and measure its radius of curvature (r) and the length of the A axis (1).

This could be done quite simply, as Photo 9.14 shows, by comparison with a prepared card of different angles. **Cailleux's index of roundness** could then be utilised, where

$$Ci = \frac{2r}{1} \times 1000$$

a) Table of results

Length (l) of A axis of stone (mm)	Radius of curvature (r) of most acute angle on AB (mm) plane	Roundness from Cailleux's formula (C_l)	Length (l) of A axis of stone (mm)	Radius of curvature (r) of most acute angle on AB (mm) plane	Roundness from Cailleux's formula (C_l)
85	2		85	2	
85	4		60	2	
30	4		90	2	
47	8		40	4	
43	6		25	2	
45	2		60	6	
65	4		55	2	
55	4		63	4	
40	6		54	4	
80	2		51	8	
55	6		39	2	
35	2		50	6	
82	6		60	4	
85	8		80	6	
55	4		45	6	

b) example of a fragment

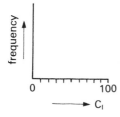

A axis

most acute angle on AB plane

c) formula

Cailleux's formula of roundness, $(C_l) = \dfrac{2r}{l} \times 100$

(NB. for a perfectly spherical stone $C_l = 100$)

d) method

1 calculate C_l for each fragment in sample
2 plot a frequency distribution of C_l (see below)
3 interpret pattern produced on graph
eg. if distribution is negatively skewed, the stones in the sample are rounded;
if distribution is positively skewed, the stones in the sample are irregular in shape .

e) frequency distribution

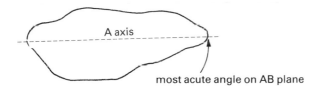

Fig 9.23 Method of calculating degree of roundness of a sample of fragments.

A perfectly spherical fragment would have an index of 100 as the length of the A axis would equal the diameter, and as that is exactly twice the radius, $2r/l$ would equal one. The more angular the fragment the lower the value of the index.

Once again, some field statistics are included, from a Lake District valley, in Fig 9.23, showing Ci for a sample of 30 fragments. The exercise beneath the figures will demonstrate how to use the statistics.

Techniques for the Professional

In addition to statements about sorting and roundness of sediment, much other information can be gleaned from the detailed study of a deposit given the time, equipment and expertise. This is true regardless of a deposit's origin, be it windborne, fluvial, marine, fluvioglacial or glacial.

In particular, two useful aspects of a sediment's history may be the climatic environment and the date or its period of deposition, for such information will help the scientist to establish a sequence of past geomorphological events in an area. Both methods usually require a core of sediment to be extracted, say from the bottom of a meltwater channel, a glaciated valley or the bed of a pro-glacial lake, so that careful analysis can then take place of each layer of the core.

The oxygen isotope method

Oxygen occurs as two isotopes, O^{18} and O^{16}, which occur in all living organisms. Many shells contain $CaCO_3$ secreted by their living organism, and within this $CaCO_3$ the **oxygen isotopes** are contained. The ratio of O^{18} to O^{16} is a good indicator of temperature of water in which the shelled creatures were living, the proportion of O^{18} to O^{16} increasing by 0.02 per cent for every

1°C decrease in temperature. If shell fragments from a core are analysed, therefore, the temperature of the environment in which their contained organisms once lived can be estimated, which may allow us to detect the onset of deteriorating or improving conditions at the beginning or end of a glacial period.

Palaeocoleoptery

A similar exercise can be carried out by the study of ancient beetles' wings, known as **palaeocoleoptery**. Beetles have many advantages for such a study. First, they are relatively common and thus likely to feature strongly amongst organic remains. Second, the wings of each species are distinctive in shape and thus easy to identify under a microscope and, in addition, remain intact for thousands of years. Third, beetles are very sensitive to temperature change, so that, as climate alters, different species will become numerous as others decline. This all means that a sequence of temperature change should be sealed into the core, awaiting its interpreter.

Pollen analysis

The third method has many similarities to the second, but is probably the most widely used of the three. **Pollen analysis**, or **palynology**, takes grains of pollen from the sediment and, according to the frequency of different types, allows the analyst to make definite statements about the historical succession of environmental conditions. Pollen, which is hardy against decay, occurs in profusion in all plants and, again under a microscope, each type is distinguishable. As Fig 9.24 demonstrates, sequences can be built up of the frequency of different types of tree pollen in the core, and if species indicative of particular climatic conditions are chosen, a clear pattern of the changing temperature of the past can be established. Such an exercise is likely to be particularly helpful in showing us how conditions changed after the final decay of the ice or even, perhaps, how temperatures deteriorated before the Loch Lomond re-advance and during other interglacials.

Absolute dating

A series of past temperatures, even if the record is continuous, does not necessarily give us the date of major temperature changes, however, and there are few accurate methods of assessing this. In existing pro-glacial lakes, a record may be sealed into the varves on the bed, each layer representing one year, its thickness indicative of the degree of melting occurring. As we can give an absolute date to the top varve, that is, the present, backdating can be carried out effectively. Varves from a Pleistocene lake, however, can only indicate conditions over a sequence of years, for we will have no absolute date to fix the beginning or end of that sequence.

The carbon isotope, C_{14}, occurs in most organic material and decays after death at a constant rate. This allows measurements of the percentage remaining to

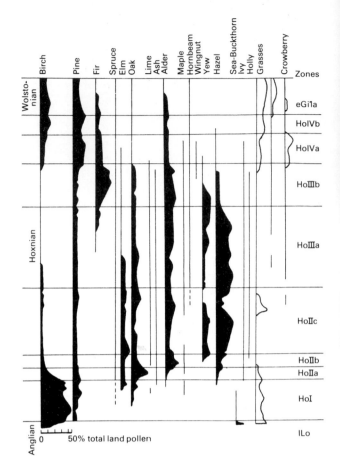

Fig 9.24 Pollen diagram from the Hoxnian lake deposit at Marks Tey, Essex.

stand as a good indicator of the age of the remains. Despite a large margin of error and various difficulties in interpreting the results, **radio-carbon dating** is relatively effective for deposits up to 70000 years old, and when used with pollen analysis can give us quite an accurate picture of the later stage of glaciation. Methods developed so far to penetrate any further than this are not totally reliable, although **potassium-argon dating**, by which the radioactive decay of 40K to 40A is assessed, has been applied successfully to older sediments to give a general indication of the beginnings of the Pleistocene Ice Age.

Questions

1 Study Fig 9.25.

(a) What relationship between meltwater production and altitude is shown by the figure?

(b) Which of the three years shown do you think experienced the mildest conditions?

(c) Is accumulation measured as a depth, volume or area?

(d) How would you calculate which band of altitude received the heaviest precipitation (snowfall) total each year?

(e) What does this diagram tell us about the mass balance of the White Glacier in each of the three years shown?

2 Study Fig 9.26.

(a) Explain in your own words the origins of the four sources of load carried by meltwater.

(b) What is the difference between meltwater entrainment and meltwater transport?

(c) What is an example of an englacial deposit becoming a pro-glacial one?

(d) In what ways can meltwater load be both an input and an output of the glacier system?

(e) Which of the four types of fluvioglacial deposition are likely to be most temporary? Why?

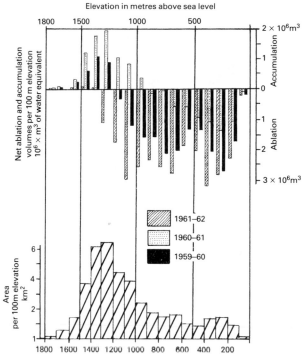

Fig 9.25 Net ablation and accumulation of the White Glacier, Axel Heiberg Island.

Fig 9.26 Flow diagram to demonstrate some of the possible paths of debris in the fluvioglacial system.

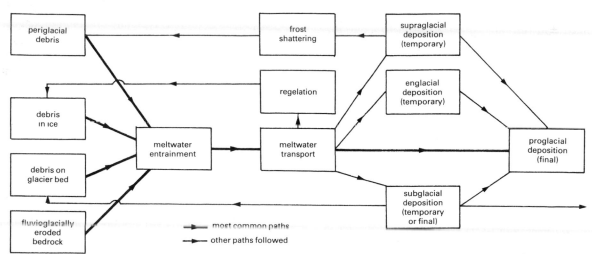

Further Reading

Sediments, D Briggs (Butterworths, 1977).

Valley Carved in the Yorkshire Moors, K J Gregory, *Geographical Magazine* 50, 276–9 (1978).

Glacial and Fluvioglacial Landforms, R J Price (Longman, 1973).

The Parallel Roads of Glen Roy, J B Sissons (Nature Conservancy Council).

The Ice Age in Britain, B W Sparks and R G West (Methuen, 1972).

Glaciers and Landscape, D E Sugden and B S John (Arnold, 1976).

Other References

Proglacial Lake Eskdale after Sixty Years, K J Gregory, *Transactions of the Institute of British Geographers* 36 (1965).

A System of Glacier Lakes in the Cleveland Hills, P F Kendall, *Quarterly Journal of the Geological Society* 58, 471–571 (1902).

Lateral Drainage Channels along the northern side of the Moltka Glacier, N. W. Greenland, V Schytt (Geogr. Annlr 38, 64–77 (1956).

Some Aspects of Glacial Drainage Channels in Britain, J B Sissons, *Scottish Geographical Magazine* 77, 15–36 (1961).

10

Periglacial Processes and Landscape

Introduction

The Meaning of Periglacial

We must not assume that it was only the areas that were actually glaciated, or covered in ice, that were transformed by the climatic change of the Pleistocene period. As the ice sheets spread out from the poles the climatic zones beyond were squeezed into the narrowing belt between ice and equator. This means that those tundra climates that today exist in northern Canada, Alaska, Lappland and Siberia would have been displaced to locations as southerly as northern France and southern England. Such areas would have been on the *peri*phery of the ice sheet, or around its *peri*meter, causing such zones to be termed **periglacial** areas. As the ice advanced and retreated during the Pleistocene these zones would have changed location, too, so that at various times the entire British Isles would have been subjected to periglacial conditions (see Fig 10.1).

It would be misleading, however, to suggest that all periglacial zones produce similar processes and landforms. The effects that are produced depend on the initial landscape, the length of time that periglacial conditions have operated, the degree of interference of man and, most of all, on the characteristics of the climate which prevails. With approximately 20 per cent of the earth's land area currently being under the influence of periglacial conditions, it is hardly surprising that there are considerable variations in climate, as indeed there would have been in Pleistocene times. A maritime or continental location would create contrasts, as indeed would wind direction – is it predominantly on to or off the ice sheet? Latitude could also influence climate by controlling the angle of the incoming rays from the sun, and the seasonal and daily variation of solar radiation.

Despite this considerable variety, it is possible to make certain generalisations about both periglacial conditions and periglacial landscapes.

Characteristics of Periglacial Areas

A periglacial climate is typically one of long, cold winters and short, milder summers. The long freeze of winter, during which temperatures may fall below $-50°C$ and very rarely, if ever, exceed $0°C$, causes the ground to become frozen solid, a condition known as permafrost. Very little weathering or erosion can occur under such conditions. Partial melting, at least, may take place in summer as air temperatures rise. Mean summer monthly temperatures are often $10°C$ and for short

Fig 10.1 The changing extent of periglacial conditions in Britain during the Pleistocene.

a) Anglian and Wolstonian Glaciations

b) Late Devensian Readvance

c) Loch Lomond Readvance

[ ] = area of periglacial activity

Seasonal variations of periglacial processes

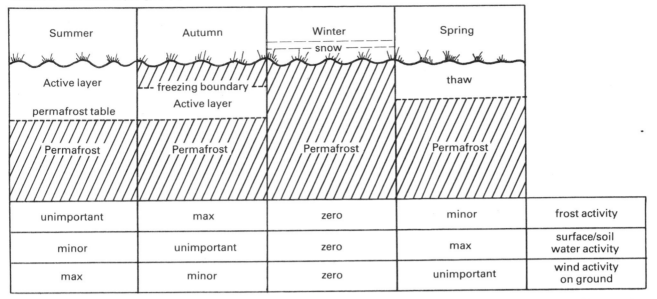

Summer	Autumn	Winter	Spring	
Active layer	freezing boundary	snow	thaw	
permafrost table	Active layer			
Permafrost	Permafrost	Permafrost	Permafrost	
unimportant	max	zero	minor	frost activity
minor	unimportant	zero	max	surface/soil water activity
max	minor	zero	unimportant	wind activity on ground

Fig 10.2 Seasonal variations of periglacial processes and permafrost.

periods of the warmer days figures may go as high as 30°C, especially in areas away from the sea. Summer melting is a vital component of the periglacial environment, for it not only feeds the rivers with great torrents of water but also enables many slope and surface processes to take place. Perhaps even more vital, though, are the transition seasons of spring and autumn, for during these periods temperatures may fluctuate constantly above and below freezing point between day and night (see Fig 10.2). Such rapid changes in temperature are responsible for many of the characteristic processes of periglacial areas, for as we shall see below, many of these are due to the action of frost.

Vegetation in these areas is limited by the extreme conditions. **Tundra** actually means 'treeless plain' and that is a suitable description for the mixture of mosses, lichens, dwarf shrubs and stunted willows that adorn the vast sweeps of northern Canada and Siberia. Such vegetation does little to impede the wind and it is hardly surprising, therefore, that wind erosion is also an important process in sculpting the tundra surface.

Periglacial landscapes, then, are not hospitable places, as Photo 10.1 ably demonstrates. They provide great difficulties for man, as places of habitation, cultivation and most of all communication. Their unevenness, their bogginess and the seasonality of their climate make them eminently unsuitable to almost all forms of surface transport, except perhaps the hovercraft.

Periglacial: a Misleading Term?

Some authors now question the broad application of the term 'periglacial' to the areas described so far. Are all the zones that experience such conditions really adjacent to ice sheets? What about those areas of high altitude, either today or during the Pleistocene, that experience or have experienced permafrost but which are far from ice sheets? What about those upland areas, sometimes known as **nunataks**, that protrude above the ice sheets and are subjected to the attacks of frost but not to the activities of moving ice? Perhaps the more general term, frost action, should be used, as Ball and Goodier suggest, for frost is common to so many periglacial processes. Frost action, however, is often used to mean freeze-thaw and seems too narrow a term to embrace the processes of gelifluxion, wind erosion and fluvial erosion that are also a part of these environments. For want of a more accurate term, then, it seems logical to continue to use periglacial as has been the case since 1909, but to bear in mind that we should not take the word too literally.

Photo 10.1   Talson River, North West Territories, Canada: a tundra landscape, unevenly drained and patchily vegetated.

Permafrost and its Associated Processes

Types and Extent of Permafrost

The term **permafrost** has been used for nearly 40 years to describe permanently frozen ground. It extends, in its various forms, across 26 per cent of the earth's land surface, although that assumes that it exists beneath all the ice cover, an assumption which many people challenge.

Permafrost's existence is largely related to the air temperature. It is unlikely to develop where mean annual temperatures are above −1°C, although, as Fig 10.3 shows, with temperatures as high as this it will probably be **discontinuous**. The further one travels poleward from the −1°C isotherm, the deeper and more **continuous** the permafrost is likely to be.

It would be too simple to suggest that the continuity and depth of permafrost are related only to air temperature. Local variations in extent may reflect the aspect of a slope, altitude, and the vegetation or the character of the soil and rock that compose the surface layers. A lack of vegetation, for instance, will mean that the ground lacks insulation and so freezing is able to proceed to a much greater depth. For the same reason, when man removes vegetation from a permafrost zone, the lack of protection means that summer thawing is able to penetrate to a much greater depth than previously. Broad stretches of permanent snow cover, and large or small bodies of surface water also provide insulation for the underlying ground, in the latter case preventing permafrost from extending beyond the coastline or beneath large lakes. Geothermal heat from below may also act as a constraint on the depth of freezing.

It has probably taken thousands of years for the deepest areas of permafrost to develop, such as those in the Yakutsk region of the USSR, where depths of over 1500 metres have been recorded (see Fig 10.4). Such areas should perhaps, therefore, be regarded as relics of a former much colder climate.

The Active Layer

The permanently low temperatures of the permafrost prevent most geomorphological processes from operating. However, few areas of the world do not experience summer daytime temperatures above 0°C, and almost everywhere, therefore, permafrost is subject to surface melting if only of the top few centimetres. It is within this melted zone, or **active layer**, that periglacial processes are able to operate. Of these processes, gelifluxion is probably the most significant in its impact on landscape, but there are many less obvious processes which distort and restructure the surface layers of the ground, and it is to these that we turn our attention first.

Cryoturbation

Despite its ugliness, **cryoturbation** is a useful word, for it literally means stirring up due to the action of frost, and it adequately summarises the various ways in which ground ice forms, and subsequently distorts, the active layer. Some of its results are as follows.

Involutions

It is important to appreciate that thawing and later refreezing of the active layer proceed from the surface downwards. This means that, as the air temperature begins to rise in spring, thawing will gradually penetrate further into the ground, its success in doing so aided or hindered by the material of the surface layers. Some of these layers will conduct heat much better than others. Eventually, by late summer, the thawing may have activated a layer several metres in depth. By late autumn, temperatures stray less and less frequently above freezing point, and the uppermost section of the ground no longer thaws during the day. The thickness of this frozen layer extends downwards with

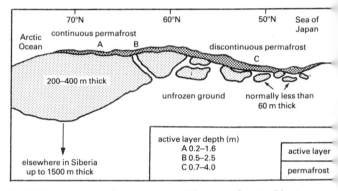

Fig 10.3 A generalised cross-section of the permafrost in Siberia at 130 degrees east.

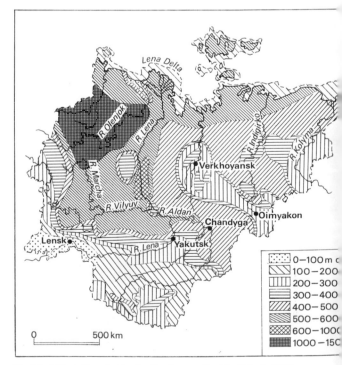

Fig 10.4 Variations in the depth of permafrost in Yakut ASSR.

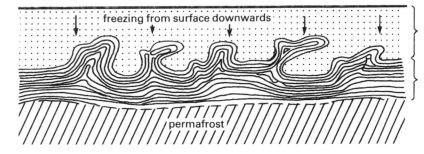

Fig 10.5 Involutions in fine sediment within the active layer.

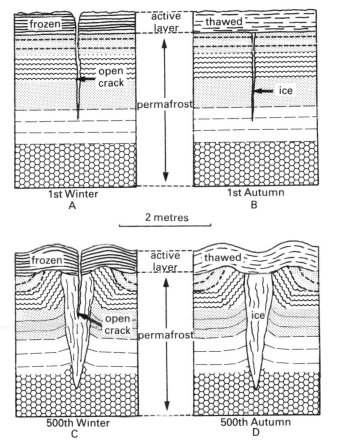

Fig 10.6 The development of an ice wedge.

cracking of the ground, not just in the frozen active layer but also in the permafrost beneath. From above, these cracks produce an irregular polygonal pattern, with polygons 30–40 metres across not unusual. Within the ground they provide a crevice into which meltwater can seep and freeze during the days and nights of the warmer seasons. These slivers of ice create **wedges** which persist during the winter freeze, their crevices providing lines of weakness which reopen as the ground contracts once more. Further layers of ice are added to the wedge which gradually widens, reaching ten metres across on some parts of the tundra, although probably taking hundreds of years to form. If the ice can resist the expansion of the ground in autumn the surrounding beds of sediment may well be contorted as they are pushed against the wedge (see Fig 10.6).

Segregated ice

From what has already been said about involutions it should be clear that the refreezing of the active layer does not occur evenly, for its speed will depend on both the various materials that compose the layer and their water content. What appears to happen in some materials is that ice forms first in particular pore spaces within the soil or sediment and then draws water to it which freezes and enlarges it. These isolated lumps of ice are often in the shape of a **lens**, and collectively are termed **segregated ice**. Experiments have shown that they are most likely to occur in materials of medium grain size, such as silts. In sediment of greater size, such as sands, freezing tends to be continuous rather than in segregated pockets, and in finer materials, such as clays, water movement is so restricted that a lens cannot be sustained. It is quite usual for a series of lenses to occur one above the other, and for some of them to be quite large. A thickness of five metres or more is not unusual and in some parts of northern Canada and Siberia extreme cases of lenses many times this size have been reported.

Once again, a feature like this is not likely to be seen by the casual observer, but its effects may well be. The formation of a solid lens of clear ice within the ground will cause the beds above it to dome up, a process called **frost heave**. Thawing of the active layer may disperse the lens and the temporary dome on the surface will

the coming of winter and, as it does so, exerts pressure on what remains of the active layer. This pressure contorts the beds of sediment, twisting them into buckled formations which are known as **involutions**. The warping of the beds in this way occurs as the finer sediments within them are thrust upwards, for with their higher water content they tend to remain unfrozen much longer than the coarse sediments and therefore are more mobile and responsive to the pressure (see Fig 10.5). These features are, of course, rarely seen until a river, or more likely man, exposes them.

Ice wedges

When water freezes it expands in volume, but if temperatures continue to drop to those typical of a tundra winter contraction will take place which causes severe

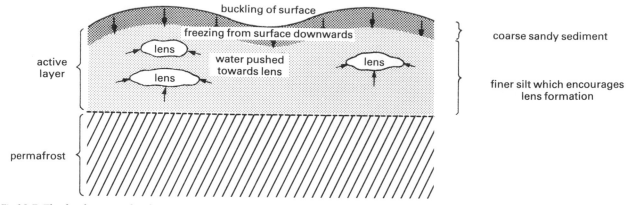

Fig 10.7 The development of ice lenses.

Photo 10.2 Pipkrake or needle ice formed in an unconsolidated surface. Catbells, Cumbria, January 1987.

Photo 10.3 Stone stripes. (See text for explanation).

collapse. A repeated annual cycle of heave and collapse will soon produce a very irregular surface of marshy or badly-drained hollows and intervening hillocks, often described as **thermokarst** because of its similarity to the pitted solution surfaces of some limestone karst areas.

Needle ice

On a much smaller scale than the lens, another form of segregated ice is **needle ice** or **pipkrake**, although these are more often due to nocturnal rather than seasonal freezing. These tapering strands of ice form beneath pebbles or stones within the ground. Ice crystals are particularly likely to develop there because of the ability of the pebble to conduct heat relatively quickly, thus accelerating night-time cooling in its immediate vicinity. Needles may be millimetres or tens of centimetres in length, and as they form and expand are likely to push the pebble towards the surface, thus contributing to the process of frost heave. Small mounds, only centimetres across, called **nubbins** may appear on the surface as a result.

Patterned ground

One of the most distinctive features of periglacial geomorphology, largely because it can actually be observed on the surface, is the intricate embroidered pattern of stones that is imprinted on the ground and illustrated in Photo 10.3. There are two questions here that need to be answered. First, why is there such an accumulation of stones on the surface, and second, why do they arrange themselves in such intricate and regular patterns?

It is largely as a result of frost heave that the stones arrive at the surface. Ice lenses, as well as needle ice, are most likely to form beneath pebbles or even larger fragments of rock. Even if the lump of ice melts seasonally, the void formerly occupied by the stone will probably be infilled with loose finer sediment collapsing into it. Stones are thus pushed ever closer to the surface, and Washburn's experiments in Greenland show that several centimetres of displacement in one year is possible.

To answer the second question is far less easy, for the process of **frost thrust** by which stones are moved laterally rather than vertically is not well understood. We need to explain why the stones are moved into networks of interlaced **polygons**, **circles**, and **stripes**. To review the many suggestions that have been made to explain stone polygons is beyond the scope of this book,

Photo 10.4   Stone circles, Iceland. (See text for explanation).

but we can suggest reasons why the pattern is perpetuated once formed.

The centre of each polygon or circle is composed of finer sediment which tends to be domed upward during winter freezing. This doming occurs because the drier stones on the polygon's perimeter freeze more readily than the wet centre; the drier stones can conduct heat more readily. The freezing of the stones exerts pressure inwards on the centre, creating the doming, and the slight gradient of the dome will then ensure that any future stone which reaches the surface due to frost heave will be transported down the gradient (see Fig 10.8). If it is not transported then freeze-thaw action is likely to reduce it in size, for the greater incidence of moisture in the polygon centre will ensure the operation of this process of weathering. In addition, in the warmer periods, meltwater will drain freely through the accumulation of stones and keep it free from fine sediment.

Stone polygons are rarely as easy to distinguish as they are in the photograph here. They may be very small, although usually they have a diameter of one to two metres, which means that they are on a quite different scale from the ice-wedge polygons mentioned above. Both types may make up **patterned ground**, but neither type is usually found in isolation. In the case of the smaller, sorted polygons, they are arranged in what are called stone nets.

Where the patterns of stones occur on slopes of more than five degrees, they form elongated polygons, **stone garlands** or even stripes. Their formation is thought to

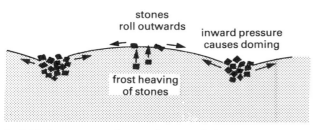

Fig 10.8 Cross-section of stone polygon or circle.

be closely related to polygons and circles. Doming within the features is once again typical, although downslope sliding of the finer, muddy centre may create a lobe within the garland not unlike a terracette banked up against the outer wall of stones on the downslope side of the garland. On steeper slopes this bank may be broken through by the flow of mud, thus leaving only stripes of stones. If the slope is greater than 30 degrees, even these may be difficult to discern for the slope movement will be so active that the pattern and segregation of stones are lost.

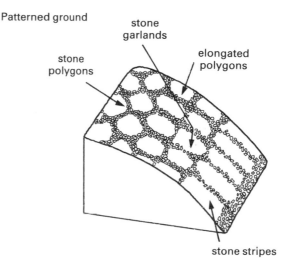

Fig 10.9 Cross-section of patterned ground to show transition of stone polygons into stone stripes.

Pingos

Several of the processes already discussed are involved in the development of **pingos**, which are small hillocks which may reach tens of metres in height but will rarely exceed 50. Their presence contributes some of the more distinctive features to the thermokarst scenery described above (see Photo 10.5).

Two contrasting theories are both accepted as explanations for their formation, the first views the

Photo 10.5   Pingos, with ice cores, north west Greenland.

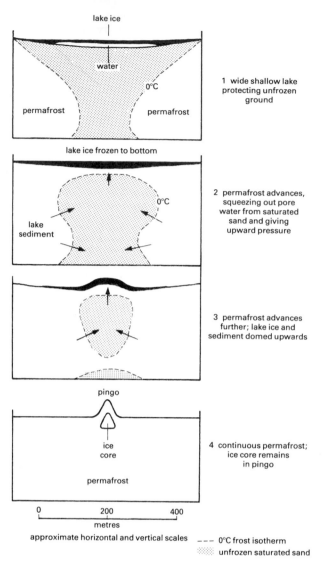

Fig 10.10 The formation of a pingo as a closed system.

development process as a closed system, the latter as an open one. More than a thousand pingos have been identified in the Mackenzie Delta of northern Canada, and this delta provides an alternative name for the closed system type.

Formation is considered to take place beneath a shallow lake over hundreds of years. Initially the water in the lake, even in winter, insulates the underlying sediments from freezing. In time the lake's depth is

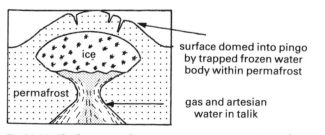

Fig 10.11 The formation of a pingo as an open system. For explanation see text.

gradually reduced with sediment from meltwater streams, thus allowing winter freezing to extend to the lake bed. Protection against freezing is no longer available for the underlying sediment, and the permafrost advances from each side. This advance exerts pressure which forces the water within the sediment to push upwards, exerting further pressure on the thin layer of permafrost beneath the lake. Doming on the surface ensues and eventually the remaining water becomes an ice core trapped within the dome. Stretching of the surface during doming may weaken it and enable melting of the ice core which will cause the centre of the pingo to collapse, leaving a boggy area which may develop into a pond or small lake (see Fig 10.10).

East Greenland gives an alternative name for the **open system type**. A body of water trapped underground after freezing from the surface has begun is called a **talik**, and pressure from the permafrost on such a water layer may force it up towards the surface. Surrounded by permafrost it may now freeze into an ice core, once again causing the surface to dome (see Fig 10.11). Groundwater under artesian pressure will continue to feed the ice core and eventually a pingo results. If pressure mounts sufficiently high, water and sediment may be erupted from the top of the pingo through cracks in the stretched ground surface.

Alases

Many of the features already described may contribute to the natural development of thermokarst. In the twentieth century, man is undoubtedly the major cause of the extension of this form of scenery for it is he who removes the trees and other vegetation that provide the vital insulation (see Chapter 12).

If thawing of the surface is continuous, ice wedges may melt and create small depressions. In areas where the wedges are particularly numerous and closely spaced, large-scale collapse of the surface may ensue to create major depressions, called **alases**. These hollows are likely to become centres of drainage, allowing lakes to form in them, which will prevent the permafrost from re-establishing itself at the surface. In Siberia, coalescence of many adjacent alases has created linear troughs, known as **alas valleys**, which reach tens of kilometres in length.

Processes of Mass Movement

Brief mention has already been made of small-scale slope processes, for material is prone to creep and flow down any dome that is created by the processes of cryoturbation. Thus, stones may move to the perimeter of stone polygons and circles, and movement within the saturated surface material of pingos may gradually reduce the angle of their slopes. In common with other climatic areas, the slope processes of periglacial areas really represent a continuum from the slow, dry movements to the rapid, saturated ones, but our study is made easier if we divide that continuum into distinct sections, thus differentiating between **frost creep** and

gelifluxion. On many occasions the two processes are simultaneous and quite indistinguishable, and quite often the former process is merely a prelude to the latter, taking place when seasonal thawing has not yet occurred to a sufficient degree to engender gelifluxion.

Almost as much time has been spent this century in attempting to produce a foolproof series of names for the various slope processes of periglacial climates as in studying the actual processes themselves. The only dispute that need concern us here is what name we give to the downslope flow of the thawed active layer. **Solifluxion** would surely suffice as a general term but as this literally means 'soil flow', many authors consider a more specific term, gelifluxion, is needed to describe the flow of thawed sediment over frozen permafrost in periglacial climates. In this chapter, therefore, it seems appropriate to reserve gelifluxion for that type of solifluxion that is found in tundra areas, but you should bear in mind that in some texts the two terms are synonymous.

Frost creep

Frost creep, the less significant of the two major periglacial slope processes, is akin to soil creep in temperate climates where, indeed, it may also occur on more exposed slopes. When frost heave occurs within the soil, particles rise towards the surface of the slope, but when the ice crystal causing heave melts they drop vertically, according to gravity. In this way the particles are able to creep downslope, by perhaps as much as 20–30 centimetres a year on steeper slopes, but certainly by as much as five centimetres in an average tundra year. Like soil creep, the movement is confined to the uppermost layer of the ground, perhaps occurring in only the top 50 centimetres and even then decreasing significantly from the surface downwards.

Gelifluxion: the process

Rising air temperatures in spring and summer cause the melting not only of winter snow cover but also of the ice contained in the pore spaces of the topsoil. Permafrost is, after all, composed of up to 80 per cent ice, in volume. The permanently frozen ground beneath the active layer plays a vital role in the process for its impermeability prevents the water from draining away from the surface layer. The saturation of the active layer which results renders it very unstable, for its shear strength is greatly reduced with the loss of internal friction and cohesion. So great is this instability that it requires a slope of only one or two degrees for the active layer to become mobile, and considerable flows, of up to several kilometres, have been observed on slopes of no more than 0.5 degrees. As the vegetation cover is rarely continuous, it is unable to make much of a contribution towards stabilising a slope. Even so, where it does exist, a mat of grass or even a patch of moss may be able to restrain movement temporarily.

Measurement of gelifluxion is not easy to carry out, for climate and terrain are inhospitable. Several metres of movement within a few days in late spring is considered possible, but is unlikely, and could be maintained only under optimum conditions of climate, slope, vegetation and sediment. A flow of less than ten centimetres a year is much more common, but that may occur in a series of dramatic, sporadic movements rather than a continuous one. Most of the movement will occur in spring when most meltwater is available, for in summer, although temperatures are higher, the surface may well have dried out.

Gelifluxion: the effects

So widespread is gelifluxion that it is undoubtedly the most important of all periglacial processes. One likely consequence of its continued operation is the reduction of relief as it removes weathered and unconsolidated deposits from the upper sections of slopes and conveys them downslope (see Fig 10.13). In this way major irregularities in the surface, and even valleys, can be infilled with deposits which can accumulate to a depth of many metres. An active river in a valley bottom may well prevent such accumulation but, if the rate of downslope movement is too great for the sporadic and seasonal river flow, its impact can be considerable. Where downslope movement is not restricted by a valley bottom, for example at the foot of an escarpment, featureless sheets or fans of material may remain. Not all surfaces are smooth, however, for terraces and lobes are also a feature of geIif!ucted slopes.

Depending on the degree of vegetation cover, **terraces and lobes** may be noticed either as buckles in the turf or as heaps of stones. Both the stone-banked and

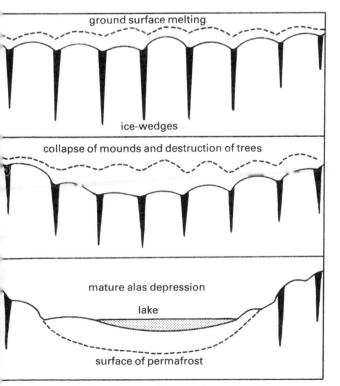

Fig 10.12 The development of an alas. For explanation see text.

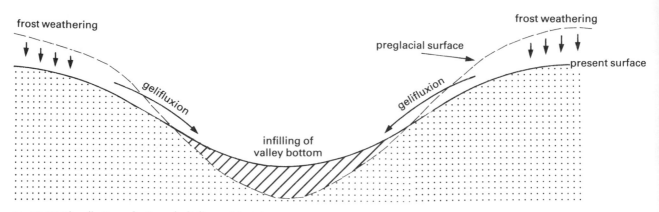

Fig 10.13 The effective reduction of relief by periglacial processes.

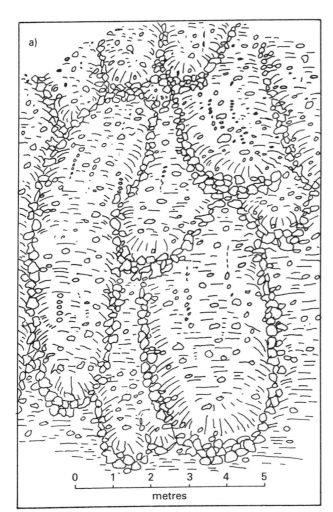

(a) Plan.

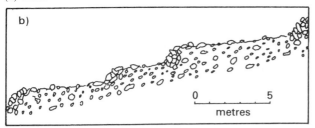

(b) Section.

Fig 10.14 Stone banked terraces and garlands

turf-banked features appear on moderate slopes, the former between 10 and 25 degrees, the latter 5 and 20 degrees. Their shape varies from a lobe to a terrace; the former has its longest axis perpendicular to the contour, the latter parallel to it (see Fig 10.14).

Stone-banked lobes and terraces: Some larger examples of the stone-banked type may have a tread of up to 30 metres and a riser of five metres, whilst smaller examples may extend only 5–10 metres upslope from a riser of less than a metre.

Stone-banked lobes are also known as garlands and their formation has already been explained in part. Stones, heaved to the surface, are likely to travel downslope faster than the finer material; they will roll and turn over and not rely only on creep and gelifluxion. If their movement is checked by vegetation, a slight change in slope or some other irregularity, the stones will build up into a small wall behind which the flowing finer material will accumulate (see Photo 10.6).

Turf-banked lobes and terraces: The **turf-banked lobe** may form a feature of similar size, but some of the turf-banked terraces are much more extensive, with treads several hundred metres in width. Insulation provided by the turf means that frost heave has been less effective in raising stones to the surface. It is thus the surface layers of turf and topsoil that are geliflucted. Again,

Photo 10.6 Stone-banked gelifluxion lobe, north west Greenland.

minor obstructions halt this movement, buckling and contorting the turf and creating a more significant obstruction which now forms the riser of the lobe or terrace.

Although creep and gelifluxion are the two major slope processes of periglacial movement, there are others, for where scree slopes and block streams occur, for instance, **rock slides** will be common. In some areas **rock glaciers** exist. On the surface these may appear as streams of angular rocks, but in fact, at depth, they are often held together by ice which means that they behave like highly loaded glaciers.

Periglacial Slope Development

The suppression of differences in relief has already been mentioned as a major effect of periglacial slope activity. A less clearly understood consequence of slope process is the development of **asymmetrical valley cross-profiles** (see Fig 10.15). The asymmetry has been studied extensively not only in areas of modern tundra but also in the chalk dry valleys of southern England, for these too are thought to have a periglacial origin. That is not to say that all asymmetrical valleys are periglacial, for many may be structural, not climatic.

Explanation is fraught with difficulty. It would be easy if the steeper slope was always the north-facing one, but research has shown that the steeper slope can face in any direction. Not only that, but in one locality there is not necessarily any consistency, and evidence from western Alaska shows that both symmetrical and asymmetrical valleys can develop in close proximity to each other. Again, it would facilitate explanation if we could decide whether asymmetry is due to the steepening of one side or to the decline of the other. Theories abound in explanation of both possibilities, and as with so many other cases there is probably some truth in all of them.

The most obvious theory, when the north-facing slope of a northern hemisphere valley is the steeper, is that lack of direct sunshine will cause the permafrost to remain frozen for longer. Gelifluxion is thus reduced in effectiveness compared with the south-facing slope, which consequently becomes gradually gentler.

Wind direction could also be a determining factor. In north-south trending valleys, a westerly wind will drive snow against the east-facing slope causing greater accumulations there. In summer this will persist as a snow patch, possibly allowing the process of nivation to attack the slope and reduce it. Alternatively, one could argue that it is the western slope which is reduced because of this, for its thin cover of snow will melt readily in summer, saturating the slope and engendering slope processes. Contrasts in snow cover need not be the result of drifting, of course; they may reflect differences in insolation.

The exposure of a slope will undoubtedly encourage weathering upon it. If this, combined with slope processes, engenders a thick mantle of debris the slope may

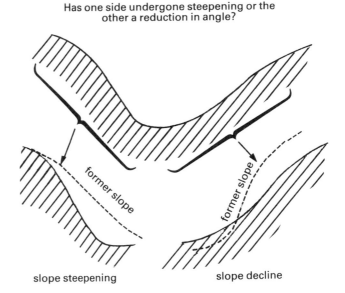

Has one side undergone steepening or the other a reduction in angle?

slope steepening   slope decline

Fig 10.15 An asymmetrical valley cross-profile.

become gentler. That debris slope could then push a river at its base towards the opposite valley wall, causing undercutting and steepening of its angle.

In addition to these climatic origins for asymmetry, ecological theories have also been put forward. Variations in vegetation cover leading to differences in insulation on the ground could create sufficient contrasts in slope processes to be responsible.

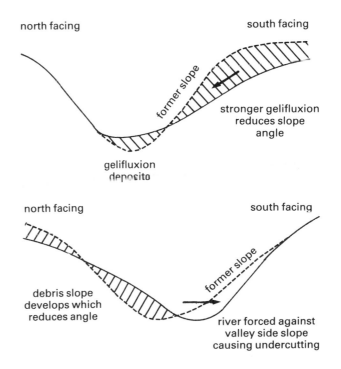

Fig 10.16 Two contrasting theories which may explain asymmetrical cross-profiles. Note how, in both cases, the former valley profile is symmetrical.

Other Processes of Periglacial Areas

Weathering

In order to produce the surface layers of unconsolidated material which slope processes transport, it is necessary for weathering processes to operate. Freeze-thaw action is the most widespread of these, for frost will be able to penetrate pores, crevices, cracks and joints of any surface (see Chapter 3). Even so, the frequency of its occurrence is easily exaggerated, for the air temperature does not actually cross freezing point all that often in the periglacial climate. In high altitude areas of the tundra it certainly does, however, and numerous scree slopes, blockfields and **block streams** bear witness to it. The latter are comparable to blockfields but occur on slopes of up to 25 degrees rather than on upland plateau surfaces.

Other weathering processes also occur. Salt weathering, employing salt crystals transported by sea winds, has been observed, as have limited forms of chemical weathering. Coatings of various chemical compounds on the surface of rocks together with tiny rounded hollows provide evidence of the latter in parts of Greenland and the Canadian Arctic. Suggestions have been made that limestone weathering is emphasised in such regions because the increased solubility of carbon dioxide at low temperatures allows carbonation to be more virulent. However, the sparse vegetation and poorly developed soil will restrict the formation of organic acids and thus reduce the possible impact on limestone. Limestone weathering may thus be no more effective than in cool temperate climates such as that of upland Britain.

Wind Action

The discontinuous, short vegetation of tundra areas combined with the drying out of the surface sediment and soil in summer and autumn allow wind to be a significant geomorphological process. Its effects can be seen in the grooved, fluted and polished rock surfaces and **ventifacts**, or wind-carved boulders, that exist in most tundra areas. Its deposits are not always easy to distinguish in current periglacial areas, but in former ones they are readily discernible in the vast spreads of **loess** that are draped across northern and eastern Europe and North America.

Nivation

Nivation is the process already described in Chapter 8 which occurs beneath snow patches. It gives rise to depressions and hollows in hillsides, the larger of which may develop into **nivation cirques**. The presence of permafrost beneath a snow patch is considered to be particularly important for it prevents meltwater from sinking into the subsoil, and by remaining on the surface it can take part in freeze-thaw action.

Fluvial Action

In common with the outwash streams of meltwater which may flow across tundra areas, periglacial streams show enormous variation in discharge during the year. For seven or eight months they may remain frozen or survive as a mere trickle, but with the coming of the spring thaw they may be transformed into great torrents capable of eroding deep gullies into the unconsolidated deposits of the surface. They will need to contend with high loads, however, for gelifluxion deposits may well block their paths. Steep gradients will need to be maintained if the high discharge is to reach an equilibrium with the heavy load.

Landscapes of Former Periglacial Areas

Few of us have, or are likely to have, direct experience of tundra landscapes and their geomorphological processes. Most of us, however, should be able to observe relics of a periglacial climate much closer to home, for many British landscapes bear the hallmark of periglacial action. Explanation in earlier chapters of features such as chalk dry valleys, granite tors, corries and screes relied heavily on the assumption that conditions akin to those of the tundra once existed in Britain.

Indeed, it is likely that they existed many times, for such conditions would have preceded and succeeded each stage of glacial cooling during the Pleistocene. Even so, the effects of each periglacial period may no longer be discernible either because glacial action has obliterated them or because post-glacial erosion and deposition have transformed them. The clearest evidence of the effects of periglacial conditions comes from the most recent occurrences of tundra conditions in Britain, that is, during and immediately after the last glacial advance. On very gentle slopes the periglacial imprint is often most distinct for it is less likely that later processes will have made such inroads into them as they have on steeper slopes.

Although we can refer to periglacial conditions in Britain, we must not make the mistake of assuming that the climate was identical to that of high latitude regions of today. Our more southerly location would mean that variations in length of day and night would not be so pronounced between winter and summer, for tundra areas of today experience little sunlight for the entire winter season. Diurnal freeze-thaw cycles would thus have been far more probable in Britain than in today's tundra. Our climate would then, as now, have been a maritime one, which would mean, for instance, that winter temperatures and depth of permafrost are unlikely to have plummeted to the depths of those in modern Siberia and Canada. Even within Britain, there were great variations in the periglacial climate. For example, during the final stages of the Pleistocene periglacial conditions stretched right down to sea level in south east England and yet, in the south west, there

Photo 10.7 Involutions – at the boundary of the Bagshot beds and the overlying iron-stained plateau gravel – in a gravel pit at West Knighton, Dorset.

Photo 10.8 Ice wedge. This cast remains in glacial sand and gravel at Stanway, Essex.

seems to be little evidence of their extending much below 300 metres above sea level

Evidence of periglacial conditions abounds, both in deposits and in landforms, although much of it is not obvious to the untrained eye for its effects on landscape are far less profound than glacial or even fluvioglacial processes.

Cryoturbation Features

Involutions and ice wedges

Involutions are often spotted when excavation of the surface is undertaken for roadworks or quarrying, or where rivers or the sea have exposed them (see Photo 10.7).

The imprint of ice wedges may be seen in comparable locations, the wedge cast preserved by the collapse of overlying material into it when the ice finally melted. These have been identified not only in southern England, but in the many parts of Scotland not touched by the last advance of the ice and, for example, in sandy deposits in north west Wales. In association with these it is not unusual to find ice wedge polygons traced into the ground, although their identification is really possible only from the air, and depends on what use the land has since been put to.

Stone polygons and stripes

One of the interesting features of stone polygons and stripes is that, in several parts of the British Isles, they are still active. Polygons on the 700 metre high Tinto Hills to the south of the Central Lowlands of Scotland have been deliberately destroyed, only to reform within a few years as a result of seasonal freezing of the ground. Ball and Goodier have studied modern activity in stone polygons at over 900 metres in the Carneddau mountain group in Snowdonia. Stone stripes, again in the Tinto Hills and also on Grasmoor in the Lake District, have also been proved to be currently active.

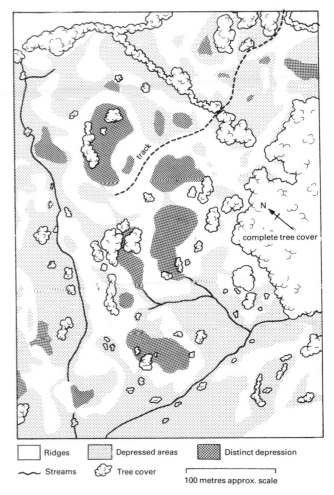

	Ridges		Depressed areas		Distinct depression

Streams   Tree cover   100 metres approx. scale

Fig 10.17 Ice mound features on Walton Common, near King's Lynn, Norfolk.

Ice mounds

The unevenness of parts of the East Anglian landscape, especially in the Breckland area of Norfolk, has sometimes been attributed to the local prevalence of thermokarst. This is a logical explanation, but not an easy one to prove. Relics of ice mounds are unlikely to retain any remnant of their doming, but the outline may well be distinguishable and may even form a minor ridge. They are particularly easy to see where the underlying rock is chalk, for the outline may then be white in colour, contrasting with the darker gravels and sands of the collapsed centre of the dome. In this way pingos have been identified in winter in East Anglian fields, and as Fig 10.17 shows, small ice mound features may stand out clearly on uncultivated ground.

The Effects of Mass Movement

Creep and gelifluxion

Once again, the effect of these processes can be seen not only by studying their imprint on relic landscapes such as the granite tors, but also by observing their occurrence, on a much more limited scale, in Britain today.

Gelifluxion will be experienced only on the coldest and most exposed hillsides. In severe winters such as those of 1946–7 or 1981–2 it may have been observed more widely, even in parts of lowland England, but it is more usually confined to locations above 1000 metres in the Scottish Highlands. The windswept Shetlands, with their consequent sparse vegetation cover, allow the process to occur on much lower slopes, even below 400 metres.

Periglacial gelifluxion in Britain is well exemplified on the chalk slopes of southern England. Fans of **coombe rock**, as the geliflucted sludge of chalk and flint is called, often adorn lower sections of escarpments, and can be particularly well seen in the gaps through the Chilterns at Wendover and Tring. Such deposits may line the troughs of dry valleys to a depth of several metres, as they may the hollows known as coombes described in Chapter 3. Evidence from the Marlborough Downs of Wiltshire and the Chilterns shows that some of this geliflucted debris was capable of moving considerable distances, perhaps 4–8 kilometres, over very gentle slopes of two degrees or less.

When chalk is not a constituent part, such deposits are termed **head deposits**, and these may be found on granite slopes on Dartmoor, along the cliffs around Start Point in south Devon, along the shores of the Scilly Isles and on many other slopes and hillsides. Their unconsolidated nature often makes them prone to landslips in today's climate.

Lobes and terraces of both varieties have been identified in the uplands of both Wales and Scotland, for example stone-banked lobes on the slopes of Lochnagar, the mountain which overlooks Balmoral, and on Carnedd Llewelyn and Y Garn in Snowdonia, and turf-banked lobes in other parts of the Carneddau mountain group. Particularly well developed terraces abound on the peaks of the Scottish island of Rhum.

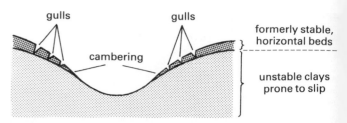

Fig 10.18 Theoretical valley cross-section to illustrate cambering and gulls.

Cambering

The convex arching of previously horizontal beds, and their slippage over the crest of a valley side slope, are another consequence of periglacial activity that has been documented in various parts of southern England, notably on the oolites of the Cotswolds. This **cambering** (see Fig 10.18) occurs where the surface rocks are underlain by clays, whose weakness under periglacial conditions causes the overlying rock to move. Joints in the surface layer may be opened up to create deeper cracks known as **gulls** which run parallel to the contours. Although they are often infilled in relic periglacial landscapes their outline may still be discernible, for example in the Jurassic uplands of Northamptonshire.

Effects of Weathering

Although many of the great scree slopes of upland Britain are still active today, they owe the vast majority of their bulk to periglacial freeze-thaw processes acting both during and after the advance of the ice (see Photo 3.2). In addition, freeze-thaw action would have produced much of the rock waste that was 'geliflucted' down hillsides, not least the coombe rock of the chalk downlands.

It is possible that some of the mountain top rock waste on the ridges and hill shoulders of Snowdonia are blockfields, but this feature is more clearly exemplified on some Scottish mountains, notably on the severely frost-riven peaks of Orval and Hallival on Rhum.

Wind Deposits

Silt-sized particles would have been blown large distances during periglacial times, and there would have been such extensive areas of dry superficial sediment from glacial, fluvioglacial and periglacial activities that the wind would have had an almost inexhaustible supply. Small wonder, then, that wind deposition of that material has created such huge areas of loess in Europe and North America. Its thickness in some regions can be gauged from the map in Fig 10.19, although these figures are by no means maxima, for in parts of Romania it has been estimated to have a depth of 80 metres. Its extent is limited by the extent of the ice cover in the last glaciation, for the winds blowing off the ice sheets most likely distributed the outwash de-

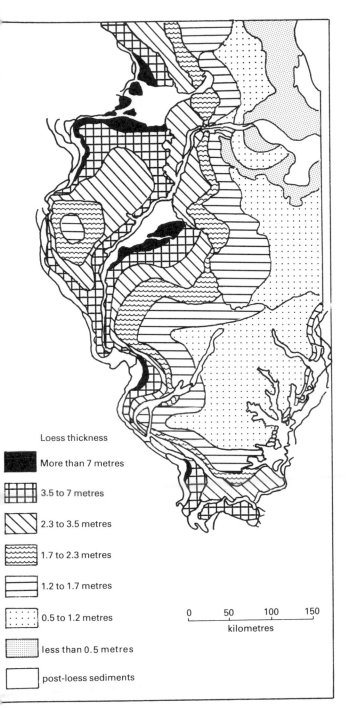

Loess thickness

More than 7 metres

3.5 to 7 metres

2.3 to 3.5 metres

1.7 to 2.3 metres

1.2 to 1.7 metres

0.5 to 1.2 metres

less than 0.5 metres

post-loess sediments

0   50   100   150
kilometres

Fig 10.19 The varying thickness of loess deposits in Illinois.

posits to those areas unaffected by ice. It thus becomes more common as one moves east across Europe and is rare in the west. In Britain there are small and discontinuous areas of loess in south-east England where it is usually termed **brickearth**. It is particularly well represented on the coastal plain of West Sussex and in the London Basin.

Its impact on scenery is not dramatic, for it tends to subdue any outstanding relief, but its impact on agriculture is profound for it breaks down into a rich soil.

Practical Techniques in Periglacial Areas

For the amateur there are few field techniques that are viable in a relict periglacial landscape such as Britain, for major excavation and sophisticated sediment analysis is often needed to derive any meaningful results. Field observation is one of the most useful techniques, for this will enable the student to get first hand knowledge of the features of cryoturbation, for instance.

If one is fortunate enough to come across stone polygons or stripes, various techniques of measurement could be employed. The mean diameter of polygons or circles could be calculated and possibly related graphically or statistically to the angle of slope on which the features appear. Transects across the polygons could be traced from which sediment samples could be drawn for analysis of size of particle or moisture content (see Chapter 9).

The positive identification of a suspected gelifluxion deposit may well be possible for the amateur for it has certain characteristics that distinguish it. For example, the long axes of stones are orientated in the direction of movement, and particles are extremely angular and are usually of the same rock type as the underlying beds, for geliflucted masses do not travel as far as glacial or fluvioglacial deposits. Careful application of the technique to determine stone orientation described in Chapter 8 may thus aid identification of a deposit. The student would be wise to choose a small upland valley for such a project for it would be necessary to sample a series of different deposits to establish the pattern of ice movement and gelifluxion in one locality.

Valley asymmetry provides the student with another possible project, preferably confined to a small area, perhaps within the chalk dry valleys of the Chilterns. Careful measurement and plotting of valley side profiles might allow one to investigate the relationship between slope angle and aspect, or slope angle and the constituent material of the slope. If one were to choose a selection of different slopes carefully, for example with and without head deposits, one might be able to suggest which of the possible theories of asymmetry seemed most plausible in that location.

Any project on a scree slope is dangerous, and one must choose one's site with care. If an active slope is chosen, one may be able to establish some idea of the rates of creep and sliding that are taking place (see Chapter 4 for techniques).

Small projects are then conceivable for the amateur and could constitute part of a more extensive study, perhaps on the granite tors of Dartmoor or chalk dry valleys of the South Downs or Chilterns.

Questions

1 Fig 10.20 attempts to divide high latitude regions into glacial and periglacial zones on the basis of certain climatic criteria.

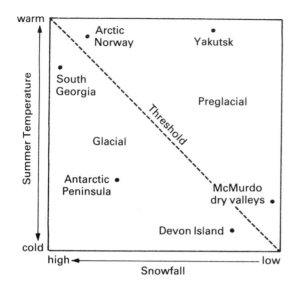

Fig 10.20 The division of glacial and periglacial zones according to snowfall and summer temperature.

(a) Why do you suppose these two particular climatic criteria have been chosen?
(b) Describe the variation in climate within periglacial regions shown in the diagram.
(c) Suggest reasons why periglacial climates vary so much.
(d) There is a useful relationship between summer temperature and amount of snowfall that allows us to differentiate between periglacial and glacial regions. What do you suppose that relationship is? What difference between the climates of the two regions does it pinpoint?

2 The two graphs in Fig 10.21 show records of air temperature and soil temperature over a six-week period at Okstindan in Norway.
(a) How does the temperature record vary for different depths within the soil at site A?
(b) Describe the extent of the differences between air temperature and soil temperature at each site.
(c) What is the major reason for the differences?
(d) In what ways could ground and soil conditions affect the relationship between air temperature and soil temperature?
(e) What implications does the relationship shown between air and soil temperature have for seasonal changes in the active layer?

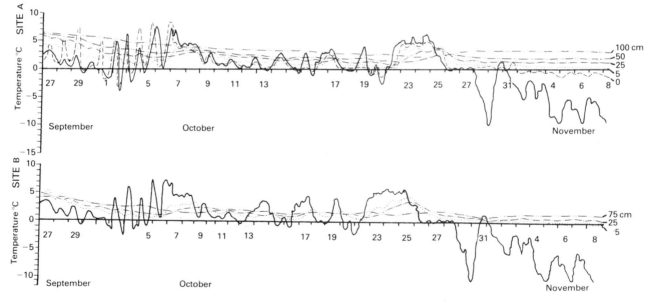

Fig 10.21 Four hourly record of soil and air temperatures.

Further Reading

Periglacial Geomorphology, C Embleton and C A M King (Arnold, 1975).
Polar Ice and Periglacial Lands, D C Money (Evans, 1980).
The Study of Landforms, R J Small (Cambridge, 1978).
The Ice Age in Britain, B W Sparks and R G West (Methuen, 1972).

Other References

Morphology and Distribution of Features Resulting from Frost Action in Snowdonia, D F Ball and R Goodier, *Field Studies* 3 (1970).

11

Arid and Semi-Arid Processes and Landscape

Introduction

Common Misconceptions and Definitions

Ask a random sample of people and their ideas and impressions of **deserts** will have more to do with the film of *Lawrence of Arabia* than with the real world, for landscapes of sand dunes loom large in most perceptions of a desert. In reality, seas of sand probably cover no more than one tenth of the Sahara's land surface and about one quarter of the total world desert surface. Ask your classmates to name as many deserts as they can and their combined list will probably amount to fewer than ten names. Popular knowledge of deserts is remarkably slim, especially if one accepts Meigs' assertion that as much as 33.6 per cent of the earth's land surface experiences arid or semi-arid conditions (see Fig 11.1).

What, then, is a desert? It is, literally, a place deserted of life. But this definition is far too broad for us, for it includes many upland areas, glacial areas, some

tundra areas and even some man-made environments. A preferable definition includes the reason for the inhospitability, namely aridity. This, as can be seen in Fig 11.2, is a function of both rainfall and temperature, but it will suffice to say here that an **arid** area is one where the amount of annual potential evapotranspiration exceeds the annual total of precipitation; in other words, where there is a permanent water deficit. Such a definition embraces not only hot deserts such as the Sahara, the Namib and the Atacama, and the cold winter deserts such as the Gobi and Patagonia, but also the ice deserts of the Arctic and Antarctic which experience drought. For reasons of space, this type of desert is not included in this chapter.

Desert Diversity

It should come as no surprise that a climatic type which extends across a third of the earth's land surface

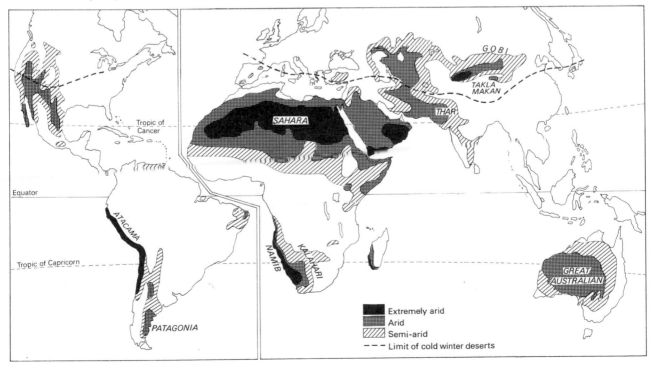

Fig 11.1 World distribution of arid areas.

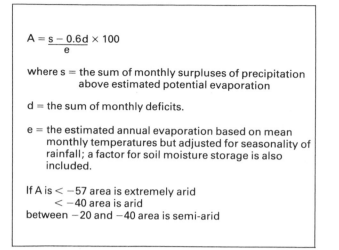

$$A = \frac{s - 0.6d}{e} \times 100$$

where s = the sum of monthly surpluses of precipitation above estimated potential evaporation

d = the sum of monthly deficits.

e = the estimated annual evaporation based on mean monthly temperatures but adjusted for seasonality of rainfall; a factor for soil moisture storage is also included.

If A is < −57 area is extremely arid
   < −40 area is arid
between −20 and −40 area is semi-arid

Fig 11.2 Thornthwaite's aridity index as used by Meigs.

contains an enormous amount of variety. Whether we view them in terms of climate, lithology, geology, topography, geographical location or even their use to man, desert landscapes are immensely diverse.

As Fig 11.1 shows, Meigs' classification of deserts recognises three types, extremely arid, arid and semi-arid, which he devised from Thornthwaite's index shown in Fig 11.2.

Within these categories there is much variety, for proximity to the sea, altitude, aspect and latitude will create anomalies in any pattern. No figure less complex than Thornthwaite's index could serve as a definition. Simple rainfall statistics are certainly inadequate; for example, whilst in southern Australia the 250-millimetre isohyet acts as a useful boundary to the arid zone, in the north of the country areas receiving as much as 500 millimetres a year are quite definitely arid.

If we examine the lithology and geology of arid areas, the variety is again apparent. Small suggests that at least five major landscape structures can be recognised, although even to do this entails great generalisation. These are:

(a) **Mountain and basin deserts**, for example in the south west of the USA that many of us know well from western films. The arid basins are surfaced with a mixture of bare rock, alluvium and sand, perhaps with the remnants of a former lake, the mountain fronts steep although often buried under boulder slopes (Photo 11.1).

(b) The **plateaux** of Libya and western Egypt, composed of horizontal layers of sandstone, which have been cut through by extensive **wadis**, many of which are strewn with debris (Photo 11.2).

(c) The **shield deserts** of Africa and Western Australia, often composed of crystalline rocks which have been eroded into plains, broken only occasionally by an isolated tor or **inselberg** (Photo 11.3).

(d) The great seas of sand and sand dunes which compose the **ergs** of the Sahara and the Great Sandy Desert of north-west Australia (Photo 11.4).

(e) The stony deserts, also known as **hamadas** and **regs**, where the surface is a confusion of rocks and stones. These could also form a component of one of the other deserts (Photo 11.5).

Other authors prefer their own classifications, but whichever we select we must remember that arid regions have the same variety of rock types, geological structures and topography as landscapes with which we are more familiar.

From Fig 11.1 it is clear that arid areas occupy a wide variety of locations. Many of the most arid ones straddle either the Tropic of Capricorn or Cancer at 23.5 degrees from the Equator. Others occupy a west-coast location, but not all, for Patagonia and north-east

Photo 11.1 The Painted Desert, Arizona, south western USA. A series of enclosed desert basins.

Photo 11.2 Aerial view of the Egyptian Sahara, showing a series of wadis 'flowing' towards the edge of the sandstone plateau.

Photo 11.3   Granite mountains on the Iran–Afghanistan border.

Photo 11.4   Erg Chebbi, Morocco: a sand desert.

Photo 11.5   Stony desert or hamada, southern Iran.

Brazil are obviously east coast. Continental interiors are another favoured location, but not in South America. As we shall see below, location is linked not only to climate, but also to the particular relief and shape of the land mass.

Finally, as resource zones for man, arid areas vary greatly in their advantages. Development often depends on location (for example, the Californian Desert benefits from the spreading affluence of Los Angeles, the Sinai from its strategic importance) or on mineral wealth (for example, the copper deposits of the Atacama, the oil of Arabia or the iron ore of Mauritania).

We should, then, be wary of making generalisations; chapters as short as this deserve to be treated sceptically. Even a textbook as long as this devoted to arid geomorphology would find it hard to avoid making certain generalisations.

Changing Desert Boundaries

At whatever time scale we choose, desert boundaries should not be regarded as anything but temporary, for at various stages of the past areas now distant from the arid zones were encompassed within them.

At the largest time scale, spanning geological periods and tens or hundreds of millions of years, continental drift has moved land masses away from arid latitudes. Thus, areas now humid were once arid and, equally, areas now arid were once much wetter or much colder. Britain, for example, was within an arid zone during the Devonian and Permian periods, giving rise to some of the rocks within the New Red Sandstone series of central England, to the sandstones of the North Sea, and to salt lakes which have left us with workable deposits of potash and table salt. Careful examination of some finely bedded sandstones will sometimes reveal that they were laid down as dunes in ancient deserts.

On a meso time scale, encompassing the climatic changes which produced the Pleistocene Ice Age, arid zones can be seen to have been squeezed into much narrower areas and then to have expanded beyond their former and present limits in a poleward direction (see Fig 11.3). Thus, areas which are now in the tropical rainy belt may previously have been arid and, conversely, at other times, present-day dry lake beds such as Bonneville in Utah would once have contained extensive lakes.

On the shortest of time scales, contained within centuries and decades, the shifting margins of the deserts continue to be noticed. Indeed, many suggest that we are currently experiencing an expansion of the deserts, possibly engendered by man's activities and tragically exemplified by the droughts of the Sahel since 1968.

The geomorphological impact of the changing desert margins is examined below (see pp. 259–61).

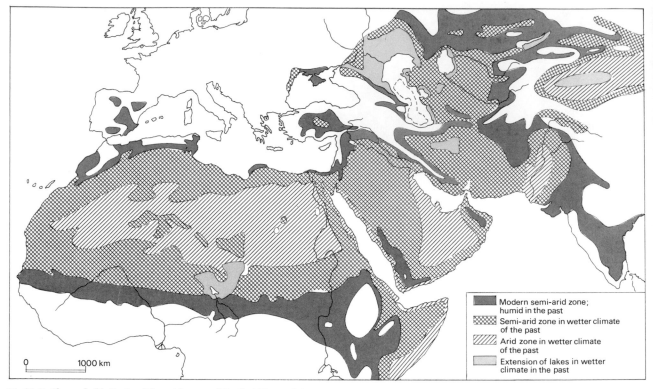

Fig 11.3 The probable limits of the arid zones of North Africa and the Middle East during a wetter climate of the past.

Legend:
- Modern semi-arid zone; humid in the past
- Semi-arid zone in wetter climate of the past
- Arid zone in wetter climate of the past
- Extension of lakes in wetter climate in the past

0   1000 km

Climatic Background

Although this does not purport to be a book on climatology, it is necessary to understand the climatic background of arid areas, for without such understanding, one's comprehension of the dominant processes is limited.

What Causes Aridity?

The major cause of aridity is the presence of bodies of stable and subsiding air which blanket all rising air currents that might otherwise produce precipitation. Even in the hottest areas of deserts, therefore, convection currents are rarely able to rise high enough to cool sufficiently for condensation to occur, let alone precipitation to form.

The **sub-tropical high pressure cells** are good examples of such a feature and their location, seen in Fig 11.4, helps to explain why so many of the world's deserts straddle the tropics. As warm air spreads out from these cells it checks any incursions of wet,

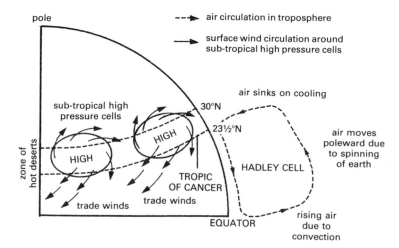

Fig 11.4 Air circulation within the tropics. Sinking air in the sub-tropics creates the arid conditions of the hot deserts.

maritime air, thus reinforcing the aridity. The peculiar distribution of land and sea prevents the sub-tropical pressure cells from amalgamating into a globe-encircling belt and this, in turn, explains why deserts do not fill a complete zone of latitude. On the eastern sides of Africa and South America, for instance, the anticlockwise circulation which the high pressure cells set up over the oceans sends rain-bearing winds onto the continent keeping aridity away from southern Brazil and Mozambique, for instance.

Aridity can also be caused by the **rain shadow** effect, where basins or lowlands in the lee of a mountain range are cut off from rain-bearing winds. This explains why Patagonia, in the lee of the Andes, and Death Valley and other basins in the south-western USA in the lee of the Sierra-Nevada are so dry.

Distance from the sea is another vital control, and it will be noticed from Fig 11.1 that those continents with interiors far from a maritime influence are very often dry, especially in sub-tropical latitudes.

Some deserts are, however, coastal in location, notably the Namib, the Atacama and the Californian. Their presence can be explained by the existence of **cold sea currents** running parallel to the coast. In south-west Africa the Benguela Current, and off the coast of Chile the Humboldt Current, allow the ascent of cold water from the ocean depths to cool any air moving towards land. Condensation and possibly precipitation take place, often in the form of fog, so that when the air eventually reaches the warmer land not only has it shed some of its moisture but further condensation is rendered impossible by the rising temperatures. A zone of aridity thus extends along the coast.

Temperature and Precipitation Characteristics

In some arid areas no rainfall has been recorded in living memory. In Arica in northern Chile the mean annual rainfall is just three millimetres. Other areas are considerably wetter, with Alice Springs, a typical example in Meigs' arid category, receiving 275 millimetres, and semi-arid locations receiving as much as 500 millimetres or more. Rainfall totals alone tell us little about arid climates. More significant are comparisons of rainfall with potential evapotranspiration (which may reach levels as high as 200 millimetres per annum in the driest areas), and the distribution of rainfall over time. Alice Springs, for example, receives an average of 34 millimetres per rain day, which means it needs only nine rain days to receive its annual total. With most desert rainfall arriving in sudden massive downpours, all mean totals, whether monthly or annual, need careful interpretation. Although rainfall totals and seasonality of its occurrence tend to increase away from the equator, its reliability from year to year does not. In all arid areas rainfall is highly variable. Study of Fig 11.5 confirms this trend.

The world's highest surface **temperatures** have been recorded within the deserts, a notable extreme being the air temperature, in the shade, of 57°C recorded in

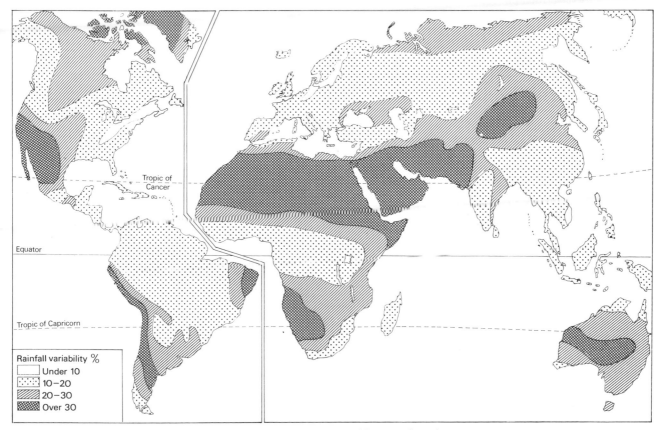

Fig 11.5 World pattern of precipitation variability. Variability is a measure of deviation from the norm.

Death Valley, California. Daytime ground temperatures may soar even higher, perhaps over 70°C. Mean temperatures, which can again be deceptive, are much lower, with Death Valley recording a July mean of 38°C and a January mean of 11°C. As most desert areas are some distance from the equator they experience distinct seasons, although only in the cold winter deserts such as Patagonia and the Gobi do winter temperatures really plummet. Urumqi in north-west China, for instance, experiences a January mean of −16°C and a July mean of 25°C.

In the warmer deserts it is not the seasonal variations but **diurnal** ones that are far more important. Lack of cloud cover means that heat radiated out from the unvegetated surfaces at night is not reflected back again, so that intense night-time cooling occurs. Daily ranges of temperature of 20°C are thus quite normal, a feature which affects geomorphological processes significantly.

Because precipitation totals are low, it does not mean that atmospheric moisture is not available. Indeed, absolute humidity levels may be very high, but air temperatures are usually sufficient to prevent the water vapour from condensing. Night cooling may cause the air to become saturated, however, and **dew** may blanket any available surface.

Justice cannot be done here to the considerable variation of desert climates. Suffice it to say that the usual effects of altitude, latitude and proximity to the sea operate to modify the general characteristics of desert climate described above.

Processes of Arid and Semi-Arid Areas

Weathering

Many library shelves sag beneath the weight of the literature that has been generated in the debate over the respective roles of mechanical and chemical weathering in arid areas. Traditionally, the lack of water caused writers to discount the possibility of chemical weathering, but since the experiments of Blackwelder and then Griggs in the 1930s, (see Chapter 3), the predominance of mechanical processes of disintegration has been repeatedly challenged.

Mechanical weathering

The presence of **insolation weathering** in deserts can be easily explained, for diurnal ranges of ground temperature may be as much as 40°C and field evidence is available of exfoliated boulders and rocks that have been broken down by granular disintegration, or fissured. Boulders that have split neatly in two, known as **kernsprung**, most likely result, too, from the repeated cycle of intense heating and cooling. Indisputably, however, the process is far more effective when water contributes to it. Barton's evidence from Egypt confirms this, for he noticed that weathering of highly polished granite monuments of a similar age was far more pro-

Photo 11.6 Exfoliation or onion skin weathering, Tsavo National Park, Kenya.

nounced in the slightly more humid conditions of lower Egypt than in the extremely arid upper Egypt. In addition, he observed that weathering was greater on the shaded sides of the monuments than on those exposed directly to the sun.

Evidence such as this, though, does not mean that insolation weathering is not an effective process in its own right, and a wide range of rocks as diverse as flint, limestone and quartzite is open to its influence (see Photo 11.6). Its predominance over chemical processes means that the physical strength of a rock becomes a far more relevant determinant of its resistance than it is in more temperate areas, which means that many limestones take on a strength that they do not have elsewhere.

Freeze-thaw action is an unlikely occurrence in most desert areas, but with temperatures frequently falling below freezing point in the cold winter deserts, its operation there cannot be ignored.

Chemical weathering

It is not only the apparent lack of moisture that militates against the operation of chemical weathering processes, but also the low occurrence of carbon dioxide in the atmosphere of the warmer deserts and the lack of organic acids in the soil due to the sparseness of vegetation. In some arid areas, therefore, chemical weathering is virtually non-existent. **Hydrolysis**, in particular, is very rare, but **hydration** certainly seems to operate. This process responds to the wetting and drying associated with sudden downpours or the spread of dew, and its effectiveness increases with the diurnal heating and cooling. **Solution**, too, has been observed on limestone surfaces and boulders.

Salt weathering

It has already been noted that chemical and mechanical weathering processes work best when operating in conjunction with each other. A classic instance of this is **salt weathering**, which is more effective in arid environments than in any other. Salt may be derived from the ocean, perhaps carried onshore in fog, or can exist in dried-up lake beds or other saline deposits brought to the surface by capillary action. When the solution of salts evaporates, the salt crystallises, perhaps within the pores or cracks of a rock. The resultant pressure physically weakens the rock. If the salt crystal then absorbs water it expands further and the effect is magnified. Porous sandstones are especially prone to this process, most of all when they occur in coastal deserts.

Whichever form of weathering occurs, nowhere in arid areas does it operate at a fast rate and reference to Fig 3.14 will emphasise this. As a generalisation it is probably fair to say that it operates most effectively in the upland regions of deserts.

Effects of weathering

Arid areas contain very few true soils, for organic matter is so sparse and the production of clays from chemical weathering so slow that spreads of rock waste or **lithosols** are the only product of weathering that even resembles a soil. Rates of weathering are such that mantles of rock waste rarely accumulate to any extent on slopes. Erosion by wind or water is likely to remove waste, especially from steep slopes, and on gentler slopes it will be prone to further diminution by weathering until it, too, is susceptible to wind erosion.

Certain minor landforms can be conceived as the products of weathering. Grotesquely sculpted rocks, known as either **zeugen** (singular: zeuge) or **mushroom rocks**, are thought to owe their narrow waists to the action of weathering. Dew and soil moisture drawn up by capillary action concentrate the attack at ground-level especially on the shaded side (see Fig 11.6). The mushroom-like cap, which may overhang by a metre or more, is usually protected by a hard crust, again the product of capillary action. Isolated blocks of horizontally bedded sandstone are particularly prone to this form of sculpture.

Hard crusts are a common feature of desert rock surfaces, and give an extra layer of resistance against

Photo 11.7 Dasht-e-Lut Desert, Iran: desert boulder sculptured by wind and water.

weathering. If the crust can be breached at a weak point, however, the weathering processes may concentrate their attack and etch out a hollow into the rock. Moisture may then collect there, especially if the hollow is on the shaded side of the rock, and this will encourage further weathering, notably hydration. One extreme result of this attack may be the complete removal of the inside of a rock, leaving only its encrusted shell, but a more typical result is to give the rock surface a pockmarked skin of tiny hollows known as **tafoni**. In some sandstones this pattern may become so regular that it resembles **honeycomb**, although in this case wind action may also be important (see Photo 11.7).

Gnamma holes are large pits, perhaps over ten metres across, which weathering processes are thought to have hollowed out, aided by the removal of debris by wind or water. They are usually found on gently sloping rock surfaces, have flat floors and may have overhanging walls.

The Development of Crusts

Many different surfaces in arid areas are encrusted with hard concretions of minerals, which are known collectively as **crusts**. They appear at many different scales, from the **desert varnish** that gives a polished and colourful glaze to pebbles and boulders, through the caps that protect zeugen and the protective layer that tops many mesas and buttes in the south-western USA, to the extensive crusts that may stretch across pediments and pediplains or old lake beds.

Desert varnish probably results from a relatively straightforward process in which **capillary action** draws salts in solution to the surface where they are evaporated, although at least partial deposition from some source external to the stone also seems likely.

Different types of the thicker crusts or **duricrusts** have been identified, largely depending on their chemical make up: they include **calcretes** (calcium carbonate crusts), **gypcretes** (of gypsum), **silcretes** (of silica) and **sodium chloride crusts**.

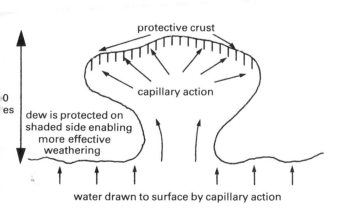

Fig 11.6 A zeuge or mushroom rock.

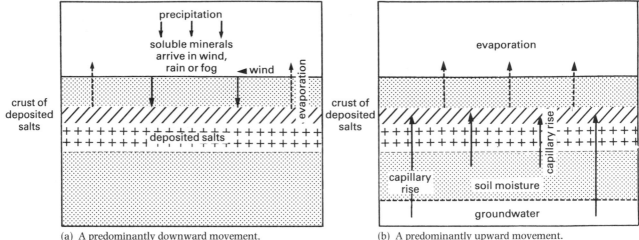

(a) A predominantly downward movement.

(b) A predominantly upward movement.

Fig 11.7 Theories of crust formation.

Calcretes are widely distributed in arid and semi-arid areas, although they form best where the rainfall is between 200 and 500 millimetres per annum. They range from 50 metre thick cap rocks to soil horizons of less than one metre.

Silcretes have been identified in the Sahara and Kalahari, but are most extensive in the Australian Desert, for example in the Lake Eyre Basin where they are up to five metres thick.

Gypcretes are less well studied than the former two crusts, but extend across large areas of the Namib and Australian Deserts, and seem to develop best where rainfall is between 50 and 200 millimetres.

Sodium chloride crusts are usually found on old lake beds in the driest areas of all, where rainfall is less than 50 millimetres.

Most of the theories put foward to explain crust formation rely on either leaching or capillary action or a combination of the two. For example, soluble minerals on the surface, that may have arrived in wind, rain or fog, will be leached to lower horizons of the soil during a rainstorm. Before any deeper percolation can take place, the rain water will be evaporated from the soil, and its contained salts deposited. Over many years these accumulations develop into sub-surface crusts, which may eventually be exposed when the overlying leached horizons are eroded.

An alternative theory suggests that salts are drawn up to the surface by the capillary rise of soil moisture or groundwater. Evaporation near the surface results in deposition. An oscillating water table that responds to desert storms may encourage this, but in many deserts water tables are too deep to be of relevance. The extent of the process of capillary rise is also under question, for it is thought to be capable of drawing water through a matter of only centimetres. Nevertheless, many sodium chloride crusts are probably created in this way, as are some calcretes and gypcretes.

The Formation of Stone Pavements

Stone mantles cover many different desert surfaces; indeed, they are so common in the Sahara that two words, **hamada** and **reg**, are used to describe the stony landscapes that occur. Hamada signifies the spreads of larger boulders and stones, whilst reg describes the blankets of finer, gravel-sized material (see Photos 11.8 and 9).

Both forms of **stone pavement**, as they are collectively known, may consist of either angular or rounded stones or a mixture of the two. Angular fragments are usually derived from the weathering of the underlying bedrock, but rounded stones imply that some form of transport, probably by water, has occurred.

Amongst the many theories of explanation, three stand out. In common with so much early desert geomorphology, a traditional explanation for the stone pavements relied on wind erosion. It was suggested that stones remained after wind had removed, by a process known as **deflation**, the finer material between them. Thus, if a soil or lithosol of some depth was gradually winnowed away, a considerable concentration of stones could remain. The weakness of the theory is that stone pavements usually protect the ground. In that case, once the pavement has started to form, how does it allow wind to penetrate to the soil beneath? Perhaps water is more dominant than early workers supposed. Sheet floods could provide a second mechanism by which **fines** are removed and pavements established.

Neither of these processes alone is thought today to be widely responsible for pavements, although both may make a contribution. More prominence is now given to the vertical sorting of stones via a process not dissimilar to that which occurs in periglacial regions (see Fig 11.8). Alternate wetting and drying of the surface causes the soil to expand and contract. Swelling of the fine material may allow stones to be heaved upwards, which are later not able to return to their position due to the collapse of finer material. In time,

Photo 11.8   The coarse surface of this stony desert, or hamada, in the coastal regions of Peru reveals concretions of salt just below the surface.

Photo 11.9   Stony desert or reg, Dasht-e-Kavar, Iran: a featureless, flat reg in which the stones are finer than in the hamada.

vertical sorting will reach a stage at which the stones are left at the surface with a relatively stone-free layer beneath them, a characteristic typical of stone pavements.

Lateral sorting of stones into patterns is another process which arid and periglacial areas have in common. Doming of the surface caused by wetting displaces stones into features known as **round gilgai**, which consist of small depressions, perhaps three metres across, encircled by low stony ridges up to one metre high. On slopes of one to ten degrees, the stony gilgai become **stepped**. Networks of both types of gilgai stretch across areas of many square kilometres in the Australian Desert.

Running Water

Passing references have already been made to the action of water in deserts, but most of the cases mentioned involve stationary water, in the form of dew or soil moisture. Little has so far been said of running water. There are two major forms of this in arid areas; first, that which results from rain storms and is temporary in nature, and second, more permanent flows of water in rivers like the Nile and Colorado which manage to sustain run-off even across very arid areas, although they, too, may be supplemented by flood water.

Flash floods

Stream floods and sheet floods: Desert landscapes encourage rapid run-off, for the lack of vegetation and corresponding organic layers in the soil, and the presence of impermeable hardpans and crusts, means that little interception or infiltration will take place. In addition, most rainfall comes in such intense storms that what stores there are quickly become saturated and begin to overflow. Water therefore spreads across the surface as a **sheet flood** or, where channels or gullies are present, becomes a **stream flood**.

Although from a distance sheet floods may appear to move as one body across alluvial fans or rock pediments, they may in fact be an amalgamation of thousands of anastomosing rills.

Fig 11.8   The formation of a stone pavement.

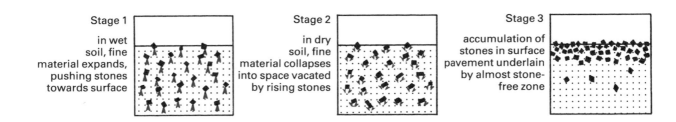

Stage 1

in wet soil, fine material expands, pushing stones towards surface

Stage 2

in dry soil, fine material collapses into space vacated by rising stones

Stage 3

accumulation of stones in surface pavement underlain by almost stone-free zone

The channels which constrict stream floods are of many different sizes and shapes. **Wadis** are the most significant (see Photo 11.10). These are steep-sided, often gorge-like, valleys which cut through upland areas. They probably owe their existence to river erosion in an earlier, wetter, geological period. Some wadis are such infrequent scenes of flooding that human settlement may have encroached upon the valley bottom. Disaster befell some of the inhabitants of Sakiet Ez Zit in southern Tunisia in September 1982 when a quite unprecedented three metre deep torrent flooded their local wadi.

Other channels, or **arroyos**, may be the result of gullying by previous flash floods (see Photo 11.11). As the natural lines of drainage, they become further enlarged by ensuing floods. They are particularly common in semi-arid areas on both alluvial and solid rock slopes and they can play havoc with man's agriculture and lines of communication.

Erosion by Flash Floods: Much debate surrounds the question of how much erosion **flash floods** can carry out. They certainly transport high sediment loads; concentrations as high as 41 per cent have been recorded from flows in the Arizona Desert. Much of this load will be the debris deposited by previous floods and weathering debris that has accumulated since. Such loads will obviously make use of the great excess of energy that the flows have and may well prevent them from eroding bare rock surfaces or deepening their channels. Even so, flash floods do seem capable of lateral erosion. Wadis may have originated as valleys, but the floods use them as channels spreading right across the valley bottom and cutting into the valley sides. This, combined with the vast thicknesses of alluvial deposits that build up in them, explains why so many wadis have a wider and shallower cross-profile than many temperate valleys. Lateral erosion by stream floods may also be responsible for the development of some rock pediments and inselbergs, as we shall see below.

Sheet floods, too, are capable of lateral erosion and may aid pediment and inselberg development, but their more usual role is to wash away loose sediment. We have already seen evidence of this in the development of hollowed boulders, zeugen and even stone pavements.

Transport and Deposition by Flash Floods: Few floods last long, although they may cover considerable distances in their short lives. Measurements from Walnut Gulch in Arizona indicate a lapse of only ten minutes between the first appearance of the flood bore and the discharge peak. It may take several hours for the entire flow to pass, however, and it may take several days

Photo 11.10   Dry wadi, Dubai.

Photo 11.11   Severe gully erosion creating badlands in the coastal desert of Peru.

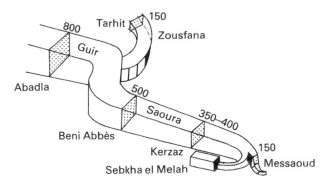

Fig 11.9 Diagrammatic representation of the flow of the Guir-Saoura in March 1959. Figures refer to peak discharges in cumecs. Beni Abbes is 150 km downstream from Abadla and Kerzaz 340 km downstream.

Photo 11.12 The Zagros Mountains, Iran: an alluvial fan emerging from a mountain front. It is unlikely that present day floods alone could have produced this feature.

before the flow completely disappears. One of the curious features of flash floods is that discharge is quite liable to decrease downstream, for tributaries may be few and groundwater contribution is probably non existent. In addition, percolation and evaporation will take their toll as the torrent is gradually reduced to a debris flow. Figures from the Guir Saoura system in northern Algeria in Fig 11.9 demonstrate this.

Such high sediment loads mean that these **ephemeral streams** accomplish a great deal of deposition. Stream beds that are churned up and scoured at the peak of the flow may well return to their former level in the later stages of the flood. Where flash floods discharge from the wadis of upland regions into the plains, the sudden change in slope may cause concentrated deposition in the shape of a fan. Such **alluvial fans** are common features of arid and semi-arid landscapes, particularly in areas like the south-west USA where steep mountains confront downfaulted basins (see Photo 11.12). They may vary in size from very

small features of less than ten metres in radius to much more significant ones of over 20 kilometres.

As the stream leaves the confines of the wadi it will be able to split into many smaller channels or distributaries, thus creating the fan shape. The actual form of the fan is very unstable and will respond to the very variable discharges of the mountain stream. This may mean that some distributaries go through successive periods of incision and deposition, some disappearing altogether perhaps. Careful lateral sorting of sediment away from the apex of the fan will create a slightly concave cross-section for the fan, as shown in Fig 11.10.

If fans continue to grow they may coalesce with adjacent fans along the mountain front, in which case a feature known as a **bajada** develops. The issue of whether fans are currently growing or are in a state of equilibrium with the processes that form them is a controversial one. Some geomorphologists believe that current rates of erosion and deposition are not balanced, but there is dissent as to whether fans are undergoing dissection or aggradation in different areas of the world. Both may well be occurring, but as we shall see below there are certainly some cases where alluvial fans cannot possibly be attributed to present day processes.

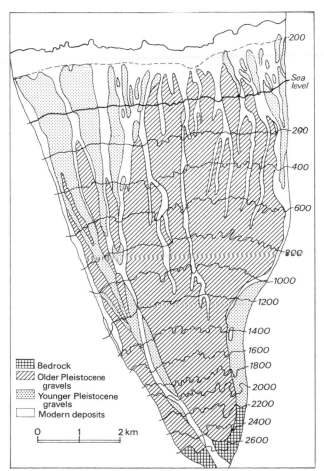

Bedrock
Older Pleistocene gravels
Younger Pleistocene gravels
Modern deposits

0   1   2 km

Fig 11.10 The alluvial fan of Johnson Canyon, Death Valley, California.

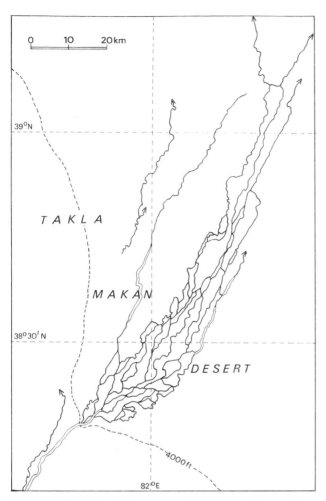

Fig 11.11 The Keriya He river system, Takla Makan Desert, China. The river flows north-eastwards. Arrows indicate where the channel peters out into sand dunes.

Permanent desert river systems

Many of the features of ephemeral streams may also occur on permanent ones. There is no reason, for instance, why some permanent river systems should not have deposited alluvial fans where they discharge from a mountain zone. Indeed, some wadis may well contain a permanent flow of water.

Desert river systems may be of two types: first, those in which flow is **endoreic** or **centripetal** into desert basins, perhaps discharging into a permanent or temporary lake so that flow does not reach the sea, and second, there are those more normal rivers, sometimes called **exogenous**, which have their source in a non-arid mountain region and flow through arid areas to the sea. The highlands of Ethiopia, for instance, provide the Blue Nile with much of its water.

From Chapter 5 it will be clear that the regimes and hydrographs of these rivers will be very different from temperate ones, not least because of the intense evaporation. Highly variable discharge as well as the large amount of bedload and the unconsolidated banks of many lowland rivers will mean that braiding is typical, and some of the most complex forms of anastomosing

drainage may be seen in deserts, as Fig 11.11 shows.

Perhaps a word of caution is needed finally about trying to differentiate too carefully between temporary and permanent drainage lines in arid areas. Many systems contain elements of each type, for example the Murray-Murrumbidgee system shown in Fig 11.12. Similarly, if one traces drainage systems of the Sahara, as in Fig 11.13, certain networks appear to have been cut off from the main lines of drainage. Permanent tributaries have been lost which may nowadays be paths only of ephemeral streams. Many have contracted towards the upland that supplies their water. Drainage systems may therefore be described as **disorganised**, and no map of a desert region can be sure of remaining correct for very long.

Wind Action

The degree to which the wind has been used to explain the form of desert landscapes says much about the history of geomorphology as a subject. In the late nineteenth century when most desert study was in Africa, wind was attributed a major role in development. Inselbergs, pediments and sand dunes were all seen as evidence of **aeolian (wind) erosion and deposition**. As research gathered pace in the twentieth century and more and more deserts became accessible, however, the role of water action was given a more substantial part. Features attributed to wind action were discovered to have other possible origins, the protection afforded by crusts and pavements over vast areas militated against active wind erosion, the virtual absence of sand dunes from some deserts and the increased understanding of the role of dew, fog and running water all helped to weaken the dominant position of wind. It was seen more as an embroiderer of surface form than as a constructor of major landscape.

In recent years, however, wind has once again been looked to for explanation of large-scale features, helped dramatically by satellite photography. Extensive areas of deserts as widespread as the Atacama, the Sahara and the Arabian have been shown to possess grooved relief which aligns exactly with prevailing wind direction (see Fig 11.14). Viewed from space, the considerable extent of some dust storms has also become apparent, and the vast sand seas as shown in Photo 11.4 are obviously attributable to wind. We can, therefore, now take a balanced view of wind, in which we see it as an important, but not always dominant, landscape process.

Wind action takes many forms. Initially, it may help to dry out a surface that has been soaked with dew or rain. More significantly, though, it winnows out fine material up to the size of sand in a process known as deflation and may carry or move it over many kilometres. This material may be taken from weathered debris, alluvial or lacustrine deposits and may then be used by the wind as an eroding tool to blast rock surfaces. Wind also deposits its load, most notably as sand dunes, and then plays with their form, continually shaping and reshaping them.

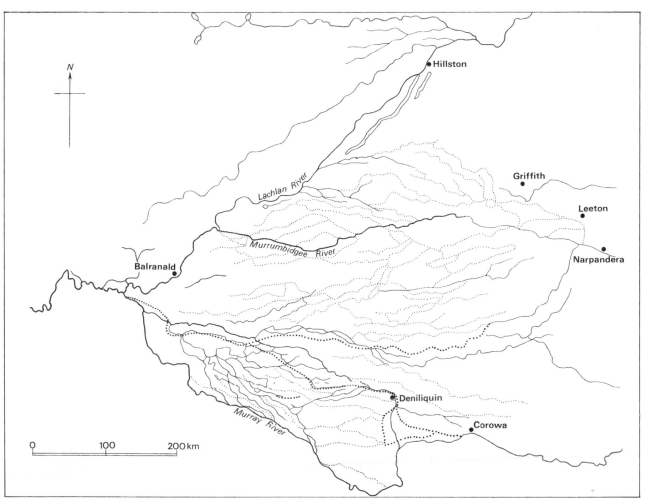

Fig 11.12 A section of the Murray-Murrumbidgee river system in New South Wales, Australia. Dotted lines show former drainage lines which may be flooded occasionally. Note how some streams peter out.

Fig 11.13 The drainage systems of the Sahara. With so much active sand the drainage systems are inevitably disorganised.

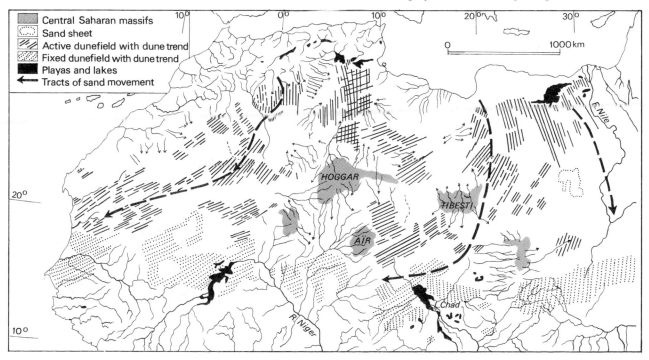

Deflation hollows

If wind is able to find a chink in the armour provided by a stone pavement, crust or cap rock, it will exploit it to the full. In time, hollows may develop which can reach a considerable size. The series of asymmetric depressions in the Libyan Desert, which include the Qattara and Kharga depressions, covers many square kilometres (see Fig 11.15).

The Qattara, for instance, measures 320 by 160 kilometres and its formation demanded the removal of over 3000 square kilometres of rock, for it delves down to 134 metres below sea level. Fluvial erosion, many millions of years ago, may well have initiated excavation by breaking through the hard cap rock of the local hamada, but wind erosion has become the dominant process in more recent times. By excavating down to the level of the falling water table, the wind has enabled other processes to occur. These make use of the available moisture by breaking up the depression floor to prepare it for further deflation. Spring sapping, solution, hydration and salt weathering may all have contributed to the extension of the hollow, and to the wearing back of the steep escarpment within some of the hollows (see Fig 11.16). Exposure of the water table may create not only an oasis but eventually a **salt pan** which may encrust and protect the floor of the hollow.

Deflation hollows are not always so large. They may form small undulations in the surface or, as in the Mongolian Desert, features of intermediate size. Here, the P'ang Kiang depressions are cut into stony plains, the importance of wind erosion displayed by the etchings of sandblast in the craggy cliff surrounds.

Wind sculpture

Although predominantly a wind-produced feature, weathering and other water-fed processes may also have contributed to sculptured sandstone surfaces such as the Borkou Lowland of Chad in Fig 11.14. Here, great ruts some hundreds of metres wide and tens of metres deep alternate with flat-topped ridges several kilometres long, the whole feature parallel to the prevailing trade winds which owe their existence to the sub-tropical high pressure cells. As the wind etches out the sand it provides itself with further tools to continue its work. Persistent attack on the ridges has isolated the more resistant sections into sharp-crested protrusions known as **yardangs**. Both their development and the initiation of the ridges in the first place have been aided by the presence of joints.

Yardangs can also be sculpted into the layers of sediment of the beds of old lakes or **playas**. These, too, are aligned with prevailing wind direction, and often show signs of undercutting by the wind. Specific features such as this occur very infrequently in arid areas though, and occurrences of rocks that have been fluted, polished or undercut by sandblasting are more common but rarely have specific names.

At the smallest scale of all, the wind is capable of shaping and polishing individual boulders and stones

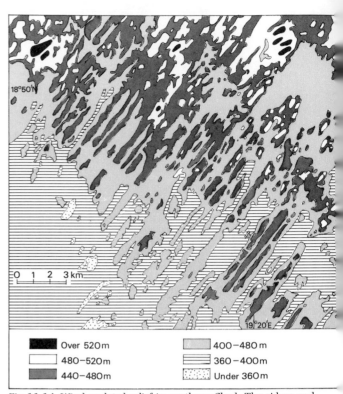

■ Over 520m	▨ 400–480m
□ 480–520m	▤ 360–400m
▨ 440–480m	▦ Under 360m

Fig 11.14 Wind sculpted relief in northern Chad. The ridges and grooves are aligned with the N.E. trade winds.

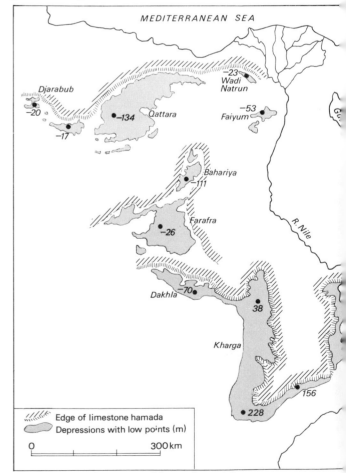

Fig 11.15 Major depressions of the northern Sahara.

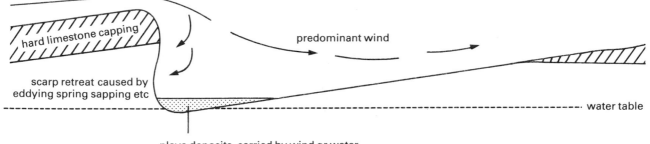

Fig 11.16 The formation of a deflation hollow.

on stone pavements. Usually known as **ventifacts**, these stones may be given distinct sides or facets by the wind, a particularly well developed type being the **dreikanter** or three-ridged stone, in shape not unlike a brazil nut.

Sand dunes

Sand transport: Sand sized particles, which range from 0.5–2.0 millimetres, are well suited to transport by the wind. Material smaller than that is likely to be in **suspension** in the air as dust, and larger grains will be able to resist entrainment.

Fine sand, up to 0.15 millimetres, may also be carried in suspension, but closer to the ground than the silt and clay sized dust, probably within a few metres. Much of the other fine sand, 0.15–0.25 millimetres in size, will move by a process called **saltation**, by which it appears to jump along the surface. Movement will commence by the wind rolling a particle along the surface until sufficient velocity is reached for it to take off into the air (see Fig 11.17).

Each hop will be of no more than a few centimetres, but as the particle lands it is likely to dislodge another which will then be entrained. Individual particles may be able to move a few metres per second in this way, although to the naked eye this will not be discernible, for the few centimetres above the surface will just appear as a blur of moving sand. Most of the movement of sand in dunes takes place by this method, although the bulk of the sand may actually move by a process called **surface creep**. As the larger grains, 0.25–2.0 millimetres, are jogged out of position by the saltating grains, they may roll a few millimetres along the surface, amounting to a movement of up to a centimetre in a minute.

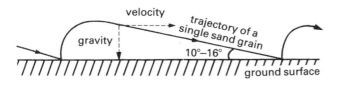

Fig 11.17 The saltation of an individual sand grain.

The fluid threshold indicates the velocity needed to engender sand movement. The impact threshold indicates the velocity needed on a dynamic surface where the impact of saltating sand grains helps to entrain other particles. Why do you suppose the threshold increases for grains smaller than 0.1 mm?

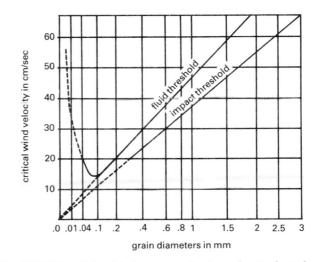

Fig 11.18 The relationship between grain size and critical wind velocity.

For the vital process of saltation to occur, a windspeed of 15 or so kilometres per hour is usually needed and there are various formulae that can be used to calculate the critical velocity of various sizes of sand (see Fig 11.18).

These processes of sand movement are most commonly found in sandy deserts where sand dunes abound, but they are also relevant to the movement of unconsolidated material from other arid surfaces, for example the winnowing of stone pavements, the erosion of lake beds and alluvial fans or the removal of weathered debris.

Types of sand dune: Although sand dunes are a rare feature of the deserts of the USA, in others, such as the Sahara and the Australian, **sand seas** form major features. Indeed, it has been estimated that the Great Eastern Erg of Algeria may cover an area greater than that of France, and the Kara Kum to the east of the Caspian Sea in Turkmenistan may be even larger. The wind-formed features of these sand seas can be viewed at various scales.

At the largest scale great ridges and mounds of sands occur, sometimes called **draa**, which may be as high as 300 metres and scattered a couple of kilometres apart. Superimposed upon these are intermediate features or dunes, which rarely exceed 30 metres in height and are tens or hundreds of metres apart. Finally, at the smallest scale, the surface of these dunes may be moulded into series of closely spaced ripples which vary from a couple of millimetres to several centimetres in height.

Not all dunes occur in sand seas or ergs; some may be quite isolated features. **Lunettes**, for example, are crescent-shaped dunes of clay or sand formed from the dried-out salt flats of seasonally fluctuating playas on their downwind side. They are asymmetric in cross-profile, the steeper side facing into the wind, and may be about ten metres high. Aggregation of the clay particles into grains of up to 0.3 millimetres allows them to be transported and deposited by the wind.

Barchans are also crescent-shaped dunes, usually found in isolation on hard, flat surfaces on plains, for example in the south Peruvian Desert. These areas tend to have a limited supply of sand, but one very dominant wind direction throughout the year. The form of a typical barchan is seen in Fig 11.19, in which it can be seen that wind moves sand up the gentle windward face. It then slides down the steeper lee face which may be as steep as 33 degrees, the angle of rest of dune sand. In this way the barchan may move forward several metres each year; the higher the dune the less far it will move. The size of the feature varies, but they may be as wide as 30 metres or more.

Although common in some areas of the Atacama and Californian Deserts, barchans are not widely distributed, accounting for only 0.01 per cent of the sand in currently active dunes.

Seifs, or longitudinal dunes, may also occur as isolated dunes in landscapes of bare rock, but they are also a common feature of sand seas. They may stretch in well ordered columns several hundred metres apart for kilometres, or even hundreds of kilometres, across the

Photo 11.13 Longitudinal dunes, Dasht-e-Lut Desert, Iran.

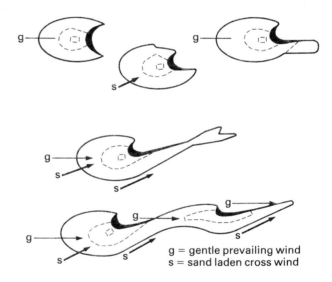

g = gentle prevailing wind
s = sand laden cross wind

Fig 11.20 The transformation of a barchan into a seif dune by a cross wind.

desert, as they do in the Simpson Desert of Australia and the Libyan Desert (see Photo 11.13).

Seifs run parallel to the dominant wind direction, and early theories suggested that they developed from barchans, through the stages suggested in Fig 11.20.

Development of dunes: It may well be true that the illustrated stages of transformation are passed through, but it seems unlikely that in the majority of cases the mechanism suggested, of cross winds blowing from a different direction from usual, is the cause of the alteration. Examples from parts of the Sudan and Libya support this simple explanation, but a more widespread explanation sees the development of a secondary series

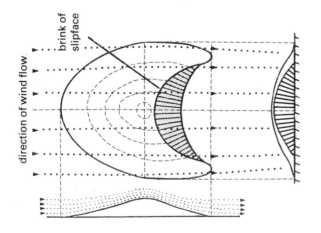

Fig 11.19 A barchan dune viewed from above, from the side and from downwind.

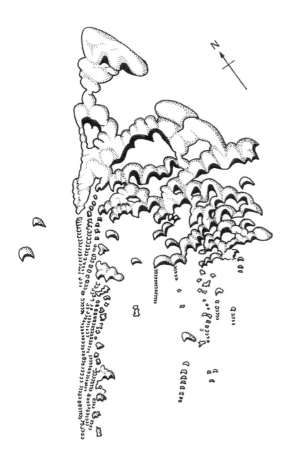

Fig 11.21 Barchan and seif dunes near Bilma, Niger.

but also from the development of corresponding lines of cumulus cloud which stretch out above the dunes. We have, then, a theory for the development of seifs quite independent of barchan formation.

Even this, however, greatly simplifies air flow patterns, for in addition to the longitudinal vortices there is also a transverse element to flow that we need to understand. Eddies developing transverse to wind direction may mould the surface sand into a series of steps, as Fig 11.23 shows. If this simple pattern is then combined with the longitudinal dunes produced by the vortices, one can envisage the development of a series of sinuous ridges as shown in Fig 11.24.

The alternating **barchanoid** and **linguoid** (tongue-shaped) sections of the ridge combine into a pattern of dunes which at their most complex are known as **akle** in the western Sahara, and which are far more common than the simple barchan. Further study of Fig 11.24 will reveal that each linguoid section is

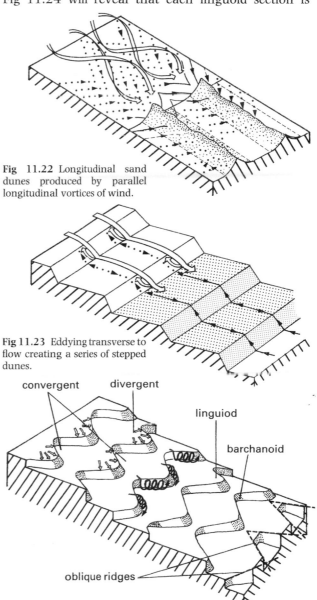

Fig 11.22 Longitudinal sand dunes produced by parallel longitudinal vortices of wind.

Fig 11.23 Eddying transverse to flow creating a series of stepped dunes.

Fig 11.24 Barchanoid and linguoid dunes.

of oblique dunes as more important. As air flows over the barchan, spiral eddies may develop which then move off at an oblique angle to left and right; Fig 11.24 may help understanding. In perfect conditions, these two oblique air flows would, presumably, create elongated sand dunes of equal size radiating out from each horn of the barchan. In the real world, however, the eddy on one side may be stronger than the other and thus extend a limb of the barchan in one particular direction. Continued development of such oblique dunes will, in time, allow them to be more dominant than the initial barchan and transform the feature into a seif. The pattern of dunes in Fig 11.21 in Niger shows a series of barchans, created by wind blowing from the north east, which are being elongated towards the south west, although some of the dunes in the north and east appear to be developing a longer eastern horn. In this area, therefore, transformation to a more longitudinal form is occurring despite the lack of cross winds.

The flow of air over a body of sand seems to consist of a series of parallel longitudinal vortices, as Fig 11.22 shows. These produce a series of alternating lanes of divergent and convergent flow. Where the air converges and slows down, sand is moulded into longitudinal dunes, and where it is diverging, further accumulation of sand is prevented in the intervening alleyways. Supporting evidence for this comes not only from observation of sand movement and wind patterns

succeeded downwind by a barchanoid curve in the ridge. This is explained by diverging and converging vortices of air which the diagram illustrates. To develop these transverse dunes a particularly large and constant supply of sand is essential; they are thus well developed in the ergs of the Sahara.

Parabolic dunes are like isolated forms of the linguoid sections of transverse ridges, with horns pointing upwind rather than downwind. They are found in semi-arid areas where vegetation has a role to play in stabilising the dunes. They probably develop as the result of the blow-out of a dune due to the burial of its vegetation. It is thought that these too may evolve into longitudinal dunes by the horns becoming elongated and the centre of the dune then being blown out to leave two parallel ridges.

It was often said in the early days of desert exploration that dunes form around the bodies of dead camels! The many billions of desert dunes would require a population of camels greater than that of human beings if this were true. Nevertheless, it is true that some dunes do owe their existence to the presence of obstacles, and a series of possible shapes is given in Fig 11.25.

Photo 11.14 Rhourds, Great Eastern Erg, Algerian Sahara. This aerial view gives some idea of the great size of these star-shaped dunes.

a) sand dune in shadow of obstacle

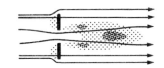

b) sand drift in lee of gap in obstacle

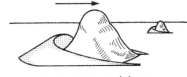

c) wrap-around dune

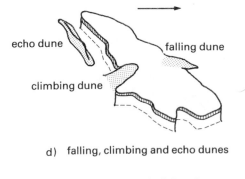

d) falling, climbing and echo dunes

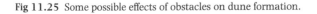

= wind direction

Fig 11.25 Some possible effects of obstacles on dune formation.

There is always danger in classifying forms the way we have here, and many sandy deserts may bear little resemblance to what has been included. In reality, patterns are a complex mixture of the forms mentioned here, with one series of forms blending into another as one moves across the landscape, or, in the most complex cases, one pattern superimposed upon another in areas where wind patterns are not unidirectional.

Large-scale features: Much attention has been paid to the intermediate scale, namely the dune. Less research has been focused on the large-scale features, the **draa**, although once again satellite observations of sand and atmospheric patterns have aided our understanding.

Draa often take similar forms to the dune, with longitudinal, transverse and crescentic patterns all occurring. Their explanation relies on larger scale movements within the atmosphere such as lee waves and convective cells, and many, once formed, help to sustain these movements and thus perpetuate their own existence. One interesting form is the **rhourd**, which is a star-shaped mound up to 150 metres high and between one and two kilometres across (see Photo 11.14). Their development has been linked with convective chimneys of rising air which draw in not only wind but also sand. Other suggestions are that they form as a result of winds blowing from several directions.

Landforms Resulting from more than One Origin

Equifinality

For very few of the arid landforms that we have looked at so far could we say that their origins are clear beyond doubt. In some cases this reflects a lack of sufficient research, in other cases it is because a theory that appears to be applicable in one area does not seem to fit another. This once again reflects the great diversity of conditions that can be found within arid regions, where local differences in climatic patterns, geological structure or the density of vegetation can completely invalidate a particular theory. It is therefore often said that a characteristic of desert landforms is their **equifinality**. This simply means that the same result can come about from the operation of quite different processes and quite different conditions. Thus, for example, it may well be true in some areas that stone pavements are the result of wind deflation, whilst in others water erosion may be the dominant process and in yet other areas the vertical sorting of stones may be the appropriate explanation for the same feature.

Another demonstration of equifinality is provided by the great depressions of arid areas that sometimes contain lakes or lake beds. The origins of deflation hollows such as the Qattara depression have already been examined above, but wind cannot explain all depressions. Many of the basins of Nevada and Utah are structural in origin, resulting from **block faulting**. The basin to the east of the Ruby Mountains in Nevada, for instance, which contains the salt lakes of Franklin and Ruby, is overlooked by a towering 1200 metre high fault scarp. **Shallow downwarping** of the surface has created the lake basin of some shield deserts, for example those of Lake Eyre in Australia and Lake Chad, although in the former case deflation has emphasised the depression. In the Hoggar Massif of the central Sahara, lakes occupy **volcanic craters**, whilst the **dayas** of Algeria are depressions resulting from the solution of the underlying limestone. In semi-arid areas, intensive animal grazing around water hollows may have created sizeable depressions such as the **vloers** of the Kalahari or the **buffalo wallows** of the USA. Finally, lake basins may be a response to deposition, of either alluvial or wind blown dams.

Equifinality, then, is a characteristic feature of arid areas, and a quick review of this chapter will demonstrate its occurrence in many different landforms. Nowhere is it more apparent, though, than in the study of rock pediments and of the isolated mountain masses that they sometimes front.

Pediments

Pediments are gentle, slightly concave, slopes cut into bedrock which extend from mountain fronts towards alluvial zones under which they eventually disappear (see Fig 11.26). They may cover a distance of many miles, and may amalgamate to form the vast erosional plains of arid areas known as **pediplains**.

The pediment surface may be bare, but not necessarily uniform, for it can traverse a succession of rock bands and it is prone to differential weathering of lithological and structural weaknesses. On the other hand, the surface may be hidden beneath a veneer of alluvium or, more rarely, coarse, stony debris. The profile is sometimes straight but more usually grades slowly

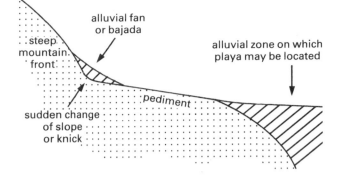

Fig 11.26 The pediment and its associated features.

from up to ten degrees at the mountain front down to less than 0.5 degrees. Where the pediment meets the mountain front there is usually a sudden and distinct change of slope, termed the **piedmont angle**. An alluvial fan or bajada may conceal this angle, and in extreme cases may completely obscure the pediment.

The four major hypotheses for pediment formation give us good cause to apply the term equifinality, for each has supporting evidence.

First is the theory that suggests that pediments result from wind action which has undercut the mountain front and then blown away the debris to expose the pediment. Although now largely out of fashion, there is some evidence that this theory is applicable in some cases.

Sheet floods were another suggestion of early geomorphologists, as they envisaged eroding floodwater emerging from the uplands, being no longer restricted by valleys. This appealingly simple process may well be

Photo 11.15   Pediment sloping towards base of distant mountains.

relevant, but a chicken and egg problem operates. How could the smooth sheet of water have formed unless there was a smooth rock surface there to support it? The presence of alluvial deposits and the concave profile typical of a water-eroded form suggest that water erosion must play a part in the development, however.

The third hypothesis supports this belief, although the actual mechanism is different, for here lateral planation by individual streams emerging from the mountains is the dominant process. Streams, particularly when in flood, are able to swing vigorously from side to side by using their excess energy to erode their channel horizontally. This idea seems perfectly acceptable, except in the many areas where there are no streams emerging from upland to pediment.

By combining the processes which cause the retreat of the mountain front with those that form the pediment, the fourth group of theories has gained wider acceptance than any of the preceding ones. At the centre of this group is King's pediplanation hypothesis (see Fig 11.27). This envisages the retreat of the mountain slope due to weathering, mostly by block disintegration. At the base of the slope, where moisture collects, the rate of weathering will be at a maximum, which will prevent the accumulation of blocks from taking over the slope by breaking them down into fine debris. This material can then be eroded by wind or by water, in any of its forms. The pediment is thus seen as a response to the need for the removal of debris, its angle capable of providing the water with sufficient energy to remove the comminuted debris. Research has suggested that surface flow increases across the slope; less energy is therefore needed to carry the same amount of load and so the angle becomes progressively gentler, producing the concave profile. The sharp piedmont angle is seen as the junction between the operation of two separate processes, the weathering and retreat of the mountain front and the removal of the fine debris.

The explanation is neat and appealing. It is not universally accepted, however, for it seems best suited to rock types such as granite, which are conducive to block disintegration. This is not too great a drawback, for many pediments are cut in granitic rocks, but a

Photo 11.16 Granite inselberg, Algerian Sahara.

more unscalable hurdle is that not all pediments are backed by retreating scarps.

We are thus unable to provide a complete solution to the problem of pediments.

Isolated Mountains

Many people associate the steep-sided mountains or **inselbergs** that project in isolation from lowland plains with desert areas. This may be a valid association for some arid and semi-arid areas, but one must bear in mind that they are not exclusively an arid landform for they also occur in savanna and tropical rainy environments. Even in desert areas they are not a uniform feature, for they vary greatly both in scale and shape. Inselbergs may be no more than isolated protrusions of rock, but may also be 600 metre high mountains. Whilst often formed of crystalline rocks, such as the granite in the Namib and Kalahari Deserts, they may also be of sandstone, such as the mystical Ayers Rock in central Australia.

The parallel retreat of the mountain front referred to in King's pediplanation theory above also provides a mechanism for inselberg formation. A much more extensive upland area of the past is envisaged which has been reduced from all directions to leave the inselberg standing alone.

A particular type of granite inselberg known as a **bornhardt** has been given a different origin, however. Bornhardts are rounded domes of massively jointed rock which appear to have been developed underground in a way not dissimilar to that which Linton proposes for the tors of Dartmoor (see page 66). Deep chemical rotting, probably in a wetter climate than is currently experienced in deserts, has attacked the

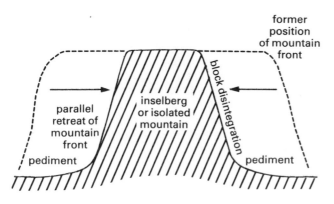

Fig 11.27 The parallel retreat of mountain fronts or King's Pediplanation Theory.

granite beneath the surface, aided by water's penetration through an extensive joint system. Where the rock is massive, or relatively joint free, it is protected from decay and is preserved underground until erosion of the weathered regolith allows exhumation (see Fig. 11.28).

Isolated mountains of a rather different kind occur in the deserts of the USA. **Mesas**, and their smaller counterparts, **buttes**, are flat-topped table-like residuals of what were once extensive plateaux (see Photo 11.17). Persistent scarp retreat caused by river erosion of past and present has isolated sections of these sandstone plateaux. Cap rocks or crusts often protect the surface from faster denudation and may produce striking slope profiles. The most striking examples of all have been used to good effect by many a Hollywood film director.

Climatic Change in Deserts

Careful reading of this chapter so far will reveal that many desert landforms cannot be fully explained by reference to the processes operating in today's climate. Crusts, varnish, wadi systems, lake basins, alluvial fans, pediments and inselbergs, for instance, can all receive more comprehensive explanation if climates of the past are also borne in mind. Climatic regimes which produce high annual totals of precipitation are usually looked to for this explanation for they allow processes to be faster acting and more prolific.

Evidence for Wetter Climates

Evidence for considerably wetter past climates is not difficult to accumulate and can be of many different types. Archaeological relics in areas which are now prohibitively dry for man's occupation are among the most interesting, not least around the edges of the vast Gilf Kebir Plateau in the Libyan Sahara, where ancient

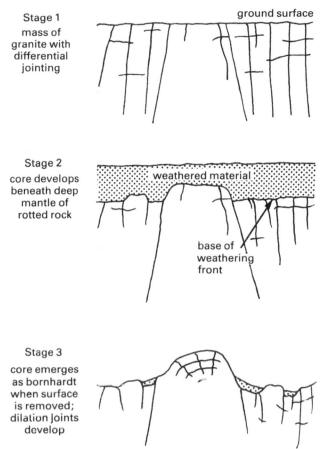

Stage 1
mass of granite with differential jointing

ground surface

Stage 2
core develops beneath deep mantle of rotted rock

weathered material

base of weathering front

Stage 3
core emerges as bornhardt when surface is removed; dilation joints develop

Fig 11.28 The development of a bornhardt. These features are not exclusive to arid and semi arid areas.

drawings of mammoth and tiger in the sandstone caves suggest that the local climate was once more hospitable. In the Valley of the Kings near Luxor in Egypt, where the elaborate tombs of the Pharoahs are concealed in the hillsides, there is plenty of evidence of fluvial scarring of the landscape; but we know that persistent water action must have ceased at least 4000 years ago for none of the tombs has been affected by it.

Biological evidence is equally convincing. Fossils of creatures that we would normally associate with tropical rain forests have been unearthed in the Atlas Mountains, for instance, and pollen analysis of lake sediments extends proof further. Some isolated desert oases contain species of fish that we associate with much wetter tropical areas; this suggests that rivers of the past provided a migration route for them.

Perhaps the most plausible evidence of all, though, is provided by the landscape itself. Underground limestone caves and great thicknesses of tufa are difficult to explain in today's arid areas of Egypt. The shrunken outlines of numerous desert lakes can be observed in Australian, American and African desert landscapes, particularly if one is aided by satellite photographs. Lake Bonneville in Utah, for example, once covered an area ten times larger than the Great Salt Lake does today (see Fig 11.29). Similar evidence can be sought

Photo 11.17   Monument Valley, USA: mesas and buttes.

Photo 11.18   Salt flat, Iran.

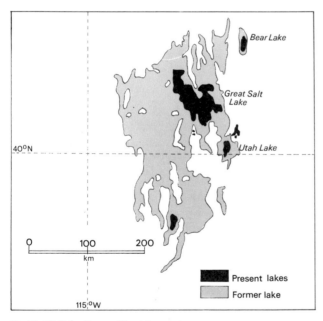

Fig 11.29 Lake Bonneville at its maximum.

as that which is used to identify former pro-glacial lakes in the British landscape, namely shoreline features such as benches eroded by waves and beaches made of gravel. Lake-bed deposits can also be examined, such as deltas of fluvial sediment or layers of clay and silt that have been laid down in fresh water and contrast starkly with the saline sediments that have accumulated above them in the playas of today.

In the Andean foothills of the Peruvian Desert alluvial fans exist, 50 metres thick, which cannot possibly be accounted for in today's rainfall regime. Optimum conditions for calcrete development appear to be when rainfall is between 10 and 40 centimetres. What, then, of the well developed calcretes in the extremely arid Tibesti Plateau in the Sahara? Some

wadi networks are so extensive that only a permanent river network could have created them. How else, for example, could the intricate dissection of the Gilf Kebir Plateau have been executed, or the wadis that radiate out from the Ahaggar Massif have been cut?

There appears, then, plenty of evidence to suggest that climates were once much wetter than today in many deserts, and that these conditions provided the processes that produced some features of the present landscape. More careful investigation, however, shows that the pattern of past climatic change is not a simple one.

Past Patterns of Climate in Deserts

Nowhere is a past-climate pattern more apparent than around Lake Chad, whose fluctuations have been studied in great detail. The water surface appears to have reached its greatest extent between 5000 and 12 000 years ago when it covered perhaps 350 000 square kilometres, some 15 times greater than today. It is not just a simple case of gradual shrinking over the last 5000 years however, for at some times it probably dried up completely and was replaced by a dune field. Space photographs certainly reveal large areas of sand dunes beneath the lake's surface. Prior to its maximum extent, the shoreline also appears to have undergone major fluctuations, with sand dunes being succeeded by flooding of the lake bed on more than one occasion.

Similar patterns of climatic change can be confirmed by the fluctuating effects of fluvial activity. Terraces in the cross-profiles of wadis in Algeria suggest a series of varying river regimes in the past, as do the various levels of planation that occur on some pediment surfaces in the Atlas Mountains. Many fluvial features, from gullies to alluvial fans, have been subjected to

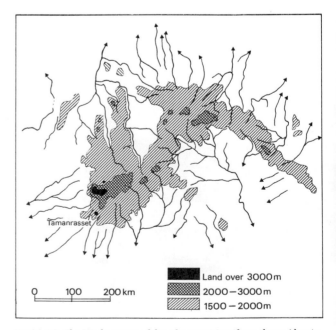

Fig 11.30 The Wadi system of the Ahaggar Massif, southern Algeria.

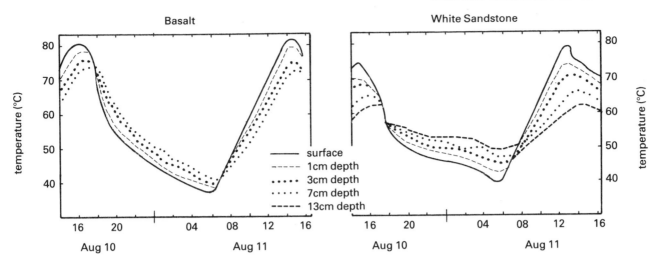

Fig 11.31 Diurnal temperature variations within a dark basalt and a white sandstone in the Tibesti Plateau, August 1961.

alternate periods of incision and infilling, erosion and deposition, degradation and aggradation. Fossil sand dunes in areas beyond today's desert margins also suggest that the arid areas were once much more extensive than at present. For example, ergs may have once covered up to 50 per cent of the land surface between 30°S and 30°N.

It is not just over time that the pattern of climatic change presents an oscillating image, for the same is true over space. Although many of the climatic fluctuations can be linked to the advance and retreat of the ice that was occurring in higher latitudes during the Pleistocene, one must not assume that all climatic belts were pushed in a parallel formation towards the equator. The change was far more complex. For instance, the shifting of the sub-tropical high-pressure cells which generate the arid areas may have altered the wind directions. This may have exposed areas to desiccating, sand-laden winds that did not previously experience them. Alternatively, it may have allowed climatic depressions to move into areas which previously they did not penetrate. It cannot always be said, therefore, that when Europe and North America were experiencing a glacial maximum in the Pleistocene, all parts of the northern hemisphere deserts were simultaneously much more arid or much wetter. Nevertheless, it does seem to be valid to say that for much of Africa, Australia and northern India a major period of increased aridity occurred between 25 000 and 12 000 years ago, which corresponds to the glacial maximum in Europe and North America of 18 000–17 000 years BP and the retreat of glaciation about 11 000 years ago. The period was not one of unmitigated aridity, however, for pluvial phases appear to have punctuated the desert climates, the last of them as recently as 9000 years ago. The pattern in the south-western USA is different, for it seems that the last period of glaciation in Europe coincided with a period of much greater humidity.

Whether or not desert areas are currently extending their boundaries is a question that has stimulated much debate and if desiccation is taking place, the precise role of man in it has yet to be clarified (see Chapter 12). What we can be sure of is that explanation of desert landscapes must resort to study of past climatic patterns, and perhaps that should not surprise us, for where would an explanation of Scottish Highland or Lake District scenery be, for instance, without resort to the climatic changes of the Pleistocene period?

Questions

1 Refer to Fig 11.31.
   (a) Describe and explain the diurnal variations in temperature that occur in the basalt sample.
   (b) Explain why the patterns of temperature variation are different for white sandstone.
   (c) In what way are these patterns likely to affect the type of weathering that takes place?
   (d) How might you go about collecting temperature statistics such as those shown in the graph?
   (e) Give as many reasons as you can to explain why basalt in Britain is unlikely to experience anything like the pattern of temperature variation shown here.

Further Reading
Desert Geomorphology, A Goudie and A Watson (Macmillan, 1980).
The Warm Desert Environment, A Goudie and J Wilkinson (Cambridge, 1977).
Desert Landforms, J A Mabbutt (MIT Press, 1977).
Arid Lands, D C Money (Evans, 1982).
The Study of Landforms, R J Small (Cambridge, 1978).

Other References
The Disintegration and Exfoliation of Granite in Egypt, D C Barton, *Journal of Geology* 46, 109–11 (1938).
A Theory of Bornhardts, L C King, *Geographical Journal* 112, 83–7 (1948).
World Distribution of Arid and Semi-Arid Homoclimates, P Meigs (UNESCO, 1953).

12

Human Impact on the Physical Landscape

Introduction

People and Landscape

If one of the aims of geographical study is to understand the interrelationship between man and his environment, then a text such as this cannot possibly ignore the imprint of man on the landscape. However, a look at the effects of human activity on the natural landscape would quickly take us into the study of interference with natural ecosystems, the creation of urban landscapes, the pollution of the atmosphere and oceans and the impact of industry and agriculture. Such a list of topics would need a series of books to do it justice, not simply one chapter. For that reason we concern ourselves here with just one aspect of that impact on landscape, that which occurs through the medium of the various geomorphological processes described in earlier chapters.

How exactly man operates via this medium will be revealed in the following pages, but one might consider a few possibilities here. Is human activity actually a landscape process in itself? Or does it merely exaggerate or speed up natural processes? Is it, in fact, so important that without it some natural processes could not take place at all? Or does it merely provide the superficial detail on a landscape whose form is largely governed by the occurrence of natural processes?

Scale

For the student of tectonic movements, mountain building and, indeed, most geological concerns, man's existence can be regarded as an insignificant dot on a continuum of geological evolution that has stretched through 4500 million years. The scratchings of human activity on the surface can have no relevance to a landscape that is shaped by the folding of the Alps and the Himalayas, the opening up of the Atlantic or the disappearance of land masses at destructive plate margins. Whilst respecting this view, one could argue that, particularly in the last century or two, man has harnessed sufficient energy to match those tectonic cataclysms. By blasting open-cast mines in the American Mid West that can be seen from space, and by creating atomic bomb craters in the deserts of the USSR, he has done

more than just scratch the surface. Nevertheless, the geological history that is locked into the rock strata of the globe occurred uninterrupted by man, and it is on the processes of only the past forty or fifty thousand years that humanity has directly intervened.

For most students of geomorphology, time scales of a human life are often the most relevant, and in this span man's impact on natural processes is immense; indeed, most of this chapter will be concentrating on this scale. Within this spectrum one can include the impact on coastal processes of a new harbour wall, the impact on run-off of a Forestry Commission plantation, or the impact on a hillside of rapid economic development or population growth in the Third World.

Certain activities may have even more immediate impact on the landscape, their results apparent after only years or months, not decades. One need witness only one or two of man's attempts to control landscape processes cited in this chapter, be they successful or unsuccessful, to appreciate that changes can be clear within weeks or months of their being effected.

The scale of the spatial impact of human activity is similarly broad, although a local outcome such as in channel cross-section, beach gradient or hillslope drainage can normally be expected. Even so, we must not ignore the regional effects, for these are often the most serious. By reducing the Nile's load of sediment, the Aswan Dam has directly contributed to the Nile Delta's degradation by the sea, even though it is over 1000 kilometres away. Many of the barrage schemes proposed for the British coast, such as the ones across Morecambe Bay and the Wash, have never been built, partly because of the concern about the impact on longshore sediment movements and currents their erection could have, with possible repercussions many kilometres from their origin.

At the largest scale, many are familiar with the theory that the earth-atmosphere system is being transformed into a giant greenhouse by the constant emission of carbon dioxide into the atmosphere from human combustion of fossil fuels. The ensuing warming of the atmosphere, although by only 0.2°C so far this century, could eventually be sufficient to melt at least part of the ice caps, which in turn would alter the entire map of the world's oceans and continents. It is

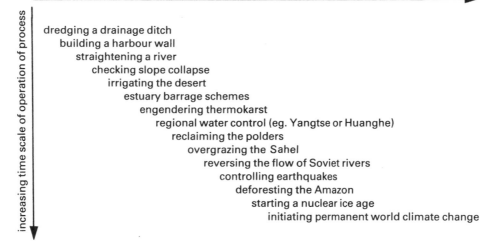

increasing scale of spatial impact →

increasing time scale of operation of process ↓

dredging a drainage ditch
building a harbour wall
straightening a river
checking slope collapse
irrigating the desert
estuary barrage schemes
engendering thermokarst
regional water control (eg. Yangtse or Huanghe)
reclaiming the polders
overgrazing the Sahel
reversing the flow of Soviet rivers
controlling earthquakes
deforesting the Amazon
starting a nuclear ice age
initiating permanent world climate change

Fig 12.1 The scale of human impacts.

Photo 12.1   Open-cast iron ore mines, Minnesota, USA.

not our intention here to evaluate such a theory or to postulate its effects in detail.

Human Control?

In any analysis of human impact on any of the earth's systems, one needs to differentiate between various human roles.

In some cases man attempts to control his environment, most notably perhaps in the damming of a river's headwaters. As Fig 12.2 indicates, successful intervention engenders a negative feedback loop, in which the human action effectively reduces the interference which the natural process has been inflicting. On the other hand, the supposed control may engender changes in hydrology, in the river channel or in the slopes around the reservoir. These may continue to have repercussions which man had never intended,

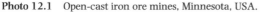

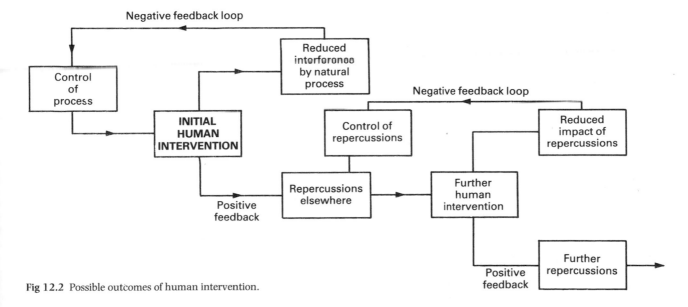

Fig 12.2 Possible outcomes of human intervention.

until a completely new and different equilibrium is reached in the landscape; a clear instance of positive feedback in operation.

Quite similar contrasts in outcome can ensue from a quite different rôle when control of a particular environmental process is by no means man's goal. In this case, man's activity, say excavating gravel from a beach or changing the agricultural land use from heather moorland to grass, may have no intention of changing any geomorphological process. However, once effected, the change may release any number of side effects in local hydrological and slope systems; it may open a Pandora's box of unwanted outcomes which completely distort the calm operation of the geomorphological system – a clear case of positive feedback.

It is no coincidence that, when geographers look for examples of positive feedback in natural systems, they inevitably revert to examples of change engendered by human activity, and so often by an action which was intended to alleviate a problem, not create one.

Human Impact on Tectonic Events

We would be implying that man had assumed godly powers if we suggested that he had anything more than a minor effect on the occurrence of earthquakes and volcanoes but nevertheless, in certain cases, human activity can be seen to make a distinct contribution to tectonic events. Sadly, though, in the future he may increase his ability to mirror the catastrophes of nature by utilising his own nuclear arsenal, or by failing to prevent disasters such as that at Chernobyl power station in the Ukraine in 1986.

Earthquakes

Mining

Inhabitants of the areas around Britain's coalfields who experience earth tremors will often attribute them to the settling of the crust which man's mining has disturbed. Relatively recent tremors in the Staffordshire coalfield around Stoke-on-Trent may be rightly attributed to such a cause, but the majority of British tremors occur along ancient fault lines associated with more significant tectonic adjustments along plate boundaries, and few can be attributed to a human cause. A more common result of underground mining in Britain is localised subsidence, especially noticeable in housing areas, as the land surface collapses into abandoned workings. In 1985 the luckless owner of a Leicestershire bungalow discovered this, as his garden sank irretrievably into oblivion.

In other mining regions of the world, similar patterns of activity may occur although sometimes on a more exaggerated scale. Gold mining in the Witwatersrand area of South Africa has been blamed for the frequent seismic disturbances in the region, which in one recent year alone amounted to over 1600 events. Earth tremors around nickel mines on the Canadian Shield near Sudbury provide further examples. In the intensively mined coalfields of Pennsylvania, from which especially thick underground seams have been removed, lawyers were kept busy for many years in compensation claims for land subsidence until new conservation techniques introduced by the state in 1966 improved the situation.

Reservoirs

There is far more convincing statistical proof that the creation of reservoirs produces an increase in earth tremors, or even, in some cases, generates sizeable earthquakes of magnitudes as high as 6.4 on the Richter scale. Although perhaps only a few in a thousand of the world's large reservoirs have such effects, as many as one in five of the deepest ones have produced seismic activity.

Although previously an area free from tectonic tremors, the states of Nevada and Arizona around the Hoover Dam experienced over a hundred significant vibrations in 1937 following the creation of Lake Mead. Continued disturbances, of some significance, accompanied the increases in the water level as late as 1942, but since then a new equilibrium appears to have been reached and seismic activity has declined.

Similar histories can be drawn for other major damming exercises, notably the Koyna Reservoir near Bombay, the Kariba Reservoir in Zambia and the Mangla near the northern frontier of Pakistan.

It would be easy to suggest that such earthquakes result from the increased loading on the earth's surface due to the vast weight of, say, over 100 metres of water, which increases the stress on existing fracture planes. Such an explanation is probably too simple, however, and seepage of water into underlying rocks may be a more relevant cause as it increases the pore pressure enabling it to overcome the previously adequate resistance to slippage along weakness lines.

It is to take advantage of this phenomenon that water has been pumped into the San Andreas Fault line, the aim being to set off a series of small, insignificant tremors to avoid one or two devastating ones. Whether the policy will achieve this or increase pore pressure sufficiently for one major slippage to occur remains to be seen.

Volcanoes

The unexpected number of deaths that occurred in May 1980 at the catastrophic reawakening of Mount St Helens gives an indication of man's inability to predict accurately the behaviour of a volcano, let alone his inability to alter it.

Nevertheless, one or two interesting attempts have been made in recent years to thwart the power of particular mountains. In 1973, on Heimaey in the Westmann Islands (Vestmannaey jar) off the south coast of Iceland, erupting fissures on the flanks of Helgafjell threatened to destroy the livelihood of the nearby town

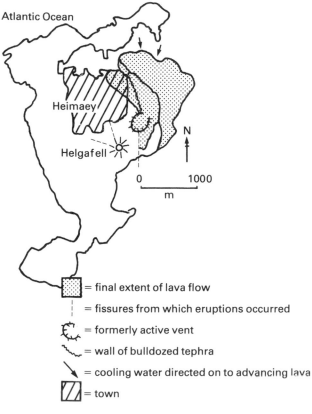

Atlantic Ocean

Heimaey

Helgafell

N

0   1000
        m

⬚ = final extent of lava flow

┊ = fissures from which eruptions occurred

ⵚ = formerly active vent

⌇ = wall of bulldozed tephra

↘ = cooling water directed on to advancing lava

▨ = town

Fig 12.3 The extent of the lava flow on Heimaey.

Photo 12.2 Heimaey, Iceland, 1973. The lava is spreading from the right of the photograph on to the town of Vestmannaey jar and into the harbour.

by engulfing it in ash and cinders and by blocking its protected fishing harbour by a slowly unfurling tongue of lava (see Fig 12.3). Whilst little could be done to prevent the submergence of many buildings beneath the tephra, an immense national and international effort allowed a series of ships to pump 5.5 million tons of sea water on to the advancing lava, to congeal it and stem its flow. So successful was this operation that the new delta of lava which threatened to block the natural bay in fact has created a harbour even more sheltered than previously for the vital fishing fleets of Vestmannaey jar. Whether this was entirely the result of man's intervention depends how far one believes those scientists who suggest that the lava flow had naturally begun to turn eastwards out to sea before the pumping operation was fully under way.

It was also the threat of economic disruption, this time to a region's considerable tourist and agricultural resources, that led to the controversial scheme of lava diversion on Mount Etna in Sicily in 1983. In March of that year a new fissure opened on its southern flank which was soon disgorging a steady ten cubic metres of lava every second and which, by the end of April, had fed a flow which extended four kilometres and covered 40 million cubic metres. To prevent further damage to villages and farms in its path, explosive charges were detonated in May to breach the solidified lava embankment which enclosed the lava flow. Some of the lava was thus diverted into an alternative channel which would lead it to an ancient crater and bring it to a halt at a much higher altitude than would otherwise have been the case. The scheme, however, was only partially successful, managing to divert only a fraction of the flow.

Human Impact on Weathering

To appreciate the effectiveness of polluted air in accelerating the rate of rock weathering, one need only observe the distorted faces of the figures and gargoyles that adorn the buildings that have survived the onslaught of Victorian industrialisation in London, Manchester or Glasgow. Emissions of sulphur dioxide and carbon dioxide combine with rainwater to produce dilute solutions of sulphuric and carbonic acids, each of which will etch grotesque scars into the face of even the most angelic stone cherub or cause finely hewn pinnacles and crockets to crumble away. The Clean Air Acts of 1956 and 1968 in Britain have played a significant part in reducing the speed of weathering of our ancient monuments and have enabled the restoration of the masonry that surmounts our cathedrals and public buildings to become economically viable. Although not yet proven, the citizens of Stockholm and Goteborg and other Scandinavian cities see the rapid weathering of their public edifices as a direct result of the acidic rainfall which reaches them, windborne, from Britain and West Germany, polluted by gases emitted from industries and power stations.

Quite a contrasting way in which man can strengthen the power of a weathering process is by removing protection from a rock surface previously provided by soil and vegetation. Open-cast mines and quarries, such as that in Photo 12.3, expose rock to much faster mechanical weathering than would previously have been the case, as does peat digging in the already barren landscape of the Outer Hebrides.

In the semi-arid areas of Africa, where overgrazing and overcropping resulting from overpopulation have caused desertification and the stripping off of the meagre topsoil and vegetation, underlying rock strata have been left open to the merciless ravages of tropical weathering, nowhere greater than on the sandstones of the Udi Plateau of south-east Nigeria where gullies 30 metres deep have been etched into the escarpment (Photo 12.4).

Whether man the tourist ought to be seen as an agent of weathering or one of erosion is open to dispute, but one need only observe the damage inflicted each year on popular sites such as Stonehenge, Hay Tor on Dartmoor, the Valley of Rocks in north Devon or the White Horse of Kilburn to appreciate that the trampling of feet, clumsy hands and graffiti 'artists' are as effective methods of abrasion as any provided by nature.

Human Impact on Slope Processes and Slope Profiles

In the early months of 1986 our television screens were once again relaying a natural disaster engendered by man, a crawling, trembling flow of mud down a Peruvian valley entraining all sign of life within it. This, we were told, was the result of rapid deforestation of the

Photo 12.3 Carboniferous limestone quarry, Horton-in-Ribblesdale, North Yorkshire. This huge quarry opens up the limestone to the ravages of physical weathering.

Photo 12.4 This 25-metre deep gully in soft sandstone in the Makran area of Iran demonstrates the potency of tropical weathering and erosion once the protective soil layer is removed.

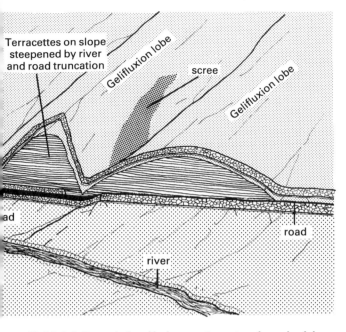

Fig 12.4 Soil creep induced by human steepening of an upland slope.

Andean foothills for agricultural development, succeeded by heavy rainfall which destabilised the deeply weathered clays. This is a story all too familiar to disaster watchers, who have experience of man-induced slope failures as far apart as Hong Kong in 1966, the Vaiont Dam in north Italy in 1963 and Aberfan in South Wales in 1966.

Almost every slope process described in Chapter 4 can be accelerated by human intervention. Of the four main variables which influence rates of slope processes – climate, rock type, vegetation and slope angle – it is the latter two which man is most likely to alter in precipitating slope movements.

Increasing Slope Angle

Slope angles are most usually increased by the construction of roads or railways, by mining, or occasionally by some agricultural practice. The construction of a modern road up the steep climb to the Kirkstone Pass in Cumbria has sliced through gelifluxion lobes on the hillside, exposing their contents and inducing soil creep and terracette formation upon them (see Fig 12.4).

Elaborate measures are commonly taken nowadays by motorway engineers to avoid the failure of the artificially steep embankments and cuttings that are created in order to maintain the gentle gradient of the road. Sub-surface drainage systems flush excess rainfall away and prevent pore pressures from threatening the low resistance of such steep slopes in unconsolidated materials. When roads are blasted out of hillsides, such as the A592 around the southern shores of Ullswater, the roadside cliff may be so steep that engineers can do little to prevent accidents except to warn of frequent rock slides with road signs.

It was the creation of an excessively steep slope on a tip of coalmining waste that produced the disaster at Aberfan which killed 144 schoolchildren and villagers. The 250 metre high tip liquefied into an horrific mud- and earthflow, the effect of recent heavy rainfall and a misguided policy of dumping waste across a natural spring line for 30 years.

Changes in Vegetation Cover

The moorlands of North Yorkshire provide ample evidence of man's acceleration of slope processes through his interference with vegetation. The forests were cleared steadily from the uplands from about 3000 BC, the destruction accelerating during the Bronze Age about 1500 years later. So complete was the clearance that by the time of the Anglo-Saxon migration into the region, the uplands were regarded as natural pastures, and, as such, pretty wild and inhospitable places unsuited to permanent settlement. Significant soil erosion downslope has thus been speeded up by certain of man's policies. Regular heather burning as part of the widespread management of grouse allows patches of upland, peaty soil to be moved downhill by wind and water, and enables gullies to be incised on the steeper slopes. Particularly serious moorland fires in 1935 and 1959 undoubtedly added to the efficacy of this process. The excavation of drainage ditches adds further to the desiccation of the peat. In periods of agricultural boom, the limit of ploughing creeps up the hillsides, as during World War II when even some hillcrests were reclaimed for cultivation. This policy of 'digging for victory' may have benefited the economy but it did nothing for the environment – the chalk soils from the crest of the Wolds' scarp near Staxton were stripped off most effectively by rainwash. A more contemporary cause of gullying are the tourists who extend the footpaths of the moors, so effectively on the famous Lyke Wake Walk that the number of hikers has had to be limited during the peak season. What better example of man engendering positive feedback can there be than when such footpath erosion leads to gullying (Fig 12.5)?

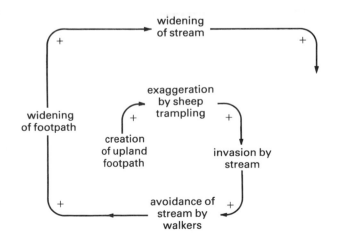

Fig 12.5 The positive feedback loop of footpath erosion.

The impact on the landscape of these effects may seem minor – headward extension of upland streams into incised gullies, the build-up of soil mounds behind hedgerows and stone walls, the thinning of soil on moorland tops – but their speed can be considerable. One stream near Levisham has been seen to dump over 0.5 metre of eroded material from uphill in just 60 years. One intense summer thunderstorm on a moorland stripped of vegetation by trampling walkers can remove centimetres of soil.

Such impacts, though, may be trivial when compared to the equivalent devastation of tropical slopes. In recent attempts to increase the agricultural output of Ecuador, for example, the government has faced considerable problems of soil erosion. On the steep-sided valleys of the southern sierras near Cuenca as much as 75 per cent of the cultivated area may have been eroded thanks to over-zealous agricultural practices. In the northern sierras to the south of Tulca, hard concretions which were formerly submerged beneath 2–3 metres of soil now form the hillslope surface. This dilemma of choice between economic development and environmental devastation faces most tropical nations, especially those which need to develop heavily forested, mountainous regions.

Other Changes

It is unlikely that man will accelerate slope processes by altering rock type or climate, but he is easily capable of inducing change in local water tables which destabilise the former balance between shear stress and shear resistance on a hillside. The Vaiont Dam disaster in north Italy illustrates this point well. Whilst it was still under construction in 1960, many experts predicted catastrophe, well aware of the instability of the surrounding slopes and their tendency to fail. Countering these suggestions, other experts claimed that the observed movements of the surface were to be expected in such a rugged, mountainous area. Bores were made to strengthen their evidence and reinforce their opinions. Nevertheless, on 9th October 1963, following a period of exceptional rainfall, a landslide of such ferocity took place that a mass of over 250 million cubic metres cascaded into the reservoir creating a wave of water which the dam was totally unable to contain. Two thousand villagers perished. As Fig 12.6 shows, the slopes comprised a series of layers of limestones and clay. The permeable surface limestone would have allowed water to penetrate to the weak marl beneath and saturate it quickly. This process would have been speeded up thanks to the already high water table which the reservoir's construction had induced. Once saturated, the natural shear resistance of the rock would no longer have been able to sustain the slope, and disaster was inevitable.

Controlling Slope Processes

With his effects so blatantly obvious, it is hardly surprising that man has devised many methods of soil conservation on slopes. The magnificent rice terraces of Luzon in the Philippines may be 2000 years old, but still today the stepped profile provides checks for water erosion. Farmers who have ploughed sloping fields have often done so at their peril, as Photo 4.3 shows.

Sub-surface drainage, cover cropping and contour ploughing, which lessens the chance of gullying, may alleviate the problem. On the moorlands of North Yorkshire careful management and supervision of all land use changes are rectifying the situation, allied with judicious planting of stands of conifers by the Forestry Commission since 1919.

Major slope movements are more difficult to prevent, even when they are induced by man, but various attempts at controlling them in the coastal environments where they are so common are looked at below.

Fig 12.6 The Vaiont Dam disaster, northern Italy.

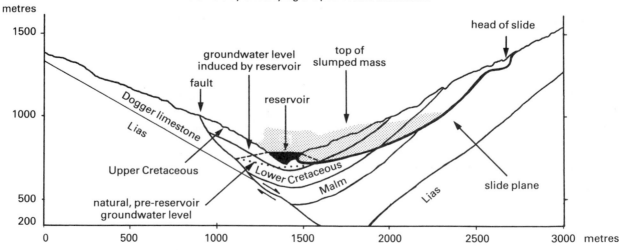

Note the water table which the reservoir raised, and the unstable clay underlying the permeable limestone.

Human Impact on Hydrology and River Systems

Every aspect of the hydrological cycle can be interfered with by man, either accidentally or deliberately, including the input of precipitation which has been manipulated, albeit rather unpredictably, by the aerial seeding of clouds with silver iodide crystals. It is his effect on the earth's surface that we are more concerned with here, however.

There are, ultimately, three aspects of a river basin's daily functioning that man is likely to affect, the rate and amount of run-off which feeds the river, the volume and rate of water discharge and the quantity and type of load it transports. Each of these, in turn, can of course then determine certain human activities, yet another case of a feedback loop.

Undoubtedly some human activities are more likely to change the hydrological cycle than others. Deforestation and afforestation, urbanisation and agriculture would be high on a list in any climatic region, but so would the provision of water and power supply, and changes brought about for recreation, navigation and industry would not be far behind. To illustrate the major points, just three activities are selected here.

Deforestation and Afforestation

Two pieces of evidence, given in Figs 5.13a and 12.7, ably demonstrate the impact of a forest. The first contrasts the size of the unit hydrograph peak from equivalent storms in two adjacent upland basins in mid-Wales, one having been planted by the Forestry Commission, the other not. The second shows how two periods of tree felling cause a river's discharge to increase considerably above the expected flow and how, in the intervening period of 23 years between the two

cuts, the flow slowly returns to normal as the young trees mature. Forests, then, increase the lag time and by doing so even out the supply of run-off to the channel by operating controls on interception, evapotranspiration, overland flow and even throughflow. They also reduce the supply of sediment to a channel by checking slope movements of soil and other debris. the reason why, for instance, a forest has been planted on the valley slopes above Thirlmere, the Cumbrian reservoir which slakes the thirst of Manchester.

Urbanisation

Urbanisation of a drainage basin transforms every suface, storage area and flow within it. Where there was once vegetation and soil, there is now tarmac; where interception was once a haphazard process of raindrops trickling through branches it is now a controlled one, siphoned from gutter down drainpipe to sewer; where surfaces once varied in colour from season to season, they are now eternally grey, their albedo permanently lowered; where water supplies were once well matched by the demands made upon them by vegetation they are now constantly under threat.

No review of the impact could be more comprehensive than that by Douglas in Fig 12.8. Careful study is essential, and consultation with Question 1 at the end of the chapter is advisable. One or two points are worth emphasising. First, that a town has an impact not only within its immediate environment but also for a considerable distance downstream. Second, that the impact may change at different stages of urban construction and growth; and third that no single aspect of the hydrological cycle is left untouched, not even precipitation.

One major downstream impact of urbanisation according to the diagram is to increase the height of the river flood. Further clarifying work has been carried out on this aspect by Hollis who has studied the fluctuating flows of Canon's Brook during the construction within its catchment area of Harlow New Town between 1953 and 1968. As Fig 12.9 shows, he demonstrated a significant reduction in lag time for both winter and summer storms and a significant change in the magnitude and speed of the river rising after a storm, as computed by the unit hydrograph. New developments increased the mean maximum monthly flood by 220 per cent and the unit hydrograph in the late 1960s reached a peak 4.6 times higher than that for the early 1950s.

Illustration of another of Douglas' points, gully development, can be made from Gregory and Park's study of the role that road construction can play in transforming a small stream channel of less than 0.5 metre depth and 1 metre width into a gully almost 2 metres deep and over 4 metres wide. Although located in a rural area of central Devon, it was an urban land activity, road metalling in the late 1940s, that caused this transformation within a period of less than 30 years.

Fig 12.7 The increase of run-off after clear felling a forest, the Coweeta Catchment of North Carolina.

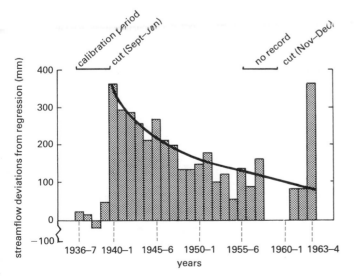

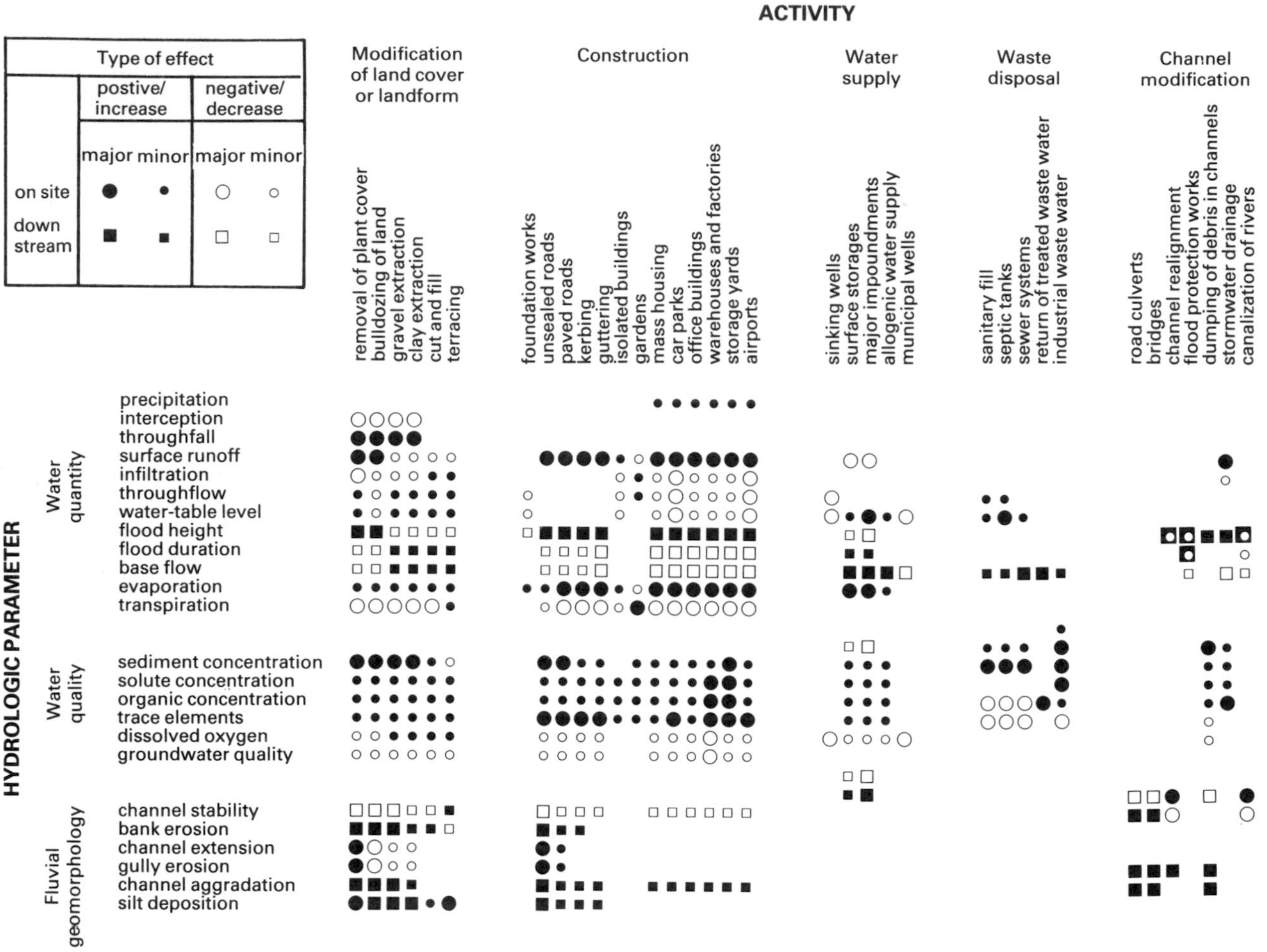

ACTIVITY

Type of effect legend:

Type of effect	positive/increase		negative/decrease	
	major	minor	major	minor
on site	●	•	○	○
down stream	■	▪	□	□

Activity categories (columns):
- **Modification of land cover or landform**: removal of plant cover; bulldozing of land; gravel extraction; clay extraction; cut and fill; terracing
- **Construction**: foundation works; unsealed roads; paved roads; kerbing; guttering; isolated buildings; gardens; mass housing; car parks; office buildings; warehouses and factories; storage yards; airports
- **Water supply**: sinking wells; surface storages; major impoundments; allogenic water supply; municipal wells
- **Waste disposal**: sanitary fill; septic tanks; sewer systems; return of treated waste water; industrial waste water
- **Channel modification**: road culverts; bridges; channel realignment; flood protection works; dumping of debris in channels; stormwater drainage; canalization of rivers

HYDROLOGIC PARAMETER (rows):
- **Water quantity**: precipitation; interception; throughfall; surface runoff; infiltration; throughflow; water-table level; flood height; flood duration; base flow; evaporation; transpiration
- **Water quality**: sediment concentration; solute concentration; organic concentration; trace elements; dissolved oxygen; groundwater quality
- **Fluvial geomorphology**: channel stability; bank erosion; channel extension; gully erosion; channel aggradation; silt deposition

Fig 12.8 The impacts of urbanisation on various aspects of the hydrological system.

The two road drainage ditches which flank the road, and which fill quickly with water draining from the impervious road surface soon after a storm, discharge into the stream immediately upstream from the 500 metre long gully. It is these storm discharges which have carried out such significant erosion.

Water Supply and Control

One consequence of increasing urbanisation is, of course, the need for increasing control and management of water supply both to provide for the urban population and to offset the more wild fluctuations of river flow that result from urban growth. It is not just urban rivers which pose a flood threat, however. Flooding can affect human activities in almost any river valley. A series of case studies is drawn here, through which various principles of river control can be exemplified.

The River Nene in Northamptonshire

Although only 145 kilometres in length, the River Nene provides an interesting study of many of the chal-

lenges of river management that face a water authority. Its course is rarely steep, rising only 150 metres above sea level, and it flows through a relatively wide valley down to Peterborough before crossing the Fens on an embanked, straightened course that keeps it four metres above the land at high water (see Fig 12.10).

River management has become even more necessary in recent years, not least due to the growth of three towns within its catchment area, Corby, Northampton and Peterborough, Enterprise Zones in Wellingborough and Corby, and the continued growth of Kettering, all of which have increased water demand and the need for industrial and residential sewage disposal. In this region of the East Midlands, the intensification of arable agriculture means more irrigation and more agrichemical seepage, which is balanced against a rising wave of concern for conservation and of interest in river recreation. Gravel has long been a major resource of the flood plain and constant demand for more extraction must concern the Anglian Water Authority. Natural hazard avoidance is another task of management, for the 1953 east coast floods severely affected the lower Nene and the town of Wisbech continues to be threatened, located as it is within the 40-kilometre tidal section of the Nene.

This leaves the water authority with multiple aims, to reduce the flooding risk to houses, roads and arable

(a) Changes in hydrograph lag time.

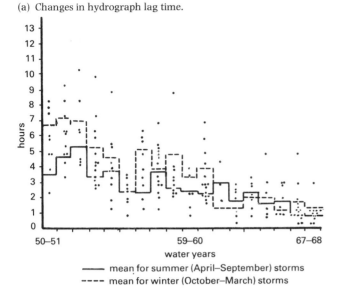

mean for summer (April–September) storms
mean for winter (October–March) storms

anyone who has a knowledge of the interactions and interrelationships of the basin hydrological cycle. A river is, after all, a cascading system in which outputs from one section are inputs into the next. It may be all very well to speed up the flow in one section to reduce flooding but it serves little point if it increases the risk of flooding downstream. A river, unlike a road system, cannot be managed individually by the county authorities and police forces through whose territory it happens to pass.

The management of the Nene has continued successfully for many decades, and notable schemes have been introduced to deal with the changes in land use. For example, the Northampton Washlands scheme, combined with channel diversion, has coped effectively with new town expansion. An enclosed area of 100 hectares on the flood plain acts as an emergency reservoir for floodwater during peak flows. A contrasting scheme carries out a similar task for Corby. Here, an on-river storage reservoir, built around the river and

(b) Increase in the maximum monthly flood.

maximum flood each month
51 months moving mean

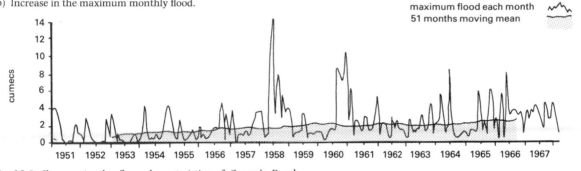

Fig 12.9 Changes in the flow characteristics of Canon's Brook following the construction of Harlow New Town.

land, to protect the needs of water consumers including those who use the Nene for navigation and, if possible, to maintain and stimulate the increase in agricultural production. Such aims undoubtedly produce conflicts, for the amount of water available for consumption needs to be maximised whilst flood control requires the reverse. It is essential that a river authority takes a look at the entire basin including its tributaries in devising a management plan, a notion that will not be lost on

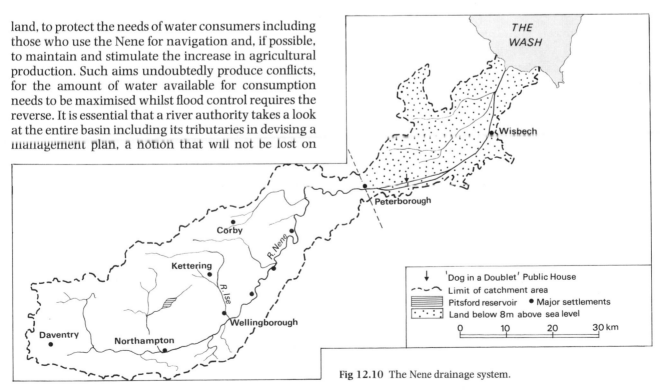

Fig 12.10 The Nene drainage system.

not beside it, allows the Willow Brook at Weldon to compensate for increased peaks of flow caused by urban expansion.

To extend its control over nature even further, the Anglian Water Authority in the early 1980s looked carefully at various proposed schemes of river management. They were:

From the source to Peterborough.

1 Increase the capacity of the river channel by widening and deepening it, by dredging.
2 Create a greater channel capacity by lowering the existing retention levels in the river between sluices.
3 Construct embankments along the river bank.
4 Reduce the peak discharges from the tributaries.
5 Make more use of the floodplain as a storage area for excess water in time of flood.
6 Automate the sluices and weirs.

From Peterborough to the sea.

1 Use Whittlesea Wash Mere as a storage area for excess water.
2 Move the tidal limit from the Dog in a Doublet much closer to Wisbech.
3 Bypass Wisbech by constructing a new channel, thus avoiding the tortuous course through the town.
4 Link the Nene with the Welland via pipes or drainage channels.

The selected scheme of management draws upon various elements of these proposals, avoiding the most controversial and expensive suggestions such as the Wisbech river by-pass and the use of the Whittlesea Wash Mere. To evaluate each scheme for yourself, see Question 2 at the end of the chapter.

Fig 12.11 The extensive system of the East and West Lyn Rivers.

The Lynmouth flood disaster

In August 1952, 34 villagers and holidaymakers were drowned as a furious tumult of water swept down the Lyn valley from Exmoor onto the coastal settlement of Lynmouth. The causes were complex, a series of interacting human and natural contributions. The flood was the climax of an exceptionally wet August which saw nearly 20 millimetres of rain fall in the first fortnight of the month, saturating the soils of the Lyn's catchment area. Of the further 30-40 millimetres that fell during an intense thunderstorm late in the day on 15th August, rapid run-off could be the only outcome, even without other exacerbating factors within the drainage basin.

Thin soils surmounting impermeable sandstones in the upper Lyn catchment on Exmoor were not able to delay much run-off and neither were the steep slopes of the incised lower valley of the East Lyn. As water approached Lynmouth, the V-shaped valley would have channelled its ferocity, for there is virtually no valley bottom or flood plain on which to disperse its energy. Hardly surprising, then, that by late evening the river in Lynmouth was rising 15 centimetres every 15 minutes. The East Lyn's major tributaries, Badgeworthy Water, Farley Water and Hoaroak Water, fall over 450 metres in under 7 kilometres, producing steep gradients, which in common with the West Lyn's, would have contributed significantly to the torrent. Although not directly to blame, various man-built obstacles certainly added to the disaster. Sited at the junction of two river systems, Lynmouth was receiving over 520 cumecs of water at the flood's peak, a figure not much below the record discharge of the Thames in London! Part of the devastation wreaked by the flood has been attributed to the waves of water which swept into the town, waves which represented the release of impounded water breaking through dams. In the upper

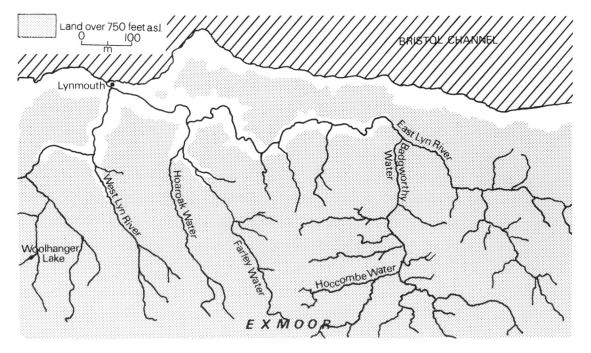

Photo 12.5(a)   Lynmouth, North Devon, today: looking up the East Lyn River from the footbridge near the harbour. Note the potential capacity of the bankfull channel and the straightened, enforced course.

Photo 12.5(b)   Lynmouth, North Devon. From above, the straight course and the harbour and beach protection walls can be seen. Note also how few buildings now flank the river.

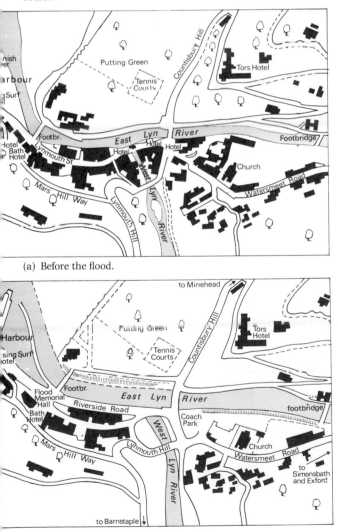

(a)   Before the flood.

(b)   After the introduction of flood protection.

Fig 12.12 Lynmouth.

reaches of the West Lyn catchment, Woolhanger Lake contained about 1.5 million gallons of water until it burst its dam at 9.10 p.m. A disused railway embankment provided a temporary dam for water upstream from Parracombe, the culvert through it having been choked with debris, until it gave way soon after Woolhanger. Uprooted trees accumulated behind bridges in the lower Lyn, creating dams that quelled the river temporarily before releasing an even greater terror. Had cottages not lined the banks of the Lyn, would the devastation have been so horrific? With hindsight we can see man's minor contributions, but the most destructive hand was undoubtedly played by nature.

Lynmouth's tranquillity today provides a stark contrast to August 1952, but that peace is maintained by various flood protection measures revealed in Photo 12.5b. The course of the East Lyn River through the town was straightened, widened and deepened to ensure the faster passage of floodwater through it. Its form is controlled by solidly constructed sidewalls which provide it with an efficient cross-section which hopefully will rarely, if ever, be bankfull. The West Lyn River has been re-routed to follow the natural course it chose on the night of the storm, as well as being widened and dredged. Land cleared by the flood to the south of the East Lyn has been left with few buildings, vehicle parks and recreation areas being considered more appropriate land uses for the vulnerable banks of a flooding river. A curving wall protects the harbour and directs discharging water out through a frequently dredged channel across the beach.

Impact of a dam construction

Some consideration has already been given in Chapter 6 to the effects of building a dam on a river system, but so important can this be to areas up and downstream that further examination is needed here. Reservoirs act as debris traps. Not only will this affect the load transported and the supply of sediment to depositional features downstream, but also the work capability of the water discharging from the dam. This water will be clear, sediment free and capable of considerable channel erosion. In addition, the flow regime below the dam will be regulated, peaks and troughs ironed out, which could mean the river is no longer able to remove the debris contributed by unregulated tributaries below the dam, perhaps reducing channel capacity in time. On the other hand, a stream that formerly braided may be less inclined to do so both because of the reduction in load and the regularisation of flow. In hot climates, where reservoirs are often most needed, their construction may lead to increased evaporation, thus reducing the river's average annual discharge, and conceivably altering local patterns of humidity and precipitation.

If one adds to this the possibility of stimulating an earthquake, altering local groundwater levels, repercussions on coastal sedimentation and delta formation and the creation of a new base level for the upper course of the river above the reservoir, one can envisage that tampering with nature to solve one local problem can prove less of a solution than one would hope.

The essential lesson, then, to be learnt from the Nene River management, the Lynmouth flood disaster and the impact of dams is that the river basin is a complex process-response system, where one man-induced change can produce feedback loops that ricochet back and forth across the catchment area and beyond it. The system can be managed only with a system that matches it in sophistication, and that has been supplied only relatively recently with computer programs capable of calculating responses that man alone could not gauge.

The success of the flood protection scheme in Kendal, Cumbria certainly justifies the money and time that were spent in designing it. A questionnaire put to people in 1986 who live and work in the area of Kendal that was most severely affected in the 1954 flood showed that most believed that there was no threat from the river. This calmness of mind is surely a just reward for the planners of the protection scheme, which was built in the 1970s (see Photo 12.6).

Human Impact on Coastal Landscapes

Coastal landscapes are no different from any other in having both unintentional and deliberate human actions piled upon them. Perhaps, first, we should look at the side effects of other human activities before examining man's usually ill-fated attempts to control coastal processes.

Side Effects of Human Activity

Cliff profiles

Despite the attempts of vegetation and weathering to hide the traces of human interference on cliff faces, the

Photo 12.6   A sediment trap at the confluence of the Rivers Kent and Mint above Kendal, Cumbria. This is one part of a comprehensive flood protection scheme in the town. The aim of the large pool seen here is to filter out some of the load, thus giving the river greater energy to move the water efficiently through the town in time of flood.

indelible print of man's hand is not difficult to discern. North from Whitby along the North Yorkshire coast stands a series of cliffs bearing the scars of centuries of exploitation. Alum, jet and even ironstone have been quarried mercilessly, leaving chasms and caves and generating landslides, although in some cases, such as at Rosedale Wyke above the tiny, abandoned Port Mulgrave, giving the cliff a bevelled profile that looks suspiciously like a natural phenomenon.

Along other coastlines, the tipping of waste obscures the natural cliff-line, most notably on the south Durham coast where the magnesian limestone cliffs are obscured by the cascades of coal waste from local mines. Excessive tourist pressure may hasten a cliff's decline by starting rock slides from overused paths on the cliff-top. Weak sandstones and chalk on the Kent

Photo 12.7   Port Mulgrave and Rosedale Wyke, North Yorkshire. The apparent slumping on the headland is, in fact, the effect of now abandoned iron ore workings.

and Sussex coasts are particularly prone. At Alum Bay on the Isle of Wight the multi-coloured sandstone cliffs attracted so many tourists to scrape the stone for seaside souvenirs that restricted access has been made essential to lessen the rôle of erosion.

Beaches, spits and bars

All three of these depositional features are dynamic landforms, relying on inputs of sediment from long-shore drift to maintain them and compensate for the losses due to erosion. Any interruption to the supply, therefore, may deform the landform or threaten its continued existence. Harbour walls, marinas, jetties and piers are the usual culprits in such cases. The inhabitants of Seaford in Sussex have battled to save their beach since the harbour at Newhaven, to the west, was built over 250 years ago, effectively ending the eastward drift of sand and shingle (see Fig 12.14). So scarce has the supply become that the beach has disappeared altogether along stretches of Seaford Head and the chalk cliffs here are retreating much faster than elsewhere. An increase in erosion is not an uncommon result of harbour wall construction for the obstacle may refract waves to a sufficient degree to concentrate their force onto a particular beach or cliff. Longshore drift relies on river-borne sediment as one of its supplies, and human interference with river discharge and load may thus unintentionally cut the supply to a coastal landform.

Beaches provide an easily accessible source of sand and gravel which many councils and contractors cannot resist. Fortunately, conservation laws often curtail such activities, but at Sheringham in Norfolk extraction has certainly occurred. The 30 kilometre long, shingle-rich Chesil Beach has attracted the interest of excavators for 700 years despite considerable research by geomorphologists to prove that the landform is essentially a fossil feature, being sustained by very little current deposition. Extraction, if continued, could in time mean the extinction of the landform. We certainly need to learn from our mistakes; the removal of half a million tonnes of gravel from an offshore bank a century ago on the south Devon coast accentuated coastal erosion sufficiently for the village of Hallsands to become its victim.

Sand dunes

Tourists, however well meaning, are the major threat to sand dunes. On any popular coast where sand dunes abound, be it Camber in Sussex, Bamburgh in Northumberland or Formby in Merseyside, footpaths are trodden in the cols between the dunes. Grass is trampled, the sand offers no resistance and the wind is quick to exploit a chink through the dune ridge and create a **blow-out**, which in extreme cases can destroy the entire dune system.

Mudflats

Rice cord grass, or Spartina Townshendii, was first introduced in the 1800s in Southampton Water. It was recognised for its property of rapid growth and stabilisation of mudflats which were particularly valuable assets in a busy waterway. What was not foreseen, however, was just how quickly Spartina would adapt to the British environment for it has rapidly spread through the estuaries and marshes of Britain, accreting mud where it was not wanted and competing far too efficiently with native forms of vegetation.

At Mont St Michel on the coast of Brittany, it is not vegetation, but another potent mix of human and natural processes that has caused mudflats to extend too rapidly. The tiny granite island sits in what was once a deep, sheltered marine bay, but mud deposition has been so extensive that the bay is seen increasingly as the estuary of the See and Selune rivers. Tidal scouring is now almost non-existent. This natural evolution has been hastened by human activity for more than a

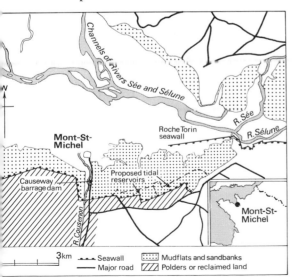

Fig 12.13 The problems and proposed solutions of Mont St Michel, Brittany.

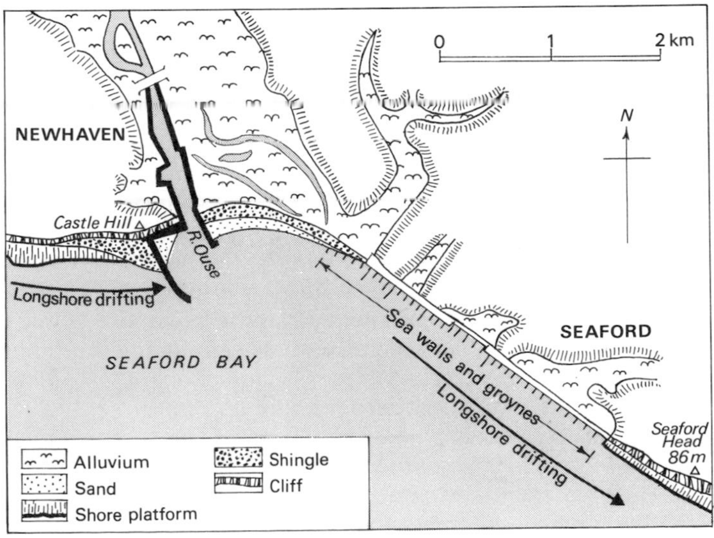

Fig 12.14 The impact of Newhaven Harbour: the supply of shingle from the west has been greatly reduced by man-made obstructions.

Photo 12.8 Boulder clay cliffs between Mundesley and Happisburgh, Norfolk. The bungalows on the cliff top are threatened unless cliff retreat is checked.

Photo 12.9 Boulder clay cliffs between Mundesley and Happisburgh, Norfolk: two parallel lines of revetments to reduce the energy of the waves.

century, since reclamation of the growing mudflats began to the west of Mont St Michel (see Fig 12.13). Natural flushing and erosion of this western area have been further reduced by diverting the River Cousenon away from it and constructing a barrage dam at its mouth. Flats to the east of the Mont have more than doubled in area in the last 30 years, a process which began in the mid-nineteenth century with the construction of a sea wall at Roche Torin to prevent discharging river water from flowing into the area. The causeway to the Mont has left these eastern mudflats almost isolated from river water and tidal action.

In 1983 the plan to re-excavate the bay and free Mont St Michel from its muddy confinement was set in motion with the removal of the Roche Torin wall. So that river water can flush out the eastern mudflat from both directions, sections of the causeway will also be removed. Tidal scour will also be augmented by trapping seawater at high tide in two small reservoirs, await-

ing release when the tide has receded. To the west of the Mont the barrage on the Cousenon will be adapted so that water stored at high tide will be released with sufficient speed at low tide to erode the mud. One only hopes that by turning the tide at Mont St Michel the engineers will not engender erosional effects which all of their detailed planning could not have foreseen.

Human Control of Coastal Processes

This pessimistic note is not as unrealistic as it may seem, for time and time again man's attempts at controlling the sea have been no more effective than King Canute's. Nowhere is this better demonstrated than in his many endeavours to control cliff retreat.

Cliff protection

Slumping of cliffs provides local councils with numerous challenges to its reponsibilities. Farmers are losing agricultural land, residents their gardens or even houses, and holidaymakers their beach chalets and cliff walks (see Photo 12.8). These are problems which are familiar to all who know the coastline at Barton-on-Sea in Hampshire or around Mundesley, Overstrand and Happisburgh in north-east Norfolk.

In Norfolk, the task of the engineers has been to design a scheme which not only protects the cliff from marine erosion but also slows down the rate of slumping. Erosion has been so severe around Happisburgh in the past that during one stormy night in 1845 a five-hectare field of wheat disappeared into the sea. The first attempt to check the devastation took place in the late 1940s when steel pilings were driven into the cliff in an unsuccessful attempt to stabilise it. By 1956, a more elaborate scheme had been devised which has operated ever since. This consists of a massive wooden revetment (see Photo 12.9), the aim of which is to diffuse the energy of the waves, and if necessary hold back the slumping cliff so as to reduce the unconsolidated boulder clay to a stable angle of rest. Along some stretches of the cliff-line a second line of defence has been needed, consisting of an embankment of reinforced concrete. Although effective against the everyday processes that operate, the defences have proved vulnerable to extreme natural events of both marine erosion and cliff slumping (see Photo 12.10). So ineffective have some of the defences been that some local experts have suggested that it would be more cost-effective not to attempt to protect the cliffs at all and to pay compensation when and where it is necessary.

Sea walls have frequently been seen as a permanent solution to marine erosion, the bigger the threat the more imposing the wall. Indeed, at Happisburgh, a wall has been proposed at a cost of £1600 per metre, at 1985 prices, to replace the present revetment. Government economies may well prevent such expenditure but if the experience at Seaford is anything to go by, this may not be a great loss. The great stone defence which was erected here to counteract the effects of Newhaven harbour has been more symbolic than effective. Whereas a beach helps dissipate wave energy, a wall allows it to be concentrated, which weakens the structure, often eventually destroying it. It also reflects the energy onto the beach beneath it, scouring it and adding to its demise, a point well demonstrated at Seaford.

Where cliff problems are less dire, sub-surface drainage may be sufficient to remove the excess water which engenders mass movement. At Whitby, an ingenious plan which incorporates drainage into the zigzagging cliff paths was instigated in the early 1980s and so far appears to be successful.

Beach protection

Almost every holiday beach in Britain is protected by groynes and breakwaters which are designed to trap sediment moving along the shore and to reduce the energy of the waves. At this they are undoubtedly effective, although by removing sediment from the system they may well be exposing to erosion the coast 'down drift' of them.

In January 1985 the shingle erosion at Seaford had become so severe that the local council was forced to consider a £10-million plan to put it right. Two sources of shingle supply are possible in such cases – dredging from offshore or transfer from a site inland. In either case, very careful preliminary research is vital, for the angle of the beach and the size and grading of the shingle must be well matched to the original if the natural equilibrium is to be maintained. Before embarking on such a scheme the council wisely commissioned a computer program to simulate the possible effects of dredging offshore sediment back on to the beach.

Photo 12.10 The breached revetments near Overstrand, Norfolk. One huge slump has completely engulfed the massive wooden structure.

Photo 12.11 The West Cliff, Whitby, North Yorkshire. To prevent the constant slumping of the unstable boulder clay, an elaborate drainage scheme was introduced in the early 1980s which involved the landscaping of the entire cliff. Note the parallel bands of gravel which indicate the lines of drainage.

Sand dune protection

The usual motive behind protecting sand dunes is an economic one, to protect the farmland on which they are encroaching, although in some worthy cases it may be ecological. At Borth, north of Aberystwyth, a series of parallel fences and brushwood acts as traps which are successfully stabilising dunes (see Photo 12.12). In other areas, judicious planting of marram grass or sand twitch is adequate, the type of vegetation depending on whether the dune is prone to marine inundation. At Culbin on the Moray Firth and at Wells-next-the-Sea in Norfolk conifer trees have been the only form of vegetation capable of preventing dune migration.

Interfering with coastal processes is, then, a precarious business, for the outcome can never be guaranteed and often varies considerably from the intention. In

Photo 12.12 The control of sand dunes at Borth, Dyfed: parallel lines of brushwood fences trap sand and so stabilise the dunes.

some cases these side effects may be beneficial, for example, since the introduction of larger cross-channel ferries in the early 1980s the churning up of the shallow waters near the entrance to St Peter Port harbour in Guernsey has lowered the sea bed by as much as 30 centimetres a year, but at the same time has exposed a long sought-after shipwreck.

Human Impact in Glacial, Fluvioglacial and Periglacial Landscapes

The more hostile the environment, the less widespread are the effects of man, but this does not mean that where they do occur they are any less intense. Indeed, so sensitively are most tundra environments balanced that even small, apparently insignificant human activities can have considerable impact on the permafrost.

Glacial Processes and Landscapes

Man is unlikely to interfere very much with glacial processes except on a global scale by altering the world climate sufficiently to cause ice caps to extend or contract. Indeed, although difficult to prove one way or the other, the pollution and local warming of the atmosphere associated with industrialisation may have contributed to the pattern of advance and retreat of individual glaciers. Increased exploitation of currently glaciated areas for tourism and for HEP may also have an indirect impact on the physical processes in operation, if only through stimulating avalanches and localised melting.

It is much more likely that human influence will be exerted on formerly glaciated landscapes. Hydroelectric power schemes (such as the Dinorwic scheme in Snowdonia), reservoirs, gravel extraction, quarrying, road construction (a recent example being the A9 improvement through the Scottish Highlands) and tourism all modify the environment which the Pleistocene Ice Age left us. Depositional landscapes may even be obliterated. These changes will often cause

Photo 12.13   Kirkstone Quarry, Cumbria. This active quarry is well disguised in the rugged scenery of the borrowdale Volcanics.

modifications in the operation of contemporary processes, although occasionally, as in Photo 12.13, man's activity itself may exaggerate the form of the existing relict landscape.

Fluvioglacial Processes and Landscapes

Where meltwater is acting within a glacial system man is as unlikely to interfere with a fluvioglacial process as he is a glacial one. Beyond the ice, though, meltwater-fed rivers may be easy prey as they cross tundra zones.

Fluvioglacial landscapes are much modified today. Man may contribute the final blow to unconsolidated deposits already ravaged by climatic changes, and land use changes may modify side slopes of meltwater channels by altering slope processes.

Periglacial Processes and Landscapes

Of all the cold regions it is probably in the tundra zones that most impact of man is seen, for the delicate thermal regime of the permafrost is easily disrupted. Fortunately, three nations whose resources are sufficiently great to finance research govern most tundra zones, namely Canada, the USA and the USSR, which means that technological responses have quickly been found to avoid repetition of initial disasters. Incentives to find solutions are provided by the vast mineral wealth that underlies the permafrost, which itself extends across 20 per cent of the earth's land surface.

Stimulation of the melting of the active layer in advance of its normal date, of the ice lenses and ice wedges within the active layer, or of the permafrost itself are the most usual effects of human interference, although results of such actions vary greatly according to local physical conditions and the extent of the activity. Clearance of land for agriculture or for the construction of an airstrip, settlement or communication line is the most likely impetus for change, but gravel extraction or other mineral exploitation may also provide it.

Thermokarst with its various features is the most likely outcome of man-induced change. Once removed, the cover of vegetation and top soil can no longer provide insulation from the extremes of temperature on the surface. The active layer will therefore extend deeper in summer at the expense of the permafrost beneath. At Inuvik, in the Northern Territories of Canada, within four years of a forest fire in 1968, the active layer was deepened by 40 per cent. Slope failure may thus be stimulated, even on low gradients, and the stages of thermokarst degradation described in Chapter 10 may be engendered to produce miniature badland landscapes which provide even greater challenges to human movement. The effect is heightened when an area is underlain by a polygonal network of ice wedges, for erosion will be concentrated along the edges of the polygons to produce a confused, hummocky surface. This is often one of the most rapid of all man-induced processes, examples from Banks Island in the Canadian Arctic showing degradation within four or five years of disturbance by oil drilling and airstrip construction.

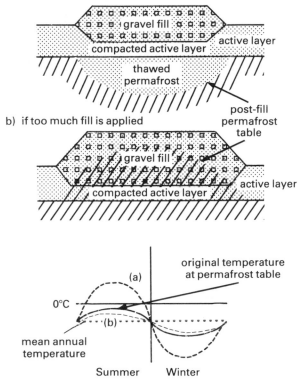

the permafrost table represents the top of the
permanently frozen ground

a) if too little fill is applied

b) if too much fill is applied

c) effects of a and b on seasonal temperature variation

Fig 12.15 The possible detrimental impacts of a gravel pad on the active layer.

By providing artificial insulation to replace any cleared vegetation or to prevent the heat from his buildings penetrating the ground, man has often been able to minimise disruption of the thermal equilibrium. Many roads, towns and even pipelines need to be constructed, therefore, on gravel pads. Their thickness varies considerably – the Alaskan oil pipeline built in the 1970s sits on a two-metre carpet of gravel – but it is critical. Too thick a pad may isolate the active layer so effectively from air temperature that it ceases to melt and the permafrost extends towards the surface. Too little fill may provide insufficient insulation and the active layer may deepen, resulting in the evolution of thermokarst which the pad had tried to allay (see Fig 12.15).

More man-induced problems may develop if he tries to excavate the gravel from a local recource without first considering its possible consequences.

Human Impact on Desert and Semi-Desert Landscapes

Human Impact on Climate

It is possible that human impact on the desert marginal areas has already created more significant changes than on any other landscape on earth, for **desertification** is estimated already to have affected 50×10^6 square kilometres of the earth's surface. Considerable controversy exists as to whether desertification, as the extension of desert conditions to semi-desert areas is known, owes its origins to climatic change induced by nature, by man, or by a mixture of both. Perhaps Hill analysed the situation most accurately over 50 years ago when he declared that: 'the Sahara has seized the opportunity of man's stupidity.'

Opinion continues to be divided as to whether drought disasters such as that in the Sahel of west Africa between 1968 and 1973 and that which affected Ethiopia and eastern Africa between 1982 and 1986 are one-off occurrences or are intense fluctuations within a long-term trend of desiccation. Certainly the Sahara has undergone long-term oscillations before, such as the humid climates which existed between 15 000 and 7000 years ago and again between 6000 and 4700 years ago. There is also evidence from northern Kenya that there is a decline towards aridity which began about 1000 years ago, an integral part of it being Lake Chalbi's drying up in the twelfth century. It may be that Sahelian desiccation is an aspect of a much shorter cycle perhaps only 200 years in duration.

The question remains, to what extent are these intensifications of the dryness natural, induced by slight changes in the position of the sub-tropical high pressure belts, and to what extent is man causing them? It is not only via the greenhouse effect of increasing the atmosphere's carbon dioxide content, but also by altering the albedo of the surface that man can do this. By his systematic removal of vegetation the surface becomes lighter and more reflective, and thus more incoming energy returns to heat the atmosphere, which decreases even further the chance of condensation or precipitation occurring. If we accept the fact that man is contributing to, or even causing, the droughts, it does not help us to conclude that the intense droughts are merely isolated events. Some authorities suggest that the pluvial phase of the Sahara ended 4700 years ago because of man's intervention, and others believe that pastoralism in north Kenya has accelerated desiccation for many centuries. Thus, it appears that man may contribute to long-term drought, not just short-term intensification of it.

Human Impact on Landscape

Whether or not man's activities modify climate it is certain that they modify the landscape and may engender the encroachment of sand dunes, soil erosion and salt encrustation, and may even increase the occurrence of salt weathering.

At the smallest scale, in common with tundra regions, the driving of a Land Rover may be sufficient to disturb the surface equilibrium, which may be the Achilles' heel of a particular feature. A more usual cause, though, is overgrazing, or overcropping stimulated by extended irrigation.

Overgrazing by nomadic pastoralists usually occurs

Photo 12.14   Massive gully erosion, Ethiopian Central Highlands.

because a falling death rate has increased human population, necessitating the need for larger or more herds, which increases the pressure on what little vegetation there is. Around traditional water holes the pressure is especially great, for trampling is concentrated into small areas, the surface becomes hard packed, its infiltration capacity drastically reduced and erosion by both wind and water greatly facilitated.

A well documented example of this occurred during the 1970s in the Awash valley of Wollo in northern Ethiopia. This valley has traditionally provided pasture for the migrating Afar pastoralists during the dry season between September and May. Since the 1960s the fertile parts of the valley have steadily been enclosed and sold off to various international and native commercial interests in order to irrigate them and produce crops for export. As the cultivation expanded, the Afar were forced on to the poorer land leading, inevitably, to overgrazing, the effects of which were exacerbated when drought hit the region in 1972 and again in 1982.

Throughout northern Ethiopia soil erosion has bitten deep into the land during the 1980s' drought, not aided by the frequent occurrence of sloping land, the intensity of the sporadic rainfall, poor techiques of cultivation and stock management and centuries of misuse of land thanks to a now outlawed feudal system (see Photo 12.14).

Extension of irrigation schemes into semi-arid areas has produced many disasters in the past, notably in what is now Bangladesh, although modern attempts are usually more successful. Evapotranspiration is increased when water becomes more available; this draws saline solutions to the surface which evaporate to leave salt crusts. In severe examples deep saline groundwater may also be dragged upwards, again encrusting the surface.

Conclusion to the Human Impact on Landscape

It seems logical to return to the questions posed in the introduction to this chapter in order to analyse the rôle of man as a geomorphological process, and the reader would gain much from pondering upon those questions again now.

Whatever the conclusions reached, one might consider the thoughts of two modern geomorphologists. According to Brown, over the last few thousand years 'man has increased his geomorphological capabilities on what would appear to be something like a logarithmic scale', and according to Selby, human activities 'have probably increased world denudation rates two or three times above the long-term geological rate and locally the accelerated rates may be 1000 times as great'. There are probably very few landscapes, then, however natural they may at first appear, on which man has left no trace.

Postscript: Landscape's Impact on Human Activities

It is not intended to give a comprehensive review of this topic as it is really outside the aims of this text. Examples given within this book, for example the Mount St Helens eruption, the Vaiont Dam disaster or the Lynmouth flood should be sufficient to make every reader aware of the impact on man of events within the landscape. It is not, however, just disasters that we must bear in mind, for effective management of day-to-day occurrences is essential if we are to be the beneficiaries of our interrelationship with the landscape.

For this reason a detailed knowledge of geomorphological processes is vital. Decision makers who effect changes in land use should thus consult geomorphologists for their opinion on the physical viability of their schemes. Is a slope stable enough for urban construction? How prone is a proposed coastal recreation site to erosion? Will land subside if underground water is extracted? How well suited is a river regime to increased irrigation use? How far flung will the effects of a particular volcanic eruption be? The Egyptian government wisely consulted geomorphologists before planning the extension of Suez City and were able to avoid areas most threatened by flooding and most liable to aggressive salt weathering. The inhabitants of New Harmony, Indiana would be wise to do the same if they are to stop their city from being undermined by the whiplash effect of the marauding and meandering Wabash River. It would seem, then, reasonable to conclude that there is no location where man can afford to ignore landscape processes for they, ultimately, will determine the success of his ventures and activities.

Questions

1 Refer to Fig 12.8.
   (a) Why is it essential that we consider the entire river basin when studying the impact of urbanisation on the basin hydrological cycle and on river processes?
   (b) According to Douglas' diagram, which aspects of urban activity have the greatest impact on the amount of load in a river? Give reasons why.
   (c) According to Douglas' diagram, which aspects of urban activity are most likely to increase the chances of a flood in the river channel?
   (d) With reference to Douglas' diagram, summarise the effects of urban activity on the processes of river erosion and deposition.
   (e) With reference to Douglas' diagram, summarise the effects of water supply on the basin hydrological cycle and river processes.
   (f) How and why do the effects of construction vary during different stages of urban growth?
   (g) Why is the management of an urban drainage basin so difficult?
   (h) How is the impact of a Third World city likely to differ from that of a city in the Developed World?

2 Refer to each of the schemes of river management of the Nene included on page 272. The question numbers correspond to the scheme numbers.

From the source to Peterborough.
   (1) What impact would this scheme have on: the likelihood of flooding, river velocity, and the peak discharge at Peterborough? How would the various land uses in the river valley be affected by the scheme?
   (2) Could the lowering of existing retention levels have any detrimental effects?
   (3) How does this scheme alleviate problems caused by river flow?
   (4) What problems may emerge if only some of the tributaries are regulated and not all?
   (5) What practical disadvantages can you envisage with this scheme? Which flood plain land uses would be most appropriate for the scheme to operate with minimum disruption?
   (6) How does this scheme alleviate problems caused by river flow?

From Peterborough to the sea.
   (1) Parts of Whittlesea Wash Mere are a wild bird reserve. How would the proposed scheme affect its use?
   (2) How does this scheme alleviate problems caused by river flow?
   (3) What detrimental effects might this scheme have on Wisbech?
   (4) What research would you need to carry out first and what statistics would you need to collect in order to ensure that this scheme is feasible?

3 Refer to Photo 12.8 of cliff collapse in north Norfolk.
   (a) What arguments would you put forward for and against introducing a cliff protection scheme in those parts of the area that do not already have one?
   (b) List the possible measures that could be taken to protect the cliff both in the immediate vicinity and within a wider area?
   (c) What techniques could you use to assess the impact of each of the suggestions you make in the previous question?

Further Reading
The Lynmouth Flood Disaster, E R Delderfield (ERD Publications, 1981).
The Human Impact, A Goudie (Blackwell, 1986).
Man and Environmental Processes, K J Gregory and D E Walling (Dawson Westview, 1979).

Other References
Man Shapes the Earth, E H Brown, *Geographical Journal* 136 (1970).
The Effect of Urbanisation on Floods in Canon's Brook, G E Hollis, *Transactions of the Institute of British Geographers*, Special Publication 6 (1974).
The Development of a Devon Gully and Man, K J Gregory and C C Park, *Geography* 61 (1976).
Slopes and Weathering, M J Selby in *Man and Environmental Processes* (see above).

Glossary

The glossary contains those geographical terms which are used in the text and which may be new to the reader but for which no explanation is provided *in situ*. Clearly the definitions here are brief, just sufficient to enable the reader to follow the sense of a particular passage. For a fuller explanation reference should be made to a geographical dictionary.

ablation: The wasting of snow or ice from the surface of an ice sheet or glacier by melting or evaporation.

abrasion: The mechanical wearing down of rock by abrasive material, such as sand, which is carried by ice, water or wind. Abrasion is the result, corrasion the process.

aeolian: An adjective which refers to the action of the wind; hence, aeolian erosion, aeolian deposits.

aggradation: The accumulation of deposits, usually within a river channel or on a beach.

alluvium: The sediments deposited by a river, whether on its bed, its flood plain, as a fan or in a lake delta.

anticline: An upfold resulting from compression in the earth's crust.

arid: Deficient in moisture, where potential evaporation exceeds actual precipitation.

artesian water: Water trapped in permeable rocks underground, usually in an artesian basin.

aspect: The direction in which a slope faces.

asthenosphere: A plastic layer of the earth's mantle immediately beneath the lithosphere.

attrition: The progressive wearing down of sediment as it is transported by water or wind.

bankfull: The stage of flow in a river when the channel is full to the brim.

basalt: A common, usually dark-coloured, fine-grained basic igneous rock.

basal weathering front: The lowest level of active weathering.

base level: The level down to which a river can erode.

bedding plane: A plane of separation between one bed of a sedimentary rock and another.

black box system: A system whose internal structure is either not known or not identified.

bluff: A steep slope; usually the river-cut cliff on the outside of a meander.

boss: A small circular igneous intrusion.

braiding: A descriptive term for a river whose course is split into separate channels by the deposition of bars of alluvium, sand or gravel.

capacity: The maximum quantity of sediment that a river or the wind can transport in a unit of time.

capillary water: Water held in a film around particles of the soil within the pores that separate them.

cascading system: A type of system through which material or energy cascades from one sub-system to another.

catchment area: The area from which a river channel receives its run-off.

channel roughness: The resistance which the channel offers to the flow of water.

channel run-off: That portion of the water output of a drainage basin that flows along the channel.

cleavage line: A plane within a rock which results from metamorphism.

climatic climax: A mature plant community in equilibrium with the prevailing climate.

closed system: A system whose boundaries are closed to incoming or outgoing energy or matter.

col: A passage between two peaks on a mountain ridge.

competence: The maximum size of grain that a particular stream velocity can transport.

crust: (i) The outer layer of the earth's surface, or (ii) a hard surface layer of the ground, common in arid and semi-arid areas.

cryoturbation: A form of frost action which churns up the surface layers.

cupola: A dome-like protrusion on a batholith.

cycle of erosion: A model put forward by W M Davis in 1899 to describe the evolution of landscapes over millions of years.

dead ice: Ice which has become detached from a stationary or retreating ice mass.

deductive reasoning: A process of reasoning which proceeds from the general to the particular by using theory to explain a specific feature.

deflation: The removal of dry, loose material, such as sand, from the land surface by wind.

deglaciation: The wastage of an ice mass.

denudation: The wearing down of the earth's surface by processes of erosion and weathering.

dilatation: Pressure release caused by the removal of a rock layer.

discharge: The volume of a flow in a unit of time.

disorganised drainage: An irregular drainage pattern in which streams appear and disappear in an unexpected fashion.

distributary channel: A channel which results from the splitting of a river, perhaps as it enters a delta.

diurnal range: The variation occurring within one day.

downwarping: A gentle, downward deformation of the earth's crust.

englacial: Within the ice of a glacier or ice sheet.

ephemeral stream: A stream whose flow occurs only occasionally, usually as a result of intense rainfall.

equifinality: The achievement of the same state or form, but as the result of different sets of conditions or processes.

equilibrium: A state of balance between the controlling forces and the state, condition or form of a feature.

erosion: The wearing away and removal of parts of the land surface by a variety of agents (rivers, wind, ice, the sea).

escarpment: A steep slope at the edge of an upland surface.

eustasy: A change in sea level due to a rise or fall in the level of the oceans themselves rather than a movement of the land.

evapotranspiration: The output of water vapour from the earth's surface as a result of evaporation and transpiration.

extreme natural event: A high-magnitude, low-frequency, natural occurrence.

fines: A general term for fine-grained particles.

flash flood: A sudden, but short-lived, increase in any flow of water.

flume: An artificially constructed stream channel.

fluvioglacial: An adjective: relating to meltwater.

free face: The section of a slope too steep for debris to accumulate.

frost weathering: Those processes of weathering that result from the fluctuation of temperature above and below freezing point.

gabbro: A dark-coloured, coarse-grained, basic igneous rock.

gelifluxion: A process of soil flow in tundra areas caused by seasonal melting of the surface layer.

geology: The study of the earth and its structure.

geomorphology: The study of the changing shape of the earth's surface.

glaciation: The advance of ice across the earth's surface from mountain ice caps and the poles.

gorge: A river valley with steep, rocky sides.

grade: A state of equilibrium reached by a river or a slope when there is a balance between erosion, transport and deposition.

grey box system: A system whose internal structure is only partially known or identified.

greywacke: A strongly cemented, coarse sandstone or gritstone, now more commonly known as a turbidite.

groundwater: The store of water contained within the pores and spaces of the rocks which form the earth's surface.

gully: A deep channel eroded by a river but only occasionally occupied by it.

halophyte: A term used to describe plants which are tolerant of salty conditions.

head deposits: A mass of unsorted material deposited by gelifluxion.

headward erosion: The extension of a river upstream, usually by the process of spring sapping.

helicoidal flow: The flow of water within a river channel which resembles the coil of a spring.

hydraulic gradient: The slope of the water table.

ice age: A period of geological time, during which glaciation and deglaciation occur.

igneous rock: A rock formed by the solidification of magma.

inductive reasoning: A process of reasoning which bases explanation on collected evidence rather than theory.

insolation weathering: A form of weathering which results from a change of temperature between day-time heating by the sun and night-time cooling by radiation.

interglacial: The time period between two major glacial advances during which the temperature increases significantly.

iron pan: A thin, hard layer within the soil which results from leaching.

isostasy: A state of balance within the earth's crust.

isotope: A form of a particular element which differs from other forms in its weight of atoms.

joint: A fine fracture within a rock which, unlike a fault, involves no vertical or horizontal displacement.

kinetic energy: The energy derived from movement.

lava: Molten rock extruded on to the earth's surface.

leaching: The removal, in solution, of minerals from the upper horizons of the soil and their redeposition in a lower horizon.

lithology: The study of rock.

lithosol: A very immature soil consisting primarily of bare rock debris.

lithosphere: The crust and upper mantle of the earth, above the asthenosphere.

longitudinal profile: The profile of the bed of a river, from its source to its mouth.

longshore: Parallel to the shoreline.

magma: Molten rock beneath the surface of the earth.

mass wasting: The downslope movement of surface materials.

matrix: The finer components of a rock in which the coarser material is contained.

metamorphic rock: A rock formed by the transformation of a sedimentary or igneous rock due to intense heat or pressure.

misfit stream: A stream of much smaller size than that required to cut the valley in which it flows.

morphological system: A system in which only the constituent parts are identified.

morphometry: The measurement of shape or form of the landscape, particularly applied to drainage basins.

negative feedback: The process by which a change is counteracted to return a system to its equilibrium.

nivation: The wearing down of rocks beneath, and around, a snow patch.

normal relief: Relief whose highs and lows reflect the anticlines and synclines respectively.

open system: A system whose boundaries are open to incoming or outgoing energy or matter.

orientation: The direction or arrangement of fragments within a deposit.

orogeny: A major phase of fold mountain formation.

overdeepening: The deepening of a river valley by a glacier, perhaps to a depth below base level.

parallel retreat: The wearing back of a slope, during which the same profile is maintained.

pediment: A gentle bedrock slope, extending away from a steeper slope towards a zone of deposition.

pediplain: An extensive area of low relief formed by the merging of several pediments.

peneplain: The product of W M Davis' cycle of erosion, resulting from the wearing down of the land surface into a low, undulating plain.

periglacial: A term used to describe the zone that borders ice sheets and glaciers.

permafrost: Permanently frozen ground.

permeability: The ability of a material to allow water to pass through it.

phreatic water: The water beneath the water table, synonymous with groundwater.

plant succession: The sequence of changes of vegetation over time.

porosity: The ability of a material to hold water within it.

positive feedback: The process by which an initial change sets in motion a further series of changes which may destabilise a system.

potential energy: The energy stored within a body of water because of its height above base level.

process-response system: A system in which components and processes, and the relationships between them, are identified.

quadrat: A square metal frame used for sampling.

recurrence interval: The average period of time between two events of a similar magnitude.

regelation: The re-freezing of water into ice, usually because of a reduction of pressure within a glacier.

regime: The seasonal variation of flow of a river or glacier.

regolith: The surface layer of rock waste and soil overlying the bedrock.

rejuvenation: The resurgence of erosional activity of a river due to an increase in potential energy.

run-off: The total quantity of water reaching a river channel from its catchment area within a given time.

safety factor: The ratio of resistance to force, usually applied to a slope.

saltation: The bouncing of sediment along the surface.

scree slope: A debris slope of angular fragments which result from mechanical weathering.

sedimentary rock: A rock formed from sediment derived from other rocks or from organic sources.

seismic: Relating to earthquakes.

shatter belt: A zone of intense faulting on the earth's surface.

shear strength: The resistance of a material to stress.

shear stress: The force operating on a material on a slope against its resistance to movement.

sial: The major constituent of continental crust; mostly granitic rocks rich in silica and alumina.

sima: The major constituent of oceanic crust, rich in silica and magnesium.

sinuosity: The degree of meandering of a channel.

slope-foot processes: Those processes operating at the base of a slope which are liable to undercut it.

slope movement: See mass wasting

soil structure: A description of the soil in terms of the size and shape of crumbs or aggregates of particles.

soil texture: A measure of the particle size of the soil.

solifluxion: The slow flow of saturated soil downslope.

sorting: The laying down of sediment in an ordered fashion, according to size, shape or density.

spring sapping: Headward erosion by a spring.

stock: a small igneous intrusion.

storage: The capacity of a component of the hydrological cycle to store water.

strandline: The shoreline of a lake.

subglacial: Beneath the ice of a glacier or ice-sheet.

supraglacial: On the surface of a glacier or ice sheet.

system: A series of components, materials or variables linked by processes or by flows of energy or matter.

tectonic: Of the internal forces of the earth's crust.

tephra: A collective name for the various solid fragments emitted in a volcanic eruption.

terracette: A small stepped feature of hillsides, thought to result from soil creep or small-scale landslides.

thalweg: The line joining the deepest points of a river channel; the longitudinal profile of the river bed.

threshold: (i) The point of transition from one form or stage to another, or (ii) the rock barrier at the mouth of a fjord or corrie.

till: The unsorted mixture of sediment deposited by ice; synonymous with boulder clay.

topography: The shape of the earth's surface.

tundra: The treeless plain of northern latitudes, between the area of permanent ice cover and the coniferous forests or taiga.

turbidite: Modern term for greywacke.

vadose water: The water contained in the zone above the water table.

ventifact: A fragment of rock sculpted and polished by the wind.

watershed: The divide between catchment areas or drainage basins.

water table: The upper level of the groundwater in permeable rocks.

weathering: The disintegration or decomposition of rock at or near to the earth's surface.

white box system: A system whose internal structure is known and identified.

Index

Abbreviations used in the acknowledgements

Amer. J. Sci.   American Journal of Science.
Ann. Ass. Amer. Geogr.   Annals of the Association of American Geographers.
Geol. Soc. Amer. Bull.   Geological Society of America Bulletin
Geogr. J.   Geographical Journal.
Geogr. Annaler   Geografiska Annaler.
Geogr. Mag.   Geographical Magazine.
J. Geomorph.   Journal of Geomorphology.
J. Glaciol.   Journal of Glaciology.
J. Geophys. Res.   Journal of Geophysical Research.
Int. Ass. Scient. Hydrol.   International Association of Scientific Hydrology
Phil. Trans. Roy. Soc. B   Philosophical Transactions of the Royal Society Series B.

Proc. 4th Conf. Coastal Engng.   Proceedings of the 4th Conference of Coastal Engineering.
Proc. Geol. Ass. Lond.   Proceedings of the Geologists' Association of London.
Proc. Roy. Soc.   Proceedings of the Royal Society.
Proc. Yorks. Geol. Soc.   Proceedings of the Yorkshire Geological Society.
Q.J. Geol. Soc. Lond.   Quarterly Journal of the Geological Society of London.
Scott. Geogr. Mag.   Scottish Geographical Magazine.
Trans. Inst. Brit. Geogr.   Transactions of the Institute of British Geographers.
U.S. Geol. Surv. Prof. Paper.   United States Geological Survey Professional Paper.
Zeit. Geomorph.   Zeitschrift für Geomorphologie.

The author and publisher would like to acknowledge that some of the maps and diagrams in this book are based on illustrations that have appeared in other published and unpublished works. They would like to thank the following individuals and organizations for permission to use copyright material:

Anderson D.L. (1980) *Earthquakes and Volcanoes*, p.46, ed. B.A. Bolt, W.H. Freeman & Co. **2.12A**

Anglian Water, Cambridgeshire **5.12, 5.14**

Bagnold R.A. (1941) *The Physics of Blown Sand and Desert Dunes*, Methuen **11.18, 11.19, 11.20**

Barringer J.C. (1976) *The Geography of Lakeland*, Dalesman **6.47**

Bascom W.H. (1954) *Proc. 4th Conf. Coastal. Engng.*, 163–180 **7.21**

Bird E.C.F. (1979) for fig. 6.6 of *Man and Environmental Processes*, K.J. Gregory and D.E. Walling, Butterworth **12.13**

Bird E.C.F. (1984) *Coasts*, fig. 49, Basil Blackwell **7.30**

Boulton G.S. (1974) *Glacial Geomorphology*, ed. D.R. Coates, State University of New York, Binghamton **8.13**

Bowen D.Q. (1973) 'Time and Place on the British Coast,' *Geography* 259 **7.36, 7.37**

Bowen D.Q. (August 1977) *Geog. Mag.*59 **8.2b, 10.1**

Brunsden D. and Goudie A. (1981) *Classical Coastal Landforms of Dorset*, fig.13, Geographical Association **7.27**

BSAC 'A Diver's Guide to the Weymouth and Portland Area' **7.11**

Buckle C. (1978) *Landforms in Africa*, fig. 5.16, Longman Group UK Ltd. **6.28a**

Butzer K.W. (1961) *Arid Zone Research* 17, 31–56 **11.3**

Carson M.A. and Kirkby M.J. (1972) *Hillslope Form and Process*, Cambridge University Press **4.8**

Catt J.A. and Penny L.F. (1966) *Proc. Yorks. Geol. Soc.*, 35, 375–420 **7.38**

Chorley Mrs R.J. (1969) *Water Earth and Man*, fig. 2.1.1, R.J. Chorley, Methuen **5.4**

Chow T. (1959) *Open Channel Hydraulics*, McGraw Hill Book Company **6.5**

Clapperton C.M. (1973) *Geogr. Mag.* 46, 83–96 **12.3**

Clark M.J. and Small J. (1982) *Slopes and Weathering*, fig. 5.5 Cambridge University Press **7.13**

Clark M. and Small R.J. (1982) *Slopes and Weathering*, fig. 1.2, Cambridge University Press **4.4, 4.26**

Clayton K.M. (1966) 'The Origins of the Landforms of the Malham Area', *Field Studies*, Vol. 2, 359–84 **3.20**

Crowell J.C. and Frakes L.A. (1970) *Amer. J.Sci.* 26 **8.1**

Czudek and Demak (1970) *Quaternary Research*, 105–20 **10.12**

Davies J.L. (1980) *Geographical Variation in Coastal Development*, figs 133 (after JRL Allen 1965) and 96, Longman Group UK Ltd. **6.28b, 7.18**

Delderfield E.R. (1981) *The Lynmouth Flood Disaster*, ERD Publications, Exmouth **12.12**

Doornkamp J.C. and Gregory K.J. (1979) *The Atlas of Drought in Britain* Inst. Brit. Geog. **5.16c**

Douglas I. (1976) 'Urban Hydrology', *Geogr. J.*, Vol. 142, p 67, Table III **12.8**

Dunning F.W. et al (1981) *The Story of the Earth*, figs 35a, 36d, 16, B.G.S. **2.5, 2.6, 2.9**

Dury G.H. (1953) *Scott. Geog. Mag.* 69, 166–77, © Royal Scottish Geographical Society, reproduced by kind permission of the Society **8.30**

Elliston G.R. (1973) *Int. Ass. Scient. Hydrol.* 95, 79–84 **9.3**

Embleton C. and Thornes J. (1979) *Process in Geomorphology*, figs 5.2, 5.3, Edward Arnold **4.9a,4.9b**

Embleton C. and King C.A.M. (1968) *Glacial and Periglacial Geomorphology*, figs 4.5, 14.1, 2.4, 2.11, Edward Arnold **8.10, 8.34, 10.4, 10.10**

Eyre S.R. and Palmer J. (1973) *The Face of North East Yorkshire*, Dalesman **9.5**

Ferrians et al (1969) *US Geol. Surv. Prof. Paper 678* **12.5**

Flint R.F. (1971) *Glacial and Quaternary Geology*, Wiley **10.19**

Galvin C.J. (1968) *J. Geophys. Res.*, Vol. 73:12, 3651–9 **7.5**

George Philip and Sons Ltd (1986) for material from *Modern School Atlas* **11.4**

Goudie A. and Wilkinson (1977) *The Warm Desert Environment*, figs 4,47, Cambridge University Press **11.5, 11.12**

Gregory K.J. (1965) *Trans. Inst. Brit. Geog.* 36, 149–62 **9.7**

Gregory K.J. and Walling D.E. (1973) *Drainage Basin, Form and Process*, figs 5.10, 3.16, 3.18, 3.22, 5.7, Edward Arnold, **5.24, 6.13a, 6.13b, 6.36**

Gresswell R.K. (1957) *Beaches and Coastlines*, fig. 8, Hutton, reproduced by permission of Stanley Thornes (Publishers) Ltd. **7.42**

Gresswell R.K. (1958) *Glaciers and Glaciation* figs 82,83,89, Hutton, reproduced by permission of Stanley Thornes (Publishers) Ltd. **8.34,9.19**

Grove A.T. (1978) *Africa*, fig. 21, © Oxford University Press **5.31**

Hagedorn H. (1968) *Erdkunde* 22, 257–9 **11.14**

Haltedahl H. (1967) *Geog. Annaler*, 49A, 188–203 **8.21**

Hare R. (1980) *Waters and Rivers*, Schools Council 14–18 Geography Project, Macmillan **5.26**

Harris C. (1974) *J. Glaciol*, Vol. 13, No. 521–33, reproduced by permission of the International Glaciological Society **10.21**

Heim A. (1919) *Geologie der Schweiz*, Leipzig, as reproduced in *The Structure of the Alps* by L.W. Cullett, Edward Arnold (1935) **2.25**

Hemingway J.E., Wilson V., Wright C.W. (1968) *Geology of the Yorkshire Coast*, fig. 6 Geologists' Association **9.6**

Hendriks E.M.L. (1937) *Quart. J. Geol. Soc. Lond.* 93, p. 322, as reproduced in *The Coast of England and Wales in Pictures*, fig. 6, Steers J.A., Cambridge University Press (1960) **7.16**

Hilton K. (1979) *Process and Pattern in Physical Geography*, fig. 435, Unwin Hyman, **6.19**

Hjulström F. (1935) *University of Upsala Geological Institute Bulletin* 25, 221–527 **6.20**

Hollis G.E. (1971) 'The Effect of Urbanization on Floods in Canon's Brook', *Trans. Inst. Brit. Geog. Special Publication* 6, **5.13b, 12.9**

Hooke J.M. (1977) for an illustration in *River Channel Changes*, K.J. Gregory, John Wiley and Sons Ltd **6.34**

Howcroft H.J. (1977) *Field Studies*, Vol. 4 **5.9, 5.10**

Hunt C.B. and Mabey D.R. (1966) *US Geol. Surv. Prof. Paper 494A* **11.10**

Hutchinson J.N. (31.3.71) Roscoe Memorial Symposium, University of Cambridge **4.10**

Hutchinson J.N. (1968) *Proc. Geol. Ass. Lond.*, Vol. 79, 227–37 **4.12**

ITV programme for schools, 'Search for Order' **7.19, 7.34**

Keller E.A. (1972) 'Development of alluvial stream channels,' *Geol. Soc. Amer. Bull.* 83, 1531–36, **6.31**

Kidson C. (1953) *Geography*, George Philip & Son Ltd. **4.13**

Kirby M.J. (1969) *Water Earth and Man*, R.J. Chorley, Table 5.1.1, Methuen **5.8**

Knapp B.J. (1979) *Elements of Geographical Hydrology*, fig. 2.2, Unwin Hyman **5.13a**

Lachenbruch A.H. (1962) *Geol. Soc. Amer. Bull.* Special Paper 60 **10.6**

Land A.E., Head of Geography, Uppingham School, for material from an unpublished work **6.2**

Leather D. (1984) *Geog. Mag.*, 554–56 **12.14**

Lewin J. (1981) *British Rivers*, Unwin Hyman **5.11, 5.13c, 5.16b**

Linton D.L. (1949) *Scott. Geog Mag.* 65, 123–51, © Royal Scottish Geographical Society, reproduced by kind permission of the Society **8.29**

Mabutt J.A. (1977) *Desert Landforms*, figs 64, 62, 73, MIT Press **11.13, 11.15, 11.25**

Meigs P. (1953) *Reviews of Research on Arid Zone Hydrology*, 203–10 © UNESCO **11.1, 11.2**

Money D.C. (1980) *Polar Ice and Periglacial Lands*, fig. 7, Unwin Hyman **10.3**

Monkhouse F.J. (1975) *Principles of Physical Geography*, fig. 106 Hodder & Stoughton **9.16**

Monkhouse F.J. (1975) *Principles of Physical Geography*, fig. 82, Hodder & Stoughton **6.28c**

Morisawa M. (1968) *Streams: Their Dynamics and Morphology*, figs 2.3, 3.2, 7.3, 1.2, McGraw Hill Book Company **5.33, 6.9, 6.35, 6.48**

National Trust for Scotland (1979) Glencoe **2.27, 2.28**

Newson M.D. and Hanwell J.D. (1982) *Systematic Physical Geography*, fig. 7.24, Macmillan **1.4**

Open University Press, The, for material used in an Open University television programme entitled 'After the Earthquake' **2.16**

Oxford and Cambridge Schools' Examination Board, for permission to reproduce A-level geography papers: 1982 Paper 2; 1979, Paper 1 **5.34, 7.15**

Peel R.F. (1974) *Zeit. Geomorph.* Supp. 21, 19–28 **11.31**

Peel R.F., Cooke R.U., Warren A. (1974) 'The Study of Desert Geomorphology', *Geography* 59, 121–139, figs 5 and 4 **11.21, 11.22, 11.23, 11.24**

Peltier L. (1950) *Ann. Ass. Amer. Geogr.*, Vol. 40, 214–36 **3.8**

Pereira H.C. (1973) *Land Use and Water Resources in Temperate and Tropical Climates*, Cambridge University Press **12.7**

Pethick J. (1984) *An Introduction to Coastal Geomorphology*, figs 4.17, 6.21, 6.15, 7.9, Edward Arnold **7.10, 7.28, 7.33, 7.35**

Press F. and Siever R. (1982) *Earth*, fig. 7.43, W.H. Freeman, **6.29**

Price R.J. (1973) *Glacial and Fluvioglacial Landforms*, figs 35,38, Longman **9.8, 9.13**

Raymond C.F. (1971) *J. Glaciol*, Vol. 10, No.58, 55–84, **8.11**

Rice R.J. (1977) *Fundamentals of Geomorphology*, fig. 17.5, Longman Group UK Ltd., © Rice R.J. **7.29c**

Sharp R.P. (1942) *J. Geomorph.* **10.4**

Sissons J.B. (1976) *Scotland*, fig. 4.3, Methuen, **9.9**

Sissons J.B. (1977) 'Devon, Valley of Rugged Rocks', *Geog. Mag.* 49, 711–4, **6.38**

Small R.J. (1978) *The Study of Landforms*, figs 62, 34, 184, 153 (after R.F. Flint) Cambridge University Press **1.2, 2.24, 7.23, 9.12**

Sparks B.W. and West R.G. (1964) *Trans. Inst. Brit. Geog.* 35, 27–35 **9.15**

Sparks B.W. and West R.G. (1972) *The Ice Age in Britain*, Table 5.1, 3.23, Methuen **8.25, 8.28, 10.17**

Sparks B.W., Williams R.B.G., Davies F.G. *Proc. Roy. Soc.* A.327 **10.17**

Steers J.A. (1960) *The Coast of England and Wales in Pictures*, fig. 12, Cambridge University Press **7.29b**

Steers J.A. (1969) *The Sea Coast*, fig. 39, Collins **7.32**

Sugden D.E. (1982) *Artic and Antarctic*, fig. 4.3, Basil Blackwell **10.20**

Sugden D.E. and John B.S. *Glaciers and Landscape*, figs 3.5, 3.2, 8.12, 12.8, 14.2, 16.2, Edward Arnold **8.6, 8.7, 8.14, 8.22, 9.25, 9.26**

Times, The (January 1982) **5.2**; (August 1952) **5.1**; (November 1983) for material based on a Royal Society report **6.18**; (April 1906) **2.13**

Trueman A.E. (1971) *The Geology and Scenery of England and Wales*, figs 5, 8, 11, Penguin **2.22, 3.22**

Turner C. (1970) *Phil. Trans. Roy. Soc.* B. 257, fig. 15 **9.24**

Vanney J.R. (1960) *Men. Reg. Inst. Rech. Sch.* 4. Algiers **11.9**

Van Rose S. (1983) *Earthquakes*, fig. 28, B.G.S. **2.14**

Ward R. (1975) *Principles of Hydrology*, fig. 8.19, reproduced by permission of McGraw Hill Book Company (UK) Ltd. **5.16**

Webb and Walling (1980) *Zeit. Geomorph.*, Vol. 36, 245–263 **6.21**

Wheeler for an illustration from *Geographical Approaches to Fluvial Processes*, fig. 5, Geobook, as reproduced in *Rivers and Landscapes*, G.E. Petts and I. Foster, Edward Arnold **6.1**

Whittow J. (1980) *Disasters*, fig. 42, Penguin **12.6**

Whittow J.B. (1977) *Geology and Scenery in Scotland*, fig. 22, Penguin **6.27**

Whittow J.B. (1984) *Penguin Dictionary of Physical Geography*, fig. 178, Penguin, **10.11**

Williams H. (1980) for an article in *Earthquakes and Volcanoes*, p. 109 ed. B.A. Bolt, W.H. Freeman & Co. **2.30**

Wills L.J. (1938) *Q. J. Geol. Soc. Lond.*, Vol. 94, 61–242, as reproduced in *British Rivers*, fig. 2.5, J. Lewis, Unwin Hyman **5.18, 6.43**

Wood R.M. (1978) *On the Rocks* figs 7.2 and 4.13 with the permission of BBC Enterprises Ltd. **3.17, 3.24**

Young A. (1972) *Slopes*, Longman Group UK Ltd. **3.12–14**

Young A. and D. (1974) *Slope Development*, figs 8 and 17, Macmillan **4.23, 4.24**

The publishers have made every effort to trace copyright holders, but if they have inadvertently overlooked any they will be pleased to make the necessary arrangements.

We would also like to thank the following for permission to use photographs:

Aerofilms 7.16, 9.11, 10.1, 12.1; Patrick Bailey 2.4, 3.4, 3.8, 3.18, 4.1, 4.6, 6.7, 6.13, 8.12, 8.15, 9.3, 10.3, 11.6; W.P. Borrett 12.8, 12.9; P.C. Brooker 8.11; J.P. Crookes 3.12, 3.13, 3.14, 4.7, 8.13, 10.2, 11.8, 11.11; D.W. Dew 4.5; Malcolm Don 12.11; Geoscience Features Picture Library 2.5, 2.6, 3.3, 3.10, 3.19, 3.20, 4.8, 7.3, 7.15, 9.1, 10.4, 10.5, 11.3, 11.4, 11.5, 11.7, 11.9, 11.13, 11.15, 11.17, 11.18, 12.2, 12.4; Heaton Cooper Studio, Grasmere 1.2; Keystone Press Agency 4.13; Landform Slides, Lowestoft 7.14, 9.10, 11.14; John and Gillian Lythgoe, Seaphot Limited 11.1; Panos Pictures 12.14; Paul Renuth 1.1; Tropix Photo Library 11.10; A.C. Waltham 2.1, 7.19, 9.7, 10.6, 11.2, 11.12, 12.3; M. Wilkie 7.13, 8.1, 8.6, 8.8, 9.2